Ambivalent Miracles

Race, Ethnicity, and Politics
Luis Ricardo Fraga and Paula D. McClain, Editors

Ambivalent Miracles

*Evangelicals and the
Politics of Racial Healing*

Nancy D. Wadsworth

University of Virginia Press   *Charlottesville and London*

To my parents, Chloe Eichenlaub and Billy O. Wadsworth,
    who each in their own way sparked my interest in fracture, ambivalence,
    and miracles, and who steadfastly nurtured my interest in writing.

University of Virginia Press
© 2014 by the Rector and Visitors of the University of Virginia
All rights reserved
Printed in the United States of America on acid-free paper

First published 2014
ISBN 978-0-8139-3531-7

9 8 7 6 5 4 3 2 1

Library of Congress Cataloging-in-Publication Data is available
from the Library of Congress

Contents

Acknowledgments

In the time it took this book to find its true nature, three American presidencies, two wars, and several stages of my adulthood intervened. For a project with relatively modest ambitions, that is a lot of intellectual debt to accrue. While I am solely responsible for its shortcomings, this book has greatly benefited from the interventions of others.

Deep gratitude goes out to my mentors and graduate cohort at the New School for Social Research, where I first stumbled upon evangelical racial reconciliation efforts and decided to make them the subject of both a master's thesis and dissertation. With insight, encouragement, and humor, Victoria Hattam, Ira Katznelson, José Casanova, and especially David Plotke guided me through the tangles of investigating such an unstudied, culture-infused subject in political science. Thanks to my peers Kevin Bruyneel, Joseph Lowndes, Priscilla Yamin, Cat Celebrezze, Lori Hiris, Bonnie Thurston, Jenny Parker, and Joseph Luders, who read drafts at various stages, cheered me on, and made me feel like a fast, efficient writer. (Ha!) I may have been the first out, but I'm the last one in, and your own accomplishments have been guiding stars.

The Carnegie Mellon Foundation provided a glorious postdoctoral fellowship at Cornell University from 2001 to 2003, where the project began to find a new framing at the intersection of race and religion in American political life. Thanks to Michael Jones-Correa, Kate Morris, Maria Fanis, the members of the faculty seminar on race and ethnicity in the United States, and especially the wise, tempered Richard Bensel for his mentorship. A decade later on the same campus, the School of Criticism and Theory provided six weeks of intellectual inspiration, and time to write the ending. Thanks especially to Hent De Vries and the students in his seminar on miracles, events, and effects. Our explorations brought me full circle on the subject of ambivalent miracles.

The University of Denver (DU) made possible the second wave of primary research, focused on the multiethnic church movement. Thanks to the committees of the DU PROF, Student Summer Research Scholarship, and Faculty Research Funds; Dean Anne McCall; the DU Salon Series; and the Department of Political Science. Arielle Finkelstein combed through three decades' worth of *Christianity Today* and helped code the articles I analyzed. Jeffrey Satterwhite and Catlyn Keenan at the Iliff School of Theology were valuable graduate editors. To Tom Knecht, Seth Masket, Susan Sterett, Hava Gordon, Caryn Aviv, and Lisa Conant, all of whom helped my work along, I am most thankful and honored to be a part of this community.

The book would lack blood, spine, and spirit without the more than sixty people who generously shared their time, hopes, insights, and critiques with me over the course of my research. In particular, Beth, Anthony, Mark, and Jason— in your different ways, you went beyond the call of duty. I hope this work can begin to represent the complexity of the worlds you introduced me to. Your faith and passion inspire me.

Lisa Dale brought sanity, laughter, grim determination, and hundreds of hours in Denver coffee shops to the final drafting process. The sound of your feverish typing will always haunt me.

For the times I didn't think it would ever end and friends were islands of relief, I am also grateful to Jim Bouchard, Janine D'Anniballe, Layla DeStaffany, Terry Freeman, Jessica Grant, Linda Kallinger, Javier Polár, Andria Marshall, Kris "Grandpa" Mattingly, Marcy Reiser, Jen Schneider, Wendy Shedd, Clé Symons, Katie Symons, and Dawn Weber. Thank you all for believing it would happen.

Anne Pogoriler, you are a brilliant editor, diagnoser of stylistic tics, and the real political scientist between us. I am so grateful for your generosity, patience, and love.

Introduction

This is a study of a growing, dynamic, increasingly influential, but little understood movement that has been unfolding in the last few decades within the diverse panoply of identities and faith-based organizations that is American evangelicalism. What I refer to here as "evangelical racial change (ERC) advocates" draw on core resources of their faith in hopes of conscientiously acknowledging a troubled past, repairing centuries-old wounds, and realizing a new, more multiracial present. They dream of transforming the segregated demographics of evangelicalism from the inside out, which means rethinking the social practices that built a racially fractured religious milieu. In this process, participants experience powerful epiphanies and social miracles, moments that transform and inspire.

Yet, puzzlingly, the movement as a whole is ambivalent about whether and how any of this should inform a politics: an explicit orientation toward the larger power configurations, policies, and party alliances in U.S. society that sculpt socioeconomic realities, including race, today. ERC advocates hope to create a Christianity faithful to what they see as New Testament principles honoring difference and diversity within the Body of Christ, and to influence the world in turn. But they are not sure that politics, as an individual or a coordinated collective response to race-related problems, is an appropriate expression of that conviction, even outside the church.

I argue that both the stunning breakthroughs this movement engenders and the curious boundaries it draws around itself are themselves products of a kind of cultural politics. Here I mean politics in the sense of the particular histories, social power dynamics, and institutional configurations that impact a given community or set of communities, which are, in turn, always in at least implicit dialogue with the larger world. Intragroup politics is situated in broader cultural contexts that constantly change. The politics of racial healing, in the evangelical case, is constructed at a crossroads where U.S. racial and religious history and the meaning-making practices of contemporary American conservative evangelicalism meet. That is a rich but fraught intersection. It teems with possibilities, including the potential for a new breed of multiracial evangelicalism to enter productively into larger national conversations about race and class in unprecedented ways. But it is also marked by anxieties about directly addressing broader power structures that impact participants' lives—anxieties that if not acknowledged and explored threaten to mute the movement's reach, influence, and overall cohesion. To understand the movement's emergence, its character, and its potential influence on American political life more broadly, we must become conversant with these complex dynamics.

The findings gathered in this book will, I hope, contribute to at least two main areas of interest. First, in the context of American political life, the ERC movement has much to teach observers about how evangelicalism, the slice of Protestantism that today represents approximately one-quarter of the electorate, has developed historically vis-à-vis the nation's racial dynamics.[1] This is a topic to which scholars have given scant attention within a mountain of research on conservative Christians.[2] It is not simply that evangelicals of all racial backgrounds have been impacted over the long term by the United States' complex racial history. That is true. But, more intriguingly, this particular social change movement sheds light on how profoundly the very categories of race and religion have sculpted the content and meaning of one another and, in turn, the religiopolitical orientations of so many who live in America. Regardless of Americans' individual associations, the complex interplay of race, religion, and politics pulses through the very backbone of our national identity.[3]

This interwovenness of race, religion, and politics, produces ongoing reverberations within American political life in the United States. For example, in the United States, in major and off-term elections, through ballot initiatives, state legislatures, and municipal bodies, religious conservatives gained ground throughout the 2000s on policy issues coded as "moral values" concerns—marriage being the preeminent one. Across the first decade of the twenty-first century, dozens of political initiatives geared toward "protecting traditional marriage" benefited from support of majorities of voters of color (Lewis and Gossett 2008; Lemelle and Battle 2004; Haider-Markel and Joslyn 2005; Egan 2005; Campbell and Monson 2008). Religious conservatives achieved a racial coalition, in part, through culturally coded rhetorical appeals and the mobilization of fears that gays and lesbians were somehow illegitimately benefiting from rights reserved for other minorities, or that the extension of rights to them would otherwise hurt families of color (Wadsworth 2008a, 2011).

In 2012, Mitt Romney, a Mormon, challenged President Barack Obama for the American presidency, with the nation's kaleidoscopic racial, class, and religious backstory functioning as constant subtext, surfacing in the coded ways candidates and citizens invoked God, nation, opportunity, freedom, and democracy (Wadsworth 2013). While the Republicans did not succeed in drawing many racial minorities to their side through the appeals they made to family values, faith, and morality, they certainly tried and, in the wake of 2012 losses, have redoubled their efforts to be racially inclusive.

These strategies and discourses did not emerge in a vacuum. For at least a decade, white religious conservatives have worked behind the scenes, sponsoring resolutions, leadership networks, church-based relationships, and other grassroots-level efforts aiming to dismantle the cultural and theological walls erected over centuries between white Christian communities and those of color. This is not to say that faith-based, cross-racial relationships were or are pursued only for instrumental reasons. Rather, political and social relationship-building efforts developed during overlapping periods, in various settings and conversations, and in some instances those intercrossings influenced political outcomes. Evangelicalism has a long, still evolving history with race, which has impacted its approach to other issues, including school vouchers battles, immigration reform debates, the politics of international poverty relief efforts, and even some foreign policy issues.[4]

Second, and beyond the world of evangelicals, this is a story about the all-too-human tensions that often attend people's attempts to create social transformation. ERC advocates yearn to change the world through what they are doing, and in many ways they want to be changed by doing it. (Indeed, the promise of experiencing miraculous personal transformation is part of the allure of evangelical Christianity.) But, like most of us, they don't want the world to change them too much, or in ways that feel threatening to their worldview and social practices. They especially don't want "the world"—a term with a particular resonance in evangelicalism—to spoil what feels rare, delicate, and special. Like any subculture, they are propelled by a worldview with its own distinctive beliefs, customs, and etiquettes. The secular political process, or at least social dynamics many evangelicals associate with politics, approaches change differently. ERC advocates realize they don't live on an island and that the formal American political system is an avenue to much of the change they seek. They are nonetheless anxious about how much difference in approach, analysis, forms of engagement, and levels of conflict can conceivably be tolerated in the room at once.

ERC efforts provide one example among countless others around the world of ordinary people engaging in social change–oriented activity while denying, avoiding, or feeling conflicted about whether what they're involved in is or should be "political" work.[5] Here we can think of cultural exchange groups that enable members of politically adversarial communities (say, Israelis and Palestinians) to get to know each other at "peace camp," institutes that promote forgiveness and reconciliation, or volunteer organizations from developed countries delivering resources to communities around the world. Families on "volunteer vacations," American college student groups trying to help out local or remote populations, or even the corporate-sponsored cast of something like ABC's *Extreme Make-over: Home Edition*, who traveled the country building new houses, schools, and community centers for people in need, reflect similar phenomena. Just about everywhere global citizens have resources, some are investing financially, intellectually, physically, and emotionally in the possibility of social change, while either dissociating such efforts from what happens in the "political" world or feeling confused about it.

Analyzing the boundaries ERC advocates draw around their activities and goals provides insights into how specific cultural resources (and deficits) inform how humans individually and collectively navigate complex issues of power, inequality, access, and rights—indeed, the concerns of politics. A study of this particular movement and its idiosyncrasies can illuminate how all of us, members of a global community, become profoundly sculpted by and attached to the lenses and habits within which we operate, and how we also continually reinvent ourselves in the process.

Scholars are perpetually fascinated by evangelical Christians, even if these true believers, in their unwieldy enthusiasms, make many of us nervous. In my case, I accidentally (or perhaps "fatefully") tripped across evangelical racial reconciliation efforts in graduate school when I was exploring writing a master's thesis on the "family values" debates emerging in the early 1990s. The topic proceeded to occupy the bulk of my intellectual life through a dissertation and postdoctoral fellowship, and in new waves of research across my years as a junior professor (though, thankfully, I did cultivate other interests along the way). After that many years, the study of conservative evangelicals trying to wend their way toward some kind of progressive racial change has simultaneously oriented me in my chosen profession and made me feel perpetually alien. Not only has my discipline, political science, lagged in studying the cultural contours of religious movements, but few nonevangelicals I've met along the way have even heard of the phenomenon, and most find the very notion of it befuddling.

I am not an evangelical Christian, or even a generic one, though both types are represented in my family. But for some handful of years growing up I was touched by "born-again" Christianity—touched not only in the sense of being acquainted with but also sometimes moved by the spiritual vitality and community I felt, for example, when a room of teenagers sang songs to a God they experienced as intimately real. I was even, at the age of twelve on a trip with my religious father, baptized (by choice) in a tributary of the river Jordan by Pastor Chuck Smith, one of the best-known leaders of the 1970s evangelical revival or "Jesus movement"—and I remember experiencing that as a powerful and hopeful, even transcendent ritual. But even that did not make formal Christianity stick. Despite my deep appreciation for the Jesus stories, whether it was a summer trip for teenagers or a Sunday night Bible study, on some level I always felt on the outside looking in among these "Believers," as they often referred to themselves. I had too many questions I couldn't resolve about the faith system, and knew too few Christians willing to grapple with them. Evangelicals would call me a "backslider," at best, though I have since found a sense of spiritual belonging in a more ecumenical faith community.

I mention my religious background up front because I have learned that most people I describe this project to, especially academics, find it hard to say anything nice about evangelicals, and assuming I must be in cahoots with them has made it tempting for some to interpret this project as an apology for the Christian Right. I certainly sympathize with the urge to scoff or dismiss. Having contributed, in the form of Religious Right organizations, more than their share to the acrimony and polarization of political discourse in the United States, and seeming to readily target others (especially members of one of my own tribes, gays and lesbians) for exclusion from the full entitlements of a modern democracy, evangelicals have angered many, including me.[6] Whatever they're up to, their adversaries often assume, must be intolerant, self-serving, or cynical. It seems disingenuous for these same social conservatives to now claim to be bridging racial boundaries and fostering multiracial community within their movement.

In some ways, to dismiss these passionate believers (or fanatics, depending on one's point of view) is easy. Yet I find it important to study this movement seriously, in a way that accurately and empathically comprehends its participants' worldview, habits, fears, and anxieties, while also trying to situate the movement critically in the broader context of a particular nation's history, the cultures and tensions entwined therein, and its multifaceted contemporary political life.

Passion and Paradox

The combination of passionate investment in more egalitarian racial transformation alongside political ambivalence seems paradoxical. Despite the milestone of having (twice now) elected a black president, the United States is anything but a "postracial" society today, and on some measures of racial inequality it has stagnated or regressed alarmingly in the past twenty years (Oliver and Shapiro 2006; Garcia Bedolla 2007; Bonilla-Silva 2010). Pervasive race- and class-linked disparities continue to impact people's life chances, educational and economic opportunities, health prospects, and net worth (Wise 2010). Meanwhile, even amid a damaging recession that has left the American poor even poorer, conservatives have made concerted efforts to denigrate the kinds of public services and programs designed to help offset these disparities. This project has been ongoing since at least the 1980s (Katz 1996, 2001; Hancock 2004). On many counts they have succeeded in stigmatizing social programs and the poor alike. Why would religious conservatives invest time, energy, and social capital in mending racial divides without participating in conversations about justice, material distribution, and fair representation for racial minorities in political policy?

From one viewpoint, observers of religion in American life might expect religious communities to produce politically ambiguous outcomes when they attempt social change. After all, it is not uncommon to hear religious people interpreting change in terms of divinely inspired miracles and "God's grace" (or punishment) rather than ordinary human achievements. In other words, certain faith lenses tend to identify real power as the jurisdiction of God, not human beings. Wariness about engaging in open political dialogue or through the formal political system also makes some sense among American religious groups who wish to avoid breaching the hallowed separation of church and state, and therefore take pains to cordon their outreach within the realm of civic engagement. Like others in religious communities accustomed to seeing their work in civic, spiritual, relational, or interpersonal, but not political, terms, it seems unsurprising that ERC advocates might interpret their work through depoliticized frames (Putnam 2000).

On the other hand, the fact that American evangelicals (of all people!) are ambivalent about political conversation and activity in the case of race and class inequalities in particular may, reasonably, raise suspicion. Again, conservative evangelicals have been among the most willing to politicize social issues other people might consider inappropriate, like prayer, abortion, marriage, and homosexuality. As a community that continues to enjoy victories on a range of political targets, haven't conservative evangelicals amassed ample resources ERC advocates could harness if they wanted to address the sorts of systems and institutions that perpetuate racial disparities? And if Christians of color are involved, which they are, don't many of those communities, especially African Americans, tend to think of religious and political justice as symbiotic objectives? Why, then, would Christians in pursuit of racial healing avoid addressing the political dimensions of inequality? What underlying biases might be reflected by such ambivalence?

Beyond ERC communities, how is it that citizens can give so much to a social change–oriented cause, invest so deeply in seeking to remedy problems they recognize as having been produced by a combination of political and socioeconomic factors, and contribute to transformative outcomes, yet cordon off their own efforts from what they see as political behavior or even political discussion? Are such "ambivalent miracles" sustainable over the long term? What are the possibilities and limits of this and other politically ambivalent attempts at social boundary crossing and healing?

Book Organization

Ambivalent Miracles employs two related interpretive approaches to answer these questions. It is, first, an empirical investigation that attempts to situate the ERC movement within a larger historical context in which nation and narrative are operative constructs. I examine the movement's historical origins, the stories its proponents tell about that history and their role(s) in it, and how the movement seems to interface with American political culture more broadly. Studying the "texts" the movement has produced, such as books, speeches and sermons, conferences, websites, and audio files, I identify the central competing narratives about race and racism that have developed in evangelicalism's particular cultural milieu over time. This allows for tracing the ways in which the movement's idiosyncratic origins, assumptions, and pivotal moments combine to produce its particular varieties of political ambivalence and its social "miracles." This approach examines the movement from the outside in.

However, to understand the visceral power of ERC efforts and why ordinary people have been attracted to and personally transformed by the movement, we must also study the movement from the inside out. A nuanced analysis of ERC efforts (or any grassroots movement) requires meeting people in the environments in which they do what they do, and paying careful attention to how they act, what they say, and how they think. The book's second and third sections, then, using ethnographic fieldwork, investigate the meaning-making practices, values, and beliefs of people involved in ERC efforts. How do people's unique cultural resources inspire and motivate but also limit their ability to think and act in certain ways? Drawing on in-depth interviews, participant-observation, local case studies, an opinion survey, and other mechanisms, I attend closely to how participants themselves conceptualize their objectives, activities, and the questions and tensions they encounter, especially with regard to the connections between race, religion, and politics, in the work they do.

Three distinctive vehicles that enable, complicate, and sometimes resist the sorts of social and political possibilities opened up by the ERC movement are *cultural histories, meaning systems* (interpretive frameworks and explanatory lenses), and *practices*. Through these, ERC participants construct their own distinctive sense of community, race, politics, and other matters. Each category is distinguishable from, but also in dialogue with, the racial and political discourses of the broader secular world and within the factions of evangelicalism. I trace different combinations of the three dimensions across the book.

In chapter 1, I summarize the main contours of the two waves of ERC efforts traced in the book and review the scholarship within which this project is in conversation, particularly work by sociologists of American evangelicalism. I elaborate my analytical claims about how particular histories, meaning systems, and cultural practices contribute to the ERC movement's startling achievements as well as its current limitations. I also discuss the value of an interpretive and ethnographic approach to the movement. Within the discipline of political science, wherein the intersections of both race/religion and culture/politics have been undertheorized, I find an emergent field of "political ethnography" particularly helpful for this project.

Chapters 2–5 concentrate primarily on histories and meaning systems that informed ERC efforts along the path to their ascent as a major discourse within evangelicalism in the 1990s. This sets up a foundation for, in chapters 6–8, layering in ethnographic fieldwork material (participant observation, interviews, and a case study) that helps us decipher, partly through real participants' stories, the complexity of everyday practices. Each chapter builds conceptually and chronologically to advance an understanding of how ERC meaning-making practices break new ground in evangelical race relations even as they foster a distinctive political ambivalence. But we can also recognize how, despite political ambivalence, a variety of applications can and do emerge from the ERC framework. These include more politicized orientations to faith-based racial change.

An understanding of *cultural histories* sheds light on why racial "justice," at least in politicized terms, is tricky to navigate for people from divergent racial and cultural backgrounds building cross-racial relationships that haven't previously existed. Within American evangelicalism, history functions as a loaded backdrop against which to engage dialogues long delayed and address racial wounds long untreated. Chapter 2 begins an overview of evangelical race history, which then threads forward across the book. A review of key elements of history from the seventeenth century forward demonstrates why the past casts a long shadow over American evangelical Christians, informing the semiotic practices racial change advocates will come to employ. This chapter describes three major religious racial traditions that bear on evangelicals as they try to transcend the past and plumbs how what I term "race-religion intersectionality" sculpts the political split personality of American evangelicalism on racial matters.

After grasping the implications of an intersectional political history of evangelical racial/religious dynamics, I begin to decipher why within the *meaning systems* of American evangelicalism *religious race bridging* is seen by practitioners as a necessary (or at least a reasonable) step toward racial healing. The distinctive, relationship-oriented race project forwarded by ERC advocates is a culturally specific attempt to draw on faith to help heal old wounds that continue to affect individuals and groups. In this context, stories matter as primary vehicles through which people explain their past, navigate their personal and social relationships, and justify their orientations to, among other factors, power, politics, and social change. Religious race bridging must be understood as a meaning system within the faith-based semiotic practices that motivate and circumscribe it.

Chapters 3–5 then explore how everyday meaning systems are intimately intertwined with cultural histories, as is especially reflected by public and semipublic discourse within evangelicalism. Chapter 3 traces how two prominent but competing meaning-making narratives about race within late twentieth-century American Christianity restricted the kinds of conversations evangelicals had about race between the civil rights movement era and the rise of the new Christian Right in the 1980s. I parse these as a racial liberation story, on the one hand, which I trace through Harlem-based African American preacher Tom Skinner's speeches in the 1970s and 1980s, and a competing, social justice–aversive story, articulated by prominent white evangelical church-growth strategist C. Peter Wagner. These figures are significant not just as symbolic spokespersons for these competing claims about how Christians ought to approach social problems like race but also as key players in the emerging racial reconciliation movement. Building from this picture, the last third of the chapter traces how an increasingly politicized evangelicalism influenced by southern diasporic communities after the 1960s attempted, often awkwardly, to navigate racial discourse, ultimately creating a discursive conundrum for the emergent Christian Right in the 1980s.

Chapters 4–6 investigate the development of new meaning-making systems and *cultural practices* through which evangelicals attempted to navigate this conundrum. Beginning in the early 1990s, white evangelical organizations began, through the distinctive religious race-bridging approach of racial reconciliation, to answer calls for change. Chapter 4 analyzes race-related coverage in the popular magazine *Christianity Today* across the 1980s and 1990s to identify why and how these change advocates, in dialogue with their counterparts of color who had been challenging them for decades, finally began to find what I call a "third way" between the competing racial discourses in American evangelicalism. In this period, the assumed "we" of the magazine's readership began to broaden as a wider range of voices joined the conversation and white evangelicals waded into the muddied waters of a deeper race discourse. Politically, though, considerable tensions simmered beneath the surface. Exemplifying this were Christian Coalition director Ralph Reed's unprecedented attempts to shift white conservative Christians' historical legacy on race. A look at Reed's navigation of historical and political frames brings into focus how the "third way" of religious race bridging exists in an uneasy relationship with the strains of neoconservatism already threaded through white evangelicalism.

Distinctive faith-based rituals within the ERC context enable racial change advocates to develop their own idiosyncratic responses to race-related experiences and to incorporate elements of the broader race discourses of American culture into their model. Understanding this requires at least a basic conversance with the content and contours of particular cultural practices, including scriptural engagement, prayer, testimony, and worship. Drawing from fieldwork conducted in 1990s racial reconciliation settings and two especially compelling stories from that data, chapter 5 examines how cultural resources within evangelicalism helped render racial reconciliation coherent to participants though meaning-making practices. We find that core aspects of evangelical culture created "epiphanal spaces," wherein reconcilers experienced things they considered miraculous and transformative. But epiphanal spaces largely rendered political conversations nonnormative if not taboo in those settings. The upshot is that the world of ERC advocates—or of any cultural group advocating social change—is indecipherable without understanding how meaning-making practices in that culture inform the rituals specific to achieving the desired change. In this case, processes encouraging apology, forgiveness, atonement, and unity building gave racial reconciliation meaning.

Chapter 6 draws on 1990s fieldwork and discourse analysis of newer treatments of race in *Christianity Today* in the 2000s to investigate how the meaning-making practices attendant to the religious race-bridging project fostered relationalism over political engagement, but then began to demonstrate more complexity in the new millennium. First, I present my findings that racial reconciliation advocates in the 1990s—not just whites but many participants of color as well—generally regarded engagement in the outside political world as contaminating in the racial context. This is partly because the political gulf between their different religious racial traditions facilitated a politics-avoidant orientation. But it is also because participants of color were distinctly leery of Christians reproducing the sorts of secular, institutionalized "programs and projects" they believed hadn't ultimately fixed American race relations. Paul Lichterman's work on the relationship between customs and social reflexivity and Nina Eliasoph's research on etiquettes and apathy provide analytical tools that help explain why 1990s ERC settings tended to be so politics-phobic. Part 2 looks at the appearance of Michael Emerson and Christian Smith's breakthrough book *Divided by Faith: Evangelical Religion and the Problem of Race in America,* which I argue both inaugurates the shift from the racial reconciliation emphasis to the multiethnic church (MEC) approach in the early 2000s and influences the evolving character and trajectory of evangelical race discourse.

Chapter 7 assesses emerging political orientations in the contemporary MEC movement, the second wave of ERC efforts. I first examine how MEC movement architects in the early 2000s employed the framework of a "spiritual mandate" to reach toward MECs in American evangelicalism. The spiritual mandate framework fosters what I call a "kindred outsider community" stance, a sense of marginalized but righteous identity, which nurtures social bonds and sponsors a measure of social reflexivity that sometimes influences participants' orientations toward politics. I then draw from results of an anonymous survey I conducted of members of a national network of existing and aspiring MEC communities and on interviews with and fieldwork among MEC participants in the 2000s to mine the nuances of their current orientations toward race-related politics. I introduce a typology of emergent political orientations in the MEC movement, finding that ERC advocates seem to be warming to political discussion and activism compared to the 1990s and to be demonstrating increased social reflexivity in these settings. A spectrum of more sophisticated and diverse sensibilities about what ERC should mean within and beyond American evangelicalism seems to be emerging, especially in relation to the topics of immigration, international rights issues, and poverty.

Examination of one particular MEC over time provides a more nuanced sense of the complex relationship between collective histories, meaning systems, and cultural practices that ERC advocates perpetually navigate. From 2008 to 2011, I followed the activities of a young MEC in Denver, Colorado, interviewing a dozen of its leaders and congregants, attending services and meetings, and meeting with its lead pastor regularly throughout the period. In chapter 8, I introduce this case study church in some detail and submit four overarching observations I suggest are applicable to the movement's current challenges and future trajectory. Within MECs, relational frameworks can and do provide paths to social action for some participants. However, this depends on important factors, like the church's stance toward the competing racial discourses within evangelicalism historically; its leaders' ability to provide forums where conflict within the congregation can be aired and discussed; and the number and type of internal subcultures within the church.

Even though the "miracles" of ERC efforts are arguably restricted by participants' ambivalence about applying these efforts to broader political situations that affect their members, it is also true that the more they enter truly multiracial communities, the less able they are to draw clear boundaries around what is and is not political. Moreover, even if most ERC advocates resist letting their churches or their movement be guided by agendas they consider political (meaning, adopting positions that align with particular parties, policies, and platforms), the fact of a multiethnic Christian community creates a range of lower-risk political opportunities. Coalition is one of these. The epilogue considers the likeliness of the ERC movement capitalizing on these.

In the United States and well beyond it, race and religion are overlapping arenas of individual identity and collective behavior that profoundly inform one another and, in turn, influence many communities' social practices and navigations with power. Like other categories of identity and agency—class, gender, sexual orientation, disability, and so on—they are also intricately entwined in the complex universes of culture(s) and politics. A careful look at the ERC movement, in all its triumphs and tensions, may bring us closer to understanding how complex mechanisms of long-term social change work.

PART ONE

What Stories We Tell

Historicizing Evangelicalism and Race

1 The New Paradigm of Racial Change

———————————————————————————————— +

Red, yellow, black, or white, all are precious in His sight.
—Traditional Christian song

There was a time when most American evangelical Christians did not have to think about race in church—or at least not about race or racism as problems within the church. For people of color, of course, the impact of a historically racialized society is impossible to avoid. But race wasn't supposed to matter among Christians: once a believer "accepted Christ" and was thereby "born again," she was "saved" and part of the Christian community whatever her background or skin color.[1] Even so, for a variety of reasons most Americans have historically joined churches filled with members who looked, racially, a lot like themselves. A long legacy of racial fracture in evangelicalism, and, later, a popular paradigm for church growth called the Homogeneous Unit Principle, created an effectively segregated church culture in the United States. Nine out of ten Christians still attend racially homogenous churches (Chaves et al. 1999; DeYoung et al. 2003; Emerson 2000, 74).

The appearance of individual taste, not systemic exclusion, as the basis for church demography gives whites the luxury of imagining the church as a race-neutral place. But the growing social movement for racial change within evangelical Protestantism has made it harder for the racially separate status quo to escape critique.[2] Within the evangelical racial change (ERC) movement, participants spotlight issues of racial and ethnic diversity (or the dearth thereof), and promote reconciliation and substantive integration inside churches and Christian organizations.[3] ERC leaders work, first and foremost, to foster a "body of believers" who know how to identify and dismantle racist attitudes, beliefs, and behaviors, and are able, wherever feasible, to thrive in racially and ethnically heterogeneous, culturally syncretic congregations in which no single worship or leadership style dominates. Such a tapestried Christian community, advocates believe, is a preview of what heaven will look like and part of a biblical command to embrace diversity.[4]

The movement can be traced to a number of historical strands and precursors. As early as there have been Christians in North America, there have been a (very) few who actively pursued the belief that their religion could foster harmony across racial divides. I focus, though, on two modern waves of racial change advocacy that sought to transform evangelicalism. These are the flurry of activities that blossomed under the concept of *racial reconciliation* in the 1990s; and the *multiethnic church (MEC) movement*, which, despite its older origins, did not begin to coordinate its collective resources until the 2000s.[5] To briefly summarize each:

Racial reconciliation focused on repairing long-standing racial fractures within evangelicalism through recognitions and apologies for racism at individual and organizational levels, new conversational forums about race relations, and the fostering of cross-racial relationships. The *MEC movement* pursues a range of models of racial/ethnic diversity, from fully integrated congregations to two or more language or culture groups holding different services under the same roof (Emerson and Kim 2003; Chaves et al. 1999; DeYoung et al. 2003; Emerson and Woo 2006; Garces-Foley 2007; Christerson, Edwards, and Emerson 2005; Anderson and Bridgeway Community Church 2004; Yancey 2003).[6] While distinct, the two waves of activity have some overlap in time, and in shared convictions and objectives. Pioneers in the MEC movement were important players during the height of racial reconciliation discourse in the mid-1990s, and racial reconciliation continues to be a refrain within many existing or aspiring MECs, though practitioners have become more circumspect about the term.

It is difficult to measure the ERC movement's exact reach in terms of how many people or churches have been involved at any given time. At this stage, the best estimates suggest that ERC initiatives constitute a minority strain, though an increasingly visible one, within the roughly 25 percent of the U.S. population that identifies as evangelical. At the peak of racial reconciliation activities in the late 1990s, over half of American "strong evangelicals" surveyed reported being aware of the movement (Emerson and Smith 2000, 127–28).[7] Racial reconciliation had its dramatic public moments: apologies by prominent leaders and organizations for histories of racism; a Christian men's movement, Promise Keepers, that emphasized racial reconciliation and caught the American public's attention; and moments of fairly public self-reflection about race in the evangelical community that critics of the Religious Right would not have expected (Newton 2005; Stricker 2001; Sack 1996; Reed 1996a). The reconciliation movement did not only "live" in particular congregations or organizations but was also carried by individual people scattered across disparate churches and parachurch organizations like Campus Crusade for Christ and Promise Keepers. Testimonies of ERC efforts became a niche literature in the evangelical publishing industry, making racial reconciliation one of the most prominent topics in American evangelical discourse throughout the 1990s.

Better numbers are available for the MEC movement. MECs are usually defined as congregations in which more than 20 percent of the members are from the minority racial or ethnic group(s) in that church. Twenty percent nonmajority members is a threshold that, proponents suggest, requires all members to substantively interact across difference. Such a congregation might be comprised of whites and people of color, or different ethnic or national-origin groups within one racial category (as race is defined in the United States), such as Latinos or Asians. As of this writing, the MEC movement counts them as constituting only 8.5 percent (De Young et al. 2003, 2) of American Christian churches.[8] That percentage would equate to tens of thousands of Americans involved (Emerson and Kim 2003, 217). Mosaix Global Network, the first national network of evangelical MECs, currently lists over 300 MECs in the United States in its directory, and at this writing claimed 1,200 individual members.[9] Mosaix sponsors local, regional, and national conferences on MEC building, produces guiding literature, and attempts to serve as a clearinghouse of resources for interested churches.[10]

Miracles and Ambivalence

While conscious of themselves as a relatively small community swimming against the tide, MEC participants see the rewards as priceless. Choosing to apply the resources of their faith—theology, beliefs about God's will for believers, rituals, and other ways of interacting in evangelical culture—to the goal of bridging racial divides, many find themselves relating differently to broader social dynamics than before. The more substantively they interact with others across differences in race, ethnicity, and/or class, the more likely they are to encounter problems of privilege, politics, and power within and beyond their immediate religious communities. But how to address such questions in multiethnic settings, and whether to consider those delicate spiritual spaces appropriate for the secular business of political engagement—or even for talk about politics—remains an unresolved issue for most.

A few snapshots provide a less abstract sense of this:

When he left his coveted youth minister position at a wealthy suburban church outside of Denver, Colorado, to plant an MEC in the inner city, Curt,[11] a thirty-five-year-old white pastor, had only the faintest idea how steep his learning curve would be. But within two years Resurrection Bible Church was hosting a motley congregation of homeless and ex-homeless people, middle- and working-class families, and a growing, multilingual contingent of Latinos, African immigrants, African Americans, and mixed-race families. After settling in the neighborhood, Curt and his wife sent their school-age boys to the local elementary school, where they were the only white students. Not long after, this pastor, who had "never been involved in politics in my life," found himself lobbying for local school reform candidates, building alliances with homeless advocacy groups, and publicly supporting immigration reform in state and federal law.

The sense of a call to engage, at a political level, some of the issues affecting community members was new to Curt. Such things were frowned upon in the ultraconservative community in which he was raised. "I come from conservative training that says you are supposed to save souls—you know, as opposed to the social gospel approach that [conservatives argue] hurt the church," he comments. "Now I'm saying, you can't separate the gospel from the work of Christ. Technically, I'm moving into social justice. It's more than social action." This new orientation raised eyebrows among some of his funders from white, wealthy, suburban churches. But Curt was willing to let the chips fall. "I know that the minute you talk justice, you're talking politics," he says. "But it's my life!"

Suzanne, who is also white, pastors an Evangelical Covenant Church in Chicago. Traditionally a Swedish immigrant denomination, and theologically closer to mainline Protestantism than some other evangelical churches, her church now hosts over a dozen first-generation immigrant communities of diverse ethnic backgrounds. As the small church grows, Suzanne is identifying a need for some kind of ministry that can help members navigate the immigration process, even as all this is new to her. "There is a huge injustice, not only in our [U.S.] system, but in the way their [countries of origin] handle them, to help or hinder them. How can we as the church make some difference in that?" she wonders. "There needs to be a space for them to know that, 'we'll stand with you.' We need to tackle this justice issue. It's a huge one."

When he came to the Multiethnic Church Track of the annual Exponential church-planting conference in Florida in 2008, James was looking for resources. An African American, James headed up a church in Crown Heights, Brooklyn, New York, that had once been a black church but as the neighborhood became more mixed, was now attracting young whites, Latinos, and Caribbean immigrants. Many longtime church members were nervous about the changes, but James saw exciting opportunities to build a new kind of community. Although identifying as dispositionally more "liberal" and "social justice–oriented" than many of the pastors at the church-planting conference, he expressed disappointment that neither the traditionally black church nor the traditionally liberal mainline churches had taken "stronger leadership in building multiracial churches," even though the African American experience made them "uniquely situated" to do so.

In setting up his church as intentionally multiethnic, James ruffled some feathers. Some of the older members even left the church. But as it has actually become a diverse congregation, he reports, "I've changed." Now, he says, "I want to see people have a relationship with Jesus Christ. But beyond that, what I would like to see happen is for the [multiethnic] church to lead the way to a society in which the common good of all people is looked out for, whether or not they are believers."

Lastly, Felix, a second-generation Korean-American, pastors a small MEC in Orange County, California, in which the average congregant is a mid-thirties professional. The church's vision statement is, as he puts it, gospel-focused and international: to "make and equip disciples of all nationalities to be Christ ambassadors to all the nations." Although his church started as 90 percent Korean, now it is more mixed; about 75 percent of the members are Asian (55 percent Korean, 20 percent Chinese), the other 25 percent Caucasian. His staff is mostly white, and his leadership team is a mix of whites and Asians. Rather than a traditional first-generation ethnic church or a second-generation "assimilationist" church, Felix tries to foster a "third culture" mix of ethnic pride, stages of accommodation to American culture, and racial intermixing, even in marriage.

His largely upper-middle-class and politically diverse congregation cares about social issues—poverty, international slavery and human trafficking, AIDS— and contributes resources in those areas. Felix believes attending to justice issues is a way to apply the gospel in practice. But as a theologically conservative evangelical, he is also wary of identifying as a "social justice" church. "I think the problem has been, among evangelicals, when you combine social justice with the gospel, that becomes the gospel. In other words, the whole liberalism— the reason that people . . . shied away from those issues is because social justice issues ate up the church."

Felix's implication that linking "the gospel" with "social justice" is potentially dangerous illuminates a peculiar characteristic of conservative evangelical Christianity in the United States, the trajectory of which I trace in subsequent chapters. The fact that the racial change advocates introduced above are squeamish about whether and how the work they do in their churches might bear on larger political questions is not a demonstration of simple apathy or disinterest. These pastors want to employ the resources they find most meaningful in order to help transform their world, and *the* world. They are usually aware that pursuing substantive racial equality and diversity in their communities may entail taking political stands on some things—say, access to equity in public education or to a fairer and less cumbersome immigration process. They know (or have learned over time) that superficial gestures toward "color-blind" Christian love often compound the problems (Emerson 2000; Loury 2002).

To suggest that conservatism explains the ambivalence would be too simple. Though most ERC participants in the movements I'm looking at describe themselves as theologically conservative, meaning committed to a literalist reading of scripture and certain biblical fundamentals, their political orientation in the aggregate differs in some respects from the larger conservative evangelical community. As we will see, with regard to certain topics like immigration, many are better described as political moderates. The movement also draws leadership and involvement from Christians of color from a variety of backgrounds and perspectives, some of whom do unabashedly identify as social justice activists. Most movement participants nevertheless embrace conservative positions toward other social issues such as marriage, abortion, and homosexuality. But even if they self-identify as conservative Republicans in general, they see themselves as part of a positive submovement within evangelicalism that purposely challenges old, "sinful" racial worldviews sometimes described as "conservative" by the people who defend(ed) them.

Yet political ambivalence persists among many individuals and organizations in the ERC movement. More precisely, as they engage in multiracial settings, they feel simultaneously drawn to and turned off by the possibility of collectively reflecting, much less acting, on their racial change–related pursuits in political (or what they often call "politicized") terms—even though the same individuals may be less conflicted about other issues, such as abortion. Some participants attempt to resolve internal ambivalence by avoiding politics altogether. But others committed to ERC work over time actually experience political awakenings and even transform into activists of one kind or another, sometimes to their own surprise. Their fellow congregants, however, are not always ready to join them because, as we will see, psychological, theological, and conceptual obstacles often stand in their way.

On one dimension, then, the ERC movement exemplifies the pursuit of the social "miraculous"—that is, exciting, out-of-the-ordinary events and processes that participants see as motivated, mediated, or directly produced by God working through faithful human efforts.[12] On another, it is about political ambivalence threaded through pursuits of transformation. Put differently, *working within a context of political ambivalence that is, for culturally specific reasons, more comfortable than engagements framed as explicitly political, people often believe they can create safer spaces for the kinds of interactions they experience as social miracles. In the process, they can produce meaningful change within their communities, yet simultaneously limit their influence more broadly.* How does that happen, and what are the benefits and costs of politically ambivalent approaches to change?

Interpreting Under-the-Radar Change

It was no small event when in 2012 the sixteen-million-member Southern Baptist Convention (SBC), the largest American Protestant denomination, elected its first African American vice president, Pastor Fred Luter Jr. (Eckholm 2012). Luter prevailed over his closest competitor, a Chinese American. While not a political event per se in the nation writ large, it is reflective of a complex process of change within the denomination over the past two decades, one that challenged the internal political climate of the SBC and gradually shifted its racial power structure and general membership profile. The ascendance of more leaders of color in formerly white-dominated churches and organizations in turn impacts the kinds of strategies evangelical elites are able to pursue on the broader political landscape, as they take stances on issues like marriage or immigration.

However, because for the most part the ERC movement has avoided identifying with traditional party positions on race and class-related policy issues, it's the sort of social phenomenon that would not register on the radar of mainstream political science, even if it *does* represent a considerable social change phenomenon. On the occasions when politics scholars and commentators notice the movement, they have tended to dismiss either its significance or its authenticity.[13] I suspect this is a product of not understanding that racial reconciliation and multiracial church–building efforts represent gradual challenges to social hierarchies long taken for granted in white-dominated conservative evangelical communities—challenges that have taken shape within the specific spaces, worldviews, narratives, and practices of those communities. To tease out the social influences at play in these intercurrences, we must search well beyond the type of information political scientists typically garner from exit and opinion polls, and delve beneath the sorts of superficial understandings of American evangelicalism facilitated by the mainstream media.

Another reason ERC efforts have been overlooked by political scientists is that there has been surprisingly scant cross-pollination between the existing literatures on religion in politics, on the one hand, and race politics, on the other. As a case in point, the wealth of research political scientists have produced on the involvement of conservative Christians in American politics has scarcely attended to the influence of race therein.[14] This is partly a result of the majority-white Christian Right's focus on matters of gender, sexual morality, and religious values over race. But because we have largely taken race for granted in studies of evangelicals (as is often the case when the racial group at hand belongs to the "unmarked" category of whiteness), we have been unprepared to explain the origins, timing, and significance of faith-based social change efforts like the ERC movement.[15] Also as a result of having produced siloed literatures on race and religion, political scientists have been relatively unaware of the extent to which the categories of race and religion have mutually influenced each other for centuries, informing many other debates in American politics.

One thing that *has* been on political scientists' radar in recent decades is the rise of American neoconservatism and the possible influence of race (or racism) therein. Neoconservatives focus, among other things, on limiting the reach of federal government institutions and rolling back state-sponsored social policies like welfare, under the rationale that such efforts interfere with liberal egalitarianism and the market freedoms valued in American democracy (Kristol 1995, 2003; High 2009; Fukuyama 2007). Some have suggested that white racial backlash, partly functioning through religious traditions, helped propel this "color-blind conservatism" (Edsall and Edsall 1992; Winant 1990, 2004; Crenshaw 1988). In this milieu, evangelical racial reconciliation efforts have been interpreted as another expression of a conservatism that refuses to grapple seriously with the legacies of racial inequality or to recognize the way structurally influenced differences in racial experiences continue to impact people's daily lives (Alumkal 2004; Stricker 2001).[16]

While this interpretation has some merit, it misses the texture, the power, and the significance of ERC efforts, and perhaps misunderstands the nature of their political ambivalence. A more nuanced reading of the movement reveals how evangelicals working against the grain of the racial divides in their faith communities manage to push the envelope of race relations *even though* evangelicalism has been influenced by the political repertoires of the various kinds of Christians involved, including neoconservatism. ERC advocates operate and perhaps inadvertently reproduce contradictory political impulses, as well as obstacles to engagement worth understanding.

Faith and the Race Divide

This study joins a growing literature beyond political science proper led by Michael Emerson that *has* looked at evangelicals alongside race and provided insight into the interplay of political conservatism therein. Although this scholarship, mostly in sociology and religious studies, illuminates much about the ERC milieu that informs this project, I seek to unravel additional puzzles about political orientations and attitudes toward engagement it does not fully explore.

Emerson and fellow sociologist Christian Smith (2000) were the first to produce a large-scale survey of racial attitudes in American evangelicalism. Their influential work, *Divided by Faith: Evangelical Religion and the Problem of Race in America,* rattled the evangelical world by exposing the deep divides between (primarily) white and black evangelicals in terms of their respective outlooks on race and related issues.[17] Analyzing a rich range of data, Emerson and Smith emerged pessimistic about the possibility for either more racially integrated or more politically progressive American evangelical race politics. Black and white evangelicals, they found, draw on practically irreconcilable theological and ideological "tool kits" through which they interpret racial inequalities and navigate race relations (Swidler 1986).[18]

Three central obstacles, they argued, inhibit the creation of an evangelical reconciliation theology that could produce a substantive social justice/change framework related to race. First, white evangelicals tend to favor "color blindness" and individualistic, unidimensional approaches to combating racism, which, typically, are relationship-oriented. They therefore tend to eschew collective and multidimensional (individual, structural, and systemic) responses. African American Christians, in contrast, are distinctly aware of racism and support the pursuit of systemic changes. Each group comes to its orientation about how social change happens through different cultural lenses, histories, and interpretations of scripture.[19]

Second, because white evangelicals are generally more attached, even through their theology, to the individualist precepts of free-will, liberal, market capitalism that hinge on the notion of equal opportunity, they tend to see ongoing racial inequality as primarily attitudinal, rather than produced by systemic structures and policies. They are thus likelier to hold minorities accountable for racial inequalities, and to believe that if people of color are subordinated, it is because they suffer from relational dysfunction and a lack of responsibility (Emerson and Smith 2000, 101).[20] Third, the development of effectively segregated, racially homogenous evangelical congregations over time contributes to the divergent demographic and racial perspectives of blacks and whites, thereby reproducing virtually irreconcilable lenses through which each group approaches race-related change. As a result of white and black evangelicals being "divided by faith," Emerson and Smith concluded that "despite devoting considerable time and energy to solving the problem of racial division, white evangelicalism likely does more to perpetuate the racialized society than to reduce it" (2000, 170).[21]

Emerson and Smith are correct about some of the fundamental obstacles that potentially beset evangelicals' racial change efforts. It is indeed difficult to navigate a "justice-related" politics if white people have trouble recognizing how systemic inequalities continue to plague some racial groups in the United States. However, *Divided* scholarship has concentrated more on evangelicals in general than on the ERC movement in particular. Members of the ERC movement may differ in terms of the interpretive "tool kits" to which they ascribe. Too, this scholarship has (reasonably) attended more to sources of division in evangelicalism than to the political attitudes and practices of evangelicals who *are* interested in racial change. A subsequent wave of research, also led by Emerson but focusing on the MEC movement, attends mainly to the theological frameworks, structures, and practices of the MEC rather than participants' attitudes toward race in *political* contexts.

Although I am influenced by Emerson and Smith's pioneering work, the research assembled here suggests something different. If we understand politics broadly as struggles over power, distribution of status and resources, and the methods by which substantive change should happen within a particular human community (like evangelicalism) or beyond it (as in a nation), even developments that ERC participants described as "apolitical" reflect more political activity than has been recognized. The series of public apologies and restructurings in the 1990s by evangelical organizations that had at some point in their history supported or tolerated racism, the early rise of multiethnic congregations, and grassroots racial reconciliation efforts in churches all demonstrate this. We might call such intragroup challenges to older, sedimented power structures "micropolitical activity."

But the phenomenon does extend beyond the insular and micropolitical. I find that, increasingly in more recent ERC settings, especially MEC forums, politics routinely bubbles through the "safe" layer of religious and social etiquettes, whether participants want it to or not. This is often true even where the sorts of relationalism that the *Divided* literature identifies (the focus on social change through interpersonal relationships) is indeed the dominant paradigm. Like Curt and Suzanne above, many participants find that the more deeply they get to know people from other ethnic, racial, and class backgrounds, the less easy it becomes to ignore or maintain a "neutral" or avoidant posture toward ongoing issues of inequality or access, in areas like immigration or education. But at the same time, as Emerson and Smith (2000) note, there are disincentives built into the worldviews and cultural habits of evangelicals that inhibit a more robust racial politics. ERC advocates find ways to navigate these realities, whether through direct engagement or measured avoidance.

Such dynamics suggest that the political ambivalence within so many ERC settings has to do with participants' cultural tool kits, but in more intricate ways than has been recognized. Interpreting issues of political engagement through religious and other cultural frameworks can impact people's willingness to engage more politically oriented conversations about race (or other social divides). I draw on sociologist Paul Lichterman (2005) to develop this point. Lichterman observes that cultural customs, including the daily practices and social expectations that characterize many conservative evangelical communities, often inhibit open engagement with and "social reflexivity" around certain kinds of disagreements, confusions, and concerns.[22] Social reflexivity is a way of imagining and talking about differences within and beyond the group; as part of that, customs can "welcome people to social criticism instead of scaring all but those already convinced" (44–47).

Within the ERC milieu, historical patterns in American evangelicalism—which, as I detail, reflect not just a religious history but a *racial history*, or more precisely several sets of interwoven racial histories—provide daunting obstacles for even confident racial change advocates to discuss race *policy* issues. Topics like abortion or protecting "traditional marriage" do not raise the same anxieties. These and other factors render many ERC participants wary of translating their vision, at least formally, to positions on racial policy and politics or even social justice matters construed more broadly. They seem to want to strike an implicit bargain: in order to protect the sacred spaces of racial reconciliation and multiethnic community, where they experience "miraculous" interactions seen as impossible in other social contexts, most (but not all) feel the need to cordon off the process from what they regard as the fraught and potentially contaminating realm of "politics." In some sense, they are resisting letting their movement be domesticated into the deeply partisan and polarized culture wars of American political discourse writ large. Still, they may be conflicted about these matters and find ways to make different individual political decisions based on their experience.

ERC efforts provide a window, then, into emerging political orientations within a social movement that does not centrally define itself politically, and even *resists* being so defined. We learn to identify factors that, for reasons specific to a given subculture, make a subject area a bit too fraught to engage, despite members' political engagement in other arenas. This sheds light on what sorts of changes occur in people's political orientations around racial and other ascribed or accreted differences (such as socioeconomic inequality) when they begin to have more cross-group social contact than they have in the past. This also challenges us to deepen our thinking about how in certain contexts political avoidance or ambivalence may itself be either an expression of a kind of political resistance, or a product of the internalized workings of political power.

Tracing Intercurrence

My reading of ERC efforts amounts to three overarching claims. Each builds on the work of other scholars; however, the combination has the potential to innovate and expand upon the analytical paradigms through which ERC efforts and other politically ambivalent social change initiatives have so far been interpreted.

First, as I have argued elsewhere, from the perspectives of history, sociology, and identity, race and religion are better understood as intersectional, *co-constituted* categories in American political life than as social categories that occasionally interact (Jacobson 2012; Wadsworth 2008b). This co-constitutionality means that each category, which represents a set of socially constructed meaning systems, has historically affected the definition and the social effects of the other. The very concept of "race" would have had little meaning in the United States without religious stories, norms, and institutions to both reinforce and challenge the ideas it represented at any given historical moment. Nor could we possibly understand American religious history without tracing the deep impact of race therein. Therefore, the development of neither racial nor religious configurations in the United States is fully comprehensible in isolation from the other category. This race-religion intersectionality is inescapable in a nation settled by Europeans who, on the whole, brought deeply held racialized and religious worldviews with them, used each to fortify the other, and through colonization, political development, and all kinds of institution building imposed power on human beings they considered inferior.

The ERC movement is one expression of how racial dynamics have impacted American Christians, and vice versa. It illuminates how racial groups argue and think about *and through* religion and, conversely, how religious communities in given political contexts have likely contended with reality partly *through* the dimension of race. I trace how American Christianity has been profoundly impacted by three distinct *religious racial traditions*, which have led to divergent faith-based interpretations of race that invariably impact political orientations. The incentives that propelled some evangelicals to try to mend racial fractures when they did emerged not so much through neoconservative trends (although those are relevant) but more squarely through the tensions that developed over time between those traditions. Because the categories of religion and/or race have impacted most Americans' identities, these dynamics influence the nation's larger social and political trajectory. In other national contexts, especially in places impacted by the waves of conquest that took place under Western colonialist, expansionist endeavors (which is virtually all of them), race and religion (or ethnicity, tribe, or class) may similarly constitute group identities and relationships.

My second claim is that ERC efforts are best conceptualized not as an expression of any single political perspective, such as neoconservatism, but as a distinctive *religious race-bridging project* sculpted within a particular cultural context.[23] A *racial project* is a conceptual framework that influences people's reactions to and/or promotion of race-related policy objectives, a set of ideas that frames the way people think about race and judge proposals for addressing race issues (Winant 2004). "Bridging," a term borrowed from social capital literature, happens when some groups engage with others, and in the process "generate broader identities and reciprocity"—in other words, cultivate ongoing relationships across their distinctive communities (Putnam 2000, 2007; Smidt 2003; Larsen et al. 2004). Such relationships can then be applied to civic objectives, like volunteering, or to political objectives, like organizing a rally. Religious race bridging, then, is a means of drawing on faith- and culture-based resources to bring members of different racial or ethnic groups together in hopes of fostering individual and corporate change within the spiritual body.

Evangelicals may participate in racial reconciliation or MECs for any number of reasons. The concept of religious race bridging helps us identify *why* participants feel there is a racial (or ethnic) gap to bridge, how they believe that gap developed, and how religious and community resources provide special resources to help them bridge it but also define the terms through which they do. Religious race bridging also illuminates how two major competing racial narratives came to circumscribe evangelical race relations in ways that render it daunting for many contemporary participants to address race relations and race *politics* in shared cultural space. The bridging that ERC manifests is produced through the idiosyncratic cultural resources of evangelicalism, which, we must recognize, are perpetually in some implicit conversation with broader historical and current discourses about race, politics, and power in U.S. culture.

Woven through the above arguments is my third analytical claim, that we cannot responsibly assess the ERC movement—or any boundary-crossing social change movement—without learning a fair amount about the cultural practices and assumptions that most participants take for granted. I pay particular attention to how, in the evangelical case, faith as a semiotic system mediates questions of identity, power sharing, and dialogue, and informs the possibilities, strategies, and tactics of community and coalition building. Whether or not ERC efforts will generate new, *formally* political coalitions among American Christians over the long run, they clearly complicate the picture of evangelical engagement in American political culture. These dynamics help reveal how social shifts within a given community are deeply mediated both by the unique cultural *habitus*—the socially learned skills, dispositions, and ways of acting of that community—and by the rings of semiotic and power dynamics that encircle it.

Examining Culture, Meaning, and Power

This book joins a growing body of scholarship working to refine paradigms for studying the intersection of culture and politics within political science. Much of this work traffics under the (productively contested) banners of "political ethnography" and "interpretive methods" (Schatz 2009; Yanow and Schwartz-Shea 2006).[24]

As Edward Schatz, one leader in the field, puts it, "ethnography often expands—indeed, it often explodes—how we understand the boundaries of the 'political'" (2009, 10). One of political ethnography's interests is investigating micropolitics, the daily and small-scale engagements with power and inequality that take place inside communities and inform how and when values and activities are embraced from broader (for example, ideological, regional, national) cultural realms, and for what ends. This involves attending to the meanings participants in social phenomena attribute to their own social and political reality. The more closely we scrutinize a set of cultural meaning systems, histories, and practices, the fuzzier the boundary between culture and politics becomes. Political ethnographers read this as less a "problem" (as some scholars invested in more mainstream, science-oriented approaches of mainstream political science might regard it) than a reality of life that our research designs need to better reflect.[25] The difference from traditional cultural anthropology (also an evolving discipline) is that political ethnography is especially interested in how cultural phenomena interact with political elements (Wedeen 2008).

Participant-observation, or "immersion in a community, a cohort, a locale, or a cluster of related subject positions," is a central approach in political ethnography (Schatz 2009, 5). Another is analysis of discourses and texts produced within the social milieu being investigated (5).[26] Analyzing how ideas are transmitted through social etiquette, speech, and written language helps us understand how meanings are produced within and through culture. This approach involves a careful balance between keenly attending to how the people whose perspective and actions we're trying to understand interpret what they're doing, and rendering an analysis through an "ethnographic sensibility" that respects but does not necessarily accept those interpretations. Across a variety of methods, most political ethnographers accept that arriving at the "truth" about social phenomena is much less a science than an interpretive effort that can never be complete (Soss 2006, 132–33).

I am especially informed by political scientist Lisa Wedeen's approach to political ethnography (1999, 2002, 2008). Drawing on research in Yemen and Syria, Wedeen proposes an anthropological conceptualization of "culture as semiotic practices" or "practices of meaning-making." Studying meaning-production, she argues, "entails analyzing the relations between agents' practices (e.g., their work habits, gendered norms, self-policing strategies, and leisure patterns) and systems of signification (language and other symbolic systems)" (Wedeen 2002, 714).[27] Such approaches involve paying attention to "what language and symbols *do*—how they are inscribed in concrete actions and how they operate to produce observable political effects" (714). Cultural meaning-making practices are always in a dialectical relationship with larger power configurations—sometimes challenging power systems, sometimes reproducing them, sometimes quietly internalizing "the way things are." These are important dynamics to attend to in a study of bridge-building efforts across different cultural arenas.

Culture as meaning-making practices also helps us inquire into cause-and-effect relationships between culture and politics—that is, when, why, and how (in this case) evangelical culture influences participants to adopt political orientations or activities and when, conversely, "outside" political phenomena (for example, federal-level advances in civil rights law) seem to inform the faith-based cultural community's meaning systems and behavior. The categories of race and religion have been both causal influences on American political movements and systems as well as effects of broader semiotic practices, institutions, and historical processes.[28] Through that interweaving of the national and the particular or local, participants in ERC settings often interpret race-related issues through guiding values not automatically accessible to nonmembers.

Meaning-making practices need to be deciphered contextually. When, for instance, reconcilers use the metaphor of Jesus's crucifixion on a cross to assert that racial reconciliation is of utmost importance for Christians, they mean something specific. When they suggest that "the world" is not interested in reconciliation and therefore it is futile to try to apply the concept beyond the community of believers, they are not talking about the same "world" we understand to exist in secular contexts. ERC advocates' conceptualizations of words like "reconciliation" and "the world" impact their willingness to weigh in on race-related issues they consider "political" but outside the jurisdiction of their communities. Studying meaning-making practices, in other words, helps us comprehend the subtle ways in which the cultures people immediately and intimately identify with inform their orientation to and navigation of broader power dynamics in the world.

To understand that meaning-making practices also reflect *effects* of broader dynamics, "of institutional arrangements, of structures of domination, and of strategic interests," surfaces myriad insights on ERC efforts (Wedeen 2002, 714). For instance, as I delineate in chapter 2, racial segregation in evangelicalism was not "natural" or biblical (though it was often defended as such) but historical: many denominations were instituted directly as a result of adherents' positions on slavery and other race-related issues. Believers raised in church communities, whether those were bastions of racism or sanctuaries for freedom-fighting, were socialized through *both* religion and race, leading to individual and collective orientations about race that, in turn, linked up with larger institutionalized power structures (for example, state legislatures, parties, school systems). When modern evangelicals began to frame racism in terms of "sin," such a conception did not represent some sudden scriptural discovery but rather encapsulated new interpretations of central symbols based on changing mores about prejudice in the wake of the civil rights movement.

Overall, the framework of culture as meaning-making practices is the best-suited means of investigating cultural phenomena with deep sociopolitical roots that bring together strands of many interwoven histories and are often, as a result, conflicted about how to engage political questions in the current moment. The ambiguities and ambivalences that emerge in ERC contexts provide interesting clues to the deeply enmeshed dynamics between politics and race, religion and culture—these practically infinite constellations of semiotic practices in the United States.

In addition to assembling empirical data about ERC advocates, their social networks, habits, activities, goals, and disappointments, then, this is an interpretive and ethnographic project in its recognition that one analyst's view can proffer no stable ontological "truths" to make sense of ERC efforts. The point is rather to better understand the distinctive epistemological frames through which participants make sense of their own efforts and come to see those frames as natural or obvious.[29] Direct observation, historical research, and interpretive analysis provide insight into how people's approaches to political opportunities, activities, strategies, and idea frameworks are informed by the various cultural orbits in which they operate—faith and ritual being, in this case, especially influential ones.

2 Evangelical Race Relations in Historical Context

—————————————————————————————————— +

With over sixteen million members, the Southern Baptist Convention (SBC) is the largest Protestant body in the United States and the largest Christian denomination outside of Roman Catholicism (ARDA 2000). It was also once a bastion of white supremacist religion. The SBC was founded in 1845 after a regional split with Northern Baptists over the issue of slavery and missions, with Southern Baptists stridently defending slavery. The denominational body resisted Reconstruction, tacitly if not actively supported Jim Crow, was slow to embrace civil rights movement era reforms, and then (as if it weren't already conservative enough) underwent a well-chronicled "conservative takeover" in the 1980s (Ammerman 1990). So it was a shock to many when the SBC became a prominent player in racial reconciliation efforts sweeping through the evangelical community in the mid-1990s. By the 2000s, the SBC had become one of the fastest-diversifying congregations nationally, with approximately 20 percent of its congregations being majority nonwhite (Green 2004; Heagney 2009). Across the country there are African American, Latino, Asian, and all varieties of immigrant communities expanding under the SBC umbrella—a phenomenon that would have been inconceivable even half a century ago. Given this growing mosaic, contemporary SBC leaders have had to walk a fine line on race-related policy issues like immigration reform, as members representing multiple perspectives demand response from leadership (Pulliam 2007; Walker 2007; Hughes 2008).

What changed? How could a tradition rife with white supremacist attachments have become a leader in intentional institutional diversity and demographic transformation? We cannot begin to answer such questions without tunneling back into American evangelical race history, a history that is central, rather than peripheral, to the broader history of racial politics in the United States.[1] Our understanding of contemporary American racial and religious

politics, and the significant role of evangelicals therein, would be greatly enhanced if this history were better understood.

It is commonplace for even keen students of American political history to
conceive of race and religion as distinct fields of ideas and struggle. This basic misperception distorts our understanding of the nation's development. To
illustrate: Imagine we are shuffling through a slide show reviewing the political
history of race in the United States. We would pass through images of major periods: Indian wars and then the removal and forced assimilation of indigenous
tribes; slavery and the Civil War; the Mexican War; the long agony of segregation; Chinese labor and other waves of immigration; the civil and voting rights
movements of various groups; and onto the present day. Next, we turn to religious political history, where images might include the Framers' debates over
religious freedom; Mormons' and other minorities' struggles for religious autonomy; the turn-of-the-century social gospel movement; and the spectacular rise
of the Religious Right in the late twentieth century. Each of these phenomena
influenced the character of American democracy, helping to sculpt the nation's
laws, policies, and political culture. But we might not think about how much one
history crosses into the other. In our historical and political narratives, and in
much scholarship, race politics seems to fall into one conceptual column, religious politics into another.

Yet if American political history can be said to have, at its heart, a story about
the struggles for democracy and inclusion within a growing empire, both religion and race are braided through that story, each element perpetually folding
into the other, fashioned in varied iterations to weave an ever-changing picture.
As the historian Mark Noll puts it, "Together race and religion make up, not only
the nation's deepest and most enduring moral problem, but also its broadest and
most enduring political influence" (2008, 1).[2] Indeed, both factors have been
inextricably embedded in the identity, mission, and political development of the
nation. But in order to grasp the ongoing relevance of this, we need to better
understand how the combination of race and religion "together" works.

In this chapter I provide a broad context for understanding how American
racial and religious history, as interwoven phenomena, created both the evangelical community's defining fractures *and* the conditions for the racial change
efforts that emerged in the late twentieth century. While not a comprehensive
index, this overview identifies road markers that signal the outlines of American
evangelicalism's distinctive racial conundrum. Along the way, I trace the racial
and religious history of the SBC and the American Pentecostal tradition, two
evangelical Protestant communities that became relevant to evangelical racial
change initiatives. This provides a preliminary sense of how the interrelatedness

of religion and race in American political development created the conditions within which evangelicals began in the latter part of the twentieth century to find reasons to attempt to repair centuries-old racial wounds by appealing to faith-based community resources.

I employ two conceptual tools to help us: the concept of *intersectionality,* and the organizing framework of *religious racial traditions.*

Intersectionality is a concept originally developed by women of color to capture the ways in which race, gender, and sometimes other categories such as class or sexuality do not simply *overlap* to influence people's lived experiences but are, more profoundly, social categories whose *very meanings are constructed through* implicit or explicit reference to one another.[3] Thus, the meaning of racial identities in the United States always contained—and indeed depended on—certain norms and expectations about gender, and vice versa. Such intersectionality meant, for example, that gendered expectations of white womanhood in the nineteenth century precluded women working outside the home; simultaneously, racial norms imposed even "male" forms of labor on black women, who were not protected by strictures of Victorian (white) womanhood.

Likewise, religion and race are, especially in the U.S. context, intersectional categories.[4] Moreover, it is impossible to disarticulate the history of race, racialization, and racism from religion in this country, and equally unfeasible to unthread American religious history from its enduring racial legacies.[5] Put differently, American religious history is profoundly a *racial* history, just as American racial history is also a *religious* history; both factors have been central to the identity, mission, and political development of the nation. When examining race in American politics, then, we must remember that racial categories themselves have been historically enacted through religious beliefs and practices; that racial injustice—but also resistance to it—has frequently been articulated through religion; and that religious values and institutions inform racial politics across multiple dimensions.

This idea of race-religion intersectionality can provide some traction for understanding political history. My use of the term refers to three dimensions of intimate interplay between race and religion. First, as I elaborate, the *foundational* categories of race and religion in the U.S. context were forged in relation to one another. Foundational, here, denotes the ways in which the meaning of and options ascribed to each category were defined at least partly through implicit or explicit reference to the other. The primary manifestation of this is that before scientific justifications for racism existed, the American racial stratification system was routinely rationalized through the dominant religion, Christianity, as a belief system that gave race meaning, as an institutional structure that implemented it, and through individual members who endorsed or challenged it. This is not to say that Christianity *itself* is inherently racist; it is not. But it provided the primary interpretive system, the basic vocabulary through which many people endorsed the racial status quo.

As a result of religion's influence on the American racial system, race and religion have come to intersect *sociologically*. The racial group into which one was assigned at birth would have some effect on one's religious options (think here of American Indians or black slaves, but also some whites, who would pay a price for subscribing to a nonnormative faith). Likewise, one's religious tradition would likely influence one's racial views through socialization, church membership, and cultural practices. The demographic history of American religious traditions thus becomes a distinctly racialized history. Indeed, the denominational and sociological configurations of American religion developed *through* racial divisions, not despite them. American faith communities have in this sense perpetually been fractured by race, often through people's racial identifications but also through their orientation to racial politics (so that, for example, abolitionism could unify some white and black Christians where race might have otherwise divided them).

Thus, as with other categories like gender and class, race and religion function intersectionally at the level of *personal identity*. Because of the legacies of Christian and racial history, what it means to be, for example, African American *and* Christian is likely quite a different political and religious experience than what it means to be a white Christian or, say, a South Asian American Hindu. But this is not always clear cut because identity intersectionality puts people into different relationships to power at different moments. Sometimes religious identity reinforces racial difference; sometimes, as in the case of new multiracial alliances, it overcomes it. But for many Americans, these aspects of identity are deeply intertwined.[6]

Through the phenomenon of race-religion intersectionality, Christianity and Christians are irrevocably (and tragically) implicated in America's distinctive brand of white supremacist traditions. But, on the brighter side, we also cannot explain the nation's democratic triumphs without appreciating the profound influence of Christianity in struggles for racial equality. Conceptualizing race and religion as intersectional, co-constituted, rather than occasionally interactive, phenomena provides a more accurately calibrated lens through which to examine the trajectory of evangelical race relations. Because race and religion are such deeply interwoven categories, groups like white Baptists could not possibly have escaped what W. E. B. Du Bois called "the problem of the color line" (1903, 19). But neither could they forever avoid having to face the long-term effects of their beliefs and actions. Eventually, both the nation's racial progress and their own Christianity demanded they deal with the past.

The framework of *religious racial traditions* provides a way to conceptually organize the intersectional story of American racial and religious history. I define a religious racial tradition as a collection of beliefs, narratives, practices, and strategies applied to racial issues in American political culture by religious individuals, groups, and institutions. Through religious racial traditions people employ a theological perspective as a lens through which they interpret and respond to some aspect of race relations (though not always in a coherent way). Even citizens who are not especially religious may be deeply informed by a religious racial tradition, as it becomes an inherited, taken-for-granted set of ideas and practices influencing their daily lives. We might think of religious racial traditions as an umbrella set of cultural meaning-making systems that get carried forward, but also modified, across long periods of time.[7]

The historian Paul Harvey (2005) identifies three major traditions defining the crossover between race and religion in the South: "theological racism," "racial interchange," and "Christian interracialism."[8] I modify these slightly to capture religious racial traditions that I suggest are applicable as ideal types to the nation writ large. In the primarily black/white context of the American South, theological racism describes "the conscious use of religious doctrine and practice to create and enforce social hierarchies that privileged southerners of European descent, who were legally classified and socially privileged as white, while degrading southerners of African descent, who were legally categorized and stigmatized as black" (2). Applied more broadly, theological racism is essentially the American Protestant expression of religion harnessed in service to the specific form of racial hierarchy known as white supremacy.[9]

Despite racial inequality, sometimes (and in the U.S. context, uniquely) believers of diverse races commingle in religious cultural settings, influencing each other's worship styles, theology, and practices. This "exchange of southern religious cultures between white and black believers in expressive culture, seen especially in music, in the formation of new religious traditions, and in lived experience," is the "racial interchange" tradition (Harvey 2005, 3). Through such moments of crossover, the culturally imposed boundaries between the races sometimes soften, though usually only temporarily, and can generate new conversations about race (and religion) as time passes and circumstances change.

Finally, "Christian interracialism," or what I term the "religious racial justice tradition," describes how Christians, white and of color, exert "self-consciously political efforts to undermine the system of southern [or, as we'll read it, national] racial hierarchy" (Harvey 2005, 3). Religious actors in this tradition (who have also included non-Christians) employ theology and material resources to fight some aspect(s) of racist policy. However, these actors are not necessarily ideologically antiracist; sometimes they fight policies (say, slavery or American Indian removal) without challenging, or even while endorsing, the racial attitudes supporting them.

Theological Racism

Theological racism expresses the "deep-rooted, interlocking system of power" of white supremacist paradigms channeled through religious traditions (Harvey 1997, 2). Using theological interpretation, imagined community, everyday speech, folklore, tracts, church services, and so forth, whites—not just southerners and not just Christians—blended various aspects of religion with the often unstable and constantly revised white supremacist project (Dailey 2004; Mathews 2004). Protestants, the dominant religious group since the nation's founding, existed at the center of this tradition, and evangelical Protestants, estimated to represent at least 85 percent of Protestants in the nineteenth century, were its heartbeat (Noll 1990).

Before scientific modernism's ascent as the primary explanatory framework for race, religious interpretive frameworks enabled Europeans to justify their status over the "dark" and therefore "sinful" others they encountered as they expanded into new territories and markets (Fredrickson 2002). Christianity's dichotomous symbology—with its binary vocabulary of salvation/sin, spirit/flesh, purity/defilement, white/black—was readily mapped by Europeans onto religion and culture to justify the oppression and later extermination of Jews in what Fredrickson identifies as the earliest expressions of racism in the West.[10] This new framework of inferiority-through-immutability extended easily to justify the persecution of other "dark," "savage," and "foreign" groups subjected to European expansion. Through theological racism, most white religious communities actively constructed and reproduced the racial categories that allowed white supremacy to function as a hegemonic norm.

In the U.S. colonial era, whites in most colonies consistently conflated Christianity with civilization and Anglo-Saxon identity in the project of nation-building. The combination of race and religion fundamentally constructed the meaningful concepts of whiteness, civilization, and savagism and the policies justified by them (Pearce 1967; Jordan 1974). Puritan notions of "God's chosen people" in the colonies justified universal land reform, representative government, rights of conscience, and notions of civic virtue, all perceived as necessary for whites to fulfill scriptural commandments (Pearce 1967, 128). Racialized national identity, anchored in a particular religious worldview with the concept of manifest destiny at its heart, led to the associated justifications for the formal, codified political exclusion of nonwhites, via the slave trade, black servitude, and American Indian genocide and removal (Tinker 1993; Morone 2003; Horsman 1981). Despite debates over religious qualification laws, American citizenship (indeed, Americanness itself) became firmly paired with whiteness and Protestant Christianity—although Jews, Catholics, and selective other ethnics could eventually be annexed on as white (DuBois 2003; Roediger 1991; Jacobson 1998). The Christianization of Africans stigmatized or prohibited most of the traditional spiritual practices blacks brought with them and forced "heathen" slaves and ex-slaves to worship in American churches. Through religious paternalism designed to "save" those perceived as existing on the lower rungs of a divinely ordained order (the so-called sill class), whites virtually extinguished African Muslim as well as Native American tribal religious traditions by forcefully imposing Christianity (Harlow 1990; Boles 1988).

Even across two Great Awakenings, which transformed the power structures of Protestant Christianity and created more egalitarian religious practices, theological racism justified slavery and other forms of racial persecution and violence through the "Curse of Ham" and other mythologies of a divinely ordained racial hierarchy (Goldenberg 2005; Daly 2004).[11] In the New World context many American Jews also found religious justification for white supremacist structures (Rosen 2000; Salzman and West 1997). The Jackson and subsequent administrations enlisted churches to execute state-sanctioned missionary projects designed to pacify and control Indians (Cadwalader and Deloria 1984; Tinker 1993). In the run-up to the Civil War, all the largest Protestant denominations fractured over slavery and/or its extension into the western frontier, with theological arguments wielded by both sides (MacRobert 1988; Lincoln 1999). Theological racism buttressed the southern "Lost Cause" after the war, supported segregation, and fortified racially separatist denominations (Ammerman 1990). It also helped to defend colonization schemes, political inequality for nonwhites, and nativism in the North.

Theological racism persisted in the twentieth century, supporting nativist and anti-immigrant policies, voting rights restrictions, religious and racial discriminations against American Indian tribes, and ongoing denominational segregation. It lived on through Ku Klux Klan–sponsored violence in the South, the tacit (and sometimes overt) support of white churches for Jim Crow, and many Christians' general inaction on issues of racial equality. It continues presently through extremist movements like Christian Identity as well as more mainstream theological perspectives that deny or justify the existence of racial hierarchies (Barkun 1994).

Theological racism demonstrates one of the ways racial ideology and practice developed intersectionally through religion to construct, perpetuate, and police racial identities, in the North as well as the South. In order to weave Baptist history into this larger picture, we need to circle back and review how theological racism played out in the South, alongside the two other religious racial traditions.

One of the first communities of dissenting Protestant sects in the early colonies, Baptists were vocal advocates of church/state separation who promoted more democratic decision making within the denomination, an activist moral ethos, and individual responsibility as an outgrowth of personal faith (Ammerman 1990, 20). During the first Great Awakening of the mid-eighteenth century, charismatic Baptist preachers like Jonathan Edwards and George Whitefield inspired mass conversions, expanding the denomination's influence across the colonies and deeply into the South. But even as some prominent Baptists preached the radically inclusive message that blacks and whites were spiritually equal and therefore could all receive salvation, many nevertheless supported slavery, and most endorsed the racial stratification structures upon which the American slave system pivoted (Emerson 2000, 25).

Until the mid-nineteenth century, evangelical Protestantism hosted a receptive white audience and a captive African one, which fostered elements of *racial interchange*, albeit within a fundamentally unequal social system. The American South has always been predominantly evangelical Protestant and heavily Baptist.[12] Southern blacks and whites had the closest daily contact, and biracial congregations—wherein Africans worshipped in the slave galleries of their owners' churches—became a routine aspect of southern life. Slave conversion was central to Christian slaveholders' self-image, as many rationalized the injustice of slavery by the salvation slaves would find in the afterlife (Gallay 1988). Because white masters mostly prohibited slaves from practicing religion independently, and because Christianity was employed as a strategy of pacification, the participation of slaves was integrated into the life of the southern evangelical church. Distinct social stratification was crucial to this ordering. However, many of the religious rituals of the Baptist community allowed for "temporary interludes of symbolic equality"—where black and white parishioners were inducted in more or less the same ways and often side-by-side (Gallay 1988). Slaves and masters attended revivals and religious festivals together, were baptized in the same ceremonies, received new members into local churches, and celebrated births and funerals as a community. Church logbooks of the period often listed the names of black and white members who participated in these rituals. And there is some evidence that the more expressive worship practices of African Americans influenced the character of some branches of southern evangelicalism in intimate ways (James 1988).

In this context, Christianity functioned paradoxically as both an oppressive imposition on slaves as well as a resource for spiritual sustenance under abysmal conditions. The evangelical faith that had provided enslaved Christians with a form of spiritual nourishment and a small measure of freedom of expression in a violently oppressive social order was eventually channeled into a resource for restoring and fortifying freed people in what remained a ruthlessly hostile culture. "For most enslaved Christians," Harvey notes, "the evangelical faith provided not so much the fuel for violent revolt as spiritual protection from the heinous system of racial subjugation supported by their white 'brethren' as God's plan to Christianize the heathen" (1997, 9). With all the privilege enjoyed by whites in the South, white Baptists "lacked the will, the fortitude, the theology, and the intellectual tools" to even contemplate accepting black believers as equals (8).

Fracture and the Lost Cause

As the institution of slavery was threatened from outside, many southern whites increasingly harnessed Christianity to their effort to protect and rationalize the hallowed "southern way of life." As the Kentucky General Baptist Association put it in 1860: "Among the white race in the Southern States there is no difference of opinion upon this subject; all are united in opinion in reference to the political, intellectual and social inequality between the colored and the white races. And the people of our Commonwealth generally feel that the present condition of the colored race in this country accords both with the Word and the providence of God" (quoted in Ammerman 1990, 36).

As early as the 1830s, even white southern evangelicals who had questioned slavery were defending it as an unchallenged orthodoxy in the face of northern evangelical critiques. By midcentury, the question of slavery fractured nearly every American Protestant denomination along sectional and ideological lines. Baptists, Methodists, and Presbyterians were rent asunder by sectional schisms that would impact their organizations permanently (Carwardine 1993). Baptist benevolent societies fractured along sectional lines as a result of battles in southern Baptist mission societies, some of which refused to be affiliated with slavery (Harvey 1997, 6; Ammerman 1990, 31). In the spring of 1845, the Baptist Home Mission Society decided to carry out its mission in separate northern and southern divisions, and in May of that year several state delegates came together to organize the SBC. It is not an exaggeration to say that the SBC was created in defense of slavery. The new denomination provided a base for white southern Baptists to organize against the abolitionist forces growing among northern Baptists and other denominations.

After establishing a newly "southern" branch of Baptist culture, Southern Baptists worked on solidifying that regional identity and attempting to secure a basic stability in the face of hostile forces to the north. The South's economic stake in slavery, and northern abolitionists' harsh criticisms of southern traditions, forced white southerners into a reappraisal of—or at least fresh justifications for—the southern way of life. Southern Baptists and other evangelicals set to work fortifying scriptural justifications for slavery (before the war) and legislating racial inequality (after the war). The racialized religious sentiments expressed by the Kentucky Baptists quoted above remained little changed for other white southerners into the twentieth century. Through theological racism white southern evangelicals set themselves above their black neighbors.

As white evangelicals in the South became self-consciously *southern* evangelicals, they set to work building new organizations and educational institutions to compete with "godless" northerners. Between 1845 and 1880, membership in Southern Baptist churches shot from 350,000 to 1.6 million, the vast majority of these churches being rural and isolated (Ammerman 1990, 32). Despite southerners' putative support of church/state separation, they jumped, as did many evangelicals in the North, at chances to translate evangelical moral values into legislation—for example, Sabbath laws and vice regulations against gambling and drinking (36).[13] Southern evangelical religion gradually became embedded as a distinct subculture within American society with its own racial twist.

By the 1850s, evangelical Protestantism had become the "principal subculture in antebellum America"—not just the South (Carwardine 1993, xvi). This nineteenth-century American evangelicalism did not represent a single community but increasingly a clash of ideologies deeply conditioned by religious beliefs and church associations. Different worldviews supported distinct party preferences, a situation that made evangelical values, discourse, and moral agendas critical to political alignments on both sides of the Mason-Dixon Line (Olson 2007). Evangelicals did not believe they could afford to avoid politics with contentious issues like slavery and states' rights at stake, and, likewise, political parties could not afford to ignore evangelicals; indeed, in both the North and the South they required them. According to Carwardine, "just as evangelical party loyalties developed out of a world view nourished by their religion, so their sectional chauvinism derived not simply from remote political developments, but from ecclesiastical antagonisms much closer to home" (1993, xvii).

The Civil War, however, demolished many white southern churches and shook theological convictions about the place of slavery in "God's divine plan." While black Christians liberated from the controlling arm of white religious paternalism constructed a new religious edifice on a hopeful foundation, white congregations concentrated on rebuilding besieged religious structures. Most took up the "Lost Cause" theology, believing that the South had been punished for a lack of humility but that it would eventually rise again. Southern Baptists worked to defend the sovereignty of their internal decision-making structures against the encroaching arm of the more integrationist nation-state and northern Baptist organizations.

As freed slaves withdrew from white churches to form their own congregations, membership in white-dominated Baptist congregations plummeted. The SBC and its churches generally supported the development of black churches and schools, partly out of altruistic motives but also inspired by fears about the social mixing of blacks and whites in integrated churches (Ammerman 1990, 36). Southern Baptists and other southern Christians overtly employed white supremacy and evangelical Protestantism as bulwarks of a segregationist order justified as part of God's plan to ensure peace and harmony between the races. Fearing northern missionaries seizing control of religious customs and ecclesiastical government, and of gendered norms about sexuality and marriage being eroded along with the racial norms, white southern Baptist organizations pursued organized efforts to block the civil rights bill of 1874.

Newly independent black Christians moved farther away from white southern evangelicals as they worked to build their church communities after the Civil War. But the long shadow of white supremacy remained. Throughout the late 1800s, African Americans were barred from membership in most of the state and national denominational organizations and had their services routinely disrupted by the Ku Klux Klan. Partly in response, the National Baptist Convention (NBC) was established in 1895. It eventually became the largest African American religious organization. Ministers increasingly involved themselves with political affairs, running for local, state, or national office. Political discourse within ex-slave communities blossomed. As membership in black churches expanded during Reconstruction, congregants debated the merits of separatism versus integration, with religious leaders positioned on both sides. The first black Christian publishing agencies were founded between 1865 and 1895, and religious centers moved from their rural origins into large cities (Foner and Schomburg Center for Research in Black Culture 1993). A direct sociological result, then, of theological racism and the racial segregation of faith-based bodies was the development of a strong and distinct African American Protestant tradition.

Religious Racial Justice—Or Not

Existing in tension with and sometimes directly countering theological racism in the United States was the religious racial justice tradition. Faith-based racial justice efforts in American evangelicalism began as a fringe minority tradition, but eventually contributed to the transformation of American political life. Initial seeds of the religious racial justice tradition included the tiny minority of American colonial Protestants who challenged the dominant white supremacist theology, and Quakers, who drew on scripture to offer counternarratives to theological racism, though both groups were largely politically impotent with regard to racist policy (Pearce 1967).

Later, the black Christian community that survived, resisted, and/or directly challenged white supremacy critically influenced the cross-racial social justice movements of the eighteenth and nineteenth centuries and helped pave the way for the modern civil rights movement.[14] Early black reform organizations drew on biblically influenced "vocabularies of Exodus," collective narratives that helped them envision and fight for freedom (Howard-Pitney 2005; West and Glaude 2003; Glaude 2000). After the denominational fractures of the late antebellum era, black denominations became a base upon which African Americans could build "a corporate identity and a political culture" and craft resistance strategies (Glaude 2000, 57). Facing a different set of circumstances, Native Americans also built traditions of political theology and revived indigenous religious practices to organize resistance to the federal government (Tinker 2004).

In the run-up to the Civil War, while southern white evangelicals were reinforcing their subculture against direct attack, northern evangelicals played a major role in antebellum party politics. Divisions between radical and moderate evangelical abolitionists influenced the Second Party System of the 1830s and 1840s as well as the election of 1860 (Carwardine 1993, 132). The more orthodox wing of evangelicalism gave the abolition movement its ballast through the American Anti-Slavery Association and eventually the Liberty Party, while other proslavery evangelicals and members of the Democratic Party sneered. Grassroots white evangelicals in the North like Charles Finney supplied abolitionists with theological frameworks critiquing slavery, though some evangelicals abandoned the cause when they saw it as interfering with their mission (Emerson and Smith 2000, 122). By the election of 1860, northern evangelicals were pushing three issues before the Republican Party—slavery, Catholicism, and political corruption—and insisted Republicans define themselves as the party of Christian witness (Carwardine 1993, 302). Mainstream Christians repudiated radical abolitionists' methods and doctrine to advocate individualist rather than systemic adjustments; these moderates endorsed voluntary manumission of slaves by their masters and assisted settlement in West Africa through the American Colonization Society.

For American evangelicals, the sundering of the Union was a blow to the millennial dream of achieving a unified kingdom of Christ on earth, but after the Civil War the hope of compromise and reunification of northern and southern evangelical schisms was suffocated. After white northern evangelicals' short-lived support for Reconstruction, however, white evangelicals abandoned significant cross-racial social justice efforts until the turn of the century (Luker 1991). In this social gospel–dominated era, mostly moderate mainline and liberal Protestants entered interracial grassroots movements seeking to provide a "better racial environment" in the wake of the upheavals caused by white backlash against black northern migration. Typically paternalist, social gospel Christianity had fairly limited goals that, while sometimes productive, often echoed state interests in control and racial subordination (for example, promoting the end of lynching; portraying blacks more positively; advocating better facilities for blacks but still in a segregated context).

In sum, strains of a religious racial justice tradition did help drive abolitionist and social gospel movements in the nineteenth century. Evangelicals who saw slavery as dangerous to American democracy were prominent among those activists, but even then, religious advocates for full-blown political equality between the races were rare. Part of the reason was that in order to launch coherent ideological critiques of racism, Christians would have had to repudiate entire vocabularies engineered to justify racial inequality through religious frameworks (whether or not those frameworks were accurate). The fact that faith so deeply intersected with justifications for America's racial system, which subordinated blacks, indigenous people, and others of color, contributed to the endurance of that system. It was not until the late twentieth century that evangelicals even began to attempt to reach across the ideological chasms forged between them during and after the Civil War. The religious racial justice tradition did not regain significant steam until the civil rights movement.

Racial Interchange: The Pentecostal Anomaly

Even as American Protestant communities became increasingly polarized into the competing religious racial justice and theological racism traditions in the late nineteenth century, periods of boundary-breaking racial interchange cropped up here and there. The story of the Pentecostal movement provides an interesting example. Pentecostalism is an American-born charismatic worship tradition that emphasizes, among other things, "baptism of the Holy Spirit" evidenced by phenomena like speaking in tongues. It is currently one of the fastest-growing segments of Christianity in the world, including in the African American community (Lugo et al. 2006; Sherrod and DuPree 1993). Most Pentecostals ascribe to a fairly orthodox (conservative and literalist) theology and are conservative on

social issues like abortion and homosexuality, which often brings them into political partnership with other evangelicals (Lugo et al. 2006, "Social and Moral
Issues" chart). They also have been well represented in conversations about racial change in contemporary evangelical communities, so their racial history
warrants a bit of a review.

Pentecostalism arose from an unusual racial interchange moment, when
members of the mainly white American Holiness movement (which broke off
from Methodism in the mid-nineteenth century) and black Christians built a
new kind of charismatic community in the late 1880s (Synan 1971). For a short
period in the early 1900s, these believers broke racial taboos to form what was
likely the first voluntarily multiracial religious movement in American Protestantism (MacRobert 1988). In 1906, William Joseph Seymour, a talented black
preacher from the South who had been mentored in Texas by white Holiness
leader Charles Parham, founded what would become the world-famous Azusa
Street Mission in Los Angeles.

For about five years (1906–11), the Azusa Street Mission was the most spiritually and racially radical American Christian development of its time (Nelson
1981). It attracted people from a remarkable diversity of race and class backgrounds; it had a nontraditional structure, with seats arranged in a circle and
Seymour preaching in the center; and it broke gender barriers by anointing both
women and men as elders and equal participants in services. White and black
pastors from all over the country came to witness the phenomenon of this Pentecostal revival, and many whites even studied under black pastors before returning to their own mostly segregated churches. Azusa prompted a huge missionary
expansion, with evangelists spreading the teachings they had learned at Azusa to
more than fifty nations within the first two years.

But theological racism cut short these huge advances in religious race relations, as the interracial equality promoted at Azusa proved too much of a threat
to white-dominated evangelicalism. Although Charles Parham spent some time
at Azusa in its early years, he had conflicts with Seymour and recoiled at the
racial intermingling in the church. By 1911, Parham publicly vilified the Azusa
community, condemning racial integration and, with other racist pastors, urging
whites to start their own Pentecostal communities or take over black churches
and vote blacks out—both of which they largely did (Synan 1971). Pentecostal
organizations became almost entirely segregated by race, despite their early integrationist efforts. Seymour led an almost entirely African American church until
his death in 1922.

Early Pentecostalism's rise and fall exemplifies a moment of racial interchange
that could not survive the pressures of racism in a segregationist religious climate.

For a brief time, the relationship between Parham and Seymour, and later Seymour's leadership at Azusa, allowed Pentecostals to overcome the impasse of the theological racism tradition. But in the end that was too great a divide, and Pentecostalism developed for the next several decades in racially separate streams. The "black" stream became the Church of God in Christ denomination, while the white stream, which excluded blacks, became the Assemblies of God, and umbrella organizations reflected those racial fractures as other denominations joined the Pentecostal "family."[15] Had race not so deeply circumscribed America's religious demographics, and had religion not been wielded so effectively to perpetuate racial stratification, interracial Pentecostalism would have been a nonissue.

Twentieth-Century Protestantism: A Battle of Religious Racial Traditions

Summarizing the major characteristics and historical markers of the three religious racial traditions in U.S. political history, we can glimpse how a sustained conflict *between* these competing traditions over a century and a half created a minefield for evangelical race relations by the late twentieth century. On the one hand, the theological racism that endorsed America's racial hierarchies and exclusions through faith-justified narratives was slow to loose its grip on the American psyche. But in competition with theological racism, the countertradition of religious racial justice provided force (albeit often outnumbered) of African American and other antiracist Christians, Jews, and others who employed faith to repudiate racist systems. Crossing both these traditions, in quotidian interludes of American religious life, were periods of racial interchange. In revival meetings, plantation churches, and itinerant crusades, whites and people of color periodically mingled across racial lines beneath the umbrella of religious belief and practice, experiencing elements of familiarity that belied the larger racial divisions that ordered their political universes.

From Reconstruction to the civil rights movement, the conflict between religious racial traditions played out in difficult conversations about racial equality and inclusion within many American religious communities, including Jews, Catholics, Protestants, Mennonites, and others.[16] However, among southern white and black evangelicals, some of the most religious populations in the country, tensions were concentrated and prolonged, illuminating the intersectional dynamic of race and religion in American evangelical life. The historian Andrew Manis (1987) describes the "clash of civil religions" that characterized the southern social and political climate from the antebellum era through the mid-twentieth century. Through civil religion, a nation or group of people professes and ritualistically reinforces its core ideals—freedom, peoplehood, democracy, equality, and so forth. Civil religion is not about religion per se; within it, religion can serve as *content*, a belief system that defines a people, or as a *vehicle*, a style of articulating a collective identity through ceremony, ritual speech forms, and cultural symbols. Though Manis does not use the term "religious racial traditions," in the Christianity-infused South a civil religions conflict is best understood as at least in part a battle over which religious racial tradition would prevail in and beyond individual Christian communities. This fight, with Southern Baptists positioned squarely at its heart, deeply affected American evangelicalism as a whole.

After the Civil War, many white Baptists clung tightly to segregation, associating it with American values, Anglo-Saxon institutions, and a homogeneous evangelical culture (Manis 1987, 80). In so doing, they drew from a symbolic universe that used religious doctrine to rebuke interracial marriage as un-Christian; to justify a divine ordering of nations and races; and to see God's hand in the development of America's unique, racially "ordered" heritage. These values fed into a vision of America as a divinely chosen, Christian democratic country that by the late 1940s and early 1950s was perceived to be threatened from the outside by atheism and Communism, and from the inside by subversion of the social order via the questioning of gender, class, and race hierarchies. Southern whites defended regional autonomy as a sacred aspect of democracy that should be protected from an interventionist state. This symbolic universe was not unique to white southern Baptists per se, but it linked up with the worldview of Baptist segregationists to promote an idealization of America that also resonated beyond the South (41–46).[17]

Black Baptists, via the NBC, tapped into a competing American civil religion that drew from a different symbolic universe to read American heritage as part of God's ultimate plan for a people. In this vision, equality was seen as a God-given, inalienable right; God chose black people as his special instruments in America and participated with them to enable the nation to achieve moral maturity and, in Martin Luther King Jr.'s terms, "beloved community." The gospel was seen as relevant to human beings' material as well as spiritual well-being and was therefore tethered to a radical social change effort. Segregation and other forms of racism were read as sins Christians had every right to oppose through civil disobedience and nonviolent resistance. Indeed, King and the Southern Christian Leadership Conference (SCLC) roundly criticized the delinquency of the white church in failing to support this righteous moral battle (King 1986b).

These contrasting visions of faith, nation, and race reflected the divergent symbolic universes in which most black and white southern evangelicals operated. Segregationist Southern Baptists, the majority of Baptist laity, equated freedom with individual liberty, choice of regional social traditions, and protection from coercive government. National Baptists, in contrast, associated freedom with democracy, equal rights, and equal protection. Whereas SBC Christians read America's purpose as protecting individual liberty in the face of grave threats to a Christian nation from external enemies (the Vatican! the Kremlin!), NBC Christians saw America as *potentially* Christian, called to embody freedom, democracy, and equality against the internal threat of hypocrisy and discrimination. Both groups regarded themselves as fighting on behalf of God's will and used biblical justifications to support their positions.

As Mark Newman (2001) explores in his study of Southern Baptists and desegregation between 1945 and 1995, although Southern Baptists struggled most acutely with segregation, all other major white denominations experienced degrees of resistance to racial change as well. Nor were Southern Baptists an entirely monolithic group in terms of race relations; the denomination gradually became more racially progressive with each new generation, and students exerted a progressive influence in the wake of the civil rights movement (166). Pastors and other leaders tended to be more progressive than the lay population. Part of the challenge for the SBC, however, was the denomination's more horizontal than vertical organization, compared to other denominations like Catholics, Episcopalians, and Methodists. SBC churches send delegates to annual conventions, where they have the power to pass or defeat resolutions impacting the entire denomination. The SBC's congregational polities required parishioner support for denominational proposals and therefore faced daunting obstacles to achieving institutional changes in race relations when progressives in the SBC were outnumbered. In contrast, more vertically organized denominations desegregated their schools and churches by order of their top leaders.[18]

For instance, when SBC leaders adopted the "Charter of Race Relations" in 1947, which sketched out the beginnings of a shift in the organizational understanding of Christian responsibility on race, most southern state conventions failed to endorse and recommend the charter. The charter proposed the following principles of conduct:

> 1) We shall think of the Negro as a person and treat him accordingly. 2) We shall continually strive as individuals to conquer all prejudices and eliminate from our speech terms of contempt and from our conduct actions of ill will. 3) We shall teach

our children that prejudice is un-Christian and that good will and helpful deeds are the duty of every Christian toward all men of all races. 4) We shall be willing for the Negro to enjoy the rights granted to him under the Constitution of the United States, including the right to vote, to serve on juries, to receive justice in the courts, to be free from mob violence, to secure a just share of the benefits of educational and other funds, and to receive equal service for equal treatment on public carriers and conveniences. 6) We shall be just in our dealing with the Negro as an individual. Whenever he is in our employ we shall pay him an adequate wage and provide for him healthful working conditions. 7) We shall strive to promote community good-will between the races in every way possible. 8) We shall actively cooperate with Negro Baptists in the building up of their churches, the education of their ministers, and the promotion of their missions and evangelistic programs. (quoted in Kelsey 1973, 253)

Unfortunately, when it came to race, parishioners tended to seize on the stream of Baptist tradition emphasizing individual morality over attacking corporate sin and evangelism in lieu of curing social ills—a tendency that would have a long-term impact on later racial change efforts (Newman 2001, 38). Pastors, paid by local churches rather than denominational hierarchies, were subject to violence and intimidation and, at any rate, likely to be fired if they preached an unpopular message. Others publicly resisted integration and defended the South's right to work out its race relations "in its own way" (Kelsey 1973, 235). Racial progressives within the SBC were thus in the position of hedging on the kinds of stronger pro–civil rights perspectives they may have preferred, in order to pacify the more conservative mainstream laity.

The progressive minority of the SBC persisted despite its losses, supporting public school integration in 1954 and, after the *Brown v. Board of Education* decision, exercising its leadership to try to persuade the dissenting majority to "conduct themselves in the period of adjustment in the spirit of Christ" (Kelsey 1973, 232). Most white Southern Baptists, however, saw the convention's adoption of a resolution to support the *Brown* decision as an affront to the separation of church and state. Defenders of the status quo used Christianity to claim that social patterns could only be changed "by regeneration in Christ," not by overturning existing (segregationist) legislation.

Meanwhile, northern Protestant denominations moved forward, directly attacking segregation, supporting fair employment practices legislation, and, in some cases, even condemning residential segregation. Verbal pronouncements did not ameliorate the segregation in their own churches, but northern racial advances put pressure on southern organizations to progress. As the civil rights movement peaked in the 1960s, most major white denominations spoke in support of civil rights while the SBC quietly tried to avoid race issues. Though the resistance to change for most white Christian organizations was a matter of degree, the difference was in the expressed intention to change: "Although non-SBC Protestant denominations remained slow to desegregate, they, unlike the SBC, which rejected a recommendation in 1964 that endorsed open churches, maintained pressure on their institutions to act" (Kelsey 1973, 182).

In the larger political theater, only one side in the battle of racial religious traditions could win the war. In the end, civil rights workers and their allies successfully swayed the federal government and, gradually, the national consensus toward basic political equality before the law. In that respect, their version of the American civil religion emerged victorious.

The Sea Change of Civil Rights

The role of religion in the civil rights movement is a vast topic addressed by several waves of scholars. I'll restrict my discussion to reviewing key dynamics that help contextualize the arc of evangelical race relations by the late twentieth century.

It is important to remember, first, that religion was not merely a handy organizing mechanism within the civil rights movement, as political scientists have tended to characterize it. Rather, it was a defining driver of the movement.[19] Noll summarizes three primary ways in which African American religion propelled the civil rights movement: through the intellectually sophisticated and theologically informed convictions of leaders like Martin Luther King Jr.; through the beliefs and energies of foot soldiers "whose religion remained close to the elemental faiths of the nineteenth century"; and through a faith community that differed in important respects from other varieties of American religion (2008, 105–6).[20]

The faith of movement elites was, as Noll puts it, "always more than just black evangelical revivalism, but never less (2008, 108)" and was seeded in the distinctive black religious thought tradition developed in the U.S. context. King and other leaders drew from strains of prophetic biblicism, faith-based liberation narratives that stretched centuries back into American history. Or as King put it in 1958, "It was the Sermon on the Mount, rather than a doctrine of passive resistance, that initially inspired the Negroes of Montgomery to dignified social action. It was Jesus of Nazareth that stirred the Negroes to protest with the creative weapon of love" (King 1986a, 16). But movement leaders were also influenced by multiple theological strands: the social gospel teachings of Walter

Rauschenbusch; the philosophical personalism of Edgar S. Brightman; the post-liberal Christian realism of Reinhold Niebuhr; and various religious and secular philosophies of nonviolence (Noll 2008, 107–14). By mining such rich theological traditions, movement architects were able to craft a coherent and powerful message that resonated even after the later movement became less attached to its theological roots.

Noll and others argue that rather than being a numbing opiate that enforced political apathy, the expressive, "fundamentalist" faith of African Americans helped transform the intellectual framework of the movement into a grassroots uprising with prophetic vision and collective power. Religious tradition and biblical stories helped people survive, interpret, and resist attacks by the forces of white supremacy. They also provided some of the strongest cultural elements at the heart of religious racial justice: songs, images, prayer, church networks, and higher biblical criticism provided coherence, force, and resilience over time (Noll 2008, 116–22).

Noll makes some crucial observations about how black American Christianity differed from white evangelical religion in its influence on the civil rights movement. These insights bear on the later emergence of racial change initiatives within the broader American evangelical community. For instance, unlike white evangelicals, who were fracturing in the mid-twentieth century over matters of biblical theology, modernism, and the United States' increasing secularism, black Christians demonstrated the capacity to collaborate to advance common social goals. Indeed, in the racially segregated universe that characterized American Christianity, they had been doing so for decades. Linking conservative theology with progressive social action was an organic step for black Christians, whereas whites had begun to congregate around these as opposing poles. For whites, theological conservatism correlated primarily with conservative social action values (a phenomenon that only deepened as 1960s-era movements expanded), leaving mainline and liberal Protestants alone on the side of racial and gender progress. Developing political solidarity under a complex religious umbrella put African Americans well ahead of whites in their ability to drive a full-blown social movement. Thus, "in contrast to the general theism of anticommunism [in the 1950s], the civil rights movement brought particularistic Christianity back into the center of American politics" (Noll 2008, 142). Somewhat ironically, this awakening of activist Christianity paved the way for the mobilization of white evangelicals around a different set of issues in the early 1980s.

De Facto Segregation, Apathy, and Fundamentalism

Once the civil rights movement found its political stride, southern white Christians who opposed federally enforced integration and other civil rights initiatives were forced to accept them, however begrudgingly. The rising tide of civil rights legislation eventually stilled the vocal resistance of Southern Baptists to integration efforts. By the time the Civil Rights Act of 1964 was passed, change had become inevitable (though anything but easy), and by 1970 all Southern Baptist colleges had abandoned racial discrimination policies. Some Southern Baptists like Billy Graham and his associate pastor, W. A. Criswell, began working to achieve a change in attitude among white conservative evangelicals in the 1970s. But for most of the 1970s, the grassroots of the SBC (and many other southern congregations) retreated to a posture of silence and apathy on race.

Historians have interpreted this silence in different ways. Manis reads it as a "mediating paralysis," in which leaders attempted to offset the disruption caused by public pronouncements about racial change questions with internal calls for "calm and clear thinking"—that is, admonitions not to react in volatile ways. Too, concern for denominational survival "contributed to a sense that peace, at almost any price, was necessary for the denomination's well being. This led even the progressive elite of the Southern Baptist Convention to phrase their pronouncements with a studied vagueness, always with an eye toward the constituency" (Manis 1987, 102). For SBC leaders who may have been sympathetic to the civil rights movement, the fear of losing standing in the white community and the knowledge that speaking out against racism in their own settings was futile may have further perpetuated their silence.

But because the mainstream of white conservative evangelicals failed to support the civil rights movement, the cultural barriers between black and white evangelicals were effectively fortified rather than dismantled in the decades after the civil rights movement era (Dailey 2004). Thus, the positioning of southern evangelicals in relation to the civil rights movement effectively created a time lag within which reconciliation efforts seemed virtually impossible. As the civil rights movement challenged American racist conventions, it also necessarily challenged white evangelical culture, particularly in the South. As the social and political relationships between whites and blacks were being rewritten, people retreated to their familiar home cultures, especially in the religious sphere, which functioned for both groups as a temporary retreat from the outside world. Whites clung to their racially homogeneous networks as their segregationist social edifice was crumbling underneath them. Blacks focused on repairing and rebuilding their own communities as they continued to work for political freedom and equitable treatment.

Between the 1950s and the 1990s, the SBC remained a predominantly white denomination. The first black congregation was granted membership in the SBC in Santa Rosa, California, in 1951, but most black Baptist congregations chose to affiliate with one of the NBCs.[21] When other congregations of color joined the SBC in subsequent decades, they were typically joining a denomination that had not yet integrated formerly white congregations, but which did offer considerable financial resources to help establish new black churches. While some pioneering leaders in the SBC worked to challenge and dismantle racist traditions in the denomination, most member congregations, particularly in the South, were entrenched in their religiously segregated patterns and preferences. Since 1989, the SBC claims to have established approximately 150 black churches a year, most of which have dual affiliations with a black denomination (Maxwell 1995a).

In the decades after the civil rights movement when basic political equality before the law had been achieved, a cultural separation between white and nonwhite conservative evangelical communities in most parts of the country became virtually—yet never officially—institutionalized. Racial division was reflected not just through white prejudice but also through patterns of denominational organization and the insular cultural associations of white and nonwhite evangelicals. In the meantime, many white evangelicals shifted their attention toward other issues that concerned them (Diamond 1995). During the Cold War (as discussed in chapter 3), they took a virulently anti-Communist stance and went to some lengths to accuse liberal church representatives of being Communist sympathizers. Gaining momentum in the early 1970s, they also worked to spread "traditional" Christian values through conversion crusades and the development of independent fundamentalist churches and schools. Some of these activities contained implicit racial politics, as exemplified by the initially segregationist Billy Graham crusade. But in many respects white evangelicals effectively avoided addressing racial issues directly and turned inward to expand and fortify their religious movement (Diamond 1995, 92–108). They sought to remove government obstacles to their propagation of the gospel in other countries through the purchase of broadcasting systems. In the 1970s and 1980s, organized white evangelicals turned their attention to threats to their traditional value system brought by the sexual revolution, the women's movement, and gay and lesbian movements, while race issues stayed "off the table." The declension of attention to racial issues reflected national trends.

A major development among Southern Baptists in the 1980s was the fundamentalist takeover of the SBC. Ammerman has observed how fundamentalists were able to democratically wrest control of the organizational infrastructure

of the denomination from the numerically smaller progressive wing. Fundamentalists were religious traditionalists concerned about what they perceived
to be the liberalization of biblical hermeneutics, pastoral authority, evangelical
missions, and social and political issues such as homosexuality and the ordina-
tion of women. They battled with progressives for support from the moderate
mainstream (who previously had been more or less ideologically split down the
middle in this battle) in a passionate effort to preserve the traditionalist integrity
of the denomination.

The fundamentalist takeover of the SBC seems to bear some relevance to
Baptist race relations, though the topic has not yet been substantively explored.
It seems probable that latent racism was an undercurrent of the conservative
takeover, though we must be cautious with such conclusions given the ideological diversity that does exist among Southern Baptists. Ammerman discovered that 87 percent of moderate Southern Baptists were broadly supportive of
the civil rights movement, while only 47 percent of conservatives were (1990,
102).[22] Newman cites another poll taken in the 1980s in which 55 percent of self-
identified fundamentalist Southern Baptists stated that they disagreed or were
unsure that the civil rights movement had led the nation in the right direction
(2001, 200).[23] But even fundamentalist leaders did not represent a monolithic
racial viewpoint. Some segregationist fundamentalist leaders objected to the racially and socially tolerant positions advocated by former progressive leadership,
and many were affiliated with New Christian Right organizations such as the
American Coalition for Traditional Values (200). Others had encouraged their
churches to desegregate in the 1970s and actively advocated racial justice.

There has been a long delay, at best, between the legal and political principles
the civil rights movement instigated and the integration of those changes in race
relations on a societal level. But for white evangelical communities, whose histories were so deeply marked by the theological, the delay was even more pro-
nounced. Nonetheless, changes brought about by the civil rights movement did
help create a new social stigma around overt racism and segregationist culture
that eventually infused even white conservative evangelicalism. As a consensus
against institutional racism was gradually enculturated, even prominent white
evangelicals came to disavow their own racist policies, in line with the changing
social climate. Billy Graham, Jerry Falwell, and others later claimed that such
attitudes represented a moral lapse among white Christian conservatives who
were raised in a segregationist culture.[24] As Graham admitted in the 1990s, "in
all those years it didn't cross my mind that segregation and its consequences for
the human family were evil. I was blind to that reality" (Reed 1996a, 68). But in

truth many conservative white evangelicals had long resisted the social changes propelled by the civil rights movement and would, it seems, not be easy to turn around.

By the 1980s, the demographic norm in evangelical communities nationwide was de facto segregation, especially due to residential segregation. Although many denominations, including the SBC, made attempts to recruit churches of color, most of these annexed churches were dually aligned with other denominations and were rarely integrated into the leadership of white-majority groups. Tokenism prevailed in SBC agencies and churches. African Americans, for their part, had plenty of reasons to be reluctant about joining white churches, including hostility from whites, different styles of worship, loyalty to traditional black denominations, and a growing separatism among some blacks disillusioned with the failure of the civil rights movement to achieve large-scale integration (Newman 2001, 194). By the 1990s, evangelicals would without irony repeat King's observation that eleven o'clock Sunday morning was the most segregated hour of the week.

In effect, white evangelicals from racially conservative Protestant traditions like the SBC and the now racially segregated Pentecostal denominations had carved a history that left them no comfortable location when it came to race relations. There were essentially wedged somewhere between the now discredited theological racism that had built many of their organizations and the religious racial justice tradition that had rightly become associated with liberal and mainline religions, African American Christians, and many white and Latino Catholics. The instances of racial interchange that had characterized earlier (and even more unequal) eras of evangelical history were now largely out of reach as racial homogeneity in church congregations became, for additional reasons I explore next, an institutionalized cultural norm. Even symbolic intermingling across race, perhaps to celebrate a Martin Luther King Jr. Day or an Easter Sunday, were haunted by the historical elephant in the room: so many whites had employed Christianity to justify and perpetuate racial inequality; so many blacks had turned to religion for solace and resistance. While the younger non- and interdenominational congregations in the West and Midwest (the Vineyards and Calvary Chapels) might have been able to circumvent such long racial shadows by appealing to a climate of postracial Christian love and acceptance, organizations that had been forged in the fires of American race history were in no position to fake harmony or even diversity. In a deeply segregated religious landscape, even many megachurch evangelicals seemed to sense that something about the racial demography of American Christians was sour.

As we will see, the quantity and tenor of racial discourse shifted appreciably in mainstream American evangelicalism in the 1990s. In that decade, evangelical Christians began seeking ways to reach across the fractures that had come to characterize their communities. But other developments were necessary before that could happen. In the next chapter, we see how two competing racial narratives became embedded within and came to characterize the tenor of evangelical race relations in the decades after the civil rights movement. Until the tensions between these narratives came to a head, and until whites found reasons to finally address them, the racial divide within evangelicalism would remain.

We cannot understand why racial change would be a fraught process within American evangelicalism without recognizing how deeply Christianity has been imprinted with the opposing religious racial projects of theological racism, on the one hand, and religious racial justice, on the other, with only occasional periods of racial interchange in between. The categories of race and religion were so thoroughly interwoven, sometimes unconsciously, into evangelicals' individual, community, and political identities and histories that crossing the divide could not possibly be simple. The concepts of race-religion intersectionality and of religious racial traditions as distinct manifestations of that intersectionality help us grasp why neither a religious nor a racial framework alone could hope to repair the fractures built over time into American evangelicalism. Yet as the U.S. racial system evolved, evangelicalism could not remain silent forever and faced increasing incentives to address those fractures. New tools would need to be developed, old histories revisited, and unprecedented risks taken to build more reconciled communities.

3 Competing Racial Narratives in the Post–Civil Rights Movement Period

We need to be bringing people together to have conversations and to have fights around these issues [race and politics]. The church can be a safe place for conflict and to push people towards power. Because I think it's important for poor and working people to have power. What that means for the churches is that *we have to challenge those, nonviolently, who are in the corridors of power.*
—African American male pastor, Brooklyn, New York, 2008

I think the problem has been, among evangelicals, when you combine social justice with the gospel, that that becomes the gospel. In other words, the whole liberalism, the reason that became—people shied away from those issues because social justice issues ate up the church.
—Korean-American male pastor, Southern California, 2008

In the world of evangelical racial reconciliation and multiracial church building, two different stories about race and power surface again and again. People told these stories in my interviews as frequently in the 2000s as they did in the 1990s, and I heard echoes of them from pulpits, in testimonials, at conferences, and in casual conversations. These are familiar stories, scripts that deliver meaning through chains of associations that resonate in particular communities and settings. They don't sit comfortably together—indeed, they are perpetually entwined in a low-grade conflict that impacts the potential political implications of racial change efforts. But each has earned a considerable degree of traction in evangelical racial change (ERC) circles, and neither seems likely to surrender soon.

Many evangelicals of color tell a redemption story, an extension of what Eddie Glaude Jr. (2000) has called the Exodus narrative. Emerging out of African Americans' long experience with persecution at the hands of whites, black Christians understand racism as one tool among many through which a devastating white supremacist system was orchestrated. Remembering it today, they (and Native American and other evangelicals as well) often articulate the story through an acknowledgment and a challenge. The acknowledgment goes something like this: "God delivered us from the long journey out from under oppression. We survived through our tenacity, our struggle, and our faith—but we survived."[1] This is a fairly familiar story, and one that resonates with white evangelicals' belief in God's ultimately liberating guiding hand.

The attendant challenge, however, names something less familiar to outsiders, a slow-healing wound inside the Christian community that still smarts when jarred. In spaces where Christians of color join white evangelicals to address issues of race, this second half of the redemption story is told, sometimes directly, sometimes almost under the breath, as if the effort of continuing to name it after so long has worn thin: "And where were all the white evangelical Christians during our struggle? Where were you then?"

In the delicate moments when this painful confrontation surfaces, white evangelicals in the world of faith-based racial change may hang their heads. They may sit in silence, humbled or at a loss. They may weep authentically, and pray for healing. They may even fall to their knees, as we will see, and beg for forgiveness in public and private settings. Some may carry the story's burden themselves, acknowledging the shameful truth that many white Christians— Christians! People like us!—not only tolerated or were complicit with but actively helped create and perpetuate the racist systems that tortured and subordinated Americans of color over centuries. Such white allies will likely offer praise to their savior for having delivered their persecuted and marginalized brethren into freedom and Christian salvation.

Yet in casual conversation, and in books, articles, small town chapels, and megachurches, white evangelicals—and not just them, many evangelicals of color, too, but rarely African American Christians—often tell another story. This is a social justice–aversive story, one that runs implicitly through race. It has its more blunt iterations:

Social justice issues ate up the church.

The church lost track of its priorities when it got in the business of social justice.

We are doing racial reconciliation for the gospel, not for social justice.

It also has subtler variations:

If we get the theology right, social justice outcomes will naturally follow.

Our movement needs to be biblical first, not guided by secular social justice concerns.

This second story delivers a criticism, always cryptic on the details, of a number of "other kinds" of Christians or Christian modes outside the confines of white conservative evangelicalism or "true," theologically correct Christianity. It distances itself from both liberal Christians and Christians of color by asserting an attachment to a particular epistemological paradigm and resistance to thinking differently.

At the core, these stories are irreconcilable. Whereas the first (redemptive) narrative reads social justice concern and action as reasonable moral extensions of the gospel, the second (defensive) story imagines the gospel and social justice at odds. Even so, both stories are, when spoken in their respective "home" settings, so deeply engrained that they have a kind of second-nature quality for those expressing them. African American Christians (especially) *know* that the shackles of a racist system were only broken through the grace of God, who ushered a weary people down a long road to freedom. Equally, white conservative evangelicals seem to recite the line about social justice hurting the church with ease (although some eventually come to question it).

Considering these stories in combination provides a glimpse of why it might be fraught indeed for evangelicals to talk about race *in politicized terms,* particularly in multiracial settings. The land mines littering the path of racial change efforts are not only born of America's sullied racial history; they are also embedded in the dual and dialectically entwined stories Christians have told to make sense of that history.

These stories have origins and spokespersons. Both narratives penetrated evangelical communities during the denouement of the American civil rights movement and other 1960s protest activities. Tracing them helps explain how racial discourse within conservative evangelical communities comes to be narrowly limited in the 1980s—the same decade that saw the Christian Right ascend as a powerful new political force. Two figures who became fairly prominent within American evangelicalism in this era, Tom Skinner and C. Peter Wagner, respectively articulate these stories (though not uniquely or for the first time) in ways that come to exert long-standing influences on the character and trajectory of the ERC movement. Between these deeply linked stories, in which religious racial meaning systems oppose and mirror one another, emerges a set of tensions that comes to draw implicit boundaries around evangelicals' conversations and thinking about race.

Identifying the cultural undercurrents that inform evangelical race discourse during a period in which white Christians don't *seem* to be very focused on race (the 1970s and 1980s) requires a way of comprehending the worlds of meaning and action that guide evangelicals *as* evangelicals. For this I return to

Wedeen's (2002) analytical framework of "culture as meaning-making (semiotic) practices" to facilitate analysis of the relation between people's actions and their matrices of meaning, which include language and other systems of signification. I employ this to inform my investigation of how race discourse in evangelical communities develops after midcentury, and how meaning systems within those conversations are asserted, interpreted, and sometimes contested by participants.

Following Wedeen, I understand *meaning-making* to imply "a social process through which people reproduce together the conditions of intelligibility that enable them to make sense of their worlds," and then, in turn, to act (2002, 717). *Practices* here simply refer to actions repeated over time; deeds and behaviors that are "learned, reproduced, and subject to risks through social interaction" (714–20). For evangelicals, examples include theological assertions, rituals, public conversations, print materials, sermons and responses to them, and quotidian activities. Cultural practices never exist in a vacuum. Rather, they interact with and may be influenced by conditions and circumstances in the social world beyond the immediate community, which makes them dynamic rather than part of some fixed subcultural universe. *Intelligibility* has to do with how people interpret signs and act in ways that make their world coherent to them in their ordinary lives (720).

The Christian Right's ascendance in the post–civil rights movement period may not appear to be a racial story. However, significant racial undercurrents informed the content and tenor of white evangelicalism's trajectory after World War II—and in turn deeply imprinted the character of reparative racial initiatives over the subsequent two decades. In this and the next chapter, I examine how an increasingly politicized evangelicalism attempts, often awkwardly, to navigate racial discourse when its constituent communities and their respective meaning-making practices are so deeply imprinted by the two competing narratives described above. As the redemptive social justice challenge narrated by Skinner and the social justice–aversive response by Wagner begin to enter into direct confrontation toward the end of the 1980s, the divergences between them generate an acute conundrum: Will whites decide to face racial tensions within evangelicalism, and the histories that produced them, head-on? As they build a political force with the potential for real influence on the American political scene, can they afford not to face the past? And will Christians of color become interested in participating in those conversations? Understanding the two competing dominant racial narratives in evangelicalism provides a foundation for examining in subsequent chapters how and why evangelical race discourse shifts dramatically in the 1990s.

Skinner's Invitation

In 1970, a small group of evangelicals made a decision. They didn't know it at the time, but that choice would become legendary among racial change advocates. Executives for InterVarsity, the national evangelical Christian college ministry, agreed at the request of a small group of African American members to sign a twenty-eight-year-old black evangelist named Tom Skinner to deliver a keynote speech at their annual Urbana '70 convention (Gilbreath 1996).

It was an era of protest movements, political upheaval, and countercultural gatherings of all sorts. Ten thousand students flocked to the University of Illinois–Urbana-Champaign campus that year, an unprecedented 500 African American students and youth leaders among them. An Afro-sporting funk ensemble called Soul Liberation surprised the mostly "straight," white crowd with songs like "Power to the People" that blended praise lyrics with Black Power grooves. By the time the young preacher from Harlem reached the podium, the crowd had gotten a musical primer on black culture and was on its feet.

With a searing delivery that remains striking today, Skinner tells a story about power and betrayal (Skinner 1970a).[2] "An understanding of world evangelism and racism in our country must begin with an understanding of the history of racism," he opens, launching a no-holds-barred account of the intimate intersection of American Christianity with white supremacy. In graphic historical detail, the former street preacher traces the ungodly marriage between theological racism, the U.S. slave system, post-Reconstruction racial oppression, and capitalist economic control. "So if you have any illusions that America was founded on godly principles," he tells his young audience, "reexamine them."

For those evangelicals who might think of racism as an anachronistic, "un-Christian" tradition, or of white evangelicals as having simply been apathetic to racism, Skinner offers no place to hide. "To a great extent, the evangelical church in America supported the status quo. It supported slavery; it supported segregation; it preached against any attempt of the black man to stand on his own two feet. And where there were those who sought to communicate the gospel to black people, it was always done in a way to make sure that they stayed cool."

Into the historical narrative Skinner then weaves his own family history, sketching what it was like for a black family to migrate from rural South Carolina to congested, slum-ridden Harlem, where he grew into a belligerent gang leader with a gift for leadership. He testifies to exploitive systems like public housing, which blacks witness and sometimes resist but which whites can often afford to assume is fair and neutral. He tells a story of an infant killed by a rat in a vermin-infested apartment. "We never arrest the landlord. We never lock up the building code inspector," he thunders. Instead, "We lock up the frustrated, bitter, sixteen-year-old brother of that two-week-old sister who in his bitterness takes to the street and throws a brick at that building code inspector." Such disparities, he argues, help explain why blacks distrust evangelical Christianity and associate it with whiteness: "Make no bones about it: the difficulty in coming to grips with the evangelical message of Jesus Christ in the black community is the fact that most evangelicals in this country who say that Christ is the answer will also go back to their suburban communities and vote for law-and-order candidates who will keep the system the way it is." Skinner takes to task the "hyper-Christian" fundamentalist who has "half a dozen Bible verses for every social problem that existed. But if you asked him to get involved, he couldn't do it." It was not white Christianity that ultimately taught black people their worth, he suggests, but rather the Black Power and civil rights movements, which "declare[d] to us our dignity. [Because] God will not be without a witness."

The American Dream. "Bootstraps" mythology. White fears of integration. Suburbanization. Skinner eviscerates the normative racial prejudices infused in each. Then, to this mostly white audience that must have stood stunned, he relates his conversion experience. Flipping on the radio while orchestrating the largest gang fight ever planned in New York City, a Christian program preempted his regular rock station and "something came through" (Gilbreath 2006, 37). He "gave his life to Christ" and ultimately managed to leave the Harlem Lords, citing his conversion. The historical Jesus, he discovered, was not some soft spiritualist, but rather a champion for social justice; "a gutsy, contemporary, radical revolutionary"; a "militant" whose entire aim was to overthrow an "infested" system in the Roman Empire and "establish his own kingdom in the hearts of men." Jesus was, Skinner argues, entirely focused on "preaching liberation to an oppressed people." Neither capitalist nor socialist, Democrat nor Republican, Christ is "Lord of heaven and earth. And if you are going to respond to Jesus Christ, you must respond to him as Lord." Only now has Skinner said something white evangelicals are used to hearing.

After this testimony, Skinner goes in for the harder sell with the Urbana crowd: the idea that following Christ means working for justice on earth. He "calls out" young evangelicals to walk the talk:

> There is no way you can talk about preaching the gospel if you do not want to deal
> with the issues that bind people. If your gospel is an "either-or" gospel, I must reject
> it. Any gospel that does not talk about delivering to man a personal savior who will
> free him from the personal bondage of sin and grant him eternal life and does not

at the same time speak to the issue of enslavement, does not speak to the issue of injustice, does not speak to the issue of inequality—any gospel that does not want to go where people are hungry and poverty-stricken and set them free in the name of Jesus Christ is not the gospel.

A Christian mission, Skinner urges, means bringing Christianity into the world "where the action is," and working toward "revolution" here and now. This application of the gospel to a social justice framework is, in Skinner's framing, a no-brainer.

I relate this speech in some depth for a number of reasons. First, in (re)telling the African American redemption story, with its attendant challenge to white Christians, Skinner tapped into well-known strains in the African American community in the aftermath of the civil rights movement. He named historical injury wrought by religious racism and the fractures it created in the Christian community. He spoke of white evangelical complicity in racist paradigms, as well as the reality of ongoing structural and systemic inequities often invisible to whites. He alluded to white Christians' fears of "losing their testimony" (veering from the primacy of their theological attachments) if they apply their gospel to contemporary social suffering in their own culture. And he exposed African Americans' deep distrust of a white Christianity that sees itself as superior while doing little to change the plight of people who have suffered under exploitive systems, including Christian institutions.

By naming these central dynamics, Skinner confronted American evangelicals with a set of hard questions that would reverberate over time. Could whites come to see race and class inequalities through the kind of faith-based social justice framework that had become second nature to African American Christians? Could blacks and other Christians of color find reasons to overcome their distrust of white conservative evangelicals who had rarely been on the side of their liberation? What would it mean for all of these communities to address the sins of the past and move forward? Was that even possible?

To understand the embedded assumptions within white evangelicalism that Skinner disrupted in his Urbana '70 speech requires a glance back at the arc of evangelical social and political activism from the Cold War era through 1980. After the 1925 Scopes trial embarrassed American conservative evangelicals as antimodern "fundamentalists," they retreated from public engagement for about three decades (Diamond 1989; Liebman, Wuthnow, and Guth 1983; Harding 1991; Marsden 1980). As a religious community with an expressed political worldview, American evangelicalism didn't rear its head again until the 1950s, gradually building ideological and material ties to political conservatism and the Republican Party. Between those developing alliances and white evangelicals' own historical race baggage, the Christian Right's rise contains within it important racial subtexts—aspects of that community's meaning-making practices—that eventually became potential obstacles for the movement. Some late twentieth-century context helps illuminate how white evangelicals' dominant orientation to race enabled them to build an awkward counternarrative to assertions about a Christian mandate to pursue social justice.

Breaking Out of the South—Or Not

There is a strain of political ambivalence that runs through American conservative Protestantism. Indeed, evangelicals have long vacillated and been divided over whether Christians are called to pursue social reform on earth. The Second Great Awakening of the early nineteenth century, with its Armenian orientation and relatively democratic notions of salvation, was optimistic about triumphing over sin and creating a more perfect human society in God's "chosen nation."[3] Rooted in rapidly growing and less institutionally hierarchical Methodist and Baptist churches, nineteenth-century evangelicalism was the heart of American Protestantism and contributed to multiple social reform movements, including abolition, women's rights, and temperance (Smith 2004; Finke and Stark 1993). (But, as noted in chapter 2, even Christian abolitionism was not immune to the racist cosmologies of the time.) As party activists and ordinary voters, evangelicals were well entrenched in the mid-nineteenth-century party systems (Noll 1990; Carwardine 1993; Wyatt-Brown 1971; Howe 1991; Himmelstein 1990, notes 24, 25).

However, at the turn of the twentieth century, as the forces of modernism began to threaten and displace meaning systems provided by religion and cultural traditionalism, what had been a mainstream evangelicalism began to shift (Marsden 1991). With industrialization, urbanization, and the continuing advance of science came changes in the way people lived and, in turn, new social problems demanding social action. The older faith- and culture-based frameworks for understanding the world were increasingly framed by secular elites as backward, with the lampooning of fundamentalists in 1925 at the Scopes trial serving as a particularly humiliating spectacle (Harding 1991).

Responses to modernism in American Protestantism divided evangelicals. What would become the increasingly secular humanist mainline denominations (for example, Lutherans, Presbyterians, Episcopalians, some Baptist and Methodist groups) saw faith as being, to some degree, adaptable to the findings of modern science and scholarship. Other denominations (Southern Baptists,

Pentecostals, Assemblies of God, Church of Christ) rejected what they saw as a compromised theology and emphasized doctrinal purity, scriptural inerrancy, and individual salvation (biblical "fundamentalism").

Even within fundamentalism, believers split between postmillennialists, who maintained that human beings could be perfected before Christ's Second Coming, and premillennialists, who predicted increasing social degeneration that Christ, not humans, would ultimately correct during his thousand-year reign on earth (the millennium) (Himmelstein 1990, 111). In what scholars call "the Great Reversal," evangelicalism effectively separated from the social reform tradition it had long advocated, while the Protestant reform churches became more secular (113, and note 27). This divide was consolidated through the creation of competing umbrella groups: the Federal Council of Churches (FCC) on the mainline side, the American Council of Christian Churches (ACCC) on the ultraconservative fundamentalist end, and the slightly more moderate National Association of Evangelicals (NAE), through which Billy Graham rose to prominence.

The upshot of these historical shifts, for our purposes, is that where white conservative evangelicalism had on the national level once been a deeply socially engaged religion, in the first half of the twentieth century it largely retreated from what it came to call "the world." Many fundamentalists turned their attention toward building new denominations or creating independent spaces within existing ones, developing new missiology frameworks (missiology being the study of Christian missionary efforts), and slowly growing their local churches (Woodberry and Smith 1998, 26–28). White, pro–social justice Christians emerged mostly from the more activist mainline and liberal wings of Protestantism and Catholicism (Wuthnow and Evans 2002). The black church, although politically associated with the liberals and mainliners, can be said to have had a foot in both arenas, based on its ties to theological fundamentalism and the charismatic traditions, such as Pentecostalism, within nineteenth- and twentieth-century evangelicalism. These historical legacies become relevant to the leadership that produces the New Christian Right.

After a few decades of relative political insularity, conservative evangelicals began to emerge from their shells in the wake of World War II, embracing a stalwart, Christianity-inflected procapitalism. Evangelicals impugned Communism for its rejection of God and the free-will individualism evangelicals associated with a divinely ordained economic philosophy. Not only did some support anti-Communist extremist groups like the John Birch Society, evangelicals also built powerful missionary campaigns concentrated in Third World, Communist, and proto-Communist nations (Wald 1994; Wilcox 1992). The concept of "spiritual warfare," in which Christians understand themselves as fighting Satan's forces across the world, developed in these soul-saving but also politically charged mission contexts. Particularly in Central America, evangelicals built extensive radio broadcasting networks—a skill that helped organize the New Christian Right infrastructure in the 1980s. Mission work abroad was supported by donations from churchgoers back in the United States who took an interest in pairing the spiritual goal of "spreading the gospel" with the political goal of eradicating Communism. As Sara Diamond chronicles, Christian conservatives' anti-Communist interests led them to engagement in the foreign military policy realm that gradually, and particularly in the Reagan era, solidified their ties to the Republican Party (1995, chapters 3 and 10). Evangelical anti-Communist efforts provide a backdrop for understanding how evangelicals came to ideologically position themselves against all kinds of state-sponsored social programs, even in the United States.

Woven into this domestically and globally oriented anti-Communism was an important demographic development: the outmigration of southern Christians of evangelical and fundamentalist veins, who moved from the South into primarily the midwestern and western states in the mid-twentieth century. Darren Dochuk explains: "Between 1910 and 1960, slightly more than 9 million people left the South for the Northeast, Midwest, and Pacific Coast with 5 million of these exiting the region between 1940 and 1960 alone" (2007, 300–301). By 1970, over 11 million southerners (about 7.5 million white, 3.5 million black) were reported to be living outside their home states. While most settled in the Midwest, California surpassed all other individual states in hosting southern-born residents, and by 1970 "more white southerners lived in Los Angeles and Orange counties than in Little Rock and Oklahoma City combined" (301). In the 1970s, the Southern Baptist General Convention of California had become the largest Protestant denomination in the state, and Pentecostal and nondenominational churches also expanded rapidly. Thousands of southern evangelical preachers relocated to serve the diaspora's growing churches.

These transplanted southerners (and here I focus on whites) brought their politics with them as they resettled. Alongside their fixation on Communism, southern evangelicals' other political bugaboo in the 1940s and 1950s was "liberal cosmopolitanism." Conservatives used the term to reference post–New Deal, state-sponsored efforts to organize the dramatic social chaos created by wartime mobilization by shoring up public education, organized labor, and urban planning, and supporting improved race relations. This reeked, for many evangelicals, of secular humanism and the dangerous power of "big government" (Dochuk 2007, 304). Hailing from a particular southern white evangelical sensibility that was, for the most part, prosegregationist in the South,[4] transplanted southern white evangelicals in places like Detroit became "an instant force" in battles over desegregation and public housing in the 1940s and 1950s (304–5).[5] Paired with the stance against liberal cosmopolitanism, the anti-Communist creed served these actors in two directions. Hard-edged fundamentalist preachers used this cause to build religious empires out of "new money and new fears generated by America's Cold War." And in the more middle-class, suburban environments of places like Southern California, anti-Communist evangelical crusaders employed a milder message of traditional values and populist antistatism that attracted followers to rapidly growing, folksy megachurches (306). In short, conservative orientations linking state-sponsored civil rights initiatives to Communism both grew churches and set the stage for a white evangelicalism hostile to "liberal" policies, which included most social justice–oriented frameworks at the time.

The racial overtones of the white evangelical diaspora became more obvious, at least in certain regions, by the racially charged 1960s. The virulently racist George Wallace drew the bulk of his support, especially in the Midwest, from transplanted southern religious activists affiliated with a group called the Baptist Bible Fellowship (BBF). The BBF represented a number of the nation's largest churches, including Jerry Falwell's Thomas Road Baptist Church in Lynchburg, Virginia (the only BBF church actually still in the South), and hosted Wallace on guest pulpits in the South and Midwest (Dochuk 2007, 308–9).

Falwell himself embodied an interesting set of tensions in this context. On the one hand, despite his sympathies with the anti-Communism of fellow conservative evangelicals, in the civil rights context Falwell preached *against* applying religion to politics. His now infamous 1965 "Ministers and Marchers" sermon articulated the retreatist fundamentalism of midcentury that defined itself against social reform Christianity:

> We have a message of redeeming grace through a crucified and risen Lord. This message is designed to go right to the heart of man and there meet his deep spiritual need. Nowhere are we commissioned to reform the externals. We are not told to wage wars against bootleggers, liquor stores, gamblers, murderers, prostitutes, racketeers, prejudiced persons or institutions, or any other existing evil as such. . . . I believe we need to rededicate ourselves to the great task of turning this world back to God. The preaching of the gospel is the only means by which this can be done. (Harding 2000, 22)

This caution against political engagement (from which Falwell later executed an about-face) didn't stop him from speaking in support of racial segregation. In one sermon, "Segregation or Integration, Which?," Falwell defended segregation on the basis of white Christians' racist reading of the biblical "Curse of Ham" story, in which blacks were condemned to second-class status. When all public schools were required to implement integration plans in 1967, Falwell opened his Christian day school, denying that the school supported a whites-only policy.[6] Thomas Road Baptist Church did not welcome its first black family and baptize its first black member until 1970 (26–27). Yet as Falwell rose to prominence as a leader of the New Christian Right, he took steps to distance himself from his prosegregationist positions.

Although racist rhetoric and liberal bashing were relatively normalized in settings dominated by white former southerners, on the West Coast southern evangelicals tended to soften their racial separatism and emphasize core conservative principles like free enterprise and Christian morality. By the 1960s, some of these southern-born evangelicals wielded their church empires to seize political opportunities available in their new regions. Bob Wells, a Dallas evangelist who came to lead Orange County, California's huge Central Baptist megachurch, mobilized conservative evangelicals against challenges to racialized patterns in housing, calling such efforts leftist propaganda (Dochuk 2007, 310–11). Outspoken in his promotion of individualism, entrepreneurialism, and the re-Christianization of America from behind and beyond the pulpit, Wells mobilized his congregants on behalf of Christian conservatism. He attacked the "leftist establishment" by targeting groups like the American Civil Liberties Union (ACLU), University of California at Berkeley radicals, and civil rights protesters, and built a legion of "concerned citizens" from Central Baptist. These Christian soldiers infiltrated a nearby California state university to monitor Communist influences, put anti–fair housing and antiobscenity initiatives on the ballot, and campaigned for Barry Goldwater outside the church. Another former Texan in Orange County, Pastor W. Stuart McBirnie, used his success as head of the large United Community Church in Glendale to become a consultant for conservative Republican politicians, including Goldwater and Ronald Reagan.

In this context, a cohort of current and former southern preachers, many of them now leading California churches, became a powerhouse for fomenting a conservative Christian revolution against the forces of liberalism and secular humanism. Californian Richard Nixon, who had long courted evangelicals like Billy Graham, began reaching out to the likes of Bill Bright, another West Coast transplanted southerner and leader of the popular Campus Crusade for Christ. Such clerics "shaped by circumstances in the diaspora threw their weight behind Nixon's southern strategy and, at least in the short term, helped to guarantee the candidate's victory" (313). After Nixon's collapse, southern diaspora evangelicals drew on their early experience in 1950s and 1960s school prayer, Bible reading, antipornography, antigay, and anti–sex education campaigns to build connections with the GOP. Future Christian Right leaders James Dobson (Louisiana-born, California-trained), Tim and Beverly LaHaye (California-based former Bob Jones University graduates), and Richard Viguerie (Californian instrumental in southern Goldwater campaigns) threw their combined force into developing new political interest groups, specialized evangelical organizations, broadcast networks, and marketing tools to advance a conservative Christian movement. California evangelical churches worked with private educational institutions like Pepperdine University to create forums for debating policy and planning strategy, and eventually coalescing in support of Ronald Reagan (314–16).[7]

The creation of the Moral Majority in 1979 was, in effect, the culmination of the influence of southern diaspora leadership on evangelical politicization. Dochuk argues that while in the 1960s race (as white backlash) combined with religion through a network of southern clerics and churches to orchestrate a conservative realignment in support of conservative Republicans, by the 1970s religion became a replacement for race as a political organizing principle (2007, 312). But Dochuk understates the complexity of the issue. In fact, this particular religious movement *needs* race, or at minimum the appearance of racial tolerance and diversity, in the changing social context of the post–civil rights movement era.

There are at least three reasons for this. First, the efflorescence of evangelical and fundamentalist churches, superchurches, youth organizations, and clerical networks from the 1950s forward produced an evangelical culture that was largely white and effectively segregated from black, Latino, and Asian churches (despite strains of evangelical theology and practice in those communities). Even denominational umbrellas were largely divided along racial lines.[8] This fact, which is partly a product of essentially segregationist church-growth models, became by the 1970s a source of some self-consciousness for whites. The fact that someone like Tom Skinner was invited to speak at Urbana '70 is itself a reflection of this.

Second, in the run-up to the 1980s white evangelicals had to grapple with the unsightly problem of racism in their own history. By the 1970s, in metropoles like Los Angeles and even relatively diverse sections of Orange County, the anti-integrationist and anti–civil rights positions of high-profile leaders like Graham (in the 1940s and 1950s) and Falwell (in the 1960s) had become a potential political liability when going toe to toe with liberals and Democrats. Certain coded iterations of racism embedded in critiques of welfare and public programs may have been tolerated, but flagrant white supremacist orientations could no longer fly.

Demonstrating this kind of rethinking, Jerry Falwell made a number of moves. In his post–civil rights movement era interviews and writings, he attempted to "backdate" his turn from segregation to a period earlier than his late-1960s reform (Harding 2000, 26 and notes 32–33). His segregationist attitudes, he suggested, were simply a product of a misguided era (even though he was reiterating them well into the 1960s). He also constructed a new narrative about his racial views: he changed because he "awakened" from the taken-for-granted racism of southern white culture to the rightness of racial equality. But in this story it was God, rather than the civil rights movement itself, that allegedly sponsored his transformation: "It wasn't the Congress or the courts that changed my heart. [The] demonstrators, in spite of their courage, didn't move me to new compassion on behalf of my black brothers and sisters. The new laws and the loud protest marchers may have helped to enforce the change and to speed it up, but it was God's still small voice in my heart that was the real instrument of change and growth for me" (Harding 2000, 25).

As he ushered his new Moral Majority—the first conservative evangelical organization in decades that explicitly sought to influence party politics—into the political spotlight, he encouraged Christian conservatives to come out of political hiding. In a truly telling maneuver, he often compared Christian Right goals to the revolutionary aims of the civil rights movement. Although he took some care to qualify such comparisons by noting that (white) Christian conservatives never suffered the discrimination African Americans did, by employing such comparisons he effectively erased the participation of fundamentalists and evangelicals, including himself, in advocating racial segregation and resisting the changes urged by the civil rights movement (Harding 2000, 23–24).

Third, from the perspective of antiracist Christians, the combination of white evangelicals' support for Southern Strategy conservative candidates in the 1960s, with their long rejection of government-sponsored social initiatives (public housing, education, welfare policies, and so forth) in the name of private-sector free enterprise, painted a clear picture of evangelical activists as hostile to Americans of color. No matter how procapitalist or theologically conservative their own individual orientations, Christians of color needed only to trace the impact of the white southern diaspora to find white evangelicals opposing practically every form of political activism by and assistance to Americans of color and poor and underrepresented populations. Moreover, whites did this, in part, by criticizing faith-based social justice efforts as misguided and theologically illegitimate.

As the Christian Right congealed into a political force on the American scene by the early 1980s, the Christian racial justice narrative through which Tom Skinner challenged white evangelicals less than a decade earlier appears to have been smothered if not entirely co-opted. Without a trace of irony, the New

Christian Right heralded itself in the tradition of faith-based moral reform, revising its racial history to concede to basic civil rights protections, while sustaining a social justice–critical orientation increasingly hostile to liberal social policies that were, in fact, extensions of the civil rights movement. This was, indeed, a delicate line to walk for a movement seeking to attract adherents across the country to a new political crusade.

Wagner's "Prophesy"

Nine years after Skinner's speech, and the same year that Falwell founded the Moral Majority, white evangelical missionary C. Peter Wagner told a different story about the relevance of social justice to the contemporary Christian community. A rising name in the growing field of missiology and a professor in the Institute of Church Growth at Fuller Seminary (conservative evangelicalism's most prominent West Coast leadership incubator), Wagner had just published *Our Kind of People* in 1979.[9] This book laid out the rationale for an "ethical" church-growth paradigm in which racial, ethnic, socioeconomic, and other kinds of cultural homogeneity in churches could not simply be tolerated but even embraced under a concept known as the Homogeneous Unit Principle (HUP).

The HUP was a social science term introduced in the church-growth context by Wagner's mentor and fellow Fuller professor Donald McGavran, who began writing about the HUP in 1936 and first published his full elaboration of it in 1955. HUP proponents found value in the idea that, as McGavran famously put it, "Men like to become Christians without crossing racial, linguistic, or class barriers."[10] As missionaries, McGavran, then Wagner, originally used the HUP to explain to Western Christian missionaries why it made sense to cater to cultural homogeneity in certain non-Western settings like India or Africa, in which tribal or caste groups preferred to practice faith within their cultural communities rather than mix with other groups (Wagner 1979, 21–22). The principle was then applied in the 1960s to American churches, under the philosophy that it was better for more people to convert and join churches, even if they circulated primarily with others like themselves, than to have to cross uncomfortable social boundaries to receive the gospel. As alarming as the HUP may sound, it is oversimplified to call it a racist framework per se—and not just because Wagner defended it as "the opposite of racist."[11] It was nevertheless received in some U.S. circles as a welcome reprieve from pressures to integrate churches along ethnic, class, and/or racial lines.[12]

With *Our Kind of People* hot off the presses, Wagner offered some predictions in a *Christianity Today* editorial about how he believed the American Christian community would develop in the 1980s (Wagner 1979). This decade, he suggests, can foster great years of church growth—a period in which American churches will potentially see significant increases in their membership rolls and thus more souls "saved" through conversion. Wagner maintained (and has continued to argue during the subsequent thirty years) that church growth, achieved through evangelism, should be the *primary* goal of Christians (17–18).[13] But growth will only occur if congregations and their presiding denominational bodies set priorities in order.

Wagner explains through a chronological review. The 1950s, he notes, were a decade of church growth in which most denominations were enjoying steady increases in membership. The 1960s, in contrast, produced "a decade of transition" because right around 1965, "the most severe decline in church membership and attendance in the history of the mainstream denominations began *as if on cue*" (Wagner 1979, 25, emphasis added). However, looking more closely at church demographics, Wagner notes, while the mainline churches lost membership between 1965 and 1975, the evangelical denominations, like the Southern Baptists and the Assemblies of God, were "growing 37 percent at the same time" (25). The 1970s, he argues, marked "a time of reassessment," as both mainstream and conservative churches reflected on why they were losing or gaining membership. Scholars also weighed in on the phenomenon.[14]

Why did mainline churches begin a steep decline around the mid-1960s? Wagner offers his reading: "What happened in the sixties? The social climate is well known. The civil rights movement, the hippie movement, the death-of-God viewpoint, situation ethics, and other social and psychological factors confused the religious world. Those already inclined to be 'public Protestants,' as [religion scholar] Martin Marty might say, particularly developed strong guilt feelings about the politically conservative nature of the American church" (Wagner 1979, 26). It is worth parsing the series of semiotic assumptions Wagner executes in the passage above. In his phrasing, the "religious world" excludes "public Protestants," by whom he presumably means liberal mainline groups and African American churches. That "religious world" is described not as part of 1960s movements, but rather a "confused" outsider witnessing them. The "public Protestants" who, Wagner's language suggests, had previously had some different outlook, developed, in the midst of these movements, "strong guilt feelings" about the American church's conservatism. It's not quite clear if this "conservatism" refers to racism and prosegregationist policies or to cultural orientations antithetical to, for example, "hippies," but beginning his description of the 1960s with the civil rights movement seems to imply at least partly a race-linked conservatism. Wagner's paragraph finishes: "Those in power used this guilt to give social service top priority on the agendas of the mainstream denominations. Some were advocating theologically that 'the world should set the agenda.' Evangelicals in general were not convinced, believing that the Bible should set the agenda" (26).

Here Wagner's story advances by mobilizing another set of signifiers: elites ("those in power," who are implicitly not the masses of churchgoers) in the liberal mainline denominations were manipulative; they "used guilt" (about Christian conservatism) to set their denominational agendas. And they crafted those agendas to prioritize "social service"—an arena that is, by implication, a "worldly" (secular) rather than a theological (biblical) priority. (In his larger opus, Wagner consistently performs a particular semantic move that carries a political connotation: he replaces the term "social justice" with the more innocuous "social service," "social issues," or occasionally "social change." Even where he's paraphrasing Christians of color who explicitly use the term "social justice," he tends to transcribe it back to "social service.") Who was not convinced of these suspicious moves, according to Wagner? Well, "evangelicals in general," for they presumably ascribed to a different set of priorities and could see through these misguided moves (Wagner 1979, 26).

Now, Wagner avers, it's not that churches shouldn't take on social service; after all, "studies show fairly convincingly that a strong emphasis on social service is not in itself a cause of decline in church membership" (Wagner 1979, 26). (Here, social service is coded as a kind of volunteering activity, not, as was the case for many mainline, African American, and even a few evangelical churches in the civil rights movement, a means of critiquing and overhauling existing racial, class, gender, and cultural power structures beyond *and within* the churches.) "Churches can be very active socially and still grow vigorously," Wagner maintains, but only "if—and here is a large if—*if they do not give social service a higher priority than evangelism*" (26, emphasis added). Here Wagner delivers the pivotal mechanism of the story. To paraphrase: churches won't grow, and they will have veered from their biblical mandate of spreading the gospel, if they focus too much on "social service." In other words, as it is translated into ordinary evangelical parlance, *social justice hurts the church.*

In the wake of this central assertion, Wagner then relates what he reads as the bright side of the misguided priorities story: the exciting evidence that fundamentalist and evangelical churches, "which by and large had not reversed priorities," are growing exponentially at the dawn of the 1980s (Wagner 1979, 26). The Southern Baptists, who are planting monoethnic churches of all stripes across the nation, grew 17 percent in the 1970s, while the American population as a whole grew only 7 percent. He recounts similar success stories for the

Pentecostals, whom he accurately predicts will lead the way of church growth in coming decades, as well as Nazarenes and the theologically conservative Lutheran Church–Missouri Synod. The mainline churches could grow, but only under a "reexamination of priorities"—that is, a return to a guiding focus on evangelism and church planting (51). In commending the evangelical churches on their rapid growth, Wagner offers no corresponding recommendation that they continue to attend, perhaps even secondarily, to social concerns.[15]

Wagner's *Christianity Today* editorial might seem an insignificant volley in the complex milieu of American evangelicalism were it not for three factors that anchor his relevance to the longer trajectory of twentieth-century evangelical race discourse. First, the McGavran/Wagner HUP model became the dominant paradigm of church growth within American evangelicalism, and Wagner its highly influential (if also controversial in some circles) proponent. Through the HUP-driven church-growth model, evangelical and fundamentalist Protestant communities grew by leaps and bounds in the 1960s and 1970s. This expansion poured money into American evangelicalism, positioning conservative Christians to mobilize resources for collective action in unprecedented ways. Today, many advocates of racial change within evangelicalism argue that the HUP-based church-growth model contributes to the persistent racial and ethnic homogeneity of American churches over time (Emerson 2001; Christerson, Edwards, and Emerson, 2005; Yancey 2003; DeYoung et al. 2003).[16] As we will see, when advocates for racial reconciliation and multiethnic church-building began to develop philosophical and theological frameworks to ground their efforts, one of their first moves was to challenge the legitimacy of the HUP *because* it had become second-nature to church leaders. This challenge, which requires pushing against the grain of a still-powerful church-growth industry, is ongoing.

Second, it is actually C. Peter Wagner, as he extended his career in missiology through an organization he built called Global Harvest Ministries (GHM), who helped develop the idea of "spiritual warfare." As mentioned earlier, spiritual warfare describes a religious confrontation with evil and a strategy for rendering "unreached" geographical areas more receptive to missionaries (Diamond 2000, 221). This became an influential principle of evangelical mission work (and political influence) in Latin America and Africa in the 1980s (Diamond 1989, 1995). Such spiritual belligerence involves activities like "casting out demons," fighting non-Christian religions and philosophies, and designing "strategic-level" challenges to "Satan's influence" over large geographical areas.[17] Diamond (1989) convincingly argues that anti-Communist frameworks of evangelical missionaries in Latin America contributed to the Christian Right's influence on the Republican Party in the 1980s.

Finally, in the mid-1990s the same C. Peter Wagner coined the term "identificational repentance," an idea that became profoundly influential, and operationalized, within evangelical efforts to promote racial reconciliation. Wagner argued that just as Christians ought to offer true repentance for their individual sins, take actions to repair the damage done by those sins, and promise not to repeat them, so should collective bodies, including nations. And, perhaps ironically given his role in perpetuating the effective racial segregation of churches, he identified the central tragic American collective sin as racism:

> The principal sin of my nation is clearly racism. The corporate sins that have established this spiritual stronghold are clear. The broadest and most pervasive sin was committed in bringing Africans to our shores as slaves—human merchandise to be bought, sold, and used for any conceivable purpose to satisfy the desires of their white masters.
>
> Beyond this, however, is an even deeper root of national iniquity; the horrendous way white Americans treated their hosts in this land, the American Indians. (Wagner 1996, 62)

Wagner argued that white Christians should be concerned about the sins of their ancestors because of "iniquity," or the "effect the sin has exercised on subsequent generations." The cycle of iniquity can be stopped, he suggested, via corporate repentance, a process of "identifying with the sin" committed by previous generations. Through identificational repentance, Christians productively advance spiritual warfare, because they "effectively remove a foothold that Satan has used to keep populations in spiritual darkness" (63). In Wagner's parlance, then, racism is both an individual and corporate sin; it is a Satanic device to promote division among Christians and thereby limit the conversion potential of non-Christians; and it is cast out through collective repentance that acknowledges the participation of white Christians in historical (and national) processes.

The Spiritual Dangers of Social Justice

C. Peter Wagner serves as an embodiment of white American evangelicalism between the civil rights movement era of the 1950s–60s and the rise of the evangelical reconciliation movement in the mid-1990s. This is an evangelicalism that managed to simultaneously distance itself from religion-driven social justice initiatives (be they mainline, liberal, or channeled through the black church) and take up the cross of acknowledging white racism—but primarily as a means of attempting to move out from under its shadow. In the 1990s, collective repentance would be offered as a way of "owning up" to an ugly racial history, even as the HUP continued to perpetuate segregation in evangelical churches, partly in the name of sympathy with ethnic minorities who want to retain their religious cultural practices, but mostly in the name of facilitating evangelism. And with "spiritual warfare" providing a meaning-making framework with global implications, the stakes of "slipping" into "worldly" social justice priorities, like church integration or challenging ongoing race-related power structures, were coded as high. Christians, Wagner and white evangelicalism asserted, can't afford to "lose their way" by turning churches into vehicles for social change—not when there are so many Satan-sponsored dangers in the world to confront. Rather, believers should concentrate on bringing others like them (at home) and cultural Others (in the missionary field) to salvation, while providing private-sector "social services" in a nonthreatening manner. Through such narratives, social justice, including critiques of racial power within and beyond Christian communities, was rendered intelligible as a dangerous temptation rather than the normative ideal that it is in the African American Christian tradition.

Through the figure of Wagner, the dialectical character of the two competing narratives becomes evident. White evangelicals construct the social justice–aversive story in an implied but not direct conversation with (or against) the African American and liberal Christian story of social justice/reform as a Christian imperative. When Wagner and other influential evangelicals assert that "social justice hurts the church," they implicitly distinguish *their* evangelical community from those *other* Christians, the ones with skewed priorities. But they are also compelled to acknowledge that the civil rights movement was right, that racism was both immoral and un-Christian, and that basic racial equality before the law is something Christians should support. Otherwise, white evangelicalism, its muddied past, and its HUP-driven church-growth model look suspicious indeed. Thus, in a dialectical sense the social justice–aversive story implicitly *depends on* the black Christian social justice story as an oppositional referent, and, in a curious way, a racial justice–phobic white evangelicalism tries to co-opt the social justice narrative even while distancing from the ongoing challenges it raises.

Wagner's 1979 editorial in *Christianity Today* serves as a place marker, shedding light on white conservative evangelicalism's hubris about race at the dawn of the 1980s. In no uncertain terms, Wagner reveals use of the social justice–aversive story as a way to justify limited interest and action in ongoing race-related and broader socioeconomic debates that continue after the civil rights movement. Wagner's editorial appeared in the same year (1979) that conservative evangelical and fundamentalist Christian leaders decided, through the creation of the Moral Majority, that they planned to lead a cohesive force into American political life despite the dangers of entering worldly politics. Through the new church-growth paradigm, conservative white evangelicals, many of whom hailed from or still lived in the South, developed a subtler way to distance themselves from the "liberal" social justice tradition while minimizing their problematic racial history and justifying their relative racial isolation.

To different degrees, and with some important shifts along the way, the two competing stories about social justice traced here continue to shape evangelical race discourse today. These stories are in dialogue with developments within American conservative evangelicalism between the 1950s and the 1980s. As streams of Christianity that could accommodate elements of modernism moved toward the social justice activism of the 1960s and 1970s, more fundamentalist variants flowed in other directions. Where many African American, liberal, and mainline Christians worked to challenge forces of social inequality, war, and other issues, many white evangelicals harnessed their energies against "Communist" and "Satanic" influences, big government, and liberal cosmopolitanism. While modernist Christians understood social and racial justice efforts as continuing a long tradition of faith-based social reform movements, more orthodox Christians worried about "losing" faith-based values—and members—to "social issues"–based priorities. But with legacies like theological racism, southern segregationism, and resistance to civil rights initiatives so embedded in white conservative evangelical history, the racial overtones of social justice–aversive narratives are difficult to deny. The problem for the emerging religious conservative movement becomes how to keep that negative legacy from being a political deal-breaker.

There has been little attention in the literature on the rise of the New Christian Right to the possibility that influences of white racism and segregated church demographics presented political liabilities by the 1980s. But there is ample evidence to suggest that white evangelicals were making efforts as early as the late 1960s to navigate this consideration. They did so through a number of strategies that are intelligible in the evangelical cultural context, but which don't always sit together easily.

There is the effort to distance from the history of racism in the white evangelical past, as Jerry Falwell did, or to silence it by simply not making mention of it. There is also the alternate attempt to justify, reframe, or redeem that history through efforts to explain some evangelicals' "misguided" or "sinful" orientations to race, particularly in the context of whites enculturated in the Jim Crow South. A third strategy of tentatively redressing the white evangelical race problem is to demonstrate interest in the activities and beliefs of Christian communities of color. (We'll soon see examples of this.) Similarly, white evangelicals might initiate selective partnerships with individual prominent evangelicals of color, usually rising-star pastors, in order to proclaim (or perform) the existence of an at least minimally cross-racial movement. Ideal forums for this include large-scale youth, Christian music, or church-growth gatherings—like the one Skinner addressed in 1970.[18] Like Falwell, many white Christian Right leaders analogize their movement to the civil rights movement, reading both movements as expressions of righteous religious activism in American politics—although this strategy carries the obvious risk of political backfire. Finally, white evangelicals may attempt to reduce the liability of their racial baggage by initiating dialogue, or at least the appearance of it, with sufficiently palatable (that is, at least pro-capitalist and theologically conservative) Christians of color as spokespersons. Such conversations might involve discussing the past in a minimally conflictual way, lauding the victories of the mainstream and faith-based wings of the civil rights movement, and inviting Christians of color to become allies in the new conservative Christian political mission. In the 1980s, white evangelicals had not yet moved into the territory of identificational repentance for their past racial sins, but as cross-racial conversations developed over the decade, this became an increasingly appealing strategy.

The historical and political context traced in this chapter enables an analysis of the articulation of these strategies, all of which are meaning-making practices, through the vehicle of evangelicalism's most prominent magazines. In the next chapter, we follow the arc of evangelical race discourse as it played out in the pages of *Christianity Today* magazine from the 1980s to the 1990s, shifting onto a new course called racial reconciliation.

Tom Skinner could not have known that it would take white evangelicals nearly twenty-five years to finally begin to utter a full-throated response to his challenges at Urbana, or that in the interim white conservative evangelicals would lead a powerful political movement. But his words, his writing, and the Jackson, Mississippi–based racial reconciliation ministry he established before his untimely death in 1994 seeded commitments among a handful of black Christians that would be influential in sculpting evangelical racial discourse (Skinner 1968, 1970a, 1970b, 1970c, 1974). The reverberations of Skinner's call eventually nudged white evangelicalism out of a comfort zone that people like Wagner and white southern diaspora leaders helped to construct.

PART TWO

A New Wave

The Turn to Reconciliation

4   Religious Race Bridging as a Third Way

I have heard very few Southern evangelicals admit they were on the wrong side of the race issues back in the fifties, sixties, and early seventies. I have never heard any of them say that they should have blocked the entrances to the jails where we were beaten and tortured, or taken a stand with us when we wanted equal access to "life, liberty, and the pursuit of happiness." In fact, over the past few years there have been only a few Southern, white, evangelical Christians who have asked our forgiveness and extended a hand in reconciliation. On the contrary, for every step we take in their direction, it seems that most take another step toward the suburbs.
—Spencer Perkins, *Christianity Today*, 1989

Only when we individually and as a corporate group renounce racism in all its forms and repent of all transgressions will God choose to use us in the future to reach all people throughout the world.
—Rev. Billy Graham, at the 150th anniversary of the Southern Baptist
Convention, 1995

Social change is often awkward and uncomfortable. Even under the best conditions it requires us to alter the stories we have been telling for generations about ourselves, others, and "the way things are"—stories we understand to be if not always *perfectly* accurate, then at least acceptable truisms that guide action. Like layers of geological sediment, collective narratives are marbled through the complex racial histories and identities in American evangelicalism. To dislodge entrenched frameworks that have provided meaning and identity for people would seem to require something akin to dynamite—a miracle, or an apocalypse. Even to *reconsider* old stories may involve feelings of betrayal of one's own family, social group, or ancestors.

At the dawn of the 1980s, American evangelicals were at a virtual standstill on racial matters. The major competing racial narratives constructed over at least a century left blacks and whites, at least, in separate and largely segregated communities. Some, like Tom Skinner and Martin Luther King Jr., understood the church as inseparable from an ongoing mission to defend and protect downtrodden communities and fight to increase political and social equality. Others, like C. Peter Wagner, saw the church as instrumental to a swift, definitive soul-saving enterprise designed to bring glory to God and ideally reform a degenerating culture.[1] Given how white evangelicals had long constructed their stories about race and religion, it was inconceivable for most to imagine being both theologically conservative *and* focused on racial justice or even racial integration in the church without straining what they saw as the central religious mission, salvation. In 1980, it was easier for most whites to imagine that the most glaring racial inequalities had receded; therefore, the choice to join a particular church did not necessarily imply that one identified with a *racial* group, even if the congregation was all white.[2] For most American Christians of color, especially blacks, such de-racialized fantasies of religious belonging were untenable, as race, ethnicity, culture, and history had long been understood as organically interwoven with religious beliefs, practices, and membership. American evangelicalism seemed locked on separate tracks.

Just a decade and a half later, however, things looked strikingly different, at least on the surface. By 1995, a person could almost flip open the most popular evangelical magazine to a random page and land on an article showcasing new racial changes occurring within the evangelical community. Racial reconciliation was on the rise, inaugurating new kinds of reflection, public and semipublic rituals of apology and forgiveness, and cross-racial dialogues within conservative evangelicalism. Suddenly race seemed to be a *positive* (if nevertheless still anxious) preoccupation. People were rethinking their old stories about race and exploring what those changing perspectives might mean for their actual social practices. Participants spoke in terms of epiphanies, collective miracles, and spiritual healing.

What changed to carve a path from stagnation to visions of divinely inspired, catalytic reconciliation? Was such change driven from outside or within American evangelical communities, and how did it impact the mental and spiritual universes of people involved? What conceptual work did the discourse of racial reconciliation do for evangelicals? What were its governing assumptions and constraints? How did racial change discourse interface with what had become a quite powerful political force in the 1990s, the organized Religious Right? And what does the turn to reconciliation after decades of resistance and avoidance reveal about human beings' abilities to creatively transform old narratives and potentially drive meaningful social change?

Fumbling toward a Third Way

In this section of the book, we turn our attention from the broad historical view to the micropolitical, investigating from a closer vantage point how American evangelicalism navigated consecutive waves of racial change at the turn of the twenty-first century. By "micropolitics," I refer to the ways in which history is told and retold, social relations are navigated and reimagined, and power is variously expressed, internalized, reproduced, contested, and disguised through social discourse among ordinary people trying to contend with a complex social issue in everyday life.[3] Here and in the next two chapters I trace how through the culturally distinctive phenomenon of *religious race bridging*, a multiracial contingent of evangelicals wove the emotionally powerful, politically ambivalent "third way" between the two major sedimented narratives of the past.

As mentioned previously, religious race bridging draws on faith-based resources to bring members of different racial groups together for meaningful cross-racial engagement and healing designed to inspire individual and corporate change within the spiritual body.[4] By employing faith and other endogenous meaning-making systems to build a common language across racial and ethnic difference, evangelicals used religious race bridging to attempt to reconcile evangelical America's past and present with their professed religious values and distinctive cultural etiquettes.[5] Although participants are influenced by the outside world as they work toward change, religious race bridging, at least among evangelicals, resists the imposition of frameworks by outside influences (for example, secular, left-leaning "social justice," academic, or otherwise foreign communities).[6]

Despite the many mistakes and awkward gestures they made as they fumbled toward this third way, through religious race bridging conservative evangelicals facilitated the first meaningful openings in racial dialogue and engagement they had produced since at least the Civil War. But for complicated reasons I disentangle, these new openings in race relations seemed, especially in the 1990s, to depend on other kinds of implicit—and sometimes explicit—closures. As they participated in bridging activities, they tended, on the whole, to encounter racial *politics* with uneasiness. Substantive racial change seemed to require a pointed avoidance of "getting political" with reconciliation. But this avoidance is informed by complex, culturally constituted layers of meaning-making within evangelical circles, and among participants different communities were—and are—motivated by different concerns.

To understand that the new racial reconciliation discourse was not just a random, isolated phenomenon in a few local churches, but rather an influential trend that registered conceptually in the larger community, in this chapter I examine the evolution of racial discourse from 1980 to 1999 through American evangelicalism's flagship magazine, *Christianity Today* (*CT*). *CT* provides an instructive measure of the racial climate within the self-identified evangelical community at large, over time. A content analysis of race-related items in the journal over three decades reveals that shifts in evangelical race discourse occurred in three main phases: a *thin pluralism* attempt in the 1980s that did not create substantive change; the much more robust *racial reconciliation* approach of the 1990s, that did; and the multiethnic church–building movement, which calls for more substantive, long-term transformations (the subject of chapters 7 and 8). Each phase built on the previous one to refine and advance religious race-bridging methods.

The *CT* material reveals how evangelical elites (pastors, denominational leaders, journalists, editors, activists, and public figures) reacted to race-related dynamics occurring at the grassroots, and how the overall perspective of the white-dominant evangelical community on race issues evolved over time. This exposes interesting sociopolitical patterns I will detail. But even close analysis of racial discourse in the magazine cannot capture how non-elite participants, ordinary believers who got involved, experienced racial change and reconciliation efforts as they unfolded. Why and how did people's racial narratives shift (or not) as they pursued change, what points of resistance arose in the process, and how were such tensions resolved? To understand these dynamics, I listened to and observed people in local settings as they pursued racial change within and beyond their communities. Chapters 5, 6, and 8 draw directly from my fieldwork with evangelical reconcilers to unpack the meaning-making systems and practices of religious race bridging in local spaces in the 1990s and 2000s.

In examining how religious race bridging worked in the 1990s, I challenge those who have minimized the significance of evangelical reconciliation efforts by interpreting them as disingenuous political strategies cynically designed to advance the Religious Right movement by either cleaning up its image, diversifying its constituency, or both. Such critics view evangelical racial change (ERC) efforts as products of whites' attachment to politically neoconservative organizations in the era of Reagan and both Bushes that espoused "color-blind" approaches to social policy and ignored structural inequalities or the need for political remedies for historical injustice (Alumkal 2004; Winant 1997, 2004; Stricker 2001; Diamond 2000). While the influence of neoconservatism on evangelicals is undeniable, neoconservatism alone is not sufficient to explain why whites were squeamish about engaging politically about race while willingly politicizing other issues like foreign policy, gender norms, sexuality, and other matters—or why many reconcilers of color also expressed political caution.

At least one Christian Right strategist, Christian Coalition (CC) director Ralph Reed, did attempt in the 1990s to tether racial reconciliation efforts to larger neoconservative goals. His efforts reflected both that a significant symbolic shift *was* occurring in American conservative evangelicalism and that racial reconciliation at the grassroots could not easily be converted into short-term political victories through narrowly neoconservative frames. More interesting and important over the long term than evangelical operatives' tactics is that the evangelical race-bridging efforts in the 1990s *and* their politically tentative character reflect how a set of social groups searched for and found a culturally specific solution to a particular set of historical, social, and political dilemmas that had developed within their communities over time. While it has never been a perfect solution, through religious race bridging evangelicals found powerful, culturally resonant ways to at least begin to traverse daunting chasms between Christian groups without immediately threatening those groups' political attachments and, interwoven therein, their home cultures, identities, and practices. Through a relational-spiritual approach to seemingly insurmountable social fractures, they found a path out of standstill. Through a level of evasiveness about power, their bridging methods attracted diverse groups to participate. Attention to how religious race bridging worked and how participants experienced and described it illuminates the cultural nuances and historical significance of the phenomenon. It also provides insight into the advantages and limitations, at least for participants, of politics-avoidant social change approaches more broadly.

Thin Pluralism in the 1980s

In the 1980s, it was easy for white evangelicals to remain obtuse to race as a Christian issue. In this context, as with other forms of long-term, de facto segregation, the dominant group has the luxury of not needing to notice the racial divide in their daily activities (Winant 1997). On the one hand, all but the most intransigent had conceded the validity of the formal and legal equality sought by the civil rights movement—but had assigned that era and their communities' actions in it to an increasingly distanced past. On the other, the church-growth movement, largely driven by the Homogeneous Unit Principle (HUP), was fast accelerating. Megachurch campuses sprung up from the beaches of Southern California to the Atlantic seaboard, while the rapidly growing Christian Broadcast Network (CBN) disseminated evangelical programming over radio, cable, and satellite (Balmer 1989; Diamond 1989). C. Peter Wagner's refrain that "social justice" activity is a distraction from soul saving—at least when such activity revolves around remedying socioeconomic inequalities within the United States—had survived intact, and the tacit acceptance of racially siloed evangelical congregations as effective ministry vehicles only cemented it.

Meanwhile, a crop of fired-up Christian conservatives were reclaiming a public voice in American political discourse after half a century of low-profile activity, to protest what they saw a morally adrift, degenerating culture (Watson 1999). Despite their earlier cautions against social activism in the civil rights context, and without a trace of irony, political strategists began assembling the resources to coordinate religious conservatives' backlash against feminism, the sexual revolution, and secular humanism. Jerry Falwell's Moral Majority ascended in 1979 and through the mobilization of a willing evangelical base helped inaugurate Ronald Reagan into the presidency, ushering in a new era of conservative activism and influence on the Republican Party (Hunter 1987; Liebman, Wuthnow, and Guth 1983; Harding 2000). Tackling abortion, challenging advances by gays and lesbians, and protecting family, religious rights, and Christian identity were the driving issues.

White evangelicals' choice of targets for religion-inspired social activism must have seemed strange from other vantage points. For Christians of color in the 1980s, the memories of faith-based resources powering the civil rights movement remained fresh. Religious practices, leaders, and values continued to influence activities like churches' support for affirmative action initiatives, poverty amelioration, after school programs, labor rights, and public school reform (Leon 2005). Consistent with the religious racial justice tradition, these Christians for the most part continued to regard social activism as an organic by-product of their religious worldviews. Such activism was not particularly interested in *restricting* rights.

Although the New Christian Right didn't conceive of itself as having anything particularly to do with race, the paucity of substantive interaction or institutional overlap between white evangelicals and their counterparts of color raised a potential liability for white evangelicals with religious or political ambitions. Rising-star pastors seek to maximize their appeal, and achieving Billy Graham–like influence in a supposedly more enlightened, post–civil rights movement era would seem to foreclose racial exclusivism. Evangelical political organizers likewise needed access to large constituencies. Their target issues weren't about race per se. Moreover, savvy operatives realized, the traditionalism of Christians of color on gender and family issues could potentially foster sympathy with some Christian Right concerns. At any rate, overt racism could attract unwanted attention, distracting from soul-saving, church-empire-expanding, and alliance-building agendas. Looking "too white" had in the post–civil rights movement era become at least a potential liability. White evangelicals seemed to understand they would do well to avoid the long shadow of their racial past. Racial discourse in *CT* magazine in the 1980s indicates how they tried to improve their public image.

CT is an apt publication through which to trace evolving race discourse in evangelicalism for several reasons. Founded in 1956 by Billy Graham as an intentional counterpoint to the Protestant mainline journal the *Christian Century*, *CT* reports on trends related to, and hosts inquiries and conversations among, an array of communities within evangelical Christianity (Smith 1998). As the print and now electronic medium with the widest circulation, longest track record, and broadest credibility within American evangelicalism, *CT* provides a useful measure of the ways in which developments within evangelical pockets of culture bubble up and circulate across the larger community.[7] The magazine averages fifteen issues annually, with two to three feature articles, one to two editorials, and dozens of free-standing news items, reviews, and small columns per issue. Although attentive to and popular among an evangelical lay audience, *CT*'s primary audience was conceived to be white male pastors in midcareer who wanted to understand developments in the larger evangelical movement.[8] Topical coverage ranges widely, from international developments of interest to the Christian community to American social and political trends, to theological debates, family and church-based advice, and local news. Through its choice of topical coverage and its editorial lens, *CT* effectively showcases the ways in which at least one important forum for evangelical public opinion approaches— or avoids—social issues in and beyond the religious community.

Every visibly race-related article listed in the table of contents from 1980 to 1989 was gathered and coded into one of the seven categories arranged in figure 1.[9] The impression created was that race was barely on the editorial radar; the magazine averaged a meager four directly race-related items per year. In general, *CT* treated race-related developments as something happening outside "our" (white) community, largely avoiding debates occurring contemporaneously. For instance, across the decade *CT* ran only one editorial or hosted discussion each on the topics of affirmative action (Spickard 1986), federal welfare policy (Skillen 1985), and illegal immigration (Tapia 1986). In comparison, it was rare for a month to pass without substantive treatment(s) of gender relations, sexuality, family values, the rising politicization of conservative Christians, or spiritual warfare as a global challenge. In a decade when debates were raging in the secular culture on race-related issues and evangelicals were mobilizing as a political force for conservative morality, such silences reflected white evangelicals' seemingly intentional racial insularity. The magazine demonstrated efforts to recognize and show some mild interest in racial and ethnic diversity among evangelicals, but seemed to be trying not to engage too substantively—a kind of careful coloring within the lines. I call this "thin pluralism."

The Tolerant White "We"

The subject of race most often appeared either in articles profiling churches, ministries, or denominational organizations of color (that is, in which most members and leaders were not white), or in reports on the ministry potential available within particular nonwhite demographic enclaves, such as the inner city or among immigrant or refugee populations.[10] Here CT reported on racial minority Christians' activities (for example, what are they doing?), or on how white evangelicals might reach non-Christians of color (how can we reach them?). Across the decade, twenty-one pieces were published in these categories, the second and third columns from the left in figure 1.

These articles generally had a charitable tone but clearly, if unintentionally, conveyed the presumption that the readership of CT—the "we" of CT—was white. While whites were indeed the vast majority of CT readers, such approaches to communities of color suggested that the CT community understood "real" evangelicalism through a white central referent, wherein other groups were viewed either as self-enclosed satellite communities or aliens in some respect. Populations of color, even if identified as Christian or even fellow evangelicals, were linguistically positioned as outsiders tentatively annexed to that "we" and its theological and cultural centrality. Consider article titling alone: in 1980 there was "The Exploding Hispanic Minority: A Field in Our Backyard," and two years later, "Hispanics: The Harvest Field at Home" (Maust 1980; Anonymous 1982). In such profiles, Latinos were not read as *also* American and *already* largely Christian, not as *members of* the existing evangelical community, but as outsiders. By 1985, the language had shifted little, as "Foreign Missions" were "Next Door and Down the Street," part of the continuing influx of low-income and immigrant populations of color into U.S. cities (Bjork 1985).[11] Articles related to Latino and other new immigrants by CT's writers, almost all of whom were white, consistently described these "others" in terms of populations ripe for the (white) evangelical picking.

Also counted within this domestic mission category are profiles of lone white evangelicals ("our" [white] representatives) leading urban/inner-city ministries. Such stories appeared roughly once a year in the 1980s. These "pioneers" tended

FIGURE 1   *Christianity Today* race coverage, 1980s

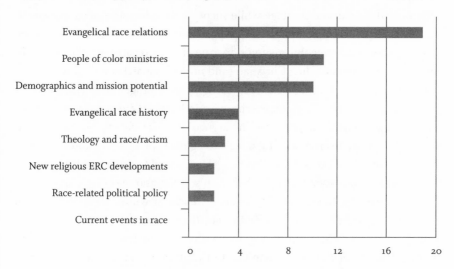

to be portrayed in admiring language, their credibility enhanced by their having dedicated their ministries to some or another unfortunate population of color. Consistent with spiritual warfare and missiology frames, in which evangelicals are portrayed as besieged warriors battling sinners and infidel religions around the world, such stories frequently presumed that white evangelicals were bringing the "true gospel" to groups not only socioeconomically struggling but also religiously misguided, vulnerable, or otherwise not quite adequate (Thompson 1984; Anonymous 1981). While the magazine occasionally ran articles countering the presumed superiority of white conservative theological frames, these were rare.[12]

The thin pluralism of the 1980s was marked by gestures of cultural tolerance alongside a distanced, abstract thinking on matters of race history, theology, and political policy. An essay by senior editor Kenneth S. Kantzer at the decade's end encapsulated this (Kantzer 1989). The March issue included an unusual "*Christianity Today* Institute" feature called "Listening to America's Ethnic Churches," in which five evangelical leaders of color were invited to write autobiographically about their respective racial or ethnic communities and developments in their churches (Maracle 1989; Smith 1989; Pang 1989; Inouye 1989). At the end of this article set, Kantzer's "Has the Melting Pot Stopped Melting?" mused on changing paradigms related to immigrant culture in the United States from his perspective as a third-generation, assimilated German American.

In the piece, Kantzer noted, and largely approved, the shift in the late twentieth century from an assimilationist model of immigration (he used the word "amalgamation") to a pluralist model in which immigrants retain important aspects of their cultural heritage while incorporating into U.S. society. Reflecting on evangelicals' orientation to the problematic melting pot, however, he repeated the broad-sweeping assumptions and elisions regarding white evangelicals' *actual* history regarding Christian (and non-Christian) populations of color that characterized CT coverage of race in the 1980s. Evangelicals (who Kantzer's phrasing implies are white unless otherwise indicated) "are committed to freedom and justice for all *in principle*," he argued, because such values are embedded in their religious doctrine (1989, 42). Religiously predisposed toward justice and equality, white evangelicals, he suggested, should appreciate the value of Christians of color worshipping in their own settings and reject racial prejudice: "So in Sunday school we sing: 'Red, yellow, black, or white, are all precious in His sight" (42). Because of this egalitarian (but HUP-consistent) orientation, Kantzer submitted, "it is our duty to make sure that the laws of our land insure the freedom, justice, and ultimate good of all human beings—not just fellow evangelicals" (42).

This was an upbeat narrative, but nowhere did it acknowledge any of the racial "sins" of white evangelical history or of evangelical whites' virtual absence in the civil rights movement. Yet Kantzer closed with a list of four things white evangelicals could do to "support the worth of all humans and seek their good." This vague list included open and public expressions of regret for past prejudice and active involvement in "removing evidences of racial and minority prejudice from our society" (Kantzer 1989, 42). Although Kantzer asserted important concerns for the white evangelical community (some of which did get taken up in the 1990s), his framing read as a distanced series of "social services" prescriptions, rather than a substantive engagement with the sources of racial inequality in and beyond the church. With Kantzer at the helm of CT's editorial board, this tepid multiculturalism, where all was assumed to be basically well and evangelicals to be oriented, by disposition, toward justice, set the tone of at least the white leadership's limited engagement with race as a *contemporary* challenge within evangelicalism.

CT did make some effort in the 1980s to educate its readership about race in evangelical history (four articles were grouped in that category), but the choice of coverage was curious. There were two pieces about black Christians: one on Booker T. Washington (not exactly a black liberation hero) at the beginning of the decade (Gaebelein 1981), and one on Martin Luther King Jr. at decade's end in a special book section (Anonymous 1989). A pair of articles about famous whites also ran. Charles W. Colson, of all people, an Alabaman who had been considered Richard Nixon's "hatchet man," penned an inspirational profile of the Christian abolitionist William Wilberforce (Colson 1985). This followed an earlier interview with another notorious Alabama conservative, George Wallace (Norton 1982a).

The Wallace exchange was hardly an exposé of the darker moments in Christians' racist past. Rather, the governor who famously stood in the schoolhouse door to defend "segregation forever" revisited the anniversary of his shooting and testified to his gratitude for God letting him survive. Like Jerry Falwell, he strategically distanced himself from the details of his legacy as a (formerly) racist Christian, in response to soft-pitched questions from the interviewer. "My attitude towards the matter of separate facilities [for blacks and whites] in schools was not valid," he commented, claiming he was never personally prejudiced, but simply raised in a system where segregation made sense at the time (Norton 1982a, 53). The piece came off as a mild apology for a once-backslidden but now harmless white southern Christian. Like the other "history" articles in the 1980s, it offered little in the way of substantive reflection about white evangelicals' participation in racist systems or worldviews.

Articles grouped directly under race relations in the evangelical community in the 1980s occupied the single largest category (at nineteen articles), though many of these were minor clips. Most commonly, small (one-half to two-column) news reports chronicled race-related events within particular denominations, churches, or local communities. For instance, in 1981 Buffalo, New York, churches "rall[ied] in response to race murders" (Anonymous 1980). Two years later, "a Christian school file[d] suit to prove it's not racist," and in 1985 "Varsity Racism" considered critiques of racism and affirmative action within college sports (Kantzer 1985; Spring 1984). Reports occasionally appeared on developments within evangelical organizations of color (Frame 1989).

Full-length articles and interviews explicitly on the topic of evangelical race relations were few and far between in the 1980s, though some substantive treatments foreshadowed deeper conversations to come. Sometimes the topic was exploratory, as in November 1981's "Can Christian Colleges Mix with Minorities?" (note: Christian colleges are presumptively white) or April 1985's interview with Billy Graham, who comments on racial segregation within American Christianity (Youngren 1981; Buursma 1985). In 1987, CT produced "Race and the Church: A Progress Report," which presented results of a poll of roughly 10 percent of CT readers' views on the state of race relations within evangelical communities (Frame 1988). The upshot was that though racial integration in the Christian community was a preference for most CT readers, it did not appear, yet, to be a "priority" for them in terms of changes they might be willing to make in order to assure it.

Only four editorials focused on race relations among evangelicals appeared in

CT in the 1980s. These often located racism among Christians either *outside* the United States or in the relatively distant American past.[13] Occasionally, however, criticism of white evangelicalism did peek out of the pages of *CT*. "Why Prolife Rhetoric Is Not Enough" explained why white evangelicals' enthusiasm for ending abortion might not automatically resonate with the urban poor and communities of color (Beers 1983). Randall Frame's "The Cost of Being Black" discussed how systemic inequalities related to poverty and unemployment among African Americans exposed racism's ongoing traction in the United States (Frame 1986). But for the most part, race relations did not yet seem to be a burning concern.

Overall, the thin pluralism of the 1980s reflected a novice and largely superficial effort to address a gulf between white evangelicals and their counterparts of color. This signaled perhaps a shift in intention, but little meaningful change from the past. In the age of the HUP of church growth, *CT* race coverage evaded the direct confrontations made by people like Tom Skinner in the 1970s and advanced a benign tolerance of racial diversity within evangelicalism.[14] Thin pluralism also entailed an abstracted, almost ahistorical, and therefore sometimes visibly strained view of Christian race philosophy wherein white evangelicals attempted to gain some distance from the overt religious racism of the past but skirted substantive self-reflection about racial attitudes, histories, and political policy. However, the creation of even minimal space in the magazine for coverage of nonwhite evangelical ministries did lead to the airing of a few sharp critiques of white evangelicalism by two influential black pastors. These challenges seemed to create a path to deeper conversations.

Piercing the Bubble

Three articles penetrated the surface of thin pluralism enough to suggest what might be coming in the 1990s. Two in 1982 focused on John Perkins, an esteemed African American patriarch who in 1960 founded what is now called the field of Christian community development, the effort of faith-based leaders to improve conditions in settings of concentrated poverty through entrepreneurism, infrastructure, health care, skill-building, and spiritual education.[15] The third was an editorial by his son Spencer Perkins in 1989. Both men were tireless leaders with unusual credibility in white evangelical circles for their work as urban mission pioneers. Both also became major figures in the racial reconciliation movement, and both took white evangelicalism to task on race even in the 1980s.

John Perkins counted himself among the black evangelicals influenced by Skinner's confrontational antiracist ministry in the 1970s (Gilbreath 2006, 63–64). This influence is almost tangible in *CT*'s 1982 interview with him, wherein he bluntly criticized the limited socioeconomic vision of white evangelicalism (Norton 1982b). While defending free enterprise and the Protestant work ethic, Perkins managed to confront the white evangelical community's oft-complicity with capitalist exploitation of the poor. Speaking of structural inequalities of opportunity, he argued:

> [The conservative church] . . . allows wealth to affect it in such a way that it refuses to challenge the free enterprise system. This economy and these workers have provided the businessman with an opportunity. As a result, he has a responsibility in terms of housing and the quality of life of the people. Businessmen have control of the lifeblood of this nation. That's a challenge. I believe such challenges will make the free enterprise system stronger. (21)

When asked to assess the role of the ascendant Moral Majority in American politics, Perkins critiqued both its narrow appeal (primarily to white evangelicals) and its inattention to broader matters of justice. "They have reduced loving Jesus down to doing nothing." "They will not put enough emphasis on social justice," he predicted, "to produce the necessary leadership to deal with the social conditions [that impact communities of color]" (Norton 1982b, 21–22). He nevertheless cited white involvement as a key to the success of urban ministry, repeatedly employing the term "racial reconciliation" as a way of identifying bridges yet to be built between black and white Christian communities. But he rejected the HUP as shortsighted at best:

> As a reconciled group, we can be more effective in society because we will know what goes into reconciliation, and our commitment will have to be to Jesus instead of race. Then our differences can call us to a fuller service to people. I don't believe we can talk about reconciliation tomorrow if we don't talk about reconciliation today. I don't believe homogeneous units will make these relations better tomorrow. (21)

As was typical in such interviews of "outsiders," the interviewer asked if Perkins believed in biblical inerrancy. Perkins responded that while he did so ascribe, black people may reasonably reject God and/or Christianity because white Christians who champion the doctrine of inerrancy "tend to be the most racist [because] they are legalistic. To us blacks, abstract doctrine and syllogisms are not as important as truth personified. The great defenders of inerrancy generally haven't shown me that they have a good sense of justice" (Norton 1982b, 22). Perkins essentially echoed the same question in 1982 as Skinner before him: where are white evangelicals when it comes to justice? But for several more years *CT* article content, focused mainly on who these "others" are and what they're doing in their own distinctive circles, didn't seem to have heard the question.

Seven years later, when the Christian Right had built a considerable alliance with the Republican Party through the Moral Majority and other activist vehicles, CT ran "The Prolife Credibility Gap," Spencer Perkins's (1989) critique of the evangelical antiabortion activism proliferating at the decade's end. Director of the International Study Center of the Voice of Calvary Ministries, founded by John Perkins in the early 1970s in Jackson, Mississippi, this second-generation Perkins was becoming an advocate for racial reconciliation (Maxwell 1998).

His editorial pivoted on a racial analysis. Spencer Perkins named the "credibility gap" blacks feel when being solicited to join a movement led by people who, historically, would have actively resisted gains for African Americans. He expressed palpable frustration, in specific terms: "Aren't some of these the same people who 20 years ago were calling Martin Luther King, Jr. a Communist? Are they not the same people who 15 years ago moved out of the neighborhood in which I live because too many blacks were moving in? Or aren't they the same Christians who opened private schools as soon as the courts ordered desegregation in the South in order to avoid any contact with us?" (Perkins 1989, 21). As they respond to the immorality of abortion, Perkins noted, whites should recognize how banning it would disproportionately impact blacks, likely increasing vicious cycles of poverty, welfare dependence, and female-headed households, particularly in urban ghettos. Therefore, "before I can pick up a picket sign and join in this parade—before I can join hands with you and sing 'We Shall Overcome,' and certainly before I can go to jail with you," Perkins suggested, he needs evidence that white evangelicals have "had a change of heart" regarding racial equality (21).

Perkins then voiced the strongest racial challenge posed in CT in the 1980s, calling whites to account:

> I have heard very few Southern evangelicals admit they were on the wrong side of
> the race issues back in the fifties, sixties, and early seventies. I have never heard any
> of them say that they should have blocked the entrances to the jails where we were
> beaten and tortured, or taken a stand with us when we wanted equal access to "life,
> liberty, and the pursuit of happiness." In fact, over the past few years there have
> been only a few Southern, white, evangelical Christians who have asked our forgiveness and extended a hand in reconciliation. On the contrary, for every step we take
> in their direction, it seems that most take another step toward the suburbs. (22)

Perkins confronted not just white evangelicals' apathy on civil rights but also their *complicity* in perpetuating white supremacy and ongoing inequalities, their insularity, and their refusal to apologize. If white evangelical pro-lifers continue to see abortion as the only justice issue worth mobilizing around, Perkins observed, black and white Christians would remain divided. "Where abortion will rank in our battle plan," he concluded, "will depend on the strength of the relationship we can establish in the future and how much your burdens and concerns, because of that relationship, can become ours" (22).

As the sun set on the 1980s, Spencer Perkins pierced the thin pluralism bubble, the wishful thinking on race that characterized most race-related CT content in the same decade that white evangelicals became a passionate political force. Where the magazine had largely reflected a benign, distanced interest in racial trends within the Christian community, Perkins reminded the readership of a giant chasm—indeed, unspoken land mines—between black and white Christian communities. Where white columnists and staff writers could routinely promote the concept of an evangelicalism that cares about racial inequality and avers prejudice, both Perkinses directed attention to the same stark realities Skinner referenced in 1970: people of color suffering poverty and ongoing discrimination while whites retreat into suburban enclaves; whites' inattention to a spectrum of race-related justice issues even as they promote new forms of Christian activism; demographic and cultural segregation; conversations that don't happen; and, thus, alliances that cannot be assumed to exist. Where CT had been telling a story of "Hey, we've come a long way," the few Christian critics of color invited into white racial discourse ultimately countered, "We haven't even started."

Waking Up in the 1990s

No single catalyst led white evangelicals to rotate from the thin pluralism of the 1980s to the much more substantive conversations, institutional decisions, rituals, inquiries, and meaning-making practices of religious race bridging. But the turnaround is well evidenced in the pages of CT. Several factors emerged as influential in this shift: continuing challenges by Christians of color, developments in the broader culture, rising editorial interest, timing within the evangelical community, the leadership of influential converts, and the participation of younger evangelicals. It is nevertheless surprising how suddenly and dramatically the new race discourse seemed to catch fire.

One influence, surely, was the topic of race in the larger culture. In the 1990s, a virtual avalanche of high-profile racial events cascaded across the American political landscape. A roughly chronological short list includes Anita Hill and the Clarence Thomas Supreme Court nomination; the Rodney King police brutality scandal and subsequent uprising in Los Angeles; the O. J. Simpson trial; Louis Farrakhan's Million Man March; President Clinton's establishment of the "One America Initiative," a national advisory board on race and reconciliation; the

New York City police brutality and racial profiling scandals in the wake of the Abner Louima and Amadou Diallo shootings; and the torture and killing of African American James Byrd Jr. by white Texas racists. Broad issues being debated in the American public included the necessity of affirmative action programs in the post–civil rights movement era; the overhaul of federal welfare policies focusing on return-to-work models; hate crimes and racial profiling laws; multiculturalism and diversity in organizations; and immigration policy.

Even if some evangelicals may have wished to avoid the nation's racial controversies, race was organically resurfacing in their communities, too. University of Colorado, Boulder, football coach Bill McCartney founded Promise Keepers (PK) men's movement in 1991 after what he described as a message from God regarding evangelicalism's lack of diversity. PK became a leading force for racial reconciliation. Race was also a hot topic on Christian colleges and throughout parachurch ministries. Major evangelical organizations initiated public responses to their racial history or current racial insularity, literally playing out Wagner's notion of identificational repentance through atonements for collective "sin." In 1996, a string of southern black church burnings prompted the CC to announce new race-related initiatives, including a "Racial Reconciliation Sundays" pledge to raise funds for the destroyed churches. At decade's end two of the groundbreakers of evangelical race relations, Tom Skinner and Spencer Perkins, died at fairly young ages, prompting further meditations on race matters among evangelicals.

In short, any CT subscriber who might have avoided taking race seriously up to that point would have found that the magazine simply wouldn't let up on race in the 1990s. Race had become an incessant discussion and religious race bridging a new reparative paradigm.

As indicated in figure 2, articles directly focused on race more than doubled in CT in the 1990s compared to the 1980s, with pieces specifically addressing race relations in evangelical communities constituting almost half of the 114 items clearly identifiable as race-related (at 56 items). The 1990s averaged over eight race-related items per year. More significant, in the 1990s the category of "race relations" had become so much deeper, broader, and more multifaceted than in the previous decade that it constituted evidence of a change in the very framing of race issues by CT. Rather than being narrowly oriented around Christians' racial attitudes and opinions, most articles about race relations now routinely incorporated more complex discussions of theology, new ministry models, and other topics. In this more blended context, I therefore did not count theology and new ERC developments as separate topics in the 1990s.

Right off, CT's coverage of racial issues seemed to be less presumptive about

FIGURE 2   *Christianity Today* race coverage, 1990s

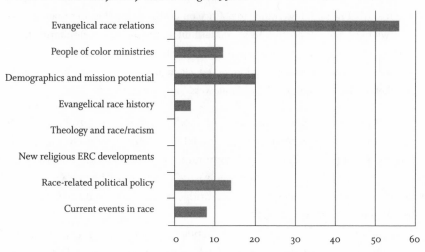

what the white evangelical community knew about communities of color. Although the predominant race framework remained black-white relations, more articles began to engage other groups, especially Asians and Latinos, in an emergent racial dialogue.[16] The more multiracial approach may have been a result of *CT* hiring a few key writers of color such as Andrés Tapia and Edward Gilbreath, whose articles addressed a wider range of race-related issues. These included the rise of Latino evangelicals; the history and sociology of charismatic denominations like the Church of God in Christ (COGIC); race relations among Southern Baptists; multiethnic church models; the ascendance of Asian congregations; race relations in Christian colleges; and the activities of civil rights movement–related figures.[17]

Two opening salvos in 1990 anticipated the new level of seriousness and the willingness of white evangelicals to at least begin to respond to calls by Christians of color to meaningfully address the past. First, in January, Philip Yancey, a best-selling evangelical writer and *CT* editor, offered "Confessions of a Racist" (1990). This was essentially a public testimony about the influence of the white supremacist religious racial tradition that had been woven through his evangelical fundamentalist upbringing in Atlanta during the civil rights movement. Yancey explained how his church, family, and southern white community in the 1960s encouraged the wholesale delegitimization of Martin Luther King Jr. He detailed the racist justifications that anchored mainstream white evangelicalism in the South. But retrospectively embracing King as a Christian "prophet," Yancey also modeled a personal confession of racial "sin" that would become an important (though not unchallenged) refrain among white evangelicals:

While Martin Luther King, Jr., lived on earth, I, his neighbor to the east, did not listen to what he said. I was quick to pounce on his flaws, and slow to recognize my own blind sin. But because he stayed faithful, in the short view, by offering his body as a target but never as a weapon, and in the long view, by holding before us his dream, a dream of a new kingdom of peace and justice and love, he became a prophet for me, the most unlikely of followers. (25)

Yancey's admissions seemed almost tailored to Spencer Perkins's 1989 challenge for white evangelicals to own up to the racial skeletons in their closet. In confessing the sins of an earlier self and community that rejected King's calls at the time, he embraced (albeit retrospectively) the black social justice vision, employing faith "in the long view" to build a bridge. In effect, he told a new story for white evangelicals (or at least *CT*).

Less than two months after Yancey's article a second salvo appeared. *CT* reported that the (overwhelmingly white) National Association of Evangelicals (NAE), of which most *CT* readers' churches were members, and the National Black Evangelical Association (NBEA) had "join[ed] to condemn racism" (Anonymous 1990).[18] Two gatherings that brought members of both groups together for the first time since their respective foundings concluded with a three-page statement condemning racism and putting whites in the hot seat. The document explicitly identified racism as a severe historical and current *sin* within white evangelicalism and called for reparative efforts firmly anchored in the Christian model of reconciliation. The statement was direct:

The white evangelical church must first repent of its sin of racism. It must examine its doctrines, policies, institutions, boards, agencies and parachurch entities and remove any vestiges of prejudice and racism. It must also enter into a meaningful dialogue with black evangelical leaders by means of establishing cultural exchanges on racism in the white community. Most importantly it must exert pressure for economic justice by witnessing within its own power structures. It must remove the institutional barriers which hinder progress for blacks and other people of color. It must work to make restitution and repair as soon as possible. (Anonymous 1990, 35)

In this process the black church was also urged to demonstrate "a readiness to forgive past wrongs," as modeled by Christ.

Notably, the NAE/NBEA statement called for "individual and corporate" repentance, self-examination, meaningful cross-cultural dialogues, *and* materially oriented social justice responses to racism. This indicates that whites were not just spontaneously offering apologies as a way of rewriting their past; rather, they were responding to direct calls to address their historical sins in meaningful, dialogic forums as a step into the present. How well they were able to hear the calls to reconsider power dynamics and recognize and respond to ongoing structural inequalities was another question.

In the wake of the NAE/NBEA statement, across the decade articles began to venture into more delicate racial territory than *CT* had navigated in the past. Whites acknowledged ugly racial histories in more complex ways, and emphasized the importance of stretching out of their racial "comfort zones" in order to address ongoing and historical problems (McDonald 1992). Articles appeared on topics more immediate and concrete than theoretical or historical, such as interracial marriage in the church; white attitudes regarding reparations for racial crimes; and how (white) evangelicals should respond to immigration issues (Zipperer 1995; Myra 1994; Marino 1998).

Perhaps the most significant early sign that *CT* editors had become willing to follow up on the NAE/NBEA statement and to risk their primarily white readers' discomfort was "The Myth of Racial Progress," a *Christianity Today* Institute feature that ran in October 1993 (Tapia 1993). Here Andrés Tapia reported on interviews with forty-one African American Christian leaders invited by *CT* to directly address the white evangelical community on issues of race.[19] This reflected a big step beyond *CT*'s cautious and noncommittal 1987 poll of its readers' racial attitudes. Long quotes or book excerpts from many of these leaders, including both Perkinses, pointedly criticized white evangelicals, even as the forum proffered some hope for reconciliation.

The feature showcased the gap between the African American racial justice story and white evangelicals' defensiveness about even terms like "social justice." African American Christians interviewed tapped four vulnerable areas for whites. They again challenged white conservative evangelicals to directly acknowledge the problem of U.S. racial history; employed the terminology of racism as, as one pastor put it, "quite frankly, sin"; linked that sin to ongoing structural inequalities; and voiced deep frustration about the possibility of substantive change by whites.

Through these critiques, African American Christians again directly *called for* repentance on the part of white evangelicals—but saw repentance as a first step on a longer journey toward faith-based social justice. Echoing Spencer Perkins's 1989 complaint, one pastor in Tapia's article lamented that "the evangelical church has never repented of these historical, social, and personal sins of racism" (1993, 19).[20] Another leveraged the call for confession to attention to structural inequalities: "Calling sinners to repentance means also calling societies and structures to repentance—economic, social, educational, corporate, political, religious structures" (20).[21] Glandon Carey from InterVarsity, however, doubted that white evangelicals would ever take racial problems seriously: "I'm tired of questions about this. I see no outcome, no real dealing with the issues, or doing what has been decided needs to be done. There has been very little fruit from the pledges of racial reconciliation made by evangelical groups, such as the National Association of Evangelicals and other major Christian agencies. These organizations continue to be white in their structure and avoid issues that concern the cities" (20).

Spencer Perkins weighed in. Refusing, as he consistently had, a reconciliation approach that ignored structural inequalities, he suggested that blacks weren't particularly interested in racial reconciliation. Rather, they're "interested in eliminating racial injustice, in confronting racism, and in ensuring that the playing field is level" (Perkins 1993, 22). Indeed, many of the pastors interviewed refused to "tone down" politics for the sake of avoiding conflict with conservative whites. "If we were practicing reconciliation, affirmative action, and level playing fields in our churches," said Cheryl Sanders of Howard University, "it would challenge our society's dominant racist values and would give Christians something to preach to others" (Tapia 1993, 23). Asked Peggy Jones of St. Paul, Minnesota, "Isn't the evangelical heritage one of social reform and speaking out against injustices as well as leading lost souls to Christ?" And why should blacks trust that whites will ever shift their reluctance to recognize the politics of race, wondered Tony Warner of InterVarsity, when "white evangelicals are more willing to pursue a white conservative political agenda than to be reconciled with their African-American brothers and sisters" (26).

In these interview excerpts, black Christians articulated a confrontational, political voice, advocating *engaged* racial reconciliation efforts, not just talk. In this forum, political themes broke through on almost every page. Even so, the editorial packaging of the *Christianity Today* Institute feature firmly veered away from endorsing politics as a solution to the racial divide around which whites had been apathetic. Interspersed among black Christians' scathing indictments of white conservative evangelicalism were a series of "Models of Reconciliation"—short profiles of friendships, ministries, and leadership partnerships of a white and an African American Christian engaged in a "reconciling" relationship. The partnership between the leaders of interracial Lawndale Christian Community and The Rock church in Chicago, for instance, portrayed a model of deep, relationship-based ministry with credibility in the African American community (Tapia 1993, 21, 24).[22]

Such portraits of collaboration seemed to emphasize the value of partnership over—or at least before—politics. Indeed, *partnership* emerged as the dominant meaning-making practice in the racial reconciliation era, a central signifier of

the evangelical religious race-bridging project. The magazine's interest in relationship-based approaches to racial change within evangelicalism appeared as
Christian presses had begun publishing a wave of reconciliation "partnership"
titles written by some of the same players mentioned above. Sometimes written
as "how-to" manuals, these accounts of the authors' personal journeys toward
reconciliation provided guidelines for how to "do the work," and explanations
of the importance of bridging racial boundaries. In them, pastors (sometimes
prominent leaders of color) cotestified about the power of and challenges to
committed cross-racial relationships. For instance, *He's My Brother: Former Racial Foes Offer Strategy for Reconciliation,* cowritten by John Perkins and Thomas
Tarrants III (a former Klansman), presented scriptural justifications and a point-
by-point plan for doing racial reconciliation (Perkins and Tarrants 1994). Others
chronicled the experience of engaging in multiracial efforts to rebuild and revi-
talize urban churches (Perkins 1995; Washington, Kehrein, and King 1997). By
mid-decade, books on racial topics flooded the Christian market, with evangelical magazines providing a steady backdrop of coverage of reconciliatory events.[23]

With cross-racial, faith-based personal relationships framed as the most
powerful means of fostering change, the answer to evangelicals' racial tensions
was presented, at least by *CT,* as apolitical. Even so, with many people of color
engaging in these partnership experiments, it is hard to call this an *exclusively*
white approach. Partnership models reflected views shared by participants of
different racial backgrounds that honest exchanges were an emotionally substantive means of beginning. Cross-racial relationships provided forums for the
sorts of meaningful attention to racial sins that people of color, especially African Americans, had been asking for, and these confessions, readers learned
through multiple examples, seemed to forge a path to deeper dialogue. The first
step to bridging the race divide, advocates repeatedly suggested, was through authentic forms of bonding through mutually approved practices. These included
admission (of sin, guilt, separation, and other hard feelings); recognition (of the
need to change); and possibly expressions of forgiveness (by people of color for
whites' racist past). Such bridging methods seemed to require setting politics
aside in order to minimize conflict. (Relationship is better than lip service, after
all.) Yet at least as *CT* approached racial reconciliation, this dominant relational
frame eclipsed the challenge repeatedly proffered by black Christians that white
evangelicals widen their political lens beyond so-called moral issues like homosexuality and abortion to include racial *justice* efforts.

Perhaps because political questions were frequently deferred in *CT*-based
race discourse in the 1990s, the emphases on atonement and relationship as
means of racial bridge-building paved the way for the steady cascade of formal

apologies and collective repentance/forgiveness rituals that developed through-out the decade. Through these, the cultural meaning-making matrix of race rela-tions in evangelicalism began to be expressed at institutional levels.

"Sorry" Seems to Be the Favorite Word

The next volley came in 1994 from Pentecostals, a denomination that, as we saw in chapter 2, had been briefly interracial in its early years before whites departed under the influence of racism. In April, CT reported on the intention of the forty-six-year-old, largely white Pentecostal Fellowship of North America (PFNA) to disband and "re-emerge as an interracial association, including the largest Pente-costal denomination, the mostly black Church of God in Christ (COGIC)" (Kellner 1994). Leaders of PFNA expressed regret that their organization formed in 1948 through exclusion of black Pentecostal churches and hope that partnering with the vibrant community of black and urban Pentecostal ministries would better the community as a whole. The monumental three-day follow-up meeting happened in October in Memphis, Tennessee, where white leaders "openly express[ed] re-grets that their history ha[d] been tainted by racist attitudes." Black leaders re-ceived whites' demonstrations of repentance through speeches, foot-washing rituals, and public embraces (Grady 1994). After PFNA board members formally dissolved their organization, the various interracial groups combined under the new Pentecostal/Charismatic Churches of North America (PCCNA). This unprec-edented bridge-building experiment became known as the "Memphis Miracle."

Following on the heels of the Pentecostal merger, the NAE and NBEA as-sembled again in Chicago in January 1995 for a four-day racial planning session to follow up on the racial changes they had promised (Morgan 1995). In break-out sessions, participants were encouraged to form "accountability partnerships" with a person of another race to build relationships and find ways to involve their organizations in reconciliation work. Climactically, Don Argue, the NAE's top leader, offered a public confession and repentance of racism within white evangelical ranks and promised to work to integrate the leadership of the new organization. Then African American leaders laid hands on the bowed, weeping man and "pray[ed] for the breaking of barriers dividing the races as well as for a new direction in the future" (48).

In CT's report on the event, black leaders expressed guarded enthusiasm, re-iterating that reconciliation rituals would have to be followed up with tangible actions. "A fragmented church divided along racial and ethnic lines is a contra-diction to the gospel itself," said plenary speaker William Pannell. "That's what's at stake here. It's not whether black and white people get together and break bread just to be nice" (Morgan 1995, 48). By the NAE's March conference, a couple of new African American and female leaders had been appointed to high posts, and plenary speakers lectured on the topic of "an evangelical response to racism" (Lee 1995). The organization also passed a resolution supporting "reasonable and just admissions policies for refugees and immigrants" and encouraged greater involvement with Latino and Asian congregations (98).

Later in 1995, the Southern Baptists, at long last, got on the reconciliation train. In Atlanta's Georgia Dome on the denomination's 150th anniversary, the Southern Baptist Convention (SBC) offered its first formal apology for "condoning" racism in the context of slavery (Morgan 1995). The SBC resolution in part stated: "We apologize to all African Americans for condoning and/or perpetuating individual and systemic racism in our lifetime, and we genuinely repent of racism of which we have been guilty, whether consciously or unconsciously."[24] Gary Frost, a black pastor and SBC second vice president, accepted the apology, stating, "We pray that the genuineness of your repentance will be reflected in your attitudes and in your actions" (53). Billy Graham, in attendance, warned his fellow Southern Baptists, "Only when we individually and as a corporate group renounce racism in all its forms and repent of all transgressions will God choose to use us in the future to reach all people throughout the world." (Here we see Wagner's idea of identificational repentance [chapter 3] performed almost verbatim.) CT reported some skepticism among blacks that such gestures might represent an effort of the SBC to "win" black National Baptists into the SBC fold, though there seemed to be little talk of such plans at the meeting.[25]

Promise Keeping

In addition to repentance ceremonies by these "big three" evangelical organizations, CT attended to similar conversations and decisions by a string of parachurch organizations in the decade. The Christian Community Development Association (CCDA), the Alianza de Ministerios Evangelicos Nacionales (AMEN), the National Religious Broadcasters (NRB), and many Christian colleges made visible efforts to bridge racial divides through hosting race summits, integrating organizations, and changing hiring practices (Carrasco 1996; Kennedy 1996; Morgan 1996). The ascendant PK men's movement appeared most frequently in this context, especially between 1994 and 1997, with CT editors taking an obvious interest in PK's sixth of seven promises, to reach across racial and denominational barriers.[26] Because PK carried the reconciliation banner more prominently than any other evangelical organization in the 1990s, it is worth noting the tenor of CT's coverage of the group's racial perspective.

Founded in 1991, PK was the brainchild of then University of Colorado, Boulder, football coach Bill McCartney.[27] McCartney claimed that his experience with players of color and direct guidance from God helped him see that the new men's movement would not be successful without the participation of Christians of color (McCartney and Halbroo 1997). By 1996, PK had attracted over one million men to gatherings in football stadiums across the country, employed a staff of over 400, and had an annual budget in excess of $115 million.[28]

An organization with relatively young membership (many PK leaders and the majority of participants were under forty years of age), PK actively challenged attendees at its events to apply the reconciliation concepts they learned through PK in their local communities. The organization hired many speakers of color on the rally circuit, assembled a full-time "reconciliation team" to build more racially sensitive materials and recruit young men of color from all the major racial communities, and by 1996 built a multiracial board of directors. That year PK announced the intentionally multiethnic makeup of its staff, which had become diverse even for secular organizations: 30 percent minority, including 16 percent African American, 13 percent Hispanic, and 1 percent Native American.[29] (I discuss interviews with PK staffers in the following chapter.)

PK demonstrated the same nervousness about politics in the context of religious race bridging that permeated other ERC efforts, and CT's coverage of it reiterated that nervousness. As PK was building momentum in 1994, CT ran an editorial by Glenn Stanton, a longtime spokesman for Christian conservative causes. In the piece, Stanton praised the "brilliance" of the PK movement and repeated a now familiar refrain: "[PK] and many others agree on at least two things: the family is in trouble, and the solution is more moral and spiritual than political" (Stanton 1994, 20). The movement, he said, faced two related challenges: to pursue social and moral engagement "without succumbing to a narrow political agenda" (though he did not specify that agenda); and to "go beyond words" in working for racial reconciliation. The best way to achieve both is to "avoid becoming politicized," because "cross-racial partnership is a safeguard against political co-optation. The best way to keep PK spiritually vital and politically incorruptible is a thorough commitment to racial inclusiveness" (21).

Curiously, Stanton did not explain how PK might be vulnerable to political co-optation or by whom, or why racial inclusiveness per se would shield the group from political corruption. He praised PK as a classic evangelical "renewal" movement focused on social problems (for example, the decline of the traditional family and men's leadership therein) through a spiritual rather than a political lens, and avoiding partisanship. "Going beyond words" on racial reconciliation would, he implied, protect the movement from some kind of unspecified takeover. Yet he asked participants to walk a fine line: delivering more than words, but less than political investment. Here again is a seemingly race-inflected fear that if (white conservative) evangelicals moved toward racial change, they would be vulnerable to being politically hijacked (presumably by the Left or by blacks) *unless* they cultivate strong cross-racial friendships. Friendships, in other words, would keep participants from entertaining political modes of redressing racial conflict. Through such reasoning, Stanton seemed to tie himself in a knot: "Nothing would sink [PK] quicker," he suggested, "than getting drawn into a mean-spirited political crusade. On the other hand, trying to stay 'above politics' can mean silence in the face of political concerns that are moral issues at heart. In this sense, PK's commitment to racial reconciliation is a strong political statement" (Stanton 1994, 21).

As if beginning to become self-conscious of this tension, in another 1995 editorial Harold Myra wrote, "Most of us who read *CT* are white. What can we say to African Americans' dashed expectations? How can we contribute to racial reconciliation?" (1995, 18). He offered four recommendations, each focused on dialogue and tiptoeing around social action. Whites must, first, "recognize our insulation" by "listen[ing] hard to understand how powerfully racism still affects African Americans." Listening might mean recognizing that "racism—even apathy toward racial injustice—is surely the antithesis of love" (18–19). While acknowledging apathy, Myra in effect prescribed listening as a viable form of action. Second, whites must determine not to caricature "the other side," such as "black believers whose politics or policy prescriptions do not agree with ours"— the implication being that whites' policy prescriptions are fixed, unified, inalterable, and always in tension with blacks'. Third, whites and (in this case) blacks must "lock arms with hopeful people," rejecting despair and listening to "each other's hopes and fears, and with goodwill go forward, knowing we have only imperfect solutions, imperfect repentance, imperfect people, imperfect love." Finally, whites must "learn to give sustained effort to racial reconciliation" because "a white evangelical mistake in the sixties was to leave civil rights at the margins" (19). As for what constitutes "effort," beyond respectful dialogue, the editorial was mute.

Myra's and Stanton's essays encapsulated how white evangelicals' excitement about the new wave of racial reconciliation activities was matched by a low-grade anxiousness about whether such efforts would disrupt their comfortable conservative political worldview by promoting public remedies to racial inequality. Religious race-bridging rhetoric enabled white evangelicals to urge, with great enthusiasm, that they acknowledge their mistakes and release any remaining racial prejudice, while cautioning against any alteration of their existing social action frames. Again, whites *were* responding to calls by people of color to show up for real, and many did so genuinely. But through emphasizing "listening," "reflecting," and "getting to know," they tried to control the terms of the third way—to keep it politically tidy, as it were. In so doing, they did begin to substantively change their racial story—and this is, indeed, a recognizable form of social change—but they also downplayed their own privilege to *avoid* racial politics and the power they had to expand their larger political agenda, if they so chose.

I return shortly to discuss how *CT's* race policy coverage became more complex as the magazine waded into welfare reform and other emerging policy issues in the late 1990s. But a brief detour out of *CT* and into the overtly political arena of Christian Right strategy underscores the simultaneous progress and ambivalence that characterized the third way, at least on the white side of the conversation. Ralph Reed's leadership of the CC in the 1990s reveals how religious race bridging could be employed in tandem, and in tension, with neoconservative politics.

Ralph Reed's Racial Jeremiad

The CC's rise and peak coincided with the racial reconciliation movement, and Ralph Reed engaged with it. Created by the Reverend Pat Robertson in 1989 as a nonpartisan vehicle for promoting Christian conservative interests from local precincts to mainstream party platforms, the CC pursued what Justin Watson (1999) calls a "restorationist" vision, to reinstate a morally degenerating society to its traditionalist, Judeo-Christian values through an agenda of faith, "family values," and faith-based social programs (130). Reed, who cut his teeth as a young Republican organizer in Georgia, was only twenty-eight years old and finishing a doctorate in history from Emory University when Robertson hired him in 1995 (Reed 1995a, 18–23). By the mid-1990s, the conservative firebrand with the elfin face was recognized as one of the keenest tacticians of the Religious Right. He helped the CC's budget increase from a reported $200,000 in 1989 to $27 million in 1996.[30]

In a sense, Reed's training positioned him at the confluence of conservative Christianity, race history, and politics, enabling him to nudge his core constituency beyond their sedimented past and help them renarrate their relationship to race—and he tried. Having written his dissertation under the guidance of southern historian Dan Carter, a formidable analyst of U.S. populism and race history, Reed understood that white evangelicals' collective moral reputation had been damaged by the racial "sins of the past." The difference between him and his predecessors in Christian Right organizations was that rather than trying to paper over the race problem, he attempted to address it directly, both with CC supporters and in the media.

After arsonists had destroyed twenty-seven southern black churches in 1996, Reed commented: "It is a painful truth that the white evangelical church was not only on the sidelines but on the wrong side of the most central struggle for social justice in this country," and announced the CC's goal of raising $1 million to help rebuild the churches (Sack 1996). In relaying this story he noted that liberal reformers, whether religious or secular, had been "correct throughout history on issues of social justice, [while] we [Christian conservatives] have been neglectful or derelict in applying the principles of faith to establishing justice in a fallen world" (Reed 1996a, 67). He couldn't have been more in sync with CT race coverage at the time.

Explaining in his books and speeches why religious conservatives should work politically to promote their vision for a more morally traditionalist America, Reed made three important conceptual moves. First, he praised Martin Luther King Jr.'s wing of the civil rights movement as an exemplar of the power of faith-based social activism. King, Reed wrote, was an "indispensable genius" and his movement "a religious movement from start to finish" (1996a, 64). Distributing voter education literature through church networks, speaking from a platform of moral conviction, protesting in the streets when necessary—these were innovations of King's movement that the Christian Right had adopted (Reed 1996b). Reed frequently described King as his own personal hero and detailed his contributions to social movement history (1996a, 56–67, 231–47). This framing rhetorically repositioned King from an icon of the Left to a religious and morally upright American, a centrist figure with whom white evangelicals could identify.

Second, Reed argued that marginalization in American politics and segregation in the churches was the costly price white evangelicals now paid for their historical racism.[31] Unlike other Religious Right strategists who avoided "dwelling" on the past, he detailed some of the ways in which white Christians used the "Curse of Ham" myth to justify slavery, Jim Crow, and failure to support the civil rights movement. In the Jeremiadic language of a fallen community that must repent its sins before an angry God, Reed cast racism as the "crucible" white conservative evangelicals carry into contemporary public life:

The past complicity of the white church in the mistreatment of African-Americans and Jews is too large a blot on our history to deny. Tragically, white evangelicals did not merely look the other way as African-Americans were denied full equality and participation in American life. They were among the most fiery champions of slavery and later segregation—all the while invoking God's name and quoting the Bible to justify their misdeeds. Why are white evangelicals accorded so little respect in the public square today? Certainly part of the answer lies in our past. (Reed 1996a, 236)

In sum, Reed scolded, "George Wallace may have stood in the schoolhouse door, but evangelical clergy provided the moral framework for his actions" (237).

He urged that white evangelicals move beyond this negative legacy by making amends for the past; forsaking racism, "both as an ideology and a political style"; and creating a more multiracial religious conservative movement (Reed 1996a, 237–40). "We must build a genuinely inclusive movement that embraces the full racial diversity of America," he grandly put it, "and makes room for our black, brown, and yellow brothers and sisters in Christ. If we flow out of lily-white churches into lily-white political organizations and support only lily-white candidates for elective office, we cannot expect the larger society to take our agenda seriously." Moreover, he maintained, "the views of minorities mark a strong departure from the liberal positions advocated by the traditional civil rights leadership" (241). Faith-based conservatives might be able to attract these estranged minorities through coalitions around abortion, school choice (for example, vouchers), and welfare reform (241–45). This would mean grooming new candidates and building organizations with greater political appeal to racial minorities, which Reed tried to do through the CC.[32]

Even as he sounded progressive notes about the value of the civil rights movement, the harmful legacy of white evangelicals' racism, and the need to repudiate it and build a more encompassing faith-based movement, Reed executed a third conceptual move, which might seem contradictory. In the capacity of CC director, he cast doubt on not just the methods but also some of the central aims of the civil rights movement, distancing his own movement from efforts to seek social justice through government redress. The civil rights movement achieved its most important gains, he argued, when voter registration efforts that helped put more black politicians into office began to replace direct actions like sit-ins. More radical activism undercuts any social movement, he claimed. "None of those gains would have been possible had the civil rights community remained committed to the tactics of sit-ins and marches. Feminist leaders have failed to learn this lesson at their hazard" (Reed 1996a, 224). A few years after leaving the CC he put it more directly, speaking to other conservative strategists at Regent University's Pat Robertson School of Government:

> I think the main [lesson] for Christians who get involved in the political arena [is] to not make the mistakes that Christians on the left did in the 1960s in thinking

that you could solve and ameliorate great social problems through political action and through government programs. You don't end racial discrimination by passing a law against it. You don't end poverty by declaring war on it. These are matters of the heart and soul. . . . The institution of government is not ordained, nor is it well suited for the task of social regeneration or formation.[33]

Using phrases like "Christians on the left in the 1960s" in the racial context, Reed reiterated the social justice–aversive bias that white evangelicals like C. Peter Wagner asserted. Despite having lauding the civil rights movement as one of the great faith-based social movements in history, Reed ultimately tethered this belated support to an ideological condition, the neoconservative precept— which syncs with white evangelicalism's social justice–aversive racial narrative— that social problems are *not* remedied through politics or government.

Of course these are ironic if not schizophrenic statements to issue from arguably the most influential Christian Right strategist of the 1990s. Reed led the CC *precisely* to lobby politicians and government and indeed declare wars on behalf of the social change conservatives sought around abortion, the preservation of traditional marriage, school choice, faith-based initiatives, and so forth; that was the point of a galvanized Religious Right.[34] But Reed's strange rhetorical juggling exposes how much white conservative evangelicals' "step forward" beyond their racial past seemed contingent on an implicit bargain: that race as a *justice* issue, a matter of pursuing concrete remedies for inequality, would be cordoned off from these others, categorically barred as a *political* pursuit, framed as *inappropriate* to the broader, moral restorationist political agenda.

Reed employed the narrative of racial self-criticism with a force and directness that would have been unimaginable for white conservatives even ten years earlier, and he did risk alienating his members by doing so. These moves, though perhaps born from genuine antiracist conviction, enabled the strategist to put temporal distance between Christian conservatives and the theological racism tradition, demonstrate to potential conservative supporters of color that he cared, and build a political bridge between white and nonwhite religious communities. Whether anyone would choose to cross it was a different question. Ultimately, the attendant framing of related justice pursuits as improper targets for political action, "matters of the heart and soul," also enabled a real exercise of power to be concealed: white evangelicals' recurrent assumption— which amounted to a decision—that race issues, but not the "traditional values" agenda, should be depoliticized and addressed in the realm of individual and cross-cultural relationships.

Weighing in on Policy

Neoconservatism's influence, with its faith in private-sector solutions to social problems, its paranoia about government intervention on certain matters, and its assertion that opportunity and success are matters of clearing the path—in "race-blind" ways—for individual achievement, is clearly an influence on evangelicals' political ambivalence around race. But, again, neoconservative ideology alone does not capture the appeal *within* evangelicalism of religious race bridging as a third way. Despite clear elements of neoconservatism running through the coverage of race issues in *CT*, it is also apparent that as the framework of religious race bridging became normative in the white evangelical community, the magazine's orientation toward these issues grew identifiably more nuanced and less insulated than it had been in the past. Sometimes awkward, often qualified and defensive, a conversation about race did move forward. The frames, practices, and flexibility of the religious race-bridging model allowed white evangelicals to shift or at least question older racial narratives to which they had been attached, to acknowledge legitimate differences in political perspective *among* evangelicals, and to largely avoid polarizing discussions across different evangelical communities that might have shut the conversation down.

The first articles identifiable as squarely related to national race policy issues appeared in 1995 and continued at a fairly steady pace through 1998, for a total of fourteen pieces in four years—more than the magazine had produced from 1980 to 1994 combined. Immigration, affirmative action, and welfare reform policy were the categories of interest, with the last receiving the most sustained attention.[35]

Discussion of national race-related policy broke into the magazine after California voters passed ballot initiative Proposition 187, a controversial restrictive immigration measure that received national attention. *CT* ran a report reviewing the deep divisions in the evangelical community around the issue (Zipperer 1995). Many Latino and Asian evangelicals, the article noted, opposed Prop 187.[36] Although most white Protestants supported it, some white evangelicals advocated a *more* pro-immigrant position, citing the biblical command to care for the "alien in your midst." In multiethnic churches, congregants were reportedly divided according to how long they had lived in the United States. A few months later, *CT* ran a feature-length and largely supportive article on immigration that advocated a "more loving," less restrictionist response (Stafford 1995).

The tenor and content of religious race bridging allowed for this. Before racial reconciliation and integration were on the editorial radar of *CT*, the neoconservative approach to immigration, which was explicit in the Republican Party and indeed had propelled Prop 187, would likely have characterized coverage of the issue. Now, however, the magazine chose to showcase diverse perspectives among evangelicals. This recognition of both evangelicals of color and whites who advocated more generous immigration policies *as members of the evangelical community* signaled a clear shift from the unconscious "white 'we,'" whose perspective CT had almost exclusively voiced in the 1980s. Indeed, acknowledging the lack of consensus on immigration, even the CC opted not to take a position on it in the mid-1990s (Jacobson 2012). In the 2000s, the ongoing diversity of evangelical opinion on immigration developed into a rich topic of conversation in CT discourse (as chapter 6 details).

Conversations about welfare reform in CT also admitted a wider range of viewpoints. After President Bill Clinton and a GOP-led Congress passed a welfare reform package in 1996 that envisioned a greater role for government-subsidized, faith-based organizations in delivering social services, CT produced a fleet of news reports, editorials, and ministry profiles in 1996–97. Some of these, predictably, angled toward issues of responsible fatherhood, parenting, and "family values," rather than race per se, and in others the racial dimensions were more implied than explicit.[37] But in general on the topic of welfare, the CT editorial board seemed to swing between delivering the neoconservative, reduced-government orientation that white, Republican-voting evangelicals might expect to read, and not losing the ground they'd worked to gain with Christians of color, whose ministries were often closer to the economically disadvantaged.

The February 1996 issue was indicative of the attempt to provide coverage of welfare-related topics that resonated with different readers. CT ran a ten-page cover story profiling Pastor Eugene Rivers, a Boston-based advocate of a "Christian black nationalism" that rejects mainstream models for rescuing the poor (Zoba 1996). In the same issue, three other welfare politics–related news blurbs ran, reflecting a spectrum of views. One reported on protests of welfare cuts by progressive evangelicals like Jim Wallis and Tony Campolo; one covered a Family Research Council–sponsored conference on welfare reform featuring top neoconservative intelligentsia like Michael Novak and David Frumm; and the third described the increasing burden shouldered by states and nonprofit organizations like churches under the new, reduced welfare benefits schema (Anonymous 1996a; Anonymous 1996b; Kellner 1996).[38]

The Eugene Rivers profile presented a kind of post–civil rights movement echo of Tom Skinner. Rivers was (and is) an intellectual, but also a credible, in-the-trenches black pastor critical of public programs "conferred by *whites*" that hold blacks "hostage" to dependency. This "hustler-turned-preacher," who managed accountability-oriented, faith-based programs in blighted areas, frequently challenged not just white evangelicals but also the black civil rights establishment and secular academics to solve social problems by building a hybrid framework of political involvement with both leftist and conservative elements (Zoba 1995, 16–17). Lest his confrontational style be threatening to readers, CT editors introduced the profile with a noteworthy call-out warning: "*CT* is committed to *building bridges* between communities, and that means dealing with issues that push us beyond our comfort zones" (14, emphasis added).

Conversant in the conservative vocabulary of collective dysfunction and individual responsibility, Rivers urged that the black church, *not* well-meaning whites, needed to lead the urban underclass out of despair. He expressed guarded support for racial reconciliation developments among conservative black and white churches, like the SBC apology—but also argued that white evangelicals, as resourced as they are, *need* black Christians if they are to build a "state-of-the-art policy intelligentsia" capable of moving beyond the narrow white evangelical policy agenda of "family values" to build a "morally consistent vision" of Christians in politics (Zoba 1996, 23).

He then moved into more delicate territory, pushing the boundaries of familiar, conservative-friendly analyses of poverty and welfare. White conservative Christians keen to diagnose the moral dysfunctions of the underclass ought to consider flaws in their moral and political lens:

> After we tell the blacks that they have to own their own issues and be morally responsible, are we then also going to ignore the biblical commands that require a redistribution of godly gain to meet the needs of the widow and orphan? There is no agonizing over the damaging effects of welfare assistance in the federal subsidies given to McDonald's and Chrysler. Nobody worries about the damaging psychological effects of welfare for the rich. So if there's no free ride for Shaniqua Jackson, then there shouldn't be any free ride for the Fortune 500 corporation that doesn't want to pay taxes. (Zoba 1996, 24)

In the end, Rivers argued, "evangelicals are in the best position to provide leadership for the country" (24) and should therefore cultivate greater face-to-face collaboration across racial groups. He nonetheless—and like Skinner before him—refused to sign on to a white-dominated agenda that ignored the background conditions unevenly impacting the urban poor.

The Eugene Rivers profile advanced the third-way race narrative attendant to the racial reconciliation phase of religious race bridging in that it focused on creative solutions and relationship building. But consistent with what many Christians of color had articulated in the magazine over the years, it rejected simple stories about whites, people of color, and the proper Christian response to social problems. In running it, and showcasing more than one perspective on welfare reform, *CT* aired critiques of white, faith-based conservatism that were ultrarare during the earlier, thin pluralism approach of the 1980s. As the focus of welfare reform turned in 1997 to Charitable Choice, the government's program for partnering with church-based organizations to provide social services, the magazine represented evangelical viewpoints from left, right, and center (Kauffman 1997; Frame 1997; Sherman 1997). Ultimately, the magazine's race-bridging conclusion seemed to be that "churches should not merely lament or laud the welfare reforms," as one report put it. "Critics and supporters alike should be in the trenches, actively assisting low-income families. Such personal engagement makes our voice in the public square more credible" (Sherman 1997, 51). The emergent recognition of multiple, viable Christian viewpoints was not a sea change, but it was a shift from a much more oblivious past.

When racial reconciliation exploded in a fairly public way in American evangelical circles in the 1990s, some outside observers wondered if the whole thing was disingenuous, some kind of strategically orchestrated stunt to make conservative Christians look less white, or less racially isolated. Such skepticism was reasonable. White evangelicals had resisted many of the nation's most important racial transformations, and then for decades remained conspicuously absent from the hard conversations that were part of the country's continuing growing pains. Why would they suddenly execute an about-face? Moreover, did these apologies and promises, prayer sessions and stadium rallies, matter in any substantive sense? Did the new racial reconciliation trend have any meaningful political implications, or was it merely evangelicals' version of political correctness?

The foregoing review of race-related conversations and events across the 1980s and 1990s in evangelicalism's largest and most popular journal reveals three important factors that must be incorporated into our evolving analysis of ERC efforts.

First, the new race discourse, while undeniably informed by trends in American culture writ large, was primarily an *inside* response to an *inside* conversation that had taken decades to crest. That does not make it any less of a demonstration of considerable social change. Indeed, it illustrates how groups navigate social change on their own terms through the vehicles of their own distinctive meaning-making systems and cultural practices. From Tom Skinner through the Perkinses through Eugene Rivers, African Americans explicitly *asked* whites for some specific things, and read their responses as signs of whites' seriousness. They challenged whites to come clean by acknowledging the sins of the past; repudiating racist attitudes, decisions, and behaviors; apologizing explicitly; atoning to God; making genuine efforts to build new kinds of relationships;

and committing to institutional change. Black Christians continued, as they long had, to urge white evangelicals to recognize the systemic and structural inequalities that perpetuated American racism—to see the politics of reconciliation. They saw such challenges as intertwined with the prospect of building meaningful, spiritually anchored, cross-racial relationships. But symbolic apologies and atonements were *named* as crucial first steps, starting places that did not immediately require overt political commitments. Anchored by a genuine willingness to see things differently, such actions, Christians of color hoped, might lead to longer-term change.

Second, religious race bridging as a social change response drew primarily on endogenous resources within evangelical communities to construct a new framework for addressing old fractures. The meaning-making practices mobilized in the new race discourse enabled evangelicals to leverage familiar, faith-based vocabulary to a persistent problem in order to build a creative third way between two older narratives that had reached a standstill. Through the concept of bridging, participants began to craft new stories, new accounts of who they were and who they could be with regard to race and racism. The emotional tenor of racial reconciliation was critical to its cultural value, and to its resonance among real people. The language of reconciliation not only drew on the central concept of Christianity, Christ's reconciliation of a sinful humanity to its creator God; it also reflected a hunger for meaningful connection across conflict, a need for healing, and a space to try. It gave conflicted whites a vehicle for publicly repudiating a racist, theologically corrupt past and moving beyond its suffocating associations. Public apologies also gave Christians of color steeped in faith-based values and perhaps disillusioned with secular solutions a certain reward: the spectacle of whites at last admitting they had been wrong, sinful, and complicit in a long chain of injuries. These processes miraculously, as participants saw it, opened hearts by providing a cathartic emotional and spiritual vehicle for the expression of feelings about racial pain rarely discussed in American political culture. Reconcilers' hopes rode on the willingness of fellow evangelicals to engage, and this was partly a matter of making the new conversations appealing and accessible.

Third, the CT material reveals that the political foreclosures of religious race bridging in the 1990s cannot be reduced to exogenous pressures by neoconservatives for evangelicals to avoid responding to race-related inequities in "liberal" (that is, governmental solution–based) ways.[39] Many white evangelicals were influenced by if not directly involved in neoconservatism, with its faith in social progress through individual relationships and in laissez-faire solutions to broad-scale inequalities, and its distrust of government to solve social problems. Certainly neoconservatives like Ralph Reed had their own incentives for trying to harness the language of racial reconciliation to particular political aims, while restraining religious race-bridging's potential to make whites reconsider their political agenda. But other factors more immediately influenced the development of evangelicalism's new race discourse and its ambivalent orientation to politics.

One was the micropolitics of power *within* evangelical settings. The proliferation of race issues in the larger culture in the 1990s, and the coming of age of a post–civil rights movement era generation that was more race-savvy, made race difficult to ignore. That did not mean that evangelical whites were ready—or even had the skills, yet—to recognize and relinquish the power they wielded within the massive assemblage of churches, denominational organizations, institutions, and cultural spaces they had built. As we saw laced through the *CT* race and reconciliation coverage, most white conservative evangelicals had massive blind spots when it came to recognizing the kinds of structural and systemic factors influencing socioeconomic inequalities to which their counterparts of color kept directing their attention. Even if they wanted to, it would be almost impossible for them to consider a political reorientation on race if they couldn't yet grasp, even after blacks kept telling them, why it might be necessary. I will examine how ideas embedded into white evangelicals' meaning-making practices made it difficult for them to see their own racial power and advantage, much less begin to respond to it in political terms—and how that began to shift when Emerson and Smith's book, *Divided by Faith*, finally got their attention in the early 2000s.

Too, political conditions at the time made it unlikely that evangelicals would approach racial change through a highly politicized lens. After all, in the 1990s the political center itself had shifted to the right. Indeed, President Clinton entered office in 1992 by cultivating compromise with an increasingly influential crop of social conservatives on his right flank who questioned the "excesses" of social programs expanded during the civil rights movement era (Blank 1997; Zuckerman 2000). Affirmative action, welfare reform, Charitable Choice, immigration rights, and gay/lesbian rights were all impacted by neoconservative arguments that once-needed policies had extended too far and must be scaled back (Gillespie et al. 1994; Bartkowski and Regis 2003). Charges of "reverse discrimination," "government dependence," "deadbeat dads," "welfare queens," "sexual deviants," and "coddled immigrants" "working the system" aroused white indignation and made it more difficult for policy makers to speak meaningfully about ongoing socioeconomic inequities (Hancock 2004). George W. Bush later capitalized on the seeming consensus that private-realm institutions could deliver services more humanely and efficiently than government allegedly could

(Segers 2003; Formicola, Segers, and Weber 2003; Black, Koopman, and Ryden 2004; Lindner 2001). In short, the containment of discussion of political policies that would address poverty, ongoing racial discrimination, or immigration rights through redistributive efforts and meaningful structural change was not limited to American evangelicalism but part of a national cultural discourse in which neoconservative frames were gaining traction.

Evangelicals interested in reconciliation had ample reasons for not letting these delicate new conversations, explorations, and rituals become entangled in political acrimony. Partly because the meaning-making practices of racial reconciliation were breaking new ground by creating a third way with diverse appeal; partly because many white conservatives could literally not imagine what a progressive *politics* born of racial reconciliation might look like; partly because whites weren't ready to see and acknowledge their own power; and partly because the larger political environment made talk of politics even less appealing, the idea of pushing farther was largely untenable. Racial reconciliation as a relational framework grounded in theological reasoning appeared in the 1990s to be the only bridge capable of bringing groups with different histories, cultural traditions, and political orientations into a substantive conversation. But even as the possibility of a more politicized religious race-bridging framework seemed to get subsumed for a time, it survived as a counternarrative in the pages of *CT* in years to come, particularly as some white evangelicals opened themselves to more self-critique around race and social justice issues through processes I explore in later chapters. By the 2000s, this counternarrative provided a basis for more complex and eventually activist evangelical perspectives among a minority of racial change advocates.

Religious race bridging was a clear step forward, *toward* substantive change after long periods of resistance, avoidance, or superficial attention to race issues among Christians. It did not guarantee any particular outcome; it did not promise anything more than a faithful beginning. But that beginning was indeed an expression of significant social change within at least an important segment of American evangelicalism. We need to understand more about the social and spiritual dynamics within racial reconciliation settings before we can grasp the contours and meaning of their political ambivalence. Having looked at the religious race-bridging framework at the level of public discourse and coverage of racial changes within evangelical organizations, we are now in a position to investigate what the meaning-making practices of racial reconciliation looked and felt like to participants in social settings on the ground. How did—and do—participants find the work personally or socially transformative, and how do they conceive of the political limits, if any, of religious racial change?

5   Epiphanal Spaces of Evangelical Culture

In the late summer of 1997, in Denver, Colorado, an African American man named Gregory Fields had a Ford van stolen.[1] Fields reported the theft to police, and a few weeks later a white detective named Colin Whitford came to his house to follow up on the case. In talking, the two men discovered that they each hunted and fished, were involved in the lay leadership of their churches, and shared a strong passion for the Bible and Christianity. Whitford brought up his recent participation in the Christian men's movement Promise Keepers (PK) (he had attended a couple stadium rallies) and mentioned the group's emphasis on fostering relationships between men of different races. Fields invited Whitford to attend services at his church, Jubilee Community Baptist.

Detective Whitford later shared that he felt as if Fields's invitation was a sort of divine appointment for him:

[Fields] is a black guy and I . . . never had hardly any relationships with anybody of any color. You know, I grew up in pretty much white, honky, middle-class America. . . . I mean, I was born out in Wyoming. . . . And he invited me to go to church, you know to come to visit their church.

. . . But I remember sitting there [at a PK conference] thinking, well, this is not really my problem, because I've never had any relationships with these people. It was kind of like, you know, God, I don't even know any black people, and you talk about going and building relationships, and, well, I don't even know any, I mean. And God kind of reached down and slapped me upside the head, and I remembered that conversation that I had with him, and he said, "Here's your chance." You know, "put up or shut up" kind of thing, and so, I think Gregory made an offer to come to church, kind of like, "Well, I'll see if I can come up to visit sometime," and "Well, we'd love to have you there."

I had that short conversation in my mind and I pulled out my pen and said, "Okay, where's the church, what time does it start? I'll come."

In late November, Whitford visited Jubilee Baptist, a medium-sized (300-seat, two Sunday services) church in what is considered a mixed-race (though traditionally black), working-class, "inner-city" neighborhood. He thoroughly enjoyed the lively music, preaching, and friendly people, and as the main service merged into another discussion, inadvertently found himself in something of a church business meeting where Pastor Darrell Brickson was discussing a financial problem the congregation was experiencing. Jubilee was faced with raising a $28,000 payment on the new church building the congregation had built after meeting in abandoned buildings and basements for the previous fifty years. The payment was due on December 31 to keep from losing the building, but the congregation did not know how they were going to raise the money.

Whitford took this information home with him and found himself troubled about it for days:

> My personality: Part of my makeup is that I have been a horse trader and a schemer from day one, and that's just sort of, something I like to do. You know, kind of a con-niver, you know, try to horse trade, "what can you do for me, what can I do for you?" kind of thing. And I said, "$30,000 bucks in order to save this building. This is not that tough, we should be able to do this." And $30,000 is a lot of money, but it's not a lot of money, you know.
>
> I went home from that Sunday service, and God just absolutely would not leave me alone. This was on my heart, it was *heavy* on my heart. And I was sitting there trying to watch the Broncos and God just kept, you know, every TV commercial I saw was geared towards white people. Every magazine I picked up was geared to-wards white people. Every newspaper I picked up was geared towards white people. And God just sort of hit me with the question, "What's it like to be a black man in a white man's world?" And again, I grew up in white honky Applewood, Colorado, I never, I mean there was one black kid in my high school, Gary Thompson, I didn't even know who he was, just cuz he was the black guy, you know. And it was kind of like, the lights came on, you know, these people have been oppressed. Their whole lives, under oppression, just because of . . . who they are. And I thought, "This is bullshit. We gotta do something about this."

A couple of days later, Whitford brought the issue to Father Mitch White, the pastor of Whitford's church, Redeemer Episcopal Church. Redeemer was an upper-middle-class evangelical Episcopal (meaning, quite theologically conservative) congregation of about 500, situated in wealthy South Denver. Whitford suggested Redeemer find a way to help Jubilee, but White reminded him that at the end of the year, the church did not have much money in its discretionary fund. Perhaps they could come up with $5,000 from their outreach budget, he suggested, but Whitford might try the Episcopal Diocese in Colorado to help raise the money.

The next day, however, Cal Tompkins, the sexton of Redeemer, reported a dream to Father White that he had while praying about an ongoing stewardship campaign the church was having. When White heard the dream, he felt something unusual was happening:

> Cal is a real prayer, he's a real intercessor, and he comes to me maybe two or three times a year, he'll come to me and say, "Now, I was praying and I had this thought or I had what I thought was a word from God or I had a vision which I think needs to be shared with the whole church. What do you think? And if you think, then I'll follow it up."
>
> . . . What he saw in this waking dream or vision was the people of Redeemer Church bringing money that somehow he knew was from selling things, it was not from their regular income, it was, somebody sold an extra car that they didn't need, somebody sold a piece of jewelry that they didn't need. It was people sort of doing away with the excess in their lives and bringing the money and putting it on the altar. And then he sort of hesitated and said to me, "and the thing was, even though I was praying about our stewardship campaign, it was that the money was not for us. It was for another congregation." Well, that just—I didn't tell him what I was thinking, I simply said to him, "You call Colin Whitford, and call him today or tomorrow, and tell him what you told me, and if you two think it's right, you come and talk to me as soon as possible."

The next day, Whitford and Tompkins met with Father White. White gave the two permission to raise the issue with the congregation the following Sunday. So at all three services Whitford spoke to the congregation for fifteen minutes about Jubilee's situation. "I just got up in front of people and said, 'Look, this is the *golden opportunity* for us to minister to some people, for white guys to minister to these black guys, just strictly out of love for one another in the body of Christ, nothing else but that. This is a golden opportunity, we cannot let this go by, we can *do* this.'" In less than a week the congregation raised about $30,000. The event was written up in the local papers.

On December 21, Whitford and forty other people from Redeemer Episcopal came to Jubilee's Sunday services to present the check to the congregation. No one at Jubilee knew it was coming. Whitford described this thrilling moment:

> So I got up and, to really be honest with you, I don't remember what I said. Just sort of that God put on our hearts to help you guys out and I had a check for you and this is not because we're rich and you're poor or something like that, it's just because we

want to help you out. You guys have a lot that you could give us and have given us and, frankly, it's more important for us to be able to give this than it is for you to be able to receive, because we need to be able to do this. And I opened my Bible and pulled out this check and handed it to Pastor Brickson.

Well, he looked at that check, and he turned away—I'll never forget this—he turned away from me, and I saw him kind of shudder, it was a sense of relief, you know, and he turned back to me and he took the microphone away from me.

Pastor Brickson described the moment in this way:

Spiritual pandemonium. It was God showing that nothing's too hard for him. God showing his sovereignty, his faithfulness, through a most unusual way. I still have not been able to put into words my feelings. I will say that God gets all the glory from that, because on either side of the coin, Mitch or myself or Gregory, there was nothing we could have done to put it together.

Lorraine Close, a member of Jubilee, also remembers the day well:

I didn't know exactly what was going to happen. I knew it was some money, but I didn't know exactly what was the dollar sign. . . . I didn't expect that kind of blessing and it just seemed like, you know, the heavens had poured out on us. You know, I've never seen our church *explode* like that!

Redeemer's bequeathing of the check for Jubilee marked the dramatic beginning of an intentional relationship-building process between these two formally unconnected congregations. The two pastors gradually built a friendship (each man's first close cross-racial relationship), as did others on each church's pastoral team. The two churches combined their men's and women's ministries for a time, and occasionally their Sunday services. They also set up a twelve-week racial reconciliation (RR) course in order to "go deeper" with the work that was begun with that initial exchange. The course was led by two African American pastors, Rev. Joseph Jackson, an associate pastor at Staff of Life Christian Center in Denver, and Bob Swanson, a lay minister heavily involved in prison ministries. A small subset of members of both churches attended the class. I attended most of the sessions, as well as several church services involving one or both churches, and interviewed most of the participants involved.

Vanda's Miracle

A few weeks into the twelve-week RR workshop provided for interested members of Redeemer Church and Jubilee Baptist, about thirty people are scattered throughout the Jubilee church sanctuary. Pastors Joseph and Bob are teaching a session on healing and forgiveness. Joseph leads into the topic with a personal story about his experience as the only black pastor at an affluent suburban white church. Although that congregation seemed to enjoy his sermons, they resisted accepting him on the more interpersonal levels of pastoring. For a long time he was embittered and felt hateful toward the people who rejected him on the basis of race. Eventually, however, "God revealed" to him that he needed to work on forgiveness toward the people he resented and to pray for the cleansing of his own heart. The lesson is still ongoing, he admits, but it was crucial to the RR ministry he eventually began out of that experience.

A woman sitting near the back of the church raises her hand. This is Vanda, a soft-spoken African American woman in her early forties. During an earlier break, I had asked Vanda what brought her to the RR course. (The members of this workshop know me as a researcher participating in the class.) She told me she had been raped by a white man as a young woman and that she was trying to find healing around that issue, but she wasn't sure where to start; the violation continued to haunt her. I told her a little about the sexual assault victims' advocacy organization I happened to be working for at the time and suggested some resources she might try to get support. Now she sits tentatively raising her hand.

"I was wondering," Vanda quietly begins, "how you were finally able to get over your feelings about those people?"

"Well, with a lot of help from the Lord," Joseph confesses. "It was a long-term process."

"But, I mean, how did you finally forgive the people that hurt you?" Her voice gains urgency. She leans forward from the pew. "What did you do? I want to know because—" her voice breaks, "I just don't know if I can forgive him."

Vanda begins to cry. Next to her, a middle-aged white couple from Redeemer begin gently laying hands on her and softly praying. People in the pew in front of Vanda twist around to join them.

Now Bob steps to the front of the sanctuary and takes the microphone. "You don't know if you can forgive who, Vanda?" he asks.

"The man who hurt me."

"What did the man do to you, Vanda?" Bob continues.

She sobs quietly. Her head is down. People whisper words of encouragement and continue praying. Vanda's body is shaking; she looks frightened.

"How did he hurt you?"

No response, just the sound of Vanda's sobs and the soft, whispering prayers.

"Did he do something bad to you?"

"Yes," she answers.

"What did he do, Vanda?"

Silence.

"Sister, can you tell us what happened?"

"He raped me," she says very clearly, then bursts into sobs.

"All right. All right now. Can people get up and lay hands on this sister right now?" Bob asks. The small sanctuary comes alive as people shuffle out of their seats and over to Vanda. Now there is a thick huddle around her. The people on the periphery touch others who are touching Vanda. She is barely visible in the center.

"We're going do something different tonight," Bob announces, his voice impassioned. The energy in the room grows even more charged.

"I believe the Lord's gonna take care of this sister's pain right now. Oh, I believe the Lord is right here with us and he will heal you tonight, Vanda, as we are gathered here together. Are you ready to be healed, Vanda?"

Vanda is now rocking back and forth, nodding her head. Black hands, white hands, male hands, female hands press against her back and arms. One tall white man stands swaying with one arm raised, palm up toward heaven, and the other opened out toward Vanda. His eyes are squeezed shut, and his lips mumble a steady stream of prayer.

"I know that God is going to heal you tonight, Vanda. There isn't going to be any more pain. There aren't going to be any more nightmares. You are not going to see this man's face in your worst dreams anymore. God is going to take all that away for you tonight. But you've got to be ready to be healed, sister. You got to be ready to give it up to the Lord. Are you ready to do that?"

"Yes," she manages, still shaking. "Thank you, Lord. Yes."

"Now," Bob says to the group, "we're going to do something here." He then directs the dozen or so men in the room to come to the sanctuary stage, facing the group with the pastors. As the men leave the pews, the women spontaneously surround Vanda. Some are crying with her, others pray aloud, others silently stroke and comfort her.

Bob barely pauses between a stream of prayer and praise. "Oh, the Lord is working in here tonight. Can you feel the Spirit with us?" he asks. His tone is black gospel now, not the earlier, drier tone of "workshop" language. People nod and pray louder. "Can you feel that healing Spirit of God in our midst?" Voices register confirmation.

"Now, Vanda, I want you to stand up. Can you do that? And I want to ask the sisters to bring her forward right now. Thank you, Jesus. I want you all to help her walk up here."

The men stand in a line facing the women. Vanda seems stunned and perhaps intimidated, but rises and walks into the aisle. The other women slowly guide her toward Pastor Bob, who is flanked by the row of somber-faced men. None appears to know what is coming, and, indeed, this is unrehearsed and unplanned.

Finally, Vanda takes a step of faith, walking forward with some of the women accompanying her, and eventually stands before Bob, weeping. The two women on either side of her squeeze her supportively.

Bob turns to the line of men. "Brothers, right now I want each and every one of you to repent on behalf of the man that wronged this sister. I want you to look her in the eyes and tell her you're sorry, in your own way, you understand? Can you do that?" The men nod.

"Vanda, do you believe you can accept the apology of these men?"

She nods her head without looking up at the row of faces. Her back is to those of us remaining in the pews, so her expression is not visible.

Now Bob walks Vanda to one end of the row so that she is face-to-face with the first man, who is white. A man who often speaks when the large group is gathered, his eyes are kind as he faces her solemnly. Gently, he opens his arms to embrace her, and she, cautiously, hugs him back. When they pull away, he continues to hold her hands and begins softly speaking to her, tears in his eyes.

As this happens, Bob continues to lead prayer, strolling in circles, gesturing with one hand, holding the microphone to his mouth with the other. "Lord, we want to lift this sister Vanda up to you right now because we know that you are the Lord Almighty, you are the Prince of Peace, Jesus, and we know that in your infinite capacity you will heal this sister of the pain that has plagued her, Lord. We know that you will touch her heart right now and give her peace, Hallelujah. We thank you, Lord, we praise you now . . ."

One by one, each man in the line meets Vanda face-to-face, apologizing personally for the sin committed against her. Each wraps his arms around her, some for a long time. There does not seem to be a dry eye in the house.

Vanda seems deeply shaken by the time she has hugged the last man and returned to Bob's side. At this point Bob faces Vanda (and again, her back is to the rest of the assembled workshop participants, who are now holding hands across the aisles). "Praise God," he enthuses. "Praise God for the courage of this sister. But we're not done. Vanda, the next question is for you. Vanda, can you forgive the man that did this to you?"

Vanda's body seems for a moment to deflate. She looks at the pastor, and then down at her feet. "I'm . . . not sure," she manages, still crying.

"Can you forgive this man, Vanda, and let go of the hatred you carry for him?" Bob asks again. "Vanda, can you get rid of it? Can you let it go? You know that this hatred will destroy you."

Vanda continues to sob, her head bowed. From my seat, I cannot hear or see her answer. But with an arm around her, Bob has turned his attention to the other women in the congregation. "Now I want the women here to step in and do this," he says. "Men, I want you to turn to these women and offer your sincere repentance. And I want the women to offer forgiveness to the men."

At this instruction, the men file back into the pews to address the women individually. As a participant-observer, no one automatically exempts me from this spontaneous ritual. Nor do I choose to excuse myself, although I am taken aback. Soon a young black man in his midtwenties approaches me. "I am so sorry," he says to me, as he wraps me in an embrace. "I forgive you," I reply to him awkwardly, and to an elderly white man who likewise apologizes. The sounds of similar apologies and pardons fill the room. This is like nothing I have ever experienced, and though it feels contrived and surreal, it is also profoundly moving. People huddle in pairs and groups, speaking softly to one another and praying. This goes on for several minutes, but feels like an eternity.

Finally, Bob reassembles the group into the large closing circle that always ends the class. Vanda joins the circle, her arms around people on either side. Prayers are offered to God in a cacophony of voices. Bob breaks out in a stream of unfamiliar syllables. I realize that he is speaking in tongues. A second woman slumps to the floor, rolling back and forth and speaking unintelligibly. Her husband kneels down next to her, gently massaging her shoulders, and the group prayer continues unbroken. Some continue to lay hands on Vanda. Then C.L., a gregarious black pastor from Jubilee, and his wife begin singing a beautiful gospel version of "Amazing Grace." The room is absolutely humming. Finally, Vanda joins in the singing and, tears streaming down her face, slowly begins to smile.

The following Sunday evening Vanda is back, and her entire comportment has changed. She wears a colorful outfit accentuated with a gold scarf, and smiles easily as she glances around the room. Showing no signs of self-consciousness or embarrassment about having been the center of attention last week, she asks Bob after regular announcements are over if she might say something.

Standing with shoulders straight, she begins to speak. "I just want to thank God and all of you all for what happened last week in here. And I want you to know that in the last week I feel like a huge burden has been lifted off of me. Every day that goes by I feel a little bit lighter because I forgave that man. And I just—I feel like a different person now."

People beam back at Vanda. "Praise God! Thank you, Lord," someone cheers, and the group applauds.

"I just feel a thousand times lighter now," she continues, and her face is a testament to her words. "And I even had a crisis in my family this week. Someone in my family committed suicide. And I want you to know that I wouldn't have been able to deal with that before—before, that would have broken me down even more. But I was able to sit down with my children immediately and talk about it openly with them. I wouldn't have been able to do that before, because I come from a family where we didn't talk about things like that. But I just knew I could because God just lifted that burden from me, and it's gone now, and I feel like a different person. So I just want to thank y'all, and thank you, Joseph and Bob, because I know that the Lord brought me here for a reason."

The joy in the room is palpable. We begin the next session of RR.

Epiphanal Spaces

The most compelling experiences that infused living rooms, churches, and other settings when RR efforts were peaking in the late 1990s came not in the form of magazine articles or formal apologies by denominational leaders, but rather in what people involved described as miracles—real-life, spiritually infused moments when something seemed to change in ways people reported they couldn't have imagined or explained without reference to God. Some spoke of feeling for the first time that real, transformative change was possible. Some described sudden healing of lifelong pain. Others noted a dawning awareness that old hurts might be resolved through new faith-based approaches. Across fieldwork and interviews with participants from different backgrounds, common themes emerged: the idea that RR was occurring in Christian communities as a result of "God's timing"; the sense that the "Holy Spirit" was moving in their midst; and the notion that a distinctively Christian RR approach provides a "new way" with the potential to forever transform the broader world.

Of course, not every day in the life of a racial reconciler looked as miraculous as all that. RR and multiracial church building are more often a matter of committing to what sometimes feels like a grinding, difficult, day-in-day-out process of building relationships across difference, and trying to navigate the conflicts and tensions that arise. But the epiphanies of reconciliation efforts, when they do come, transform and motivate participants in ways that make them want to try.

Below I draw on ethnographic fieldwork to contextualize, in a different dimension than I have so far, how the ideological systems and cultural practices of evangelicalism ground and propel the "miraculous moments" that seem to hold these racial change efforts together. I was constantly struck by the emotional power of these moments, and their impact on the people involved. Drawing from Vanda's miracle, the Jubilee-Redeemer story of cross-racial, church-based reconciliation, and other fieldwork stories, I examine how core meaning-making practices in evangelical culture sculpt evangelical racial change (ERC) advocates' experiences, viewpoints, and activities in ways that would not be immediately decipherable to outsiders. What I call "epiphanal spaces" of ERC settings draw together the conceptual frameworks and physical arenas in which reconciliation processes come to feel miraculous and transformative to people who seriously engage in them. This provides insight into the cultural "motors" that seem to guide ERC efforts on the ground, informing participants' perspectives on what kind of change will or should come out of those efforts.

Deriving from ancient Greek, "epiphany" denotes a sudden manifestation or appearance of something powerful, possibly of divine origin. Epiphanies may signify that one has "seen the light" or "found the last piece of the puzzle" that brings a larger picture into focus. In the Christian tradition, it refers to the adoration of the Magi, in which the infant Christ was seen to be the miraculous incarnation of God. I employ the term to capture phenomena that help explain why evangelical RR processes registered as so meaningful to people who participated in them, regardless of the different racial "tool kits" they brought to the process. The awakenings so many evangelical reconcilers described were invariably interpreted in ERC settings as divinely guided breakthroughs; participants linked those experiences to a broader story about God's plan for the Christian community. The epiphanal quality of these settings, especially at the height of RR in the 1990s, fueled the movement's appeal among ordinary evangelicals. To understand how ERC advocates on the ground explicitly understood, and understand, race in relation to power and politics, the beliefs, values, norms, and expectations they tend to take for granted must be rendered more visible.

Understanding how epiphanal spaces function in evangelical culture helps explain why most evangelical reconcilers in the 1990s tended to perceive politicized expressions of reconciliation processes—that is, racial change objectives that engage an overtly political critique or political activities like organizing—as threatening. RR settings provided feelings of safety and accessibility that enabled unique modes of racial interaction. RR processes also depended upon a sense of spiritual meaning and cultural belonging difficult to replicate outside the community boundaries. Such insider experiences helped create the "miracles" and "epiphanies" of cross-racial healing processes. At the same time, drawing on specific cultural meaning-making practices helped believers avoid engaging, in their religious cultural spaces, in the sorts of conflict, struggle, and argument that they already negatively associated with the secular world. Part of the attraction of reconciliation processes was that they compelled participants to transcend ordinary (secular) ways of engaging race in favor of interactive modes that felt more satisfying and more natural to their cultural orientation. Interpreting these dynamics requires reviewing some of the intimate details, so to speak, of evangelical subcultures.

Here Lisa Wedeen's (2002) concept of culture as meaning-making practices can be parsed into its two constitutive components: meaning systems and practices. *Meaning systems* are idea sets socially exchanged through norms, lessons, symbols, and stories that convey specific kinds of meaning in cultural contexts. Below I focus on epistemological frameworks such as theology, religious doctrine, and notions of who is and isn't a part of the cultural community. *Practices* refer to activities that, while not necessarily identifiable through physical expression (for example, prayer can be internal and invisible), are repeated behaviors understood by participants in a culture as important to the goal(s) at hand.

Interwoven with both of these is a third factor that informs evangelical meaning-making practices, especially in racial change settings: ritual. Although ritual could reasonably be categorized as a subset of cultural practices, I separate it out in order to highlight how it mobilizes both meaning systems and practices through physical actions that require some form of culturally mediated interpretation. Lisa Schirch's understanding of rituals as "symbolic actions that communicate a forming or transforming message in a unique cultural space" is useful here (2005, 16–17). This definition of ritual helps us analyze how evangelical RR settings became epiphanal spaces capable of producing transformative experiences and allows us to identify how participants attempted to define the socially acceptable limits of their own activities.

Through a combination of theological framing, emerging spiritual conviction, and "hands-on" epiphanal experiences, reconcilers came to be convinced in visceral ways of the power of RR and committed to it, at least for a time. The opening stories of this chapter provide points of reference to exemplify these dynamics. I next review a set of defining aspects of evangelical religious culture that contextualized and facilitated the meaning systems and practices operative in RR settings. These include comprehensive community, biblical authority, a relational God, the Holy Spirit, evangelism, prayer, and testimony. I then identify a set of theological beliefs evangelical reconcilers consistently named as "guiding principles" motivating their desire to reconcile across race. Advocates constructed the RR framework such that reconciliation folds into a larger Christian mission in which all believers are called to participate. This working knowledge of the conceptual reconciliation framework then enables a discussion, in the last third of the chapter, of how three core practices common to reconciliation settings—admitting, trust-building, and apology-forgiveness rituals—facilitated epiphanal spaces that emphasized relationalism while sweeping more potentially political conversations under the rug.

For easier tracking, figure 3 lists four categories of meaning making most deeply influencing the character of RR efforts on the ground in the 1990s. The remaining chapters on ERC efforts in the 2000s build on familiarity with these categories.

The top two boxes in figure 3 list six conceptual systems and two practices common to American evangelical religious culture that influenced how RR settings functioned as distinctly epiphanal social spaces. These are elements I observed in the field, which interviewees frequently referenced when describing their experiences in RR settings, and which also appeared in first-person written accounts by evangelicals about RR. Reconcilers generally took most of these beliefs and behaviors for granted as part of the ordinary aspects of their religious world and often referenced them off-handedly when discussing racial change activities. Indeed, the fact that they felt "second nature" to participants was a good indicator of how culturally embedded they were. For outsiders, however, they require some translation. I provide brief descriptions to help establish the cultural context in which specifically reconciliation-related activities took place.

The bottom two boxes list meaning-making systems and practices evidenced specifically in RR processes. The four conceptual systems in the left box comprise the core elements of RR theology I observed during the 1990s fieldwork, and the three practices on the right the main steps that participants emphasized in interviews and in the live settings. In the 2000s, none of these disappeared in the multiethnic church–building settings I observed, but the emphasis often changed and other elements emerged as priorities, as we see in chapters 7–8.

Common Systems

The six common systems described below generate the concepts, norms, and beliefs that influence life in evangelical culture. Comprehensive communities provide a sense of togetherness, safety, and socialization while differentiating the religious community from "the world" outside. A common sacred text provides authoritative guidance and mechanisms for interpreting experiences and events. Personal spiritual experiences of "God's will" and the Holy Spirit context reinforce (at least ideally) the connection between believer and community while also reiterating the belief that the community has a special relationship to the divine. Each meaning system helps constitute RR settings as safe sacred spaces for believers—literal and conceptual spaces pregnant with spiritual possibilities and anointed by a God that works daily miracles in ordinary lives.

COMPREHENSIVE COMMUNITY   Something nonevangelicals might not realize is that to a degree rarely seen in other Protestant traditions, evangelical

FIGURE 3   Meaning-making among evangelical racial reconcilers

COMMON SYSTEMS
Comprehensive community
Biblical authority
Personal God
Anointing
Holy Spirit
Evangelism

COMMON PRACTICES
Prayer
Testimony

RECONCILIATION THEOLOGY
God-human and human-human relationships
Separation as sin
In-group reconciliation
Eschatology

RECONCILIATION PRACTICES
Admitting
Intentionality
Apology-forgiveness rituals

churches often serve as comprehensive arenas of community. Many contemporary churches pursue what sociologist Donald Miller (1997) called the "new paradigm" church model, in which a church offers enough wrap-around services for members to be around other believers any day of the week. This is typically true for large megachurches (with weekly attendance over 2,000), but many small evangelical churches also offer a menu of programs and ministries aimed to serve the "whole" Christian (Putnam 2000; Putnam, Feldstein, and Cohen 2003; Thumma and Travis 2007). Wrap-around services could include a church day care, school, and bookstore (some megachurches even have restaurants and theaters), but also Bible study groups, counseling and recovery services, finance classes, and programs for members' special interests (for example, motorcyclists, small business owners, and so forth) (Miller 1997, 138–140).

Comprehensive church communities can provide a sense of safety and normalization, reflecting and reinforcing members' religious beliefs through manifold socialization opportunities for all ages. Modes of religious expression accepted without justification or explanation, such as weeping or hollering during church services, comforting and being comforted by others, or praying aloud can flourish when community members don't have to defend or interpret such

activities to outsiders. Each of the reconciliation settings I visited attempted
to be comprehensive communities, despite having different levels of material
resources to accommodate programs and services.[2] The comprehensiveness
of evangelical church communities allowed believers to let their guard down
through spiritual and social immersion in their religious faith—all of which
helped foster environments in which participants could experience epiphanies.

BIBLICAL AUTHORITY   Among evangelicals, the Bible is the foremost source
of authority.[3] This was confirmed both in the monoethnic and multiethnic congregations I studied. Conservative evangelical Christians typically read from the
Bible more than two to three times per week and understand it as the inspired
word of God (Hunter 1987, 24).[4] Believers are taught to learn the text in its en-
tirety, read it regularly, and employ it as the primary source of guidance in all
aspects of life. To gain this knowledge, guided Bible study groups are almost a
prerequisite for membership in evangelical church communities and a common
form of socialization for new members (Roose 2009). Reconcilers I interviewed,
both pastors and laypersons, routinely recited biblical passages from memory
during their interviews.

Yet even while emphasizing literal interpretation of the Bible, evangelicals
maintain a dynamic relationship to scripture, regarding the text as a living document, a source of wisdom that provides direct insights on daily life. A common
refrain is that all truths are available in the Bible, and therefore all requisite guidance for living is revealed to diligent seekers of "God's *living* word." In this sense,
evangelicals' relationship to their sacred book sometimes seems to require a kind
of delicate balance: believers profess that every word has literal, permanently
relevant meaning, but also make use of the Bible like an oracle, a vehicle through
which God speaks authoritatively and directly to them.[5] In the reconciliation
context, evangelicals employed the Bible as the theological authority, but also
mined it for immediate guidance, inspiration, and direction. As the preeminent
textual authority in RR settings, the Bible provided an infinite source of spontaneous insights and fresh "discoveries" for believers about why and how they
should pursue racial healing.

THE PERSONAL GOD   Although the Bible is positioned as the dominant authority guiding evangelical life, believers' subjective experiences of God are also
granted a considerable measure of authority in evangelical culture. Evangelicals
passionately exemplify Protestantism's notion of a direct, unmediated relationship between individual believers and Jesus Christ or God. The personal experience of "God's will and direction" is so common in the daily speech practices of

believers as to constitute the primary narrative form evangelicals use to articulate their subject experience. When describing the most basic changes in one's life, believers use the language of personal experience with God. Examples are ubiquitous: "God laid it on my heart," "God was speaking to me through my wife," "I knew God had put us there for a reason." Such statements are so embedded in the discursive habits of evangelicals as to be rarely challenged by church members and leaders (at least in public, in my experience). So it was not especially unusual that when Father White perceived that God had spoken directly to both Colin Whitford and Cal Tompkins about raising money for Jubilee, he brought these men before the rest of the congregation to "manifest the work of God." Likewise, in Vanda's story, both her individual experiences of transformation and answered prayers and the collective experience of the group were subsequently read by the group as evidencing "God's work" in the context of racial healing.

An interview with Jim, a member of Redeemer Church, captures the language of personal and collective experiences of God's will, partly in answer to prayer. Note how he framed his epiphany as a *miraculous* outcome that could only have manifested through his pursuit, through prayer, of "God's will":

> [Before the raising of the Jubilee money] I was thinking more in a traditional, "yeah, we'll get our act together, we'll do something" [about race relations] kind of approach. But what happened here was quite literally an answer to a prayer from God; it was not anything any of us could have dreamt as a script. And the whole notion that when people pray it's a blessing to everybody they're praying for, was answered. Because if you look at the response of the church, three-quarters of the response comes from people who were not in [an earlier RR] class, had nothing to do with the class. But it still, from a spiritual point of view, was evidence—you know, it resonated that, the way we see it, there was a blessing to that congregation, that people's hearts were touched, people's eyes were opened, period.

Jubilee's pastor Darrell Brickson was likewise convinced God's hand directed the whole matter with Jubilee Baptist. "It's certainly divine intervention," he remarked, "in the sense of we could not have orchestrated that, we could not have planned it, we could not have put it together." Where secular people might frame momentous events in their lives in terms of "coincidence," "serendipity," or "fate" (or perhaps just good planning), evangelical Christians invariably testify to evidence of God's hand.

ANNOINTING   Related to evangelicals' experiences of a direct discourse with God is the notion of divine anointing—the idea that God has chosen to work through an individual or group in service to some divine goal. The term "anointing" may be used in numerous contexts: to acknowledge the talents and contributions of an individual ("God has anointed Mark to lead our youth ministry"); to reaffirm a decision ("we see evidence of God's anointing in John and Amy's work with our partners in Kenya"); to validate a new direction ("Charles has been called to found a new branch of the church"). The evidence of anointing may be revealed through prayer, through testimony (as a believer shares about the journey she or he has been on), through visions from leaders (especially pastors) granted a measure of authority in the community, and so forth.

Many racial reconcilers expressed that they, their church, or their organization had been given a special anointing by God to address racial issues within the Christian community. This was especially true for PK members, most of whom used the word "anointing" in their interviews. Raleigh Washington, the head of PK's RR division at the time of our interview, captured a common refrain:

> I believe that my calling and involvement in reconciliation is a calling that Almighty God gave me. I think it was a special measure of grace and favor. That measure of grace and favor and calling allows me to interact and to do battle on racial issues without becoming disjointed, angry, or out of proportion, and so that's a special measure of grace, I have a special measure of patience and endurance, and *passion* for dealing with it. . . .
>
> . . . God gives Promise Keepers favor to minister to anyone for reconciliation. There's nobody else out there who has the same measure of favor as we have to address this area of reconciliation. And so just the special favor, I feel that we have to address it.

Beyond the issue of specific anointings in the ministry of RR, there was a sense among evangelical reconcilers in the 1990s that whatever was happening in their lives related to reconciliation was a product of divine direction. Even people who worked tirelessly to build cross-racial relationships between churches attributed the success of that work to divine intervention.

HOLY SPIRIT   There is a thin line or a blending in evangelical culture between believers' direct experiences of God and the idea of the working of the "Holy Spirit." The Bible provides intellectual grounding for an evangelical's faith, but as believers describe it the Holy Spirit or the active presence of God-in-spirit propels that faith on more viscerally experiential levels. Some evangelical traditions such as Pentecostals and Charismatics and inter- or nondenominational communities (for example, most New Paradigm churches) integrate "*acts of the Spirit*" such as prophesy, glossolalia (speaking in tongues), and healings into their regular worship services, interpreting these as continuations of the first-century church at Pentecost (Miller 1997, 144–148). Others de-emphasize these practices, but still see "the Spirit" manifesting in a wide variety of ways. In believers' narratives, the Holy Spirit is identified as the force that allows one to hear "God's will" for his or her life. It provides conviction and inspiration, generates energy, activates healing, and manifests miracles (144–148). Witnesses to Vanda's story and the Jubilee-Redeemer relationship alike described those events as evidence of the miracle-working presence of the Holy Spirit.

EVANGELISM   The sixth common meaning-making system that sculpted evangelical reconciliation efforts is the concept of spiritual salvation. Evangelicals ascribe to the idea of substitutionary atonement, the belief that Jesus Christ was the son of God, sacrificed on the cross in order to reconcile a disobedient humanity to God by atoning for human sin and thereby bringing eternal salvation to believers in Christ. (We'll shortly see how this concept of Christ's reconciliation deeply informs RR theology.) Salvation through Christ is a central tenet of all Christian theology, but evangelicals place an especially strong emphasis on the command from Matthew 28:19–20 to proselytize: "Go therefore and make disciples of all the nations, baptizing them in the name of the Father and the Son and the Holy Spirit, teaching them to observe all that I commanded you."[6] Evangelicals believe that all Christians are compelled, like the first-century apostles, to "spread the Good News" to others, regardless of others' cultural or religious traditions, in order to save their souls from eternal damnation, which is hell. Proselytization, then, is seen as a spiritual directive and a gift of love, because through it nonbelievers might be "saved." Evangelical communities, including all those represented in my fieldwork, employ a variety of mechanisms for reaching out to the unsaved, facilitating conversion, and educating the new believer in the tenets of the faith.

But even when proselytization is not the focus (as in RR settings), the centrality of salvation theology in evangelicalism promotes a Christian/non-Christian dichotomy that suffuses evangelical speech. The experience of being a Christian among non-Christians and trying to influence others to Christianity is a regular part of life for most evangelical believers. In this meaning framework, nonbelievers tend to be regarded with a heady mix of suspicion and interest. Believers are trained to fortify their own faith so that they might be better witnesses without succumbing to the world's temptations. They are also warned of the grave responsibility to make Christianity vital enough to persuade others—especially believers' own loved ones—thereby rescuing them from permanent misery outside of salvation. Discursively, the unconverted soul is a constant presence in conservative evangelical settings—a reminder that some "walk with God" and others don't; some will be with God in heaven while others will not because their "hearts were closed."

To some degree the salvation paradigm restrains reconciliation efforts, because evangelical reconcilers often assert that non-Christians possess neither the spiritual resources nor the motivation for pursuing reconciliation. On the other hand, as I will elaborate, evangelical reconcilers framed RR itself as an important means to increase the Christian community's credibility and thereby facilitate proselytization.

Common Practices

Next I turn to prayer and testimony, two common cultural practices within evangelicalism that serve to fortify the broad meaning-making systems I have reviewed.

PRAYER   As in many religious traditions, prayer is understood as a communication or spiritual communion (sense of connectedness) between the believer and God. However, due to evangelicalism's understanding of a relational God, prayer serves an especially active role in the culture. Prayer is seen to forge and sustain not only the bond between the believer and the divine but also relationships between believers, and bonds to the larger religious community. While prayer does bookend formal moments (for example, ceremonies, sermons, special events), believers are also taught to apply prayer to all aspects of their daily lives and to pray for one another openly, intimately, and at any given moment of pain, joy, or need.

As a ritual practice in the evangelical context, prayer requires some contextualization. Here I find helpful David Kertzer's definition of ritual as "action wrapped in a web of symbolism" (Schirch 2005, 16). As Lisa Schirch elaborates, symbolic acts are physical actions that are not directly decipherable, as opening a door to exit or enter a room would be decipherable, but require interpretation. The message in a symbolic act depends on a web of myths, metaphors, and symbols "that can convey multiple, ambiguous messages to different people" (17). So when people bow their heads, close their eyes, retreat into silence, or do some of these while speaking aloud or holding hands, such activity, while familiar to many kinds of religious practitioners, would not be universally and automatically interpreted in all cultures or contexts as prayer. Rituals often (though not always) take place in unique spaces, are set off from everyday life, and "aim to form (build) or transform (change) people's worldviews, identities and relationships" (17). *Formative* rituals, in Schirch's terms, reiterate a social status quo in one or more of the aforementioned realms, whereas *transformative* rituals aim

toward change. Prayer in evangelical culture can serve both formative and transformative functions.

Consider the following comment from a PK staffer in the late 1990s, explaining the importance of building cross-racial relationships among pastors:

> I'm suggesting that to start the ball rolling, you need to go beyond your comfort
> zone and start to establish some relationship with another pastor or pastors of a
> different group, and one of the things we say is "start in prayer." Because I believe,
> personally, that you can know a person by the way they pray, and as we begin to pray
> together and we begin to depend on each other for God to speak to us together, then
> that changes our perspective. So pray together, interact, communicate. *Then* start
> programs, then start events—but the relationship needs to drive the events, not the
> other way around, see.

This statement captures both the socializing (formative) function of prayer and
the potentially transformative uses of it in evangelical culture. Prayer is read by
this reconciler as simultaneously so ordinary that each participant can be assumed to know how to do it; a vehicle for getting to know someone else, building
a bond, and (indirectly) communicating; and a channel for the transformational
workings of God.

The stories presented earlier indicate how deeply prayer is integrated in
evangelical culture. In the moment of Vanda's spoken pain, prayer played a transformative function for the reconciliation workshop by facilitating a socially safe,
epiphanal space. As a collective response both orchestrated by the workshop
leaders and automatic to participants, prayer facilitated an immediate outpouring of compassion and love, which people may not have been able to express had
the topic of Vanda's rape arisen in a different way. Through prayer, people in the
room, regardless of race or gender, could express identification with their fellow
believer by addressing God rather than Vanda directly. They thereby held Vanda
up for specific, immediate healing without asking questions or reacting in a way
that required an immediate response from her. Also in the way he guided the
group prayer, Bob was able to direct the collective mindset toward a spontaneous
healing without claiming to embody the role of healer himself.[7] Vanda's subsequent testimony about the healing enabled participants to see her transformation as a direct result of that collective prayer intervention, thereby creating a
new testimony for every individual who had been present at the event.

TESTIMONY   Testimony—when a believer shares with others some element
of his or her personal experience as a Christian—is another core practice with
ritual elements. Testimony anchors the practice of prayer and folds into the

command to evangelize by "testifying" to the power of the Christian message and experience. We might think of testimonies as a cultural mode of storytelling that believers may practice within and/or beyond the boundaries of Christian community. Although testimonies are often verbal, many evangelicals are taught from a young age to write out their faith testimony, particularly their story of "getting saved," and to practice sharing it with others. The recording and retelling of such conversion testimonies serves as a particularly important vehicle for (re)commitment for those believers who converted as adults or after a "fallen" or "sinful" period.

Testimonies in evangelicalism tend to have a common arc. Believers attest to some aspect of the power of God in their lives. God is represented as a force that pulls believers through the darkest times, helps them overcome obstacles they believe they could not otherwise have surmounted, and generally works miracles. Through testimony, believers often describe a darkness they were in prior to the spiritual intervention, and corroborate fellow believers' experiences of being touched and guided by a (or "the") living God. Believers also employ testimony to confess personal shortcomings and doubts, to speak about where they may have fallen short and require support or encouragement. As a cultural practice, testimony is a formative, socializing ritual. Indeed, it is perhaps the great *reinforcer* of evangelical belief, and therefore part of the lifeblood of evangelical cultural practice. Testimony also entails a potentially transformative element, as one might feel changed by the act of telling one's story before others.

The RR experience is typically framed by personal testimonies large and small. Vanda's story involved two: her admission of being raped and of her subsequent feeling of hatred toward white people (a testimony of hurt); and her story of personal healing in the days after the group ritual—which she described in epiphanal terms as God's intervention. Likewise, after the initial Jubilee-Redeemer "miracle" of the fund-raising, testimony from those involved became a major means through which members of both churches asserted that God was working in their midst and that cross-racial relationships needed to be further nurtured between these two communities. The practice of testimony becomes an important channel for other practices at the heart of RR, especially admitting, apology, and forgiveness rituals.

Reconciliation Theology

The theological framework of RR does not stand apart but rather draws its emphasis and character from the aforementioned systems and practices embedded in evangelical culture. Selecting a particular set of theological elements from a complex field of possibilities evident in reconciliation efforts involves some interpretive effort. I focus on four areas of conviction that most frequently, visibly, and/or passionately emerged as foundational in the narratives of interviewees, as evidenced in interview transcripts and in groups. So as not to clutter the presentation of these beliefs with too many of the scriptural references that undergird them (references that reconcilers cite routinely), I present them in layperson's terms and, where possible, in the direct language of reconcilers. They are the ideas of the proper God-human and human-human relationships; separation as sin; reconciliation as a *uniquely* Christian incentive; and reconciliation eschatology.

GOD-HUMAN AND HUMAN-HUMAN RELATIONSHIPS   When asked why they advocated RR, participants in the 1990s (and in later iterations of the racial change movement discussed later) most often answered by employing two New Testament Christian commandments. These are, as one reconciler put it, to "love God with all our heart, mind, and soul," and to "love our neighbor, regardless of race, creed or color, as ourselves." Reconcilers largely interpreted obeisance to both commands as central to being a Christian. In the words of one Latino PK staffer, "If everybody who called themselves a Christian lived out the two basic commandments . . . there would be no need for affirmative action. . . . But because the Christian community is not incarnating [them], I question if any minority would ever have a fair shake."

Many also explained these commands through the Christian cross metaphor. Here the vertical axis of the sacrificial cross represents the proper God-human relationship, and the horizontal axis the proper human-human relationship that should result from belief in and love of Christ. As an African American PK leader described it:

> To love our neighbor as ourselves means we give preference on them. To love our neighbor as ourselves means we consider the needs of our neighbors more important than ourselves. To live out the principle of reconciliation from a biblical point of view, then, I must sacrifice my own desires and give preference to the desires of my neighbor. . . . So the Christian principle, the DNA for a Christian, what a Christian is supposed to be from his biblical principles, makes him a subject to be a reconciler and an influencer. So God is saying my love for Him is validated primarily by how I demonstrate it in loving other people—white people, brown people, red people, yellow people, different people.

In religious terms, then, racial reconcilers articulated reconciliation as the proper, loving relationship among humans and between humans and God as a result of Christians' commitment to follow Christ's command to love one another.

SEPARATION AS SIN   Reconcilers routinely cited teachings of the first-century Christian apostles as the primary biblical examples of how to reconcile across traditionally impenetrable boundaries. (These theological arguments become more sophisticated in the multiracial church–building context of the 2000s.) Early apostolic missions aimed to secure the unification of Christians across the cultural divides that prevailed at the time—especially the ethnic Jew/Gentile boundary. "The Bible says clearly that Christ destroyed the wall of division between us," explained Jorge, a Latino PK reconciliation leader. "He says in Ephesians, there is now no Greek, there's no Jew, there's no male, no female—across the board. So he's saying, in essence, that when Christ died he did not only atone for a reconcilement to God, but he also reconciled us to each other. It's the cross experience."[8] Thus, Christians need to reconcile themselves to Jesus (again, addressing the vertical relationship) in order to reconcile with their fellow humans (correcting the horizontal relationship). In other words, reconcilers perceived RR as an explicitly Christian project. As one white pastor reflected, "It's interesting: Paul's closest churches were cross-racial; they were Greeks, the church of Philippi, and yet we [white Christians] never piece that together." Joseph and Bob's RR course focused heavily on the stories of how Paul and the early Christians worked to break down formidable cultural walls and radically challenge tradition through a new unity.[9]

Within this interpretation, the specter of human sin perpetually haunts the biblical call to reconciliation. As several interviewees explained, breaches of either the vertical or the horizontal relationship result from sin. And in evangelical meaning systems, sin both expresses and engenders separation; indeed, separation constitutes a "state of sin." Thus, when one relational dimension is breached, damage is done to the other. Said one pastor:

> The antithesis of reconciliation is separation, and that's *sin*, so we've [Christians] been living in a state of sin because we have been separated from each other—to which God says you are ambassadors of my desire to have people reconciled, you see. Now, when we [stray from] this, that vertical relationship is impaired. If we have a relationship with God that is authentic and affirming, then we will be reconciled as a people of God.[10]

Another dimension of the sin-as-separation concept is the notion that there can be no "true" reconciliation between *any* people outside of a God-human relationship. Most reconcilers made this explicit in interviews by differentiating their (Christian) perspective from what they saw as non-Christian or secular orientations. For example:

So people who don't understand the spiritual implication of reconciliation are not going to see it in that light, they're going to see it from a strictly humanistic, human plane. Most people want to use terms like "integration." Most people want to use terms like "unity"—to quote Ol' Rodney King, "why can't we all just get along?" Well, the problem with that is that if you exclude the vertical and try to develop the horizontal, you'll have a thwarted cross, and Christ didn't die on a thwarted cross. If one of those [is] off, something else is going to be off. If my relationship with God is off, then my relationship with man is going to be off. If my relationship with man is off, then my relationship with [God] is going to be off. Reconciliation, as I said, is a spiritual journey; it cannot be legislated.[11]

Two concepts are expressed here: the exclusivist idea that non-Christians never have the proper incentives or spiritual resources to pursue "true" reconciliation; and the concurrent assumption that secular approaches (here, "legislation") to RR are inherently inadequate *because* they are not driven by the Christian perspective.[12]

The construct of the cross metaphor of relationship contributes to one of the richest conceptual chords running through the RR narrative: the idea that racism, both inside and outside Christian communities, is fundamentally a problem of the heart. As the RR refrain often went, "racism is a *sin* problem, not a social problem." (Or the variant, "racism is a sin problem, not a skin problem.") This construction designates a social problem as something society, and particularly government, attempts to redress through programs or legislation—a problem the answer to which is sought outside of individuals and their relationship with God. As one white interviewee put it:

I guess the way of analyzing the validity of the definitions is if [racism] was a social problem, purely a matter of structure or money or whatever, then we would be making progress. But the fact of the matter is that the sociopolitical efforts to solve the problem have had as many negative fruits as positive, and some would say even more negative, because you have a level of dependency that did not exist forty years ago.

As I discuss in chapter 6, most racial reconcilers in the 1990s were disinclined to frame racism as a social problem because, as they continually emphasized, programmatic or governmental responses to racism would always fail by virtue of their incapacity to address the underlying sin problem. The speaker above, a Yale- and Berkeley-educated lawyer from Redeemer Church, critiqued what he called a leftist "power and privilege" analysis of racism, "because it excludes the spiritual element. . . . Really, reconciliation involves both people taking personal responsibility before God for their own state of mind and their own actions." In other words, to "get right on race," people need to overcome sin and correct their relationships with God (the assumption being that the racial sins are equivalent on all sides). Only then will they be able to address the flaws in their relationships with other individuals and groups of people.

In-Group Reconciliation   The theological articulations of RR among evangelicals depended on the exclusivist conceptual system referred to earlier: the idea that non-Christians can't grasp reconciliation without embracing substitutionary atonement. Not only were non-Christians understood to lack any incentive to reconcile across racial or other divisions without a belief in Christ-as-reconciler of humanity, but even if non-Christians desired to pursue reconciliation, reconcilers assumed they lacked access to the spiritual resources that propelled such efforts. A white member of Jubilee explained it thus:

> We [Christians] do have something different and that's why we're able to do this, because my relationship with Christ affects my relationship with every single person that I come into contact with. . . . And so without that relationship with him I don't know how it could happen on a real level.
>
>   . . . The world is full of sin and I think that when you're outside of a relationship with Christ, your relationship to other people is really different and a lot of those opposites of the fruit of the spirit won't allow you to reconcile with any people, I don't think. Because there's hate and jealousy and that competitive drive of pushing other people down and those kind of things. I think—I hope—you have that on a greater scale outside the church than you do within.

Gary, a white PK staffer, argued that non-Christians aren't faced with the command to reconcile:

> [If] I consider God to be my Father, I have no options, obedience is required. . . . But the average white suburbanite on the street, if he doesn't have any Godly perspective and any Godly obedience as part of his life, hey, you're penetrating his comfort zone, he doesn't like it, why should he get involved? . . . [For the non-Christian] there's no reason for them to stretch themselves.

With the exception of one reconciler I met who believed other religious groups did have theological incentives to reconcile, most reconcilers regarded reconciliation itself as a distinctively Christian concept.

Again, the flipside of Christian exclusivism in the reconciliation context was the notion that Christians needed to become a community unified across racial and ethnic divisions *in order* to influence non-Christians to convert. Black PK leader Raleigh Washington explained:

> If I love my neighbor, I want my neighbor to know that I believe I'm going to live eternally, so I want to try to show him what I believe and why, and have him consider it. But also, I have a mandate to live as one with my neighbor, especially if he is a believer. So, as a Christian, I am concerned about my community, but not as much as I'm concerned about my church and my Christian community, because I'm under a mandate [by] God as a Christian to be at one with all other believers. Now, if the church was truly the church, if the church looked like the church, if the church looked like the face of our population, if the church was a diverse body standing arm and arm, if it said "we are one"—if that happens, then the world will look at the church and say, "they got it." [Laughs.] Huh? *That's* the answer, and we would influence the world.

Through this somewhat circular logic, Washington expressed a refrain often expressed by 1990s reconcilers: becoming a model of a racially reconciled community would help Christians attract new adherents by illustrating the uniqueness of Christianity to facilitate harmony.

ESCHATOLOGY   The fourth element of reconciliation theology expressed by 1990s reconcilers builds on the three concepts described above.[13] Drawing upon the ideas of the cross metaphor of Christian reconciliation, the potential of human sin to violate that relational ideal, and the uniqueness of a Christian framework to facilitate reconciliation, many reconcilers interviewed cast RR in an "End Times" (eschatological) context. RR at that particular historical moment, many claimed, was part of a divinely guided imperative to gather Christians into a cohesive community in anticipation of the Second Coming of Christ and God's impending judgment on the unbelieving world. Reconcilers frequently cast their work within an understanding that they were living in the "Last Days," a biblically prophesied millennial era marked by global disasters, geopolitical breakdown, final battles between good and evil, the rapture of believers, and the return of Christ (not necessarily in that order).[14]

Reconcilers expressed two streams of eschatological thought, which sometimes existed in tension (simultaneously) within individual narratives. Both streams held that the phenomenon of RR among evangelicals was part of "God's plan" to attract more souls to Christianity before the final judgment. The more optimistic *revivalist* stream asserted that as the world becomes more sin-saturated and volatile, Christians begin to unify across former divisions and thereby become magnets for accelerated soul-saving and revival. The more foreboding *apocalyptic* stream expressed the belief that in the End Times political systems would break down, racial and ethnic conflicts would escalate into increasing violence, Christians would be persecuted, and God would judge the church for falling short of biblical commands to be reconciled. Both streams read RR as a direct product of "God's timing."

Through the revivalist lens, racial reconcilers expressed excitement that they were living in a difficult but miraculous era and that RR folded into God's ultimate plan for saving souls. PK hewed to this orientation, and in the late 1990s promoted a plan called Project 2000, designed to coordinate and inspire a massive "coming out" of Christians. As one African American reconciler explained:

> Our vision 2000, is for, really, the Body, the Christian Body, for that one day to be visible, to come out from behind our doors and to be visible for the whole world. I think we're headed into spiritual warfare like we've never seen before because we're calling the church from around the country, not just from one location. . . . I mean, I know for sure the world will watch what the Lord will do.

Consistent with the "spiritual warfare" framework, revivalist reconcilers tended to read RR as a powerful tool in the arsenal of winning converts in an escalating war among faiths. In this framing, the influence of Christians in political arenas is important because Christian visibility is assumed to challenge an increasingly immoral world and attract adherents. Here RR is understood as fueling forms of Christian influence not achieved in previous revivals:

> I'm of the faith that there is a rapture of the church that's coming and that it's coming soon, so because of God's timing, because of God's nature, and the need to deal with some of these things before he comes—that's why it's happening now. That's why it's not just happening in this country; that's why it's going to be a force in the world.
>
> . . . To a certain degree, what Promise Keepers is, is not the only but a tool that God is using to cause a great stir in men, and if we don't break through with racial reconciliation, we're going to miss it here too![15]

The revivalist stream paid special attention to the influence of "Generation Xers" (people born between 1961 and 1981), who capitalize on the increasing cultural boundarylessness to cross divisions that had flummoxed Christians in the past. Gen Xers, revivalists argued, would help usher in the racially reconciled Christian community.

The concept of "God's [ideal] timing" for RR in the 1990s rested a bit uneasily alongside the equally persistent claim that willful human *sin* has kept Christians from reconciling before now. Reconcilers vacillated on this issue without seeing their accounts as inconsistent. On the one hand, they read the historical perpetuation of racial divisions by Christians as an obvious sin. On the other, most reconcilers were convinced that the impulse to reconcile in their lifetime as opposed to in earlier generations was clearly a part of God's plan; if God had needed it to happen earlier, the logic went, he certainly could have arranged it. Thus, through the evangelical cultural lens in which all events are a product of God's hand, or at least occurring under an all-knowing God's gaze, the idea that RR was a product of God's specific timing made sense.

The apocalyptic stream also articulated a concept of God's timing, but in more cataclysmic, retributive, and politically ambivalent tones. During the Last Days (the confirmation of which people saw in current events), the narrative went, Satan has a wider reign and the world becomes increasingly wicked. Secular systems like government cater to sinful behavior, and social structures fail to effectively curb the chaos that unfolds on local, national, and global levels. Cultural divisions play into Satan's strategy of wreaking havoc in the world, and this is reflected among Christians as well. Part of the proof of the Last Days will be heightened racial explosion—"wars and rumors of wars"—against which secular systems fail. Meanwhile, Christians will be increasingly persecuted:

> The Bible tells us things are gonna get worse. They may get better for a period, but as we get closer to the end of the age, they will get worse, and much worse, and much worse. Therefore, the political structure, the political solution, will not work, because the definition of great evil are those world systems that are in place, that will persecute the church and the believers in all forms, so whether it's pro-life, or whether it's racial reconciliation, whether it's the basic foundational ability of the church to gather—those things will all be persecuted by the government, and no matter how much we protest, it says it only gets worse and the age of the martyrs will be upon us for those who would die for what they believe, for what they value.[16]

In response to the coming storm, these Christian martyrs, the account went, will have to increasingly separate from the world in order to fortify their faith community in the face of the ultimate persecution.

Martyrs, though, are not inured from divine retribution. Tied to the apocalyptic narrative was the anxiety that during or after his return, God will judge the church for the places it has fallen short of his commands. Even a reconciler who spoke in optimistic revivalist terms about the likeliness of converting more souls during the End Times period veered into a cataclysmic narrative about RR being linked to divine judgment (or deflection of it): "God says winning [souls] comes before destruction, and I sincerely believe with every fiber of my being that we're headed for God's judgment because of what we've done, and I think [reconciliation] is God's attempt to save us before that happens to us." Here again, RR was identified as part of a last-ditch chance for Christians to "get themselves together" in order to influence the world before it's too late.

Within the apocalyptic narrative, however, most reconcilers seemed unclear about where the reconciling church would be situated relative to sinful secular systems. One Latino reconciler suggested the church would move into politics and government:

> The church, who [sic] is supposed to be His church, that is supposed to be pure and white and without mark, is not in the place it should be, so [reconciliation is] forcing the issue and it's crossing barriers. So it's going into politics, it's going into governments, so we're going into other countries because of that preferred time schedule that God has.

By "going into politics," this reconciler suggested occupying elective office and serving visibly as Christian citizens. Another, however, cast the church as culpable for the nation's sins as a whole, due to being both too sinfully invisible to and entwined with the secular world:

> When does judgment come? When does revival come? . . . Who am I to say? But I do know this: that the church of Jesus Christ—I feel strongly about this—the body of Christ is largely to blame for the condition we see our country in today. Because we have not been salt, we have not been light, we have not stood for the truth of God's word. We have been lethargic, we have been materialistic, we have gotten in bed with the world. And we have all these crystal cathedrals and things like this, which just flies in the face of who Jesus was. We have not been what we should have been and there is no health in us, we are disease-riddled. I think [reconciliation trends] are the kind of things we see that are the beginning of restoration, wholeness.[17]

This notion of God's judgment of the church (in this case for sinful errors like racism and other forms of separation) repeats the time-worn evangelical rhetorical ritual of the "jeremiad" (Bercovitch 1978; Howard-Pitney 2005). Jeremiadic rhetoric entails a guilty lament about a community with a contractual relationship with God (here, Christians) having strayed and needing to correct its own shortcomings in the face of the punishment of a father figure who has laid the terms of right and wrong in his word. This darker eschatological stream maintained that evangelicals are compelled to enact RR under the threat of judgment from God for their collective sin.

Through this theological framework of RR, reconcilers in the 1990s made meaning of the work they were doing and why it mattered. Because RR discourse built on concepts central to evangelical Christianity—the idea of the cross, of sin as an obstacle, of Christians having a special gift for the world, and of impending final days—reconcilers believed that much, indeed the very destiny of the world, depended on their efforts. This also meant, at least for some, that apathy toward RR came with a frightening cost—the possibility of engendering divine punishment on the Christian community. By emphasizing both spiritual urgency and biblical importance, reconciliation theology helped construct RR efforts as high-priority initiatives capable of simultaneously transforming Christians as a community and facilitating the conversion of others. Tethered to the meaning-making systems and practices already ingrained in evangelicalism, theological frames gave conceptual force to RR efforts as epiphanal, miracle-working spaces.

Practicing Racial Reconciliation

In this final section, I turn to the three central practices around which on-the-ground RR efforts in the 1990s seemed to revolve: admitting, intentionality, and apology-forgiveness rituals.[18] Each of these was conceived of as reparative, and each informed how RR processes were understood as distinctly relational, rather than political. Through these core practices participants experienced the personal and collective epiphanies that infused RR efforts with meaning and power. Those practices, in turn, drew their significance and power from the cultural vocabulary, practices, and theological frameworks I have so far described as being intrinsic to the conservative evangelical worldview.

Admitting   In workshops, "how-to" manuals, written testimonials about RR efforts by church leaders, and interviews with reconcilers, admitting participation in the "sin" of racism was consistently identified as a first heart-opening step on the path to RR. To put it in evangelical parlance, admitting is the moment in which God presses something so clearly on the believer's heart that she or he can no longer avoid it and must directly acknowledge its presence. Admitting could come in the form of acknowledging (to oneself, God, or other Christians) personal race-based prejudices or misdeeds; contributions to historical injustices by individuals or groups; racial or ethnic insularity; or simply benefiting from race privilege in a way that perpetuates it. The admitting framework drew from core meaning-making practices in evangelicalism, especially the narrative form of testimony and the concept of sin as an obstacle to human and divine relationships. Such practices reinforce admitting as a prerequisite to "getting right with God."

The RR course offered for members of Jubilee and Redeemer churches exemplified what admitting often looked like in RR settings. Because admitting was framed as a first step in an RR process, public admissions were encouraged, and participants may have even felt some pressure to confess subscribing to divisive racial attitudes. One striking feature of the admitting emphasis, from a secular standpoint, was that it continually encouraged people of color, not just whites, to confess their own contributions to the reinforcement of racial isolation within the Christian community. For instance, the first lesson from the course materials packet defined racism as "an attitude of superiority, that your race is superior to any other." While this message was delivered with an obvious thrust toward white racism, the workshop facilitators, Joseph and Bob, used daily examples to illustrate how people of color could also be guilty of racism. In one lecture Bob interrogated himself for his own assumptions that a black man should naturally win a neighborhood slam-dunking contest he attended. (In fact, the only white contestant won.) "The spirit of racism is showing favoritism based on race alone," he read from the workshop materials. Then, quoting the Bible: "But 'if you show favoritism, you sin and are convicted by the law as lawbreakers.'"[19] Many reconcilers said admitting that favoritism was applicable to members of both sides of a racial boundary was a requirement for reconciliation.

As Vanda's story illustrates, hearing the testimony of a member of another racial group could often facilitate an outpouring of admitting in RR settings. This is partly because admitting is so deeply socialized as a formative ritual in evangelical culture. In small-group discussion, I watched participants demonstrate great enthusiasm about admitting ways in which they realized they perpetuated race favoritism. In one exercise called "The Need for Accountability," people in the RR course were asked to consider the question of interracial marriage applied to *their* immediate families. In my small group, this led to a discussion of the rationale cited by both blacks and whites to justify discouraging their children from interracial dating. When the large group reconvened, a lively discussion occurred. Several people expressed resistance to interracial dating, yet by the end of the discussion came to "admit" that (with the expressed provision that both the child and the suitor were Christians) such attitudes exhibited racial favoritism and were therefore sinful. One white man, after using the discussion to process the scope of his feelings before the group, made a fairly prominent display of confessing that he had been "blind" and thanked the group for bringing his unconscious prejudice to his attention.

The fact that in RR settings admitting was understood as a multisided act—something in which both whites and people of color could and should participate—was not accepted without some tension. Participants of color in interviews noted whites' trouble recognizing how they or their organizations perpetuate racism, and—since white racism was at the core of the church's racial divisions—bristled at the idea that people of color had as much to admit. As Sammy, a Latino Promise Keeper, put it, white Christians are often "in denial: 'it's not a problem—my uncle did it, my father did it, but I don't do it.'" Yet a breath later, he turned the admitting lens back on his own family. His South Texan father was, he said, "very racist against whites," and Sammy's Anglo wife experienced some very direct racism from Mexican Americans when they visited his hometown. Sammy described admitting dialogues as an important process that helped him resist replicating his own inherited racial resentments.

For many reconcilers, the act of admitting produced powerful epiphanal moments. For prominent white reconciler and author Tom Tarrants, who was an active Ku Klux Klan member in the 1960s, it was the moment in prison when, while reading the Bible, he realized that his virulent racism stemmed from a deep need for peer approval (Mitchell 1998). For white reconcilers I met, it was the point at which they realized that racism did reside somewhere in their hearts or that they had never reached out to a person of another color. Many Christians of color named the admitting moment as the point when they decided that their hatred, anger, or resentment toward whites was strong enough to constitute a sin and needed to be relinquished in order to "act from love."

Part of the epiphanal power of admitting came through a dynamic that may seem truly foreign to outsiders. Admitting rituals in evangelicalism function more catalytically than analytically. In other words, in RR settings, admitting was conceived as an act that sets a process in motion, rather than an occasion to pause and investigate larger social questions about *why*. (At any rate, the evangelical response to "why racism?" tended to generate the umbrella answer for every violation or shortcoming: "because of sin." When sin is at issue, further investigation seems beside the point.) As a social behavior, then, admitting essentially discouraged political conversations about race, because the emphasis on naming *attitudes and behaviors* in order to "move beyond them" circumvented reflective discussions of, much less arguments about, broader institutional patterns and political outcomes that resulted from or perpetuated racism.

Put another way, admitting individual sins or even one's negative racial inheritance is not the same as investigating how racial sins have impacted some groups far more negatively than others, or how institutional and structural racism works to reproduce and magnify the effect of individual attitudes. Because admitting functioned through a cathartic *spiritual* rather than analytical frame, reconcilers admitted with the aim of acknowledging a sin and then proceeding onward toward reconciliation and redemption. That process fostered a strong forward momentum that continually repressed cognitive reflection, inquiry, and open conversations about power and politics.

INTENTIONALITY   In the 1990s, racial division in the evangelical Christian community was generally conceived as a by-product of broken trust between individuals and groups as a result of "sins" like prejudice, un-Christian behavior, and conscious or unconscious racial separation.[20] RR settings and literature promoted admitting as a step toward building or repairing trust. Rituals of apology/forgiveness and the pursuit of cross-racial relationships were encouraged as even more meaningful efforts toward trust-building. But in between and across these steps was the important concept of intentionality. Under the principle of intentionality, reconcilers were instructed to listen to God's direction in their lives for reconciliatory possibilities (again, note the relational God concept) and then work toward manifesting those possibilities in conscious, effortful ways.

In a PK workbook on reconciliation written by Raleigh Washington and Glen Kehrein, his white ministry partner in a multiracial church, the principle of intentionality occupied an entire lesson and a critical step in a small-group reconciliation process. A graphic inset affirmed for reconciling men that "experiencing a committed relationship with my brothers requires purposeful, positive, and planned activities that facilitate reconciliation" (Washington, Kehrein, and King 1997, 89). This is because "developing a committed relationship with someone of a different race or denomination in the body of Christ does not happen by accident" (89). Such intentionality, the manual explained, cannot be simply a product of human effort, but rather a "God-centered" act of faith:

> Many people may try to be intentional about relationships. But in their human
> strength and wisdom, they won't accomplish lasting, Godlike results. Unless you
> stay related to Jesus so He can work through you, you'll be able to accomplish nothing of kingdom value. For intentionality to be fruitful as God intends, it must be
> God-centered. Then God the Father gets glory for what results. (92)

In sum, as the workbook put it, "If reconciliation and unity were a train, intentionality would be the engine" (93). Consistent with evangelical beliefs about the role of the Holy Spirit, the workbook offered examples of well-meaning but too self-reliant, too self-satisfied, or too secular attempts at developing relationships, versus efforts that are inspired by God and "give God the glory."

Examples of intentionality included planning activities to bring different people together (even if it is simply making friends with one person from another background), and leaving one's individual "comfort zone" to venture beyond his ordinary boundaries. Colin Whitford's effort to help raise the $30,000 for Jubilee Church fit perfectly into the framework of intentionality, as did the friendship he and Gregory Fields eventually developed from their initial meeting. Meeting Fields presented Whitford with an opportunity that his attendance at PK rallies had encouraged him to seek: a chance to *intentionally* step out of his comfort zone and befriend the black Christian brother. Fields, too, described making an intentional decision to build his first close friendship with a white man despite whatever reservations he may have had.

In interviews, whites tended to express the notion of intentionality in terms of cultivating equal relationships with people of color. Reconcilers of color also emphasized relationship but connected it to other goals like fostering substantive organizational changes. Many reported keeping a lookout for evidence that whites were serious through the choices they made "on the ground" at the relational level. From this vantage point, intentionality cut in both directions: institutional changes risked being superficial without relationships grounding them, and true cross-racial relationships should lead to institutional changes. César, a Latino leader from PK, linked intentionality to action and action to trust, as did other Christians of color in the RR movement:

> When you're a minority, you know when people blow smoke. You know when people communicate good intentions, and good intentions aren't enough. I've learned to give people the benefit of the doubt, but I'm also cautiously optimistic and say, "Okay, I want to see you walk the talk. You're claiming this, you're professing this, but in time I want to see what intentional things will you do to shake up your board of directors, your leadership, your staff. That's where you begin to really tell me if you're serious about this." Because every minority's going to be looking at those things. You know, "talk is cheap" is one of the things that we say a lot. Talk is cheap. Don't blow smoke. Don't communicate good intentions; I want to see the intentionality lived out and incarnated—that's what we're going to be looking at, we're going to judge you on that.

Intentionality was consistently described by reconcilers of color as what propels tangible, proactive commitments to working for reconciliation on levels that extend beyond individual relationships (which are hard enough) to church, organizational, and community relationships.

In 1990s RR settings, the dedicational thrust of intentionality followed quickly on the heels of the cathartic act of admitting. The emphasis on admitting drew from the confessional vocabularies of sin and testimony, while intentionality tapped into evangelical emphases on long-term commitment, listening to God's will, and piety. Both admitting and intentionality ushered reconcilers toward the truly epiphanal steps of offering authentic apology and/or generous forgiveness.

APOLOGY-FORGIVENESS RITUALS   Easily the most dramatic reconciliatory rituals at the local community level were the enactments of apology, repentance, and forgiveness between ordinary people trying to address racial divisions through their spiritual frameworks. Expressions of apology went a good step be-yond admitting a sin to lamenting and seeking forgiveness of it. On the receiving side, extending forgiveness to someone willing to "own" a negative racial belief or behavior drew equally cathartic emotions from RR participants. Both as-pects of apology-forgiveness dialogues drew deeply from the well of evangelical meaning-making practices and thereby reinscribed the relational paradigm of racial change promoted by evangelical reconcilers. By facilitating the release of painful race-related emotions like guilt, anger, resentment, and sorrow, apology-forgiveness rituals privileged epiphanal spaces of spontaneous "healing" over the uncomfortable alternatives of sustained discussion, conflict, or debate.

Given the functions of a sin- and salvation-oriented worldview, testimony as a narrative ritual describing a believer's evolving "walk with God," eschatological beliefs about Christians' need for unity, and emphases on admitting shortcom-ings, apology-forgiveness rituals were almost, but not quite, second nature to evangelicals participating in them. Even if participants weren't used to engaging apology or forgiveness dialogues around race per se (which was the uncomfort-able part), apology and forgiveness constituted a familiar cultural form because the core narrative of evangelical Christianity pivots around both. This dynamic drives to the heart of evangelical theology: for believers, Christ's redemptive power lies precisely in his model of forgiveness of all sinners, including his own detractors and crucifiers. With an all-forgiving salvation figure as the central ref-erent, would-be reconcilers are culturally and religiously primed to embrace the practice of forgiving as a redemptive act, despite what the historical and con-tinuing injuries may be, and regardless of whether the perpetrators are actually offering an apology.

Reconcilers in the 1990s typically linked the need for race-related apology and forgiveness back to the idea of God's "divine plan" for Christian unity. In the context of "loving unity," all forms of reconciliation in any conflict between be-lievers require a nonnegotiable process of owning up to one's individual actions. As Gary from PK said:

> There has to be a recognition of the offense, there has to be a willingness to ac-cept responsibility—genuine responsibility; I'm not saying taking on other people's responsibility, but, you know, if I did something personally to someone else then I need to be aware of that and I need to be sorry for that and I need express that. I also need to ask for forgiveness for that, and, in some cases, make restitution. If I've cheated somebody financially or in some other way, I need to actually make a point of making restitution. So that applies across the board, including the racial side. And that's part of God's plan, period, and we have no [other] option.

Many reconcilers of color reiterated this framework. Gregory Fields from Jubilee, for example, testified to some of the lessons he had learned in his growing relationship with Colin Whitford. He discussed apology in the context of airing feelings:

> I appreciate the apology and I accept apology as well as our congregation and I would give any type of apology for whatever I have done, because I'm not a perfect person either, I have my faults also. And there were times I felt real bad and *I* was prejudiced towards people because of some things that happened in *my* life. But I had to let that go as an adult, as a Christian first of all, and have the love of the Lord, say "love ye one another," it just doesn't matter what the situation is.

Gregory Fields articulated a popular line of reasoning that learning to forgive is a basic requirement of an observant Christian.

This is not to say that Christians of color accepted apology-forgiveness rituals uncritically. Skepticism about the authenticity and long-term effectiveness of white apologies were not uncommon. Nevertheless, the power of evangelicalism's theological framework to cast forgiveness as the mark of a mature Christian seemed to consistently reroute resistance. Jack, a Native American PK staffer, expressed the skepticism many Native Americans feel about white apologies. "It's rhetoric!" he exclaimed. "We hear it all the time. And again, as you say, 'broken promises.' Words on paper mean nothing to us. You know, just words." Nevertheless, as he explained to me, his Christianity did not allow him to avoid offering forgiveness:

> If you're not mature in the Lord, if you're an Indian you would say, "They've finally done it, they finally admitted it, thank God, and let's move on." But as a mature Christian, [forgiveness] has to be appropriate because we see what Christ did, and as a mature believer that's what I have to do. Because as a Native American, I understand maybe a lot of the history from the denominational/spiritual sense of it, all the wrongs that have been done, but I still gotta forgive them because Christ has forgiven me. So it's almost impossible [not to]; you have to do it if you're really growing in Christ. You have to forgive. You know, he's forgiven us!

Similarly, Marcus, an African American PK staffer, recast forgiveness in the American black-white context, analogizing blacks' forgiveness to Christ's "outrageous" and revolutionary model:

> Reconciliation to God did not come from the offending party. It came from the party that was offended. God was offended. He didn't do anything to us, everything that was done wounded him. . . . If reconciliation is going to come in this country, it won't come from white guys; it'll come from black guys. That's the only way it will

come because, you see, reconciliation is an *exquisite* emotion, it's exquisite, it's too much for common man to deal with, and it has to be given outrageously—that's the only way God can take it and use it, and break down—see, you can't fight a man, you can't beat a man who won't fight you back. That's what Gandhi, his whole non-violence—that was what it was based upon, the principle of Christ, that he forgave, even though forgiveness was unwanted. That is *outrageous,* for you to say to any-body; it's outrageous to hear coming out of my mouth!

These reconcilers of color spoke to the pull of conscience engendered by evan-gelical theology's emphasis on forgiveness, as well as to the potential catalytic power of forgiveness in the context of reconciliation as people responded to apologies freely given.

Some reconcilers of color expressed skepticism about organizational apolo-gies for racism (for example, the Southern Baptist Convention's apology in 1995). These reconcilers emphasized that organizational apologies would mean little until/unless they are backed up by intentional action. As PK's Raleigh Washing-ton remarked in the context of the Southern Baptist Convention's public apology for slavery,

It was a wonderful first step. But most African Americans in that denomination on the sidelines said, "What you did was long overdue. We appreciate it; Praise God. But what does it mean?" . . . So if the Southern Baptists say, "we're going to now start encouraging our pastors of multiple churches and whites of their communi-ties to bring on ethnic pastors on their staff and we're going to start seeing white churches, you know, call ethnic people there and instead of having people go out, they will submit to the leadership of that." I think, now, if you're serious, this is your next step. And I've made that statement publicly.

Or, as Aimee from Jubilee put it, "That's fine that you want to apologize, but you can *show* me better than just saying 'I'm sorry.' And when I say show me, just in your acts." For Aimee, Redeemer members' efforts at building a relationship with Jubilee were the proof in the pudding: "They're being themselves and they're try-ing to come together and they're just being a family with us. That's an apology in itself, you know." Like Aimee, most reconcilers who expressed skepticism about collective apologies indicated that true relationships, more than organizational changes, would reflect the sincerity of apologies.

That said, some reconcilers of color did see apology as an aspect of recon-ciliation that could productively work in two directions. When asked what a black man would have to apologize for in the race context, Terrance, from PK, answered,

I think because if I'm holding anger, that's wrong. And I have to deal with that, I have to deal with that when I walk in a place and I see a lady react differently than she would a white man walking around. That begins to work on me and there's an anger that begins to boil in me, and so, I would have to ask forgiveness for that anger and just the meanness in me. You know, I'm big and I'm black, so I know I can intimidate people, and sometimes I use that, and it's not right.

PK's Jorge expressed forgiveness as a means by which individuals can relinquish their personal agendas in service to a larger Christian purpose:

A lot of times the reconciliation issue is focused on Anglos making it right, but it's from both sides, from all sides. It's not just white/black or white/brown; it's sometimes black/brown and Asian/Asian, brown against brown and so forth. So it isn't a matter of skin, it's a matter of sin. So I get forgiveness for my sin and you get forgiveness for your sin and we forgive each other and we're forgiven of God, then we can start on a clean slate.

At the very least, then, the repentance/forgiveness model was the device that attempted to move the reconciliation conversation beyond blame and guilt to the potential for deeper discussion and relationship building. As a way of "wiping the slate clean" and building a ritual that allows for starting over, reconcilers saw it as a necessary and productive practice.

But what does it mean for the slate of racial prejudice and the anger and hurt that may result to be "wiped clean" by repentance and forgiveness? As the ritual surrounding Vanda's rape story illustrates, as a set of symbolic practices apology, repentance, and forgiveness served as vehicles for release. When Vanda confessed that she harbored hatred toward all white men for what one man did to her, she was led spontaneously, and without objection from witnesses, into a creative, improvised ritual whereby others could voluntarily assume that man's burden of guilt, offer repentance, and provide her the opportunity to forgive. That symbolic collective act, which drew on the theology of reconciliation as well as the larger meaning-making systems of evangelicalism, presented her with an epiphany opportunity on a silver platter. Her confession did not prompt a discussion of the personal or social factors surrounding her injury. No one brought up issues that might have been raised in other settings, such as the legacy of white male rape of black women, of rape in general, or the stereotypical image of the black male rapist. Participants did not pause to consider what understanding those things might mean for the reconciling Christian community. Nor was Vanda asked to describe or elaborate her feelings about having been victimized or to share anything with the group other than what she volunteered. She did not solicit anyone's personal perspectives, opinions, or social analysis; indeed, she was not seeking any kind of cerebral, analytical experience, and none was provided for her. What she appeared to seek, and what was offered her in that spontaneous moment through the very Christian concept of her male brethrens' substitutionary atonement, was a safe space to relinquish the pain and anger under which she was suffering in order to move forward in her life.

In the evangelical worldview, apology-forgiveness rituals constitute spiritual-cultural mechanisms for *release* of behavior or emotions perceived to stand as obstacles to a full spiritual and interpersonal reconciliation. This would be true for most any other issue that might arise in an evangelical setting—for example, drug abuse. Testimonial frameworks encourage the repentant "sinner" (for all have sinned) to acknowledge before God or other humans and release, through repentance and/or forgiveness, the internal and external ramifications of his or her sin or hurt. Follow-through certainly might require work and dedication, but that is not the point of testimony or repentance. The moment of repentance is *not* a moment for the believer to appeal to social or personal factors to explain where he or she has been and why. Rather, repenting means assuming full responsibility from that moment on, regardless of the reasons for the fall, and signaling the believer's faith in God to guide the way forward. Likewise, to forgive an injury means to draw on faith (and perhaps the Holy Spirit) to release all resentment at that moment, as Christ forgave all sinners. Thus, as with the more preliminary step of admitting, the point at which a person or group recognizes the need for repentance and/or forgiveness is a catalytic opportunity to *transcend* the conflicts/injuries/sins that have been generated over time. This is an epiphanal moment, a juncture for the expression of insight, release of a burden, and connection with a spiritual experience—all in one.

In ordinary communities in the 1990s, evangelicals participating in RR efforts cocreated unique spaces for individual and collective epiphany, spaces where extraordinary things could happen. Observing these spaces in action, it appears that one of their key assets is precisely that they feel both "safe" and emotionally and spiritually compelling. On the one hand, epiphanal spaces were removed from the potential conflicts and debates of more formally analytical settings that might require self-justification, collective reflection, or expression of secular ideological attachments (such as which political party is doing the right thing about racial inequality). On the other, such spaces attracted participants and allowed them to risk emotional discomfort because they drew consistently and powerfully from the faith-based language, concepts, and practices that already gave American evangelical culture its ballast. They galvanized participants' convictions that miracles could and should happen.

RR efforts did not gain traction as they did in that decade as a result of evangelicals suddenly "seeing the light" of ongoing secular antiracism or multiculturalism initiatives, or even because some prominent evangelical leaders were demonstrating interest in RR and being showcased in popular Christian magazines. Without the contextual factors of evangelicalism's emphasis on comprehensive community, biblical authority, a relational God, an interactive Holy Spirit manifesting contemporary miracles, and a community mandated to help save souls around the world, RR efforts might seem too ambitious to attempt. After all, "the world" had already tried to mend race relations and come up short. But with those things (plus prayer and testimony) and with Christians of all colors involved, reconciliation seemed like a challenge cut out for evangelicals. By tapping into the theological backbone of evangelicalism, reconcilers could mobilize meaning systems that rendered RR not only a Christian imperative but also one specifically tailored to the Last Days. Finally, through the familiar rituals of admitting, urging intentionality, and apology-forgiveness processes, RR could be constructed as taking place on familiar and emotionally satisfying territory. Each of these aspects of evangelical meaning-making systems facilitated RR as not burdensome and draining (though many reported it sometimes was) but spiritually rewarding and emotionally cathartic.

PART THREE

Bridging the Future

Culture, Politics, and Today's Multiethnic Churches

Troubled Waters under the Bridge

Avoiding Conflict through Customs and Etiquettes

The meaning-making systems and practices described in the preceding chapter served multiple functions within evangelical racial reconciliation (RR) settings in the 1990s. They also provided a first step toward religious race bridging. Guided by rituals of admitting, trust building, and apology/forgiveness practices, the epiphanal spaces of reconciliation settings emphasized relationship and spiritual intervention, and pointedly evaded more politically oriented conversations.

At the tail end of twentieth century, these conversations took a new turn. Christian sociologists Michael Emerson and Christian Smith conducted what would become the signature study of racial attitudes among U.S. evangelicals, and their results questioned whether any of the reconciliation hoopla made a difference. *Divided by Faith: Evangelicals and the Race Problem in America* (2000) drew on a national phone survey of 2,000 evangelicals and follow-up interviews with 200 to paint a sobering picture. The racial chasm between black and white evangelicals remained daunting. Even those evangelicals active in RR efforts, Emerson and Smith concluded, were not likely to meaningfully impact racial division, due to whites' overemphasis on relationalism and attendant inability to recognize and address the structural underpinnings of inequality. The book exposed white evangelicals' internalized biases and urged Christians to adopt a more critically engaged and proactive response to American racial divisions. Outside of the Bible itself, *Divided by Faith* would become one of the most influential resources in the evangelical racial change (ERC) movement.

As we have seen, figures like Tom Skinner, John Perkins, and (on the left) Jim Wallis had long been asking how white conservative evangelicals could profess genuine interest in race relations while avoiding, if not outright rejecting, the pursuit of policy-based remedies to racial inequality. Emerson and Smith explained in accessible terms how this could happen.[1] They laid out the history of race relations in evangelicalism, reminding readers of the extent of white evangelicals' complicity in racist systems like slavery and Jim Crow, then explained how such legacies fostered long-term racial segregation in the churches. Using believers' own accounts, they demonstrated how Christians draw from disparate religio-cultural frameworks to interpret social inequality in the United States, especially with regard to race. Their research revealed and rebutted a number of sacred cows in evangelical culture, including the "miracle motif," which as we saw demonstrated in the 1990s interviews, holds that as more individuals convert to Christianity, social and personal problems will be solved automatically (Neff 2000). They concluded that the system-changing components advocated by early reconciliation proponents like Skinner had been diluted by popularized versions of RR adopted by whites, with the result that whites' ongoing power and advantage tended to drop off the radar even of reconcilers.

Key among *Divided*'s achievements was its exposure of white evangelicals' difficulty recognizing how the long-term developments in American social and political structures (not just historical inequities but things like ongoing differential earning capacities, access to business and status networks, and so forth) continue to unequally impact people's opportunities and social mobility. Recognizing the systemic roots of racism and advocating politicized approaches to racial problems would challenge the "voluntaristic absolutism" to which white evangelicals tend to be theologically and practically more attached than other Americans (Emerson and Smith 2000, 97). The study painted an unsettling picture of the ongoing functioning of white privilege within a particular community, and of an American evangelicalism that through its specific theological hermeneutics and cultural attachments—its particular cultural "tool kit"—perpetuates racial inequality without realizing it. Emerson and Smith urged white evangelicals to awaken to this reality and reflect on what it would take to change.[2]

It would be negligent not to engage *Divided by Faith*'s findings, especially with regard to how white evangelicals' version of relationalism inhibits recognition of and responses to structural inequities related to race. However, it is worth noting that Emerson and Smith drew most of their conclusions based on data from evangelicals (data limited to blacks and whites) who were *not* active in race-bridging efforts at the time, whereas I looked exclusively at participants in the ERC movement. To interact with this pivotal text, then, I inquire whether and to what degree active participants in ERC efforts on the ground, then and now, differ from the majority of Emerson and Smith's respondents. Does the analysis in *Divided by Faith* satisfactorily explain the tendency of even committed racial reconcilers in that era to avoid politics, or is there more to it?

Although *Divided*'s assessment identified critical dynamics in grassroots RR settings in the decade, it overlooked other important cultural dynamics worth understanding that informed reconcilers' idiosyncratic orientations to politics. I make three modifications to Emerson and Smith's analysis that help develop a more nuanced and perhaps confounding picture of political avoidance among ERC advocates. These interventions uncover culture-based practices that became habitual in many 1990s reconciliation settings, but which, as chapters 7 and 8 reveal, show signs of changing in multiethnic church (MEC) settings in the decade after *Divided*'s publication.

Drawing on the work of sociologists Paul Lichterman (2005, 2008) and Nina Eliasoph (1998), I suggest, first, that the cognitive frames informing white evangelicalism's orientation to race, such as free-will individualism, were not the only critical factors propelling a relational approach to race bridging in the 1990s. Just as important, relationalism is a product of specific cultural *customs*—boundaries, bonds, and speech norms anchored in the meaning-making practices of evangelicalism broadly, and which have their own expressions in ERC contexts. The preceding chapter mentioned some of these, such as the Christian/non-Christian dichotomy, but here I examine subtler social dynamics. In the 1990s, the customs of the RR model fostered social *etiquettes* that socialized RR participants to certain kinds of spiritual, religious, and social bonding and speech, but effectively inhibited civic and political talk by rendering it suspicious—at least in the context of race. As a result, even if some reconcilers might have wished that more open conversational forums existed in which to discuss political differences, socioeconomic inequalities, and so forth, the etiquettes of epiphanal RR settings did not lend themselves to asking about or creating such forums.

My 1990s interviews with reconcilers surfaced a second phenomenon Emerson and Smith minimized: that core customs within ERC settings influenced not only most white reconcilers' inability to think and speak about racial inequality in more political terms but also many reconcilers *of color's* interest in doing so. Those reconcilers of color who expressed resistance to approaching RR through more political avenues—and, to my surprise, most I met did so—often drew on different critiques than their white counterparts. They nonetheless expressed attachment to depoliticized, relational approaches to racial change, which we much recognize as also rooted in evangelical cultural customs. While these reconcilers could and did understand the ongoing impact of structural and socioeconomic inequalities in the United States, they were often not interested in their RR communities responding to those problems through "programs and projects"—that is, through politics. In fact, they worried about it. This finding suggests that perhaps it is not simply that the *white evangelicals'* tool kit lacks mechanisms for imagining reconciliation beyond relationships to broader societal interventions, but that spiritual and social etiquettes are read by a cross-racial range of participants as more valuable, more transformative, and *deeper* than an arena coded as "political" or "programmatic." Moreover, there are incentives for privileging a relational orientation to social change, among them access to meaningful relationships and a minimization of interpersonal and organizational conflict.

Third, I suggest that Lichterman's concept of *social reflexivity*, the ability of group members to "engage in reflective talk about the group's concrete relationships to the wider social world" (2005, 45), is helpful for interpreting these findings. Social reflexivity is necessary to groups' abilities to consider engaging in political conversation and action. Observing cultural customs exposes aspects of evangelical culture that inhibit social reflexivity. My data confirm that evangelical race-bridging settings in the 1990s encouraged a kind of social reflexivity at the person-to-person level, as individuals were guided to use faith-based relationships to broaden their awareness of cultural differences and areas of commonality. However, such settings largely discouraged the kind of reflexivity that would allow reconcilers individually or in groups to reflect openly on the kind of structural and political dynamics factoring into America's racial divides. To collectively genuflect on how their own religious community may perpetuate structural racial inequalities even *through their reconciliation efforts*, as Emerson and Smith observed, would indeed have been a stretch for most reconcilers (especially whites) in the decade. Therefore, considering how a reconciling community might direct its already socially risky enterprise *toward* political solutions or even into conversations with other groups was virtually inconceivable for most of these actors.

The upshot of the above interventions is that not only the ideological frames (what Emerson and Smith called "tool kits") but also the cultural *skills* to foster such forms of social reflexivity were underdeveloped in the settings I visited. Reasonably, Emerson and Smith criticized evangelicals, including racial reconcilers, for lacking intellectual tools or idea structures for understanding structural and systemic bases of racial inequality. But I maintain that beyond intellectual tools—and even for those who had access to critical frameworks—many well-meaning evangelicals' social *skills* came up short, because their customs and etiquettes tended to deflect even "beginner" levels of conversation about race that touched on politics. Politics was the troubled water under the bridge of RR because many different aspects of evangelical culture rendered politics suspicious. This seems to have been doubly so in the delicate context of reconciliation settings. These dynamics provide insight into why groups working for social change in other contexts might avoid "going there" with approaches perceived as politically charged. They may not be antipolitics orientationally, but they may not have access to the customs, etiquettes, and skills that would make political engagement accessible or desirable.

After incorporating the above insights into Emerson and Smith's analysis of American evangelicals and race, in the final section of this chapter I suggest that *Divided by Faith* itself impacted the trajectory of the ERC movement at the turn of the twentieth century. Emerson and Smith challenged white evangelicals to a kind of self- and social contemplation that made pointed demands of them—contemplation that, in Lichterman's terms, would constitute social reflexivity. *Divided* essentially held up a mirror to the American white evangelical community and asked it to take a hard look. In so doing, the book fostered at least the beginning of an observable shift in American evangelical race discourse in the first decade of the 2000s, which is visible in the evolving treatments of race in *Christianity Today* (*CT*). The question then becomes, are participants in the MEC movement more likely to move beyond the dominant, relational race-bridging paradigm in evangelicalism and respond differently—more self-reflexively—to the kinds of structural and systemic inequalities that Emerson and Smith identified? Chapter 7 considers these questions.

Customs, Etiquettes, and the Safer Context

Emerson and Smith and others diagnosed the limits of the evangelical relational model for racial change, but it is worth knowing more about why even many committed reconcilers would embrace cultural practices that promoted relationalism and downplayed political conversations as a matter of course.[3] I begin by using the concept of *customs* to illuminate aspects of evangelical culture not fully captured in Emerson and Smith's notion of tool kits, then discuss *etiquettes* as an aspects of customs. Interview data illuminate how specific customs and etiquettes rendered certain kinds of conversations about race unlikely even among reconcilers who weren't ideologically opposed to political solutions to racial inequality.

In *Elusive Togetherness*, Lichterman studied bridge-building efforts among a range of faith-based groups in the northern Midwest. He found that groups' customs or *habits of navigating the world through boundaries, bonds, and speech norms* had great bearing on their ability to reach in nonsuperficial ways across difference, and to think and talk about complex social issues (Lichterman 2005, 145–50). We could include both customs and etiquettes as subsets of activities under the umbrella framework I have so far employed of meaning-making practices. "Customs" here designates a wider range of activities than "etiquettes" captures (as "etiquettes" primarily relates to habits related to talk and silence discussed below), but nevertheless *includes* etiquettes. Figure 4 provides a diagram of this.

Customs, Lichterman explains, are distinct from, though certainly influenced by, "cognitive grids," "tool kits," or what other scholars describe as conceptual worldview, theology, and/or ideology. But rather than capturing idea frameworks per se, customs also designate habitualized practices—ways of conceiving connections, drawing lines, talking, and relating.[4] Group-building customs, "routine, shared, often implicit ways of defining membership in a group," are relevant to ERC advocates (Lichterman 2005, 15).

Customs not only cultivate norms of expected positive behavior, they also foster more subtle "quiet barriers," areas of silence or tension emerging from social inhibition or *lack* of accessible vocabulary through which members might approach a topic. Group customs can "encourage members to discount or silence" not just their speech but also "their other ways of viewing the world" (Lichterman 2005, 15). Customs can facilitate, complicate, or inhibit processes of speaking and interacting with and especially approaching conflict between groups with different backgrounds and attachments. The concept of customs provides an analytical tool "sensitive to the ambivalence that illuminates how the back-and-forth of discussion in groups hit[s] up against quiet barriers"—in other words, dynamics that people are subtly discouraged from discussing or feel ill equipped to engage (144).

This is helpful for understanding how the boundaries, bonds, and speech norms that accompanied RR settings in the 1990s created an atmosphere in which not just racial politics but socioeconomic differences in general tended to be difficult for participants to discuss, and when people did discuss them they expressed deep ambivalence about the value of such analysis. As we have seen, in the RR context of the 1990s, evangelicals interested in RR and/or MEC building tended *customarily* to read socioeconomic inequalities on the larger social scale as either transcendable through divinely guided faith interventions (which Emerson and Smith call the "miracle motif") or simply not relevant to the goals at hand. These patterns were especially demonstrated through the speech norms that surfaced in interviews and in "live" RR settings, presented shortly.

For our purposes, we can think of *etiquettes* as unspoken social expectations that influence how talk does and doesn't happen in a community, patterns always informed by the larger meaning-making practices in, and woven into the customs of, that community. Studying how political apathy is produced through norms of American culture, Nina Eliasoph (1998) uses "etiquettes" to refer to people's "companionable ways of creating and maintaining a comfortable context for talk" in a given sphere (8). Etiquettes help define what people can

Figure 4   Meaning-making frameworks

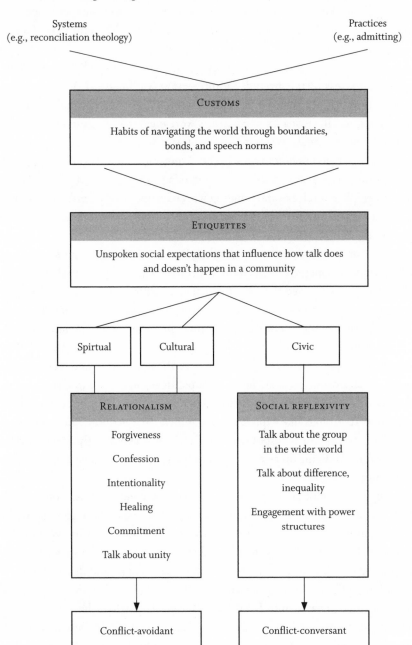

comfortably say and, perhaps more important in the case of ERC advocates, the areas where speaking becomes uneasy or regarded as unnecessary and members seek alternatives to talk, such as silence, prayer, or ritual. The etiquette of a particular context gives participants a sense of "footing" (to borrow a term from Erving Goffman), a constant, unspoken process of determining what membership requires and assessing the grounds for interaction (Goffman 1979).

The 1990s RR settings I visited exhibited a distinctive social etiquette. Through epiphanal RR spaces participants were encouraged to employ spiritual resources (prayer, ritual, testimony, and so forth) to release racial fears and resentments, reach across boundaries, and concentrate primarily on building new kinds of interpersonal and faith community relationships. Importantly, this emphasis on epiphanal release and bonding worked hand in glove with, and indeed *entailed,* a certain pointed distancing from more political responses to racial disharmony.

This is more easily described by dividing RR etiquette of the 1990s into three smaller etiquettes operative within the RR context: spiritual, cultural, and civic. In RR settings, I witnessed that the spiritual and cultural etiquettes were vibrant and accessible to participants. In contrast, the civic etiquette—a shared footing for talking about public, political issues, including evangelicals' relationship to other communities—was an anemic, underdeveloped arena. The effect of these unevenly developed etiquettes was that talk of RR flowered in and was directed toward a relationship context, not a sociopolitical one. Indeed, speech habits and silence in the RR context stigmatized dynamics that might be acceptable in a civic context—things like expression of conflict, debate, discussion of political orientation, and political responses to inequalities—as not only inappropriate but dangerous. Drawing on references from the 1990s material, each etiquette is briefly outlined below.

Through the *spiritual etiquette* in evangelical communities, comfortable speech is guided by experiences of relationship with God and the Holy Spirit, of religious communion, ritual, and reference to scriptural authority. Within this etiquette, believers have access to a shared language for exchanging personal experiences, listening and speaking to their spiritual leaders, and describing their explorations of the Bible itself as a source of the "will of God" in their lives. Such language extended easily into RR processes, especially when the conversations were framed in terms of "God's will," interpersonal relatedness, individual struggles and victories, and spiritual experiences related to race and attendant differences (ethnicity, class, and occasionally gender). Reconcilers strove to identify, manage, and ideally relinquish race-related sin in their lives and to learn how to fulfill the divine commandment to love one another. The hope was that as cross-racial or cross-ethnic relationships began to take root, believers could then bond over the broader challenges of living Christian lives.⁵ Such bonding was facilitated by the ubiquitous, familiar etiquette of spiritual talk.⁶

As we have seen, the evangelical community setting functions as a kind of "home space"—a haven from "the world" outside, which is variously coded as lost, hostile, alienating, and/or hopeless. In spaces like church, Bible studies, small groups, workshops, and Christian schools, believers greet each other, express themselves, listen, and address conflict in a variety of ways. They are welcomed, supported, admonished, or even bid farewell as family members; they express an ethic of care and love for one another; they make use of supportive spaces in which to admit shortcomings, share personal failings, and express pain; and they participate in rituals intended to nurture, release, and heal. Communities also interact with other groups and communities as neighbors, allies, and even adversaries. Within the *cultural etiquette* of evangelical settings, believers discuss a wide range of things, everything from one's well-being to the decision making of the church as a body or the moral character of the American president. Within these conversations, cultural norms of appropriateness influence how and when people speak to one another, as well as the range of acceptable topics. For example, friends at a church picnic may tell stories that might not be appropriate to share in a small Bible study group, or speaking in tongues may be encouraged at a worship service emphasizing gifts of the spirit, but more awkward in the middle of a Sunday sermon.

The *civic etiquette* of evangelicals, as with any other community, is operative in the space where members might raise and discuss questions that affect not only themselves as individuals and communities but also citizens in a larger, more diverse community. Civic etiquette would provide a way of asking, how should we get involved in our society as a result of our religious beliefs and convictions? Also, should we extend our community involvement (for example, volunteering or doing church-based outreach) into the dimension of political organizing or advocacy? Conservative evangelicals have used their civic etiquette to discuss, strategize, and build alliances around other issues they value in political contexts (for example, anti-Communism, creationism, abortion, traditional marriage, Israel). Conservative white evangelicals, as a rule, have not generally applied such civic etiquette to racial problems, although, as I discussed in chapter 4, they seemed to be fumbling toward new language in the late 1990s around welfare reform and immigration.

The compatible concepts of customs and etiquette are useful for tracking the ways in which cultural meaning-making practices, not solely the ideological frames Emerson and Smith describe, elevated relationships as the solution to the racial divide and nearly foreclosed the kinds of conversations about difference and inequality that more political approaches would require. A central obstacle was the apparent lack of etiquette that would foster sufficient social reflexivity to generate basic "starter" political questions, like how do we reconcilers in the room approach questions of politics differently? Again, many reconcilers of color in the 1990s demonstrated this pattern as obviously as their white counterparts.

Mechanisms of Avoidance

The emphasis in RR settings on epiphanal activities like confession, intentionality, and forgiving—activities that mapped onto the spiritual and cultural etiquettes of evangelicalism—loaded the experience of building new cross-racial relationships with visceral emotional value for participants. To the extent that an interpersonal relationship evolved into a commitment, 1990s reconcilers tended to assume, this value could serve as a catalyst for other modes of growth. As one Denver reconciler and Promise Keeper in the 1990s I interviewed put it, "The interesting thing about racial reconciliation was that the guys [involved in Promise Keepers (PK)] are hungry. They want to know about racial reconciliation; they want to do intentional things about it. They don't know how to do it, but they don't want to be sermonized or seminarized. . . . They want the roll-up-your-sleeves, get it in and be in relationship [experience]. They want to know how to do that."

Relationalism, here, was not just a product of abstract frameworks in evangelicalism that called Christians to connect with one another through the "horizontal relationships" discussed earlier. It was also a vehicle to satisfy a longing expressed across a variety of evangelical cultural settings for personal relationships as evidence that "through Christ," as believers phrase it, reconciliation and healing are possible. This longing was expressed even by those who had been involved with other kinds of racial change activities (activism in the 1960s, secular organizations, and so forth) but had not thought that those activities fostered "real" relationships.

Against the grain of Emerson and Smith's discussion in *Divided*, in interviews, workshops, and sermons racial reconcilers of color expressed such sentiments almost as often as whites. As they explained, the appeal was not about relationship for the sake of it, but rather the emphasis placed on commitment. Reconcilers in the 1990s often likened cross-racial relationship to marriage, casting it through cultural and spiritual speech norms that emphasized showing up when it was hard, giving conflicts to God, and being willing to go the distance. In a Christian movement that worked to fortify male-female relationships, the marriage model represents perhaps the central social custom among evangelicals. Thus, a PK reconciliation workbook continually applied the language of "love relationships" between Christian brothers and sisters to nonromantic contexts. In the language of the workbook, "Genuine" reconciliation happens when a relationship has a commitment to resolve differences. The analogy of a marriage is helpful. A marriage is, above all else, a commitment to another person. Successful marriages are not those in which conflict never arises—no such marriage exists. A solid marriage is one in which the partners share a commitment to resolve conflict. The commitment says, "I'm going to hang in there and resolve this problem." "Divorce is not an option" is a central motivating idea (if not always practiced) in evangelical culture. During a period in which a primary thrust in conservative evangelicalism was building and publicly defending stronger traditional "family values," likening one-on-one cross-racial relationships to good marriages synced with customs of committed, faith-based bonding.

Sammy, a Latino PK leader from Texas, related an experience illustrative of evangelical customs applied in the RR context, placing faith in the power of committed personal relationship to change people at the deepest levels. He testified that the most powerful manifestation of RR in his own life has been a long-term friendship with another Christian man. "My best friend right now is a six-foot-four-inch, redneck, Baptist, Texas preacher. So there you have a culture, you have a people group, and even denominational [differences]—because Baptists and Pentecostals, historically, have had a lot of conflict—the people groups of white and brown in Texas still is a huge problem," he said.

Sammy met Don at a funeral, and the two started a pastors' prayer group, which was six years old at the time of the interview. For Sammy, one of the greatest benefits of this friendship was the opportunity for understanding through communication, even if conflict arose in the process:

> So once you begin to communicate, the first thing that happens after you're willing to be honest with someone and say, "What do you mean by this that the Pentecostals believe?" or, "What do you mean by that that the Baptists believe?"—the first thing that happens is conflict, because there everybody's pushed in the corner to say, "Well, this is what I believe." But that conflict, as you continue to communicate, causes understanding. And my friend and I have come to the agreement after we've discussed a lot of things including family and personal needs and just the whole thing, that we have much more in common than we thought before we actually communicated, but it involves investing time, it involves relationship.

This willingness to engage conflict, but within the etiquette of commitment, was repeated in interviews with other reconcilers of color. Sammy explained: "When you commit to a relationship, whether it's a marriage, whether it's a relationship with a friend, with another people group, you need to commit, and relationship involves time. My friend Don and I have committed almost eight years of time. We go out to dinner as couples once a month, we share a church group, but that didn't happen on the first time we met; it took an openness and an awareness to commit to relationship. And in the course of relationship all these things come up." Sammy described his relationship with Don as stronger than his relationships with his own brothers.

Emphasis on commitment as a means of ultimately resolving conflict reflects an important tendency underscored by custom: in evangelical culture (at least in all-white and many multiethnic settings), conflict is not customarily valued as a particularly positive or fruitful thing, as something that can lead to other social "goods" in the community. For instance, it is not customary for evangelicals to organize debates in Sunday school or among the congregation, part of the reason being that they're socialized from a young age to respect and not challenge religious and familial authority.[7] Rather, conflict is often suppressed, particularly in settings marked by unfamiliar forms of difference or in which power relationships are at stake. Racial difference heightens this dynamic. In Lichterman's terms, the *bonding* put forth as necessary to sustain the strains entailed in cross-racial friendship fosters drawing certain *boundaries* around conversation.

In this context, the speech norms (etiquettes) of RR settings fostered emphases on values like unity, togetherness, and harmony over question-asking, self-reflection, critique, and argument—at least when it came to differences that might bear on politics, such as party identification. Participants in RR settings might mention that there were "both Republicans and Democrats in the room," but I never heard them create space or raise the need to discuss what those differences might mean or whether they signaled competing perspectives worth exploring in the RR process. Cross-racial friendship testimonies often revealed that the evangelical RR or MEC model does not teach individuals or groups how to *explore* conflict and learn about difference, social power structures, and so forth through a principled openness to conflict. Rather, the idea is that committed, faith-guided, "God-centered" relationships teach people how to *overcome* conflict. Through relationalism, ERC advocates tended to hang their hopes on the ability of relationship to transcend the complicated, historical, and *still conflict-ridden* wounds of and across communities. And there is some basic social sense to this: especially people building the first cross-racial relationships of their lives might feel resistance to engaging with the messy, volatile social and political questions that might disrupt the pleasure of new friendship.

Social Reflexivity and the Threat of Conflict

In order for bridging groups to become politically engaged, Lichterman asserts, they need customs that can "welcome people to social criticism instead of scaring all but those already convinced" (2005, 5). Through relationalism and other conflict-avoidant approaches to social interaction, however, certain kinds of social reflexivity or "reflective talk about the group's concrete relationships to the wider social world" are discouraged (45).[8] He provides an example from a middle-class evangelical volunteer group, Adopt-a-Family, whose goal was to assist families on welfare by building care-based relationships with them. The group had very little ability to map the families' *own* sense of how power and culture worked in their social worlds, or to talk about racial or culture-based differences between their (the volunteers') and the families' ways of navigating the world. Through a vocabulary of relationship-based, Christ-like care, the volunteers kept trying to "look past" or not see difference, but as a result they had no way to talk about inequality. "The program was predicated on a server-served relationship in which the two sides ultimately may be moral equals but were clearly not social equals. So to keep the relationships from being threatened, volunteers would try to 'know another person's world' as the program guide had put it, while avoiding encounters that confirmed the difference in privilege" (159).

Lichterman noted that although the Adopt-a-Family group involved evangelicals who may have had some conservative ideas about welfare policy, it was not their *ideology* that elicited so little discussion among them about the larger social dynamics involved, like poverty. The customs of their group made them feel they were breaching the etiquette of their model of compassionate relationships if they asked deeper questions about poverty, or how the welfare bureaucracy worked, or had conversations about politics.[9] This lack of social reflexivity seems to have factored into the program's ultimate dissolution. In the end the group was not able to sustain long-term bridging with the communities they hoped to help.

In addition to the persistent emphasis on relationalism, the etiquettes that governed RR settings in the 1990s fostered two discursive mechanisms that enabled participants to articulate an avoidance of politics. One of these I call the *antiprogrammatic* argument. This overlaps with what Emerson and Smith term "antistructuralism," but contains a more specific critique than Emerson and Smith identified, a critique that racial "programs and projects," whether church- or state-sponsored, are short-sighted. Through the antiprogrammatic argument, 1990s reconcilers opined that secular political approaches to racial change such as legislation and social programs had not created "true" transformation because they lacked a spiritual component. Real change, they argued, could only be achieved through a Christ-centered model for reconciliation.

The other mechanism, the *contamination* argument, built from evangelical meaning-making practices in describing the world outside evangelicals' own spiritual communities as inherently fraught, ineffective, or potentially contaminating for Christians, and therefore to be engaged with great caution. Again, as I detail shortly, my interviews revealed that not just whites but participants *of color* in the MEC movement employed all three of these politics-avoidant means of approaching race relations in faith-based contexts.

Problematic "Programs"

Relationalism was firmly ensconced as the dominant frame that fit with evangelical social customs, but it was anchored by an antiprogrammatic framing of race issues in the speech settings of reconcilers. The recurring line, indeed the almost canned response to questions about politics in my interviews with 1990s reconcilers, was that while institutional and political changes around race had their place, they would invariably be hobbled if the relationships to sustain them did not exist. Both white reconcilers and those of color expressed this, but with significantly different inflections.[10]

The common way of phrasing this idea was through the tautological reasoning that institutionalized efforts, necessary though they might be as short-term solutions, were incapable of producing the "heart change" that could lead to long-term social transformation. (Heart change was therefore coded as not institutional; institutional change was inadequate because nonrelational.) Institutional responses to racial segregation and inequality, whether based on law, state policy, or efforts by private institutions to foster equality, could not create heart change because such initiatives had "no spiritual core" and did not attend to building committed relationships. As this (Latino) reconciler put it, "Understand that institutional racism became institutionalized because of individual racism. So if you want to change institutional racism, you don't start from the institution, you start from people. Because the very people that created the problem are the people that can change it. In some sense, you have to hit it from both ends to turn this humungous ship around. But the greatest influence and effect that you can have in terms of a change agent is at the one-by-one, man-to-man, woman-to-woman relationship."

Were such sentiments to come only through the voices of *white* reconcilers, it would be easy to interpret them as expressing a kind of "veiled" racism that rejects truly reparative political solutions to race problems.[11] Indeed, neoconservative dismissals of structural responses to race problems did serve as handy frameworks for many white reconcilers. But the critique by reconcilers of color of church-based or secular "programs and projects" designed to create racial change as typically "white" and therefore inadequate approaches contained a distinctive critique of *white* approaches to social change. Three examples from different interviewees express this:

> Anglos, for the most part, are programmatic, whereas people of color are relational . . . if you really want to understand them, you've got to be in relationship with them. (African American PK leader)

> I think a lot of times, the government viewpoint with our Native Americans is to somehow pay them off with programs or projects, and both those issues aren't going to work. . . . The government basically tried to I think somehow cover their guilt and shame and turn us into programs, economical things, school programs, clothing programs and so on. . . . They realized it didn't work, so they gave us over to the churches to deal with. . . .
>
> Instead of turning us into programs, [the churches] turned us into projects. . . . In the early or mid 1800s, they divided Native America, so that major denominational groups would take over different parts of the Indian nations. . . . That's how they tried to somehow give us restitution or restoration—turning us into programs and projects; programs from the government viewpoint, projects from the church viewpoint. (Native American PK leader)

> The body of Christ has become very programmatic, so we want to program reconciliation, and that's very similar to legislating reconciliation. When it reality it's got to be founded on the establishment of relationships. (Latino PK leader)

The above statements come from staffers of PK, which worked to maintain a nonpolitical, nonpartisan identity. But such statements were routine across the interviews. These reconcilers employed an antiprogrammatic framework to critique what they read as a white style of pursuing racial change, whether through churches or secular institutions. They argued that such programs objectified and paternalized people of color and neglected the more important issue of fostering equal relationships, values they described as especially important to *people of color.*

In a questionnaire about their background and political orientations, many interviewees of color described themselves as Democrats, supporters of the civil rights movement, "economic liberals," or simply "not conservative on race issues." Yet they expressed a common wariness about allowing their movement to be "co-opted" into a political mode. These reconcilers seemed willing to entrust their faith in a spiritually based reconciliation model to challenge divisive be-liefs and attitudes, partly because of their disillusionment with approaches they believed had been tried all too often at the expense of people of color. "There's never been true ownership [with government-sponsored programs]," said a Na-tive American PK leader. "There's a lot of compassion, but if you put compassion with programs and projects you get paternalism. . . . But if you put compassion with, say, a working together, an interdependence where [people] feel it's theirs, then you begin to get a lot of confident people in power." Or in the words of one Latino, with programmatic responses to racial problems, "what we do is gener-ate a cycle of dependency, and we demoralize people—that's what the welfare system has done. I've seen it firsthand."

Through the antiprogrammatic critique, most evangelical reconcilers of color maintained that politicized racial change models, though necessary at certain historical periods (such as Reconstruction or the civil rights movement), could not cut through the attitudes, beliefs, and behaviors that anchor racism. They explained in interviews and RR settings that the spiritual arena offered a more penetrating approach. "Affirmative action was the right thing to do because you had to force people to do the right thing," said a Latino reconciler. "But the rea-son it didn't work was that relationships were not a part of it." The same person maintained, as did others, that the Christian community had abdicated its social responsibility to care about poor and minority communities, and this was why Christians had to get involved with civil society–based social change efforts on the ground. "So now we expect the government to take care of the poor and needy," he complained. "But God didn't assign that role and responsibility to the government; he gave that role to us as Christians."

In short, many evangelicals of color drew on evangelical customs for their own specific purposes. Their embrace of a relational model for change was ar-ticulated partly as a critique of the limits of programmatic, institutionalized, le-galistic responses to inequality attempted by both secular and Christian whites. These reconcilers of color effectively challenged white Christians to get "on the ground" where the action is, rather than attempting to control it from "on high," and to see if they could apply their faith to face-to-face friendships over the long term. They also expressed strong sentiments that the faith-based relational model, when rooted through real relationships, felt significantly more rewarding, more equal, and more likely to create transformation in two directions. Through such arguments, reconcilers of color often appealed to relationalism as a means of refusing distancing and indeed pushing whites out of a certain comfort zone (perhaps a long-demonstrated custom of American Christianity) of whites' at-traction to institutionalized "outreach," "missionary work," and programs and projects that people of color interpreted as paternalistic or worse. Reconcilers of color advocated, in other words, closing off this comfortable, "typically white" option.

In contrast to many of their counterparts of color, whites I interviewed in the 1990s often articulated a critique of "programs and projects" through an unself-consciously conservative orientation about socioeconomic social policies in general, which is more consistent with Emerson and Smith's conclusions in *Divided*. The perspective of many white reconcilers was that although institutional/policy responses to things like poverty and racial inequality had an appropriate place in society, such initiatives "simply" lacked the spiritual elements to foster long-term substantive change. White ERC advocates (especially those focused on reconciliation activities) did not seem to think that they needed to explain to an interviewer (a white one, at least) why relationship-based approaches to racial change made more sense than "political solutions"; the viewpoint was nearly second nature to them. This idea came through less in direct defensiveness about programmatic approaches and more often in a redirecting of answers toward the deeper value of the relationship-building model they promoted.

A common trope through which white reconcilers articulated antiprogrammatic arguments was the "getting off-track" idea: that if people move from relational bridge-building activities to policy commitments, they risk veering away from their "focus on Jesus Christ." This idea appeals to the evangelical meaning-making practice (reflected both through behavioral customs and speech norms) of bringing everything "back to God"—that is, letting one's personal relationship with God magically sort out whatever internal misgivings, doubts, and external temptations might be troubling a person. It also implicitly mobilizes the customary boundary evangelicals draw between themselves and "the world." Racial politics and policy are read under these norms as external to the immediate faith-based community and relevant to the other "kingdom"—the kingdom of man, or the secular world.[12]

Often encoded in the "getting off-track" narrative was an anxiety that whites (or perhaps conservatives) might have their *own* social vision altered if they went down that road of translating reconciliation efforts to policy positions. Detective Colin Whitford, whose initial efforts led to the relationship between Redeemer Church and Jubilee Baptist, provides an example. Considering running for the Colorado House of Representatives when I interviewed him, his antiprogrammatic response sounded like this:

> I think the political ramifications [of RR] are probably going to be inevitable, but our focus, as always, needs to be on Jesus Christ and what he calls us to do, and on

the body of Christ. Not on how that is going to change our social agenda, how it's going to change our picture. *I think that our focus needs to remain correct. Once you shift from trying to bring healing inside the body of Christ to trying to create more jobs for people that feel like they deserve this because of what color they are or whatever, you know, then you're treading dangerous waters.* I think that if people were behaving the way they should in the first place, these wouldn't be issues. (emphasis added)

This comment reflects Whitford's discomfort with trying to apply his newly acquired vision of RR to the political realm. Here the prospective white, Christian officeholder hints at the idea that if Christians (or reconcilers, at least) were to enter that discursive arena, they might quickly get sucked into the "dangerous waters" of confusion, conflict, and a programmatic agenda, which he implies is promoted by *other* types of people. He also implies that reconcilers' agenda is directed primarily to the body of Christ, not the world beyond or that world's policy concerns. This was a curiously politics-avoidant perspective to adopt for a politically active white conservative Republican who was staunchly pro-life and supported a "pro-family" platform. The message expressed was that defending these positions (anti-abortion, pro–traditional marriage) in the civil realm did not risk throwing evangelicals off-track—but thinking about race and other socioeconomic issues in political terms did.

Whitford's comments exemplified the sorts of silences and ambiguities that often lurked in white reconcilers' narratives (and in racial discourse in *CT*). Whom did he have in mind when he referred to people who wanted to "create more jobs for people that feel like they deserve it," and what exactly would be dangerous about treading that water? Such inquiries rarely surfaced in reconcilers' conversations, sermons, or reconciliation courses, nor did individuals seem comfortable talking about them when I raised them directly. That they did not is a function of the fact that the etiquette of the RR setting consistently guided participants to talk about relationships, faith-based interactions, and the miraculous racial healing God delivers to committed reconcilers, and to avoid discussion of conflict-inducing topics like how to shift unjust policies, what political platforms might be relevant, and how to participate politically in race-related matters.

"Contaminated" Politics

As Whitford's comments indicate, core customs within evangelicalism led many reconcilers to portray the political realm as potentially destructive to Christians, and to the RR process itself. The contamination argument, which was distinguishable from but compatible with the antiprogrammatic argument, regarded the political realm as characterized by conflict and dominated by non-Christian interests. This line of reasoning draws on the meaning-making practices described in chapter 5, especially the Christian/non-Christian dichotomy and the apocalyptic narrative. In one way or another, reconcilers (and here, not just whites) often expressed the desire to preserve a line between the formal realm of politics and the cultural realm of RR.

Some of this was rooted in a religious worldview. Many evangelical reconcilers doubted that the secular world, or any other religious perspective, is capable of engaging in RR. They perceived Christianity specifically as uniquely providing them the necessary tools that they believed other perspectives could not provide. Again, whites weren't the only ones expressing this. Raleigh Washington, PK's chief of RR initiatives in the 1990s, articulated this in the context of having spoken to President Clinton's Advisory Panel on Race in 1997 (a panel that aimed to identify and find modes of redressing ongoing racial conflicts in the United States). Washington's view was that the religiously inspired "incentive to love one another" could not be replaced with "political logic." "Inside the church," he said in our interview, "we teach love your neighbor as yourself. The president says he wants a One America campaign, we ought to have relationships—but nothing drives it. . . . So this is how we do it from a secular viewpoint: we gear up for the fight. When the church is saying that the answer is we must love one another . . . But how do you love? I think you need a power within yourself that's greater than yourself to do something that you would not naturally do yourself."

Washington's comments succinctly made a number of moves through the etiquette of RR. He reiterated a meaning system (Christian love is the answer to conflict); identified an us/them boundary through assertion of a norm (the secular world "gears for a fight" whereas Christians know "we must love one another"); and asserted the impossibility of a meaningful civic response to racial conflict (because "they" don't have access to a power greater than themselves through which to create change). Washington's stance should be understood in the context of PK's public refusal to etch out a political position on RR, but it also reflects how the etiquette of RR operated to code the secular realm as both limited and contaminated. As another member of PK put it, "we can always be challenged with the seductiveness, power of politics as different political factions may try to challenge us as an organization to take a certain stance," but the more proper position for a Christian organization is not to succumb to the temptation.

The extreme version of this wariness was the eschatological orientation—the idea that political engagement is fruitless given that the tribulation is imminent anyway. Some ERC advocates suggest that Christians should not be too attached to political responses to *any* issue because secular systems will ultimately become corrupted. Christians, then, can only hope to influence government for a period of time. But even this apocalyptic narrative contained ambivalence. Many ERC advocates urge that Christians should pray for the leaders and systems that govern them without being invested in the success or failure of secular political systems. As one Asian American reconciler I interviewed in the 1990s put it, "God also encourages us to pray for authorities that are existing—they are there, God established them for our good, but there is a point at which God allows those things to pass so that we don't put our trust and hope in politics, but we put it [on him]." In other words, Christians should keep a basic connection to things secular and political, but be willing to relinquish that connection once the secular world has turned against them. This is a fragile vision at best.

Another way of framing this tenuous orientation to the larger civic and political culture is that evangelical religious race bridging in the 1990s was a "public-minded" discourse (the term one reconciliation leader used with me) that focused on and, by its own admission, could only effectively speak to one public, Christians, but could inspire non-Christians in the process. There is certainly a cynicism to the evangelical view that only "believers" are compelled by an authority beyond themselves to create "true" reconciliation.[13] But there is also a genuine belief, persistently socialized into evangelical culture through semiotic systems and the etiquettes they produce, that that is true. When I asked one white PK reconciler if RR was possible outside Christian settings, he replied frankly, "Not effectively. No matter what my opinion is, I still have to hear what God has to say and if I consider God to be my Father, I have no options; obedience is required. Do you obey apart from love? No, you can't. . . . It's not that racial reconciliation can't happen at all [outside Christianity]. It just won't happen in a widespread fashion because people aren't willing to go there. . . . There's no compelling reason for them to stretch themselves."

Etiquettes and the "Safer" Space

In sum, interviews with and observation among reconcilers in the 1990s revealed that, in the group process–oriented context of RR activities, the customs of evangelicalism provided valuable inspiration, practical resources, and rules and guidelines for race bridging. These were channeled primarily through spiritual and cultural etiquettes. The prioritization of these functioned to foreclose certain kinds of discourse—in effect, to inhibit means of talking about race issues *as political issues*. This rendered a civic etiquette virtually irrelevant to race-bridging efforts. Race and race relations were interpreted as not properly political topics—at least not political topics *for reconcilers*—and instead belonging to the realm of emotional and spiritual issues to be addressed in a cultural (and personal/individual), *relational* context. The epiphanal atmosphere of reconciliation settings fostered modes of interaction that depicted the spiritually anchored, relationship-building model for crossing racial and ethnic divides as deeper, more rewarding, and therefore better for creating long-term social change than other racial change models they identified as political. In short, under relationalism, one of the core customs of evangelicalism, the pursuit of the "self-transforming, heart-changing relationship with Jesus Christ" becomes elevated as a model for all other relationships (Lichterman 2005, 143).

Compounding this, etiquettes of RR culture foreclosed more political discussions of race through specific speech norms. First, neither the spiritual nor the cultural etiquette allowed for the open expression of extended conflict, debate, or public-minded conversation in the immediate community setting. This is not to say that ERC settings directly censored such conversation. Rather, the constant, positive emphasis on certain subjects like friendship and overcoming distance subtly deflected inquiries into others. This provides a sense of how customs produce not just activity but also silence and avoidance. Individuals and groups involved in RR almost never referenced topics related to race as relevant to the civic realm where the etiquette governing controversial or political discussions would apply—except to discount that realm as either fruitless or dangerous. This speech norm, pervasive among reconcilers, implicitly reinforced bonds among reconcilers and boundaries against non-Christians. The overriding assumption, which some interviewees made explicit when questioned, was that no one came to a reconciliation course, a reconciliation-related job, or a new cross-racial relationship to "talk politics." Rather, reconcilers assumed, Christians came to interrogate the state of their own hearts and to participate in possibly difficult, emotional, spiritual conversations with the guidance of one another and the resources of their religious or faith-based organization leaders and their God.

Second, the evangelical ("Christian" in participants' terminology) approach to RR was constructed as a more powerful and effective *alternative* to politics. In other words, the value of faith-based RR processes was asserted in stark contrast to civic and political approaches, and structural analyses of inequality among them. Within both the spiritual and the cultural etiquettes, the political realm figured as a world that existed "outside" of, and in some sense in contrast to, the community of believers/reconcilers, especially in regard to racial issues. Because the spiritual and cultural etiquette organized spheres that felt safe, ordered, and supervised (by God and community), the constant, underlying implication was that the political context is a place of discomfort, disorder, and ineffectiveness.

Two fully functioning and one underfunctioning or at least deemphasized realm of etiquette had the powerful discursive effect of creating a binary opposition between relationships and politics in the narratives of 1990s reconcilers. This is because the etiquettes of both the spiritual and cultural realms consistently directed would-be reconcilers toward relationship as the means *and ends* of a "real"—meaning authentic and substantive—reconciliation process. In contrast, politics figured for the bulk of participants as, at best, a secondary by-product of reconciliation that would "naturally" emerge from a more racially united Christian community and, at worst, a contaminating realm of interaction. To conceptualize this differently, relationship figured rhetorically as the realm of the "true"—tangible, authentic, meaningful, and grounded. Politics in the context of RR figured closer to the "suspect," for not only does it entail interacting with a secular world that evangelicals deeply distrust, but reconcilers read it as often inauthentic, limited, groundless, and fraught with irreconcilable conflict. Relationship, in short, was framed in RR etiquette as both deeper and *safer* than politics, and avoided substantive discussion of race politics and the conflicts that discussion might raise.

Divided by Faith as an Intervention

Although the thrust of Emerson and Smith's book seemed to understate the complexity of evangelical customs on the race divide and to overlook the cross-racial appeal of relationalism as a solution, it is hard to imagine a work that could have delivered the critique of white evangelicalism with more care and credibility than *Divided by Faith* did. Emerson and Smith were accomplished sociologists at top research universities as well as professed Christians, which granted them a respectful audience among evangelicals. From my vantage point, their observations visibly impacted the trajectory of evangelical race discourse by synthesizing and rendering more public and data-grounded a conversation that had been simmering for decades. This constituted a move with social change implications inside American evangelicalism.

Divided by Faith provided several critical interventions. It exposed culture- and ideology-based systems that thrive under the insidious auspices of moral neutrality. It leveraged rigorous research in the interest of awakening white Christians to the power inequalities that their thinking tended to systematically render invisible to them. Analytically, it exposed the luxury of white evangelicals' ability to assume racial issues in the United States had little to do with them, and argued that racial and socioeconomic questions immediately concerned white evangelicals regardless of their social locations. "Using their cultural tools,"

Emerson and Smith noted, "evangelicals apply universalism *interpersonally* to the exclusion of other strategies, such as working for more just laws" (2000, 118, emphasis added).

Divided explicitly pressed white evangelicals toward greater social reflexivity by urging reconsideration of customs long taken for granted; rethinking of habits of speech and action; and action in response to information. The freewill individualism that feels natural to so many whites, the authors argued, "eliminates their ability to see [their own] advantage" (Emerson and Smith 2000, 91) and allows them to shift the blame for inequality to historically disenfranchised groups. Surfacing embarrassing insights had its risks, but part of the deftness of *Divided* was the judicious delivery of its conclusions. On the one hand, Emerson and Smith made plain the damaging effects of the white evangelical tool kit.[14] The situation, they wrote, is "a rather dismal portrait of the realities of and prospects for positive race relations among American Christians in the United States" (170). On the other, while the authors seemed personally convinced that the most important way to address racism is to address structural issues like integrating residential neighborhoods, they acknowledged that white evangelicals were nowhere near embracing such strategies immediately.[15]

Thus, they pitched their prescription where their research suggested the most hope might exist: integrating congregations. When they collected their data, only a bare majority (53 percent) of white strong evangelicals selected integrating congregations as a good way to address racism. However, Emerson and Smith also found that those white evangelicals who *did* feel empowered to address structural racism were people whose social networks enabled substantive, long-term interactions with people socioeconomically different from themselves. The MEC community, therefore, reasonably emerged for Emerson and Smith as the most likely place to seed a shift. "If white evangelicals were less racially isolated, they might assess race problems differently and, working in unison with others, apply their evangelical vigor to broader-based solutions," they suggested (Emerson and Smith 2000, 132). Between evangelicals' enthusiasm for interpersonal relationships, their theological vigor, and the strong slap on the hand *Divided* delivered, the hope seemed to be that the community might stand a chance to become less racially isolated.

As an indicator of the perceived significance of *Divided* among many evangelical elites, *CT* dedicated a special section to the book after its publication in 2000. The issue included an editor's overview and editorial, a book excerpt, a pastors' roundtable discussion, and a related feature about a white, social change–oriented pastor in a tiny African American church in West Texas. The editorial board seemed more than receptive to Emerson and Smith's critiques. *CT* editors underscored the authors' core interventions: observations about white evangelicals' denial of the racial problem in the United States; their blame of the media and minorities for "refusing to forget the past"; and their "individualized theological worldview that blinds many white evangelicals to certain societal injustices" (Anonymous 2000, 34). Editor David Neff's preview of the *Divided* issue even quoted Michael Emerson saying, "We have an artificial division among Christians—that of personal responsibility, accountability, and change versus macro change and justice. They are both of God" (Neff 2000, 117).

The roundtable moderated by Edward Gilbreath, one of *CT*'s regular race relations writers (and long the only African American on staff) and Mark Galli, *CT*'s managing editor, set an interesting tone for racial discourse in the 2000s. The four participating pastors mostly endorsed *Divided* as an important corrective to evangelical race discourse, agreeing that evangelicals should be more concerned with racial justice. Gilbreath prompted participants to address the critique that white evangelicals' tool kits tend to inhibit their ability to recognize or respond to socioeconomic inequities and racial injustice in the United States (Ellis and Lyon 2000). The pastors did not challenge this finding, though some questioned whether evangelical theology is "predisposed" to racism or whether evangelicals have simply been too individualistic in their applications of it.[16] The pastors critiqued American evangelicals' overattachment to materialist, "American Dream" values, which, in combination with Homogeneous Unit Principle–driven church growth, deepen the racial divide.[17] Robert Franklin, who headed the largest historically African American seminary in the United States at the time, argued that "the greatest sin in the pulpit today is one of omission and not commission on the issues of race and justice. . . . We rarely hold America accountable or critique what our government is up to" (Ellis and Lyon 2000, 45). Charles Lyon, a white pastor of an MEC, offered criticism of white evangelicals who try to host cross-racial events, missions, or campaigns without building the relationships required to sustain them.

Overall, the *Divided* discussion orchestrated by *CT* did seem to sponsor social reflexivity among the pastors, setting a contemplative tone. However, it (or at least the portion *CT* published) also veered toward the somewhat easier topic of how churches could build more substantive "bridges" out of their comfort zones and get more engaged in meaningful "service" projects, rather than whether they should shift their energies toward a greater activism.[18] One pastor (Franklin) did say he wished Emerson and Smith had dealt more with "how to move towards a transformational ministry" in which congregations could have a more "diagnostic conversations in which we address issues of reconciliation and justice" (Ellis and Lyon 2000, 47).

The consensus in the special issue on *Divided* seemed to be that evangelicals ought to take Emerson and Smith's critiques seriously and work on addressing race and other forms of inequality in more structural, less individualistic terms. The discussion perhaps reflected a yearning for a more developed civic etiquette within racial discourse. But it also indicated how the relational customs of evangelicalism rendered it easier to respond to these new insights in terms of "conversations" and "relationships" rather than through politically conversant, justice-oriented responses to social problems.

Christianity Today Race Discourse, 2000–2009

CT's initial coverage of *Divided by Faith* suggested that at the least evangelical elites (pastors, *CT* editors and writers, for starters) supported Emerson and Smith's analysis of the racial divide in evangelicalism. In the wake of that, race coverage in *CT* became visibly more nuanced, complex, and self-reflexive in the first decade of the 2000s, as if the gatekeepers of evangelical race discourse had been waiting for Emerson and Smith's critiques. From 2000 to 2009, ninety-two directly race-related articles appeared in the magazine, almost as many as during the height of reconciliation discourse in the 1990s.

However, there were noteworthy differences in coverage compared to earlier decades. One was that race-related articles had become less generalized and now regularly and substantively addressed other thematic categories. This indicated that the topical range of evangelical race discourse was deepening and diversifying.[19] In the 1980s and 1990s, race coverage in *CT* focused mainly on social dynamics or divergences between evangelicals, with topics like public policy only given minimal attention in the process. In the first decade of the 2000s, however, such generalized "race relations" coverage declined, while specific areas such as MECs and cross-racial alliances among evangelical groups received deeper, more extended treatments. As another example, whereas in previous decades profiles of "ethnic" churches or mission work constituted interest areas in and of themselves, now treatments of these topics routinely included a simultaneous attention to race-related policy issues (for example, AIDS, debt relief, refugee law) or social justice (for example, poverty or rights questions). Coding categories were reorganized in order to reflect such evolutions of race discourse in the magazine.

Table 1 provides a count of race-related articles organized by the primary thematic topic into which the article was coded, with 1980s and 1990s numbers included for comparison. Main coding changes worth noting are that "current events" articles in the 2000s tended to focus on specific subjects like race-related policy, social justice, and demographics and mission potential, so were counted in these areas. In the 1990s, the topic of MECs usually appeared within broad articles on race relations, so were coded there, whereas in the 2000s MECs had become a prominent stand-alone topic. The topic of faith-based "social justice" efforts emerged as a regular coverage area in the 2000s, and articles were coded based on whether they had a U.S. or foreign/international focus. Whereas "demographics and mission potential" articles were generally grouped together in the 1980s and 1990s, they were coded into more specific categories in the 2000s like MEC or racial change ministries.

For the 2000–2009 period, coded under "race relations" broadly were CT's now-standard discussions about real or perceived racial differences among Christians (or Americans), explorations of how groups can "get along" more harmoniously or productively (for example, RR articles), and how Christian congregations and organizations might address past error or trauma in order to heal and move forward. While part of the difference is in the mode of counting, the number (17 items) is more balanced on the whole than in the 1990s when 56 of 114 (over 49 percent) articles matched the criteria of the umbrella category. Also included in this category were most articles related directly to Emerson and Smith's *Divided by Faith*.

In 2003, Curtiss Paul DeYoung, Michael Emerson, George Yancey, and Karen Chai Kim released *United by Faith: Multiracial Congregations as a Response to the Racial Divide*, a companion to *Divided* (DeYoung et al. 2003). *United* followed through on Emerson and Smith's earlier assertions that racially and ethnically heterogeneous social networks guided by a theology of diversity were the best path to *real* social change. This intervention fueled (and followed) the burgeoning MEC movement by developing a theological defense of the multiracial congregation as "an answer to the problem of race," as the book jacket put it.[20] *Divided* and *United* joined a handful of nonbiblical sources I heard regularly mentioned in ERC and MEC settings. (I discuss the influence of *United* on the MEC movement in chapter 7.)

CT paid considerable attention to the MEC movement, which appeared to be a ripe venue for new expressions of social reflexivity. From its first review of *United*, CT ran a steady series of book reviews and profiles of attempts at fostering multiethnic ministry. At mid-decade it hosted two roundtable forums on multiethnicity in the church (Gilbreath 2004, Gilbreath and Gallay 2005).

In some of these forums, as with the shift from the *Divided* to the *United* framework, the focus was less on the problems of socioeconomic inequalities being unevenly distributed across race and more about the practical and cultural obstacles to creating truly integrated evangelical communities when less than 10 percent of American churches meet Emerson and Woo's (2006) definition of

Table 1   Race-related themes in *Christianity Today*

	2000–2009	1990s	1980s
Race relations in evangelical community	17	56	19
Race-related policy issues (e.g., immigration)	16	14	2
Social justice–focused ministry (e.g., poverty)	12	—	—
Multiethnic church ministry (U.S.)	10	*	*
Multiethnic or social justice ministry abroad	9	*	*
Ethnic group profiles (general or theological)	7	12	11
Cross-racial political alliance	7	—	—
Demographics and domestic mission potential	4	20	10
Racial change ministry profiles	3	*	2
Evangelical race history	2	4	4
Current events in race	*	8	0
Theology and race/racism	*	*	3
Other race-related	5	—	—
Total	92	114	51

Note: Dashes indicate categories in which not enough articles substantively addressed the theme to be counted in it. Asterisks indicate where the topic may have been visible, but was better coded into other primary categories.

multiracial. However, these forums also showcased examples of dawning awareness of where evangelicals had been myopic and how ministries could engage in the world differently than they had in the past. For instance, Bill Hybels, leader of Willow Creek, one of the largest megachurch networks in the country, confessed that *Divided by Faith* was a personal "wake-up call" and led him to redirect Willow Creek toward a multiethnic vision:

> I was like the stereotypical person that *Divided by Faith* talked about. I didn't view myself as being racist in any way. I therefore felt that there was no issue I was responsible for. If it was ok with me and *my* individual multiracial friendships, then it was *all* ok. And when I got to the section about the ongoing structural inequities, it devastated me. I thought, *how could I have not seen this?* And that was the beginning of my journey. I felt so badly about being a pastor for 25 years and having been as oblivious as I was to these kinds of issues. It was embarrassing. But these days I'm trying to make up for lost time. (Gilbreath and Galli 2005, 38).

Hybels discussed how he subsequently solicited guidance on building a more multiethnic vision at Willow Creek, hiring more diverse leadership, creating Spanish-language and simultaneous translation services, and working to incorporate a greater multiracial social justice perspective into the mission work the church does domestically and abroad. A profile of Hybels's ministries in Africa later in 2009 looked at how Hybels bypasses nongovernmental organizations and instead partners with tiny churches on the ground to fight poverty and AIDS in Third World countries (Galli 2009).

The racial critique and attendant call for more racially integrated Christianity offered by Emerson et al.—and by a long line of African American and other social justice–oriented Christians before them—seemed to be making its way into the consciences of influential white evangelical leaders. Saddleback's Rick Warren, the Southern Baptist Convention's Richard Land, Richard Stearns of World Vision, as well as popular Christian musicians, long-standing youth organizations (InterVarsity), seminaries, and media forums (*CT, Christian Century*) not only regularly mentioned racial and other socioeconomic divides within evangelicalism, including whites' history of isolationism, in the 2000s, but they also seemed to be at least exploring ways to address them.[21] In the process, whites expressed more self-reflexive disclosures about what they *don't* know, and asked more questions. People of color spoke more openly about their own hesitations about "crossing the divide," whether within or beyond their racial group (Olsen 2004). And Christians involved in MEC-building efforts spoke more openly about how much more difficult it can be than they imagined. Evangelicals were still defining themselves against "the world" in many respects, but they articulated growing sensitivity to the divides, power structures, and inequalities within their own communities.

By the 2000s, *CT* had come some considerable distance from the 1980s, when editors could without compunction run titles like "The Mission Field in Our Back Yard" when describing Latino immigrants. Now ethnic group profiles were no longer treatments of "others" who might be captured by enthusiastic white missionaries ready to bring them to God. Instead, coverage had become more respectful of difference, more integrated into broader topics (for example, refugee struggles in the United States), and driven by the voices of the community members profiled. *CT* covered issues like challenges faced by Haitian refugees, Korean Christians' responses to the Virginia Tech massacre, and Latinos' responses to the 2000 U.S. Census (MacHarg 2000; Alford 2007; Carrasco 2001). Similarly, articles coded under demographics and domestic mission potential constituted a much smaller, more focused category encompassing issues like middle-class blacks leaving the inner city and how small local communities are reaching out to immigrants (Carnes 2003; McGill 2007; Zylstra 2009).

These emergent sensitivities, while not earth-shattering from a secular per-spective, are indicators of expanding social reflexivity. They display much greater awareness than in the past of evangelicals as a racially diverse community, of the relevance of larger social and political dynamics to members of that community, and of the community's connection to other groups around the world who may not be Christian.

Policy and Politics

The expansion of directly race-related *policy* articles in *CT* indicates that evan-gelicals were at least *beginning* to treat issues of structural and systemic racism more seriously in the wake of *Divided by Faith*. Sixteen articles directly focused on race-related political policy (such as immigration law) appeared between 2000 and 2009, compared to only two in the 1980s and fourteen in the 1990s. Relatedly, articles that centered on race-related social justice issues (such as pov-erty) rose to twelve (a topic not robust enough to merit a category earlier). Seven articles explicitly examining cross-racial political alliances also appeared.[22] Many of these topics were simultaneously entering discussions in racial change settings on the ground and were echoed in my interviews with and survey of MEC participants.

The race-related policy thread in *CT* encompassed a few subjects.[23] One was the question (to which white evangelicals appeared sympathetic) of whether high abortion rates in low-income communities represented a kind of racist, modern eugenics trend (Trammel 2007; Blunt 2003).[24] Immigration emerged as the race-related policy topic given the most sustained, in-depth coverage in *CT*. Indeed, it seemed to be the pivotal vehicle through which white evangelicals explored possibilities for cross-racial political alliance building. *CT* articles on immigration in the 2000s reflected greater receptivity to Christians of color's viewpoints (if not leadership from them) and more willingness to depart from conservative Republican Party positions.

In 2006, immigration debates dominated the news, as coordinated grassroots policy reform demonstrations occurred across the United States. In 2003, *CT* reported on the Hispanic Churches in American Public Life (HCAPL) study, which showed that Latinos were both interested in politics and public affairs and wanted their religious leaders to try to get more involved (Sellers 2003).[25] Prominent leaders like Jesse Miranda, founder of the Alianza de Ministerios

Evangelicos Nacionales (AMEN), were quoted urging that Christians get more involved in advocating friendlier immigration policy. By 2006, immigration became a major interest area for the magazine; fourteen articles on the topic appeared through 2009.

First, in January 2006 *CT* posted a story from the Religious News Service on its website critical of prominent (largely white) evangelical groups being "conspicuously mum" on proposed new immigration legislation (Macdonald 2006). By March, the conversation became more complex. *CT* reported on how Hispanic pastors and churches were approaching the legal and spiritual dilemmas (and opportunities) that arise with unauthorized immigration (Scheller 2006). Pastors interviewed challenged the white evangelical church to rise to something they call the "Leviticus 19 Principle," urging their parishioners to stop seeing illegal immigration as "sin":

> The verse says, "The alien living with you must be treated as one of your native-born. Love him as yourself, for you were aliens in Egypt. I am the Lord your God."
>
> [Samuel] Rodriguez [of the National Hispanic Christian Leadership Conference (NHCLC)] interprets the command this way: "We have a moral, biblical, God-given obligation to take care of the disenfranchised, the alienated, and the foreigner. How they got here is not our issue." He . . . asks, "Was it sinful for the Europeans to kick the Indians out and put them on reservations? Is it sin for a father to cross the Rio Grande because his family is impoverished?" (Scheller 2006, 49)

Rodriguez advocated that the white evangelical church issue "clear-cut statements" that would resonate with the Leviticus 19 principle while balancing the value of (and Latinos' own advocacy for) protecting the borders. Another Latino pastor pointed out that some of the damaging U.S. immigration laws were passed with the support of white churches. A few whites were quoted acknowledging immigration as a "moral dilemma," but the piece as a whole conveyed strong interest in and representation of Latino pastors' voices.

In April, *CT* ran a middle-of-the-road editorial acknowledging the legal and moral complexity of the immigration issue and two other pieces that captured disagreement among evangelicals without siding with the traditional white, conservative "rule of law" position (Anonymous 2006). In "Blessed Is the Law—Up to a Point" (Galli 2006), *CT* actually adopted a position mildly supportive of the pro-immigrant view: "While security, overtaxed healthcare, and other issues also desperately need to be addressed, *CT* thinks legislative reform should give some slack to those who have entered our land illegally. Some will remain unconvinced."

In September, *CT* profiled Samuel Rodriguez (the head of the NHCLC), who discussed obstacles between whites and Latinos related to immigration and

other issues. Rodriguez actually called out white evangelicals for soliciting Latinos' support for other political issues while evading a coherent immigration
position:

> "We need to know from white evangelical leaders," Rodriguez was quoted saying in
> *The Washington Post*, "why did they not support comprehensive immigration reform,
> why they came down in favor exclusively of enforcement [of immigration laws]
> without any mention of the compassionate side, without any mention of the Chris-
> tian moral imperatives? So down the road, when the white evangelical community
> calls us and says, 'We want to partner with you on marriage, we want to partner on
> family issues,' my first question will be: 'Where were you when 12 million of our
> brothers and sisters were about to be deported and 12 million families disenfran-
> chised.'" (Stafford 2006).

Perhaps to offset Rodriguez's viewpoint, later that month *CT* ran a more nativist,
conservative response to these immigration-friendly editorials (Edwards 2006).

Through the immigration policy debate, *CT* seemed to find a means to discuss
a race-related issue that bore on the sorts of systemic and structural inequalities Emerson and Smith urged whites to begin to address. While representing a
range of possible positions among evangelicals, *CT*'s leadership seemed willing
in a way they rarely had in the 1990s to consider immigration policy in social
justice terms, through the leaders and organizations covered. To a degree, coverage reflected white evangelicals' general confusion about the proper Christian
position on immigration. Perhaps more significant, *CT* editors facilitated Latino
evangelicals' influence on the discussion. Across the decade they became more
outspoken and far better represented in *CT* forums than in the past—reflecting
at least a measure of growing social reflexivity on whites' part.

For instance, in 2007 the magazine ran "Solution Stalemate," a piece that
put Rodriguez from the NHCLC in dialogue with Richard Land from the Southern Baptist Convention. Land worried about border security and pathways to
citizenship (Pulliam 2007). A few months later, *CT* polled its readership on the
matter, reporting that a whopping 81 percent of respondents believed that Bible
verses on "welcoming the stranger" should guide responses to the U.S. immigration debate (Anonymous 2007). Fifty-four percent supported a path to citizenship as a solution, and a surprising 31 percent supported blanket amnesty. Only
15 percent of *CT* readers advocated enforcing current laws.

Following up on this, *CT* ran a piece noting the GOP's declining support
among Hispanics, and again showcased Latino evangelicals' perspective that
"immigration is a family values issue" (Hughes 2008). By this point (January
2008), Richard Cizick from the National Association of Evangelicals appeared

as a bridge-builder, suggesting that the right-wing's take on immigration was misguided and offering to help evangelicals find common cause. The following year, CT carved out a position in support of an immigration reform program that aimed to balance stronger border security with more pathways to citizenship and better programs for guest workers. The editorial board suggested that churches draw on their strong social capital and long experience with refugee settlement to provide a faith-based partnership with the federal government supporting assimilation of formerly undocumented immigrants (Anonymous 2009). Less a call for activism and more a call for engaged volunteerism, this was nevertheless a socially considered stance. The magazine then continued to cover Latino Christians' protests of what some considered inadequate immigration reform (Walker 2009).

Admittedly, the immigration reform conversation in CT tended to be framed largely through a Latino-white construct (as it was in the United States as a whole). CT did cover other groups on the topic of immigration (Asians, African refugees, and others), though less in relation to policy debates. But this shift out of a black-white race conversation seemed to open up some fresh discursive paths. Through it whites (CT journalists at the very least) exhibited a new measure of social reflexivity by giving new immigrants' perspectives credence and resisting biting a GOP platform hook, line, and sinker. This was an advance from 1990s-era discussions, when most race issues were framed almost exclusively as "minority" (not white) issues. There was an emerging sense in which even white evangelicals had an obligation to respond to immigration in both moral and social-structural terms even if it put them in an uneasy alliance with their traditional political allies.

The immigration debate was an important indicator of how racial discourse in CT did seem to have changed in the new century. Broader shifts were undeniable. It is significant that among American evangelicals in the 2000s, the term "social justice" is no longer a phrase almost exclusively reserved for historical treatments of abolition or the civil rights movement. At least a dozen articles in the U.S. domestic context and another nine in the international field profiled evangelicals, many of them white, who embrace rather than distance themselves from the term "social justice." Under this theme we now find evangelicals (of various colors) asserting that volunteer efforts to help the poor that neglect to respond to the structural sources of poverty are "unjust" (Moll 2005). We also see evangelicals pursuing public advocacy and legal activism to redress social inequality. High-profile megachurch leaders like Rick Warren and Bill Hybels apply terms like "activism," "partnership," and "international justice" to their mission projects; authors advocate a stronger social justice theology in evangelicalism;

and others promote service models in Christianity that involve more substantive sacrifice on the part of privileged whites and middle-class Christians than in the past.[26] While it would be overgenerous to assume all of this is representative of substantive commitments and not just savvy public relations, much of the discourse around mission work or helping the world seems to have become considerably less objectifying of nonwhite and non-American cultures, as well as less distanced and paternalist.

The meaning of observable shifts in the tenor and content of racial discourse over time in a forum like *CT* should not be overdrawn. White evangelicals on the whole did not undergo a revolution in their thinking about the connection between race and systemic inequalities as a result of books like *Divided by Faith* and *United by Faith*. Most did not become politicized social justice activists, ready to change the world (though a few did). But in the wake of the picture Emerson and his colleagues painted of an evangelicalism racially fractured in large part because of whites' limited ability to recognize privilege, power, and inequality, the conversation did seem to evolve toward more nuanced and socially reflexive engagement with race than had existed in previous decades.

Perhaps we can say, based on my observations, that evangelical RR settings before the publication of *Divided by Faith* comprised a first phase of racial change activity, one more personally than socially reflexive. The customs, etiquettes, and cultural vocabulary that developed in RR settings in the 1990s allowed people access to interpersonal, confessional styles of interacting across race while providing subtle disincentives for more political discussions. The contamination and antiprogrammatic arguments were two such mechanisms, which whites and people of color tapped into for different reasons. The relationalism Emerson and Smith criticized did foster a kind of personal reflexivity about race with emotional depth to it—but also discouraged open inquiry into evangelicals' "concrete relationships to the wider world" (Lichterman 2005, 45), including complex issues like privilege, power, and structural inequalities. It is not just that white evangelicals were blind; even many reconcilers' "tool kits" did not train them in skills that fostered political conversations about topics in which there is *not* an automatic assumed consensus, where there is the possibility of ongoing disagreement.

Divided by Faith and the related MEC movement seemed to make social reflexivity about race in evangelicalism at least a little easier. They provided the community with rigorous but culturally sensitive research by credible experts not seen as outsiders (surely it helped that Emerson and Smith are white), and surfaced social dynamics sensed but rarely spoken. Too, perhaps at a time when white evangelicals were readier than they had ever been as a result of the RR frenzy of the 1990s, these developments (which could be interpreted as leadership within the community) gave them permission to openly explore differences in political orientation without shutting down. The evolving treatment of immigration policy in *CT* suggests how a community that in the past had managed to either avoid open disagreement or ignore such issues altogether found new ways to acknowledge substantive diversity of opinion, multiple theological perspectives, and even tension—to, in an important sense, embrace ambivalence. Evangelicals in this period also become more politically conversant and socially reflexive on matters of global poverty, social inequality in the United States, and diversity within their own community. As a wider range of voices entered the conversation, even some influential individuals and organizations broke free from the politics-avoidant etiquette that was paradigmatic in the 1990s.

7 Politics, Culture, and the Multiethnic Church

—————————————————————————— +

Barbara and her family moved to Colorado to help build something different than anything she'd been a part of before. An old friend, Curt Cutler, had followed his dream of planting a multiethnic church (MEC) in the heart of the city and asked her family to come join their lay leadership team. Having grown up a pastor's daughter in an all-white church in the South, she was excited about the vision of a young faith community that would unite to "glorify God" across differences in class, race, and national origin. Industrious, keenly intelligent, and curious, Barbara, forty-four years old during our interview, was also an attentive mother of four internationally adopted children of color, a trained musician, and a free-lance writer. Many Sunday mornings would find her playing keyboards and singing background vocals with the church's makeshift band.

Barbara didn't see herself as someone who knew much about politics. But in our two-hour interview, she expressed a thoughtful struggle about it. Like a number of Pastor Cutler's supporters, she'd been raised in a very fundamentalist denomination that, while deeply conservative, generally rejected the idea that the church should get involved in politics in "the world." "I was basically taught that everyone on the outside was kind of dangerous and questionable," she said. "Questioning for me wasn't really an option." From that perspective, even "helping the poor was kind of viewed as a dangerous slide toward the social gospel."

She did have a streak of social justice activism in her, though. While a student at the ultraconservative Bob Jones University, she helped organize a successful overturning of the school's interracial dating ban, learning a lot about institutional power in the process. Years later, after moving her family into the inner-city neighborhood in Denver, Colorado, enrolling her children in the local "majority minority" public school where they were among less than 5 percent of nonblack pupils, and getting to know her neighbors, she found herself rethinking the values she'd inherited. Her experience in conservative churches made her concerned about unstated expectations that parishioners ascribe to a particular party orientation. "We [early joiners of Resurrection Bible Church] discussed this ahead of time, a group of us. We are not about politics, we should be involved, but we are not about—you know, Christian does not equal Republican. . . . Be a member of society, be a citizen, be, you know, involved, but we are not here to tell you from the pulpit how to vote, what you should believe in, all that stuff—as long as it doesn't—where the Bible is silent, we are silent." Of her former fundamentalist friends who expected conservative Christians to have a particular political party orientation, she said, "I'm just like 'get over it, it doesn't matter.' See, because politics is not why we're here—it's a useful thing, it helps organize society, whatever; it should be a tool for good. That's exactly what the Bible says, 'the government is given to you as an agent of good.'" But she didn't like the idea of judging people based on their political affiliations.

At the same time, Barbara wondered where the stigma on "social gospel" in conservative churches came from. Why had her hometown fundamentalists been reluctant to "get involved" in matters of social inequality, or willing to intervene only in a selective range of issues like abortion? The challenges she was becoming aware of in her new neighborhood—homelessness, the needs of new immigrants, the impact of gentrification on a historically African American community, the problems single-parent, lower-income families faced—seemed like relevant issues for Christians. When asked whether some kind of political engagement should be part of Resurrection's vision, she said, "It should. If it's the right kind of church, we are to be doing this. We're supposed to help the poor, the fatherless, the widows. We have to be, you know?" She wasn't sure what getting involved meant, but, returning to scripture, as was her way, she rolled some ideas around. "Well, Christians are supposed to be salt and light. Salt being preserving, enhancing the flavor of; light being shining light on, being a positive influence. We've lost sight of that largely, and so I think like what Curt's trying to do—we need to look around and go, 'I am part of this community, I need to be involved, you know, I need to be out there,' whatever. Being involved in the schools, sweeping broken beer bottles off the sidewalk, whatever, interacting with your neighbor, trying to make sure that, you know, [affordably priced] housing stays." While she didn't feel a personal call to political work per se and figured she should leave it to more informed church leaders to make those decisions, Barbara had a sense that maybe the church could do more to engage in public life.

Barbara's interview reflects compelling dynamics that emerged to different degrees and with different ramifications among participants in the MEC movement in the 2000s. At the beginning of a potentially long journey, she, like many of her peers in MECs, found herself trying to simultaneously make sense of her present, reconsider the indoctrinated values of her past, and imagine a different kind of future while navigating a new religious collective identity with its own evolving customs, etiquettes, and tensions.

How do people who choose to join multiethnic faith-based communities think about power, politics, and social change? Do the time-worn racial narratives and histories of American evangelicalism still haunt them? Are they attracted to more socially reflexive approaches to change than the racial reconciliation models of the 1990s provided? Do the meaning-making practices and experience of being involved in an MEC community influence the orientations of evangelical racial change (ERC) advocates toward politically informed responses to and conversations about race problems? Or does building multiethnic faith-based community hinge on an ongoing avoidance to politics?

In this and the next chapter, I draw on four sets of data collected in MEC settings to explore emerging answers to these questions in a culturally textured way. I first examine how MEC movement architects in the early 2000s employed the framework of a "spiritual mandate" to reach toward MECs in American evangelicalism wherever possible. The spiritual mandate framework fosters what I call a "kindred outsider community" stance, a sense of marginalized but righteous identity, which nurtures social bonds and sponsors a measure of social reflexivity that sometimes translates into participants' orientations toward politics. I then review results of an anonymous survey of members of Mosaix Global Network (MGN), the national network of existing and aspiring MEC communities. This surfaces patterns of apparent softening to at least the idea of politicized approaches to social change. The final section draws on interviews with and fieldwork among MEC participants to mine the nuances of their current orientations toward race-related politics. A typology of emergent political orientations in the MEC movement allows me to identify the perspectives that place participants on different points therein.

In each of the research contexts, I broadly defined as political engagement any of the following:

- recognition, interest in, or conversation about race- and class-related structural and systemic inequality issues that might surface in churches through their impact on members, such as immigration policy, homelessness, and fair access to housing, quality public education, jobs, and opportunities;
- collective action on such matters, framed by participants as an outgrowth of MEC philosophy;

- discussion or promotion, at the congregational level, of political party platforms or particular policies, locally or nationally;
- support for or critique of political officeholders, addressed in the context of the MEC's mission; and/or
- alliance building or collaboration with other organizations in some sociopolitical context.

Findings from the survey, interviews, ethnography, and local case study illuminated much about the benefits, costs, challenges, and tensions attendant to MEC building in evangelical communities (Wadsworth 2010). The following four observations stood out. In this chapter, I focus on the first three observations. In chapter 8, which draws in greater depth on the case study church, I explore the last.

1. *All data sets produced evidence that evangelicals involved in racial change efforts such as MECs are becoming more comfortable than they have been in previous decades with political conversation and even activism, either as options within or natural outgrowths of faith-based racial change.* One reason for this may be that the way the MEC movement defines its mission asserts a critique of American evangelicalism, a critique with political reverberations of a sort *within* the evangelical world. Through that critique and the kindred outsider community stance it entails, solidarity is fostered among MEC advocates. Other possible explanations for what seems to be increased openness to political approaches to racial change, such as cross-cultural contact and more open customs and etiquettes, are also explored.

2. *The current phase of ERC efforts reflects markedly increased social reflexivity in comparison with the 1990s.* The ability of group members to "engage in reflective talk about the group's concrete relationships to the wider world," including questions of power, seems to be growing in MEC settings (Lichterman 2005, 45). Increased social reflexivity may be influenced, in part, by *Divided by Faith*'s interventions, as many MEC leaders referenced that book's ideas. Too, multiethnic settings almost invariably bring Christians into conversations with communities with whom they may not have had substantial contact in the past, dynamics that often breed both tensions and openings. Identification with a kindred outsider community seems, for many, to be a path to increased social reflexivity, as from that position participants begin to ask questions about power that often awaken them to issues they may have not previously considered. But, as in the 1990s, there are other conceptual frameworks, customs, and etiquettes operating in MEC settings that seem to impose limits on social reflexivity.

3. *A wider range of orientations to social justice and race politics is visible in the MEC movement than during the racial reconciliation phase.* Even so, reluctant or

ambivalent orientations toward political responses to race issues continue to be evident in the 2000s. Certain meaning-making practices such as the Christian/ non-Christian dualism and the social justice–aversive racial narrative continue to influence such ambivalence. The typology of MEC movement participants' political orientations toward racial "social justice" issues helps identify factors that seem to move participants from more to less politics-avoidant perspectives on racial change.

4. *MEC communities can indeed provide a path to the sorts of expanded social change–related engagements Emerson and Smith and MEC architects hoped the MEC might create.* Political activism seems more likely to the degree that participants build relationships beyond the church and in racially and socioeconomically diverse communities. The more extensive their *personal* investments in multiethnic settings beyond the church (in local neighborhoods, for instance), the more inclined participants seem to be to start thinking about race-related political problems and responding to them. Chapter 8 probes this hypothesis through the Denver case study.

The Rising Multiethnic Church

After the peak of racial reconciliation efforts in the 1990s and in the wake of *Divided by Faith*'s critiques of a racially fractured Christianity, the thrust of ERC efforts pivoted from ceremonial reconciliation dialogues, workshops, organizational rituals, and cross-racial church partnerships toward reenergized efforts to create intentionally diverse Christian communities at the congregational level. The MEC movement was on a mission to change the face of American Christianity.[1]

Pioneers in the MEC movement had for years experimented with and written about various models of racially diverse churches, and advocated that evangelicals break out of the monoracial church mode (Ortiz 1996; DeYoung 1995b; Becker 1998). A research literature on the phenomenon was even emerging by the late 1990s (Foster and Brelsford 1996; Yancey 1999; Stumme 1995; Becker 1998). But it was not until the 2000s that MEC advocates began to coordinate a professional network through which they could share resources and establish a more visible presence as a movement within evangelicalism. It was in this context that *United by Faith* was published in 2003 (DeYoung et al). Alongside *Divided by Faith*, it became a major resource on the bookshelves of ERC advocates.

Leading the project was Howard University theologian and pastor Curtiss Paul DeYoung and a multiracial team of Christian researchers invested in the value of MECs: Michael Emerson, George Yancey, and Karen Chai Kim. They argued that embracing ethnic and racial diversity within Christian churches was not just a good idea; it was necessary in order to honor a *spiritual mandate* at the heart of the New Testament. Building from one of *Divided*'s central claims that the segregation of social networks, especially in American churches, renders most Christians impotent to shift racial inequality and stratification (Emerson and Smith 2000, 168), *United* urged that multiethnic congregations could make a difference. "The book issues a call for the emergence of a movement. . . . The twenty-first century must be *the century of multiracial congregation. Christian congregations, when possible, should be multiracial*" (DeYoung et al. 2003, 2).

United by Faith reviewed the history of racial division and the legacy of monoracial congregations, made a theological case for the urgency of a multiracial church movement, compared types of multiracial churches and MECs, and responded to arguments against them. The book's analytical tone was milder than Emerson and Smith's pointed critique of white evangelicals' blindness to systemic patterns of racial inequality. It concentrated instead on the MEC as a site for demographic and attitudinal social change within evangelical communities and as a powerful means of attracting converts. Against the grain of established church-growth patterns based on homogeneity, the authors held that meaningful diversity jibes with the first-century church's radical message of cultural inclusion (DeYoung et al. 2003, 134).

Acknowledging the concern that multiethnicity could undercut the sense of solidarity often fostered in monoethnic churches of color (for example, the traditional African American church), DeYoung et al. suggested racial isolation may not fully serve long-term social justice goals either. White members of MECs are more likely to be more progressive than other whites, so not to engage them could be a missed opportunity. Multiracial congregations offer the opportunity to influence whites in reform directions and to build viable cross-racial networks that can be channeled toward the pursuit of greater equality. Multiracial congregations, then, "must duplicate the role of these [social justice–oriented] uniracial congregations [of color] by impacting society with an agenda for inclusion in mainstream life and a call for accountability in issues of racial injustice" (DeYoung et al. 2003, 136). *United* pivoted its recommendations on the hope that the MEC can create "parallel communities" of refuge and resistance in a racially stratified society, through which Christians can challenge power structures and promote racial justice as natural extensions of the multiracial community (chapter 8).

Although interested in the amenability of MECs to a social justice–oriented Christianity, DeYoung and his colleagues focused more on developing a theological rationale and strategy for church building than on the social justice component. But they raised compelling questions in passing. One is whether whites' interaction with persons of color in MECs helps shift white attitudes about social inequalities, or whether more progressive whites simply self-select toward multiracial congregations in the first place (DeYoung et al. 2003, 136–37). Another is whether "the dominant [white] group's perspective that faith and politics [with regard to socioeconomic issues, at least] are unrelated" constitutes an obstacle to the pursuit of activism as an extension of multiracial church membership (137). A third concerns whether Christians' experience belonging to largely monoracial churches may foster racially divergent orientations to social reform and justice issues that can't successfully coexist in an MEC.

Such inquiries about the political potential of the MEC movement guided my investigations. In 2008–9, I interviewed twenty-four members of MGN.[2] MGN functions as a clearinghouse of information and resources, and an organizer of local, regional, and national MEC forums, two of which I attended in 2008. Through the network, members share theological frameworks, practical strategies, experiences, lessons, and advice for creating successful MECs within a larger evangelical subculture that offers them little guidance. Members receive information through e-mail newsletters, blog forums, live phone calls, and podcasts. Interviewees represented regions across the United States.[3] I was able to interview most during or after MGN-sponsored regional, multiday workshops, where I also conducted participant observation.

Overlapping with this, for two and a half years (2008–11) I closely followed the progress of the church Barbara attended. A brand-new, small (approximately 300-member) MEC planted in a multiethnic, mixed-class urban neighborhood in the Denver metropolitan area at the time, Resurrection Bible Church joined the MGN network during its first year and consulted with its leaders along the way.[4] At Resurrection, I conducted fieldwork and formal interviews with thirteen members, including members of the church's core leadership. During the case study, I also conducted longitudinal interviews with the lead pastor, Curt Cutler, and some of his staff.

The "Mandate" for the Multiethnic Church

Like Barbara, most advocates for MECs don't see themselves as carrying a political cross. Far from it: they still describe themselves as participating in something that has little to do with politics. But at the heart of the mission to build churches that nurture a diverse mix of ethnic, racial, class, and cultural groups is a micropolitical critique with implications within American evangelicalism. By "micropolitical," I mean that the critique renders visible, analyzes, and challenges entrenched social dynamics, established patterns, and power structures within community institutions that haven't as a rule been self-reflective about race.[5] In particular, MEC movement architects challenge one meaning-making practice that, as we have seen, deeply impacted evangelicals' ability to traverse racial divides: the Homogenous Unit Principle (HUP) of church growth promoted by Donald McGavran and C. Peter Wagner. MEC advocates persistently assail the HUP, asserting that is not only short-sighted and outdated but, more important, *unbiblical*.[6] In confronting a practice that has accrued considerable power and status to prominent evangelicals, they carry forward a strand of political critique within evangelical culture.

Even in the mid-1990s people like Manuel Ortiz, a Christian researcher and early proponent of MEC building, delivered the vision of multiethnic Christian community partly through a direct rejection of Wagner's well-entrenched paradigm (Ortiz 1996). "I believe HUP has been a hindrance to race relations and to racial and ethnic reconciliation in the Christian community," Ortiz wrote (45). This critique appeared consistently in the field. Mark DeYmaz, MEC pastor and MGN leader, urges audiences of current and aspiring church-builders to reject HUP-based church planting to the degree that their local demographics provide an option. At an MEC workshop in 2008, he said, "We must no longer allow the Homogeneous Unit Principle to inform church growth and development. This [movement] is an intentional step, to reject that teaching. . . . There is nowhere in scripture that gives us a mandate to plant specific ethnocentric churches. And the question should never have been how fast can you grow a church; it should have been how biblically can you grow a church."[7]

Likewise, Curt Cutler, Resurrection's pastor, noted in my first interview with him, before the doors of his church had officially opened, that critical to planting his MEC was a rejection of HUP-based church design. Referencing McGavran, he derisively called this the "Domino's Pizza for Jesus" model.[8]

Through such critiques, MEC leaders read HUP-based churches as a hindrance to the racial bridging required to produce authentic community among a diverse body of Christians. This impugning of ossified assumptions inside the evangelical world carries social and political risks, given that it implicitly challenges the influence of people in high places—and aspirants to similar paths. For decades, the largest church-planting conferences in the country have promoted formulas and strategies either explicitly or implicitly based on the HUP. The MEC movement's counterstand casts doubt on legacies in which a measure of status and success, particularly for lead pastors and within networked nondenominational churches like Vineyard, has been the rapid growth and size of a congregation (Miller 1997). I saw this risk evidenced in 2008 at the annual Exponential conference, the largest national gathering of evangelical church planters, in Orlando, Florida. There, leaders of the "Multiethnic Churches" track, a new track within the conference, were well aware that the content of their panels challenged the conventional church-planting models that were drawing hundreds of people to keynote lectures in the primary curriculum.

The claim that MECs are a sounder blueprint for Christian community than most monoethnic or monoracial churches (no matter their racial makeup) potentially casts suspicion not just on white but also on African American, Latino, Asian, and other ethnic churches—a stand that creates potential adversaries. MEC advocates assume this risk even while acknowledging, and readily enumerating, the higher social "costs" of membership in racially diverse congregations.[9]

MEC proponents justify such a choice through the idea of a biblical mandate for MECs to live out the vision of God's "kingdom" on earth. (This is often referenced as "kingdom theology."[10]) This theological anchoring is a necessary move in the context of an evangelical faith culture that, as I discussed in chapter 5, puts more stock in biblical anchoring than secular arguments.[11] Interpretations of the theological justifications for MECs are offered in most of the "how-to" manuals on building MECs. Two that pitch the matter explicitly through the goal of propelling an MEC movement come from *United by Faith* and DeYmaz's *Building the Healthy Multiethnic Church* (2007).

Central to the theological mandate argument is the idea that Jesus Christ's ministry was fundamentally a bridge-building enterprise, a model for Christians of the values of radical inclusivity. As an outsider himself (born in a manger, a Jew with many Gentile associations, and so forth), MEC advocates point out, Christ's ministry was inclusive of people who would normally not be sitting at the same table—people like women, tax collectors, sinners, Gentiles, and untouchable classes. Preaching an inclusive gospel that included the poor and oppressed of Israel and expanded beyond the nations to become a "house of prayer for all nations," Jesus "broke all the rules" of his society (DeYoung et al. 2003, 16–17). The power of the Christian faith, goes the narrative, was revealed as communities in and after Jesus's earthly ministry bridged cultural and racial differences thought virtually insurmountable at the time. MEC architects like DeYmaz look to the Gospel of Paul at Antioch to anchor the idea of multiethnicity as a mandate for Christians. Galatians 3:2 is a particular favorite: "There is neither Jew nor Greek, slave nor free, male nor female, for you are all one in Christ Jesus." Christ not only transcended the cultural barriers of the time, he called his followers to do the same. Therefore, as the *United* authors put it, "Jesus' inclusive table fellowship and vision of a house of prayer that was for all the nations was a precursor to what we call multiracial congregations. Jesus' 'congregation' of followers was multicultural" (20).

In this framework, the value of "Christian" as a potentially revolutionary identity and community precedes the goal of "justice" in any secular sense. As in the 1990s, the claim of the biblical mandate for multiethnicity is not that Christians should fight for racial justice in "the world" *in order* to be better Christians (though many MEC proponents would say individuals should), or in order to attract multiethnic congregations by virtue of being justice-oriented. Rather, the call is to build MEC communities because Christ himself promoted a faith community undivided by cultural differences, and because MECs as a model of the unity Christian faith makes possible will inspire *others* to become Christians. Such a framework reflects the evangelical view that "the world" cannot achieve racial unity because it lacks a Christian framework.[12]

As a theological explanation of multiracial church building, the biblical mandate concept seems to justify the political risk of challenging the American evangelical mainstream. Proponents insist that the benefits and rewards of MEC communities outweigh whatever difficulties the process entails, for if crossing cultural lines through faith is a divine mission, the reward is in fulfilling the commandment to create diverse community in the church "as it is in heaven." In this spirit, *United* authors strike down common pragmatic, theological, activist, cultural, and sociological defenses of monoracial churches with a mixture of theology and scholarship. They conclude, "We have held the high standard of what it means to be an authentic multiracial congregation. We do not apologize for this. We do recognize that multiracial congregations are a result of a commitment to take a long and difficult journey toward authenticity. So we call for a movement toward more multiracial congregations" (DeYoung et al. 2003, 143; see also their chapter 8).

Difficulty, even intense discomfort, is framed here as a natural and valuable part of the MEC process. Indeed, it is *required* in the sense that discomfort reflects that people are engaging substantively with others from outside their home culture. DeYmaz put it bluntly at a 2008 church-planting conference, in the context of incorporating multiple musical styles in a multiracial church: "If you're doing it right, 30% of folks in your church will be uncomfortable 30% of the time. And that's good!" MEC advocates argue that the outcome of a process done right will be deep growth, for individuals and for a community.

Kindred Outsiders

The biblical mandate idea combined with an embrace of cost and discomfort provides a strong sense of *kindred outsider community* among MEC movement participants, a sense of collectively resisting the hegemony of monoethnic church communities that other Christians largely take for granted. Nearly all MEC participants I met saw themselves as participating in something nonnormative and quite radical in evangelical church culture.[13] People spoke of the "relief" they felt simply being in a forum in which they could share their experiences and hear from others who could relate. They spoke about pursuing a vision that they did not get much tangible support for from other churches and denominational organizations—even, sometimes, from members of their own church who resisted the changes brought by the MEC approach. Like kin, they sometimes argued over approaches to or priorities within MEC building. But the perception and reinforcement of the messages that they were being faithful to scriptural authority and engaged in a righteous, though sometimes painful, struggle helped fortify their identity as outsiders working to create positive change in the Christian community.

In some ways the risk of the kindred outsider experience is that in their identity as believers following a biblical mandate for diversity rather than embracing a notion of multiculturalism imposed by the secular world (which to many smacks of religious relativism), MEC proponents might have a kneejerk tendency to see secular approaches to social change as distractions, tools of an unbelieving world, and so forth. On the other hand, when people move from monoracial settings to multiracial ones and start to see themselves as rebels and pioneers vis-à-vis the larger evangelical community, they may be more inclined to build a climate of solidarity with new communities. For example, people from Resurrection who moved into the local neighborhood near the church began to "have a heart" for the poor and homeless living in the area. Through empathic identification, they explored avenues for getting involved, which brought them into conversations with people and groups in the city with whom they might not otherwise have built connections. Other patterns emerge here, such as MEC members' experiences of realizing that their churches of origins may have been "wrong" on issues of race—an insight that, for many, seems to trigger a cascade of reconsiderations about the church's proper role in society. Dogmatic assumptions seem to decompose in this mode of dawning insights, replaced by new openness.

Surveying Mosaix Global Network Members

As we saw in chapter 6, *Christianity Today's* coverage of immigration debates and other matters from 2000 to 2009 signaled the possibility that what used to be an identifiably white evangelical community had become less homogeneous in terms of the voices, experiences, political perspectives, and public engagements represented in its own discourse than in the previous two decades, and seemingly more tolerant of a range of Christian responses to social problems, including those that concern race. Informed by patterns emerging in the case study and interviews from MEC participants, I developed an online survey of MGN members in 2010 in order to probe broader attitudes about how and whether MEC communities should approach race-related social change issues, including politically. One hundred and twenty-six people, or approximately 10 percent of MGN's membership list at the time, responded. The pattern of growing willingness to speak about race issues in political terms—at least with regard to policy matters like immigration—and to reconsider previously taken for granted "white" conservative perspectives on these matters was echoed in the survey results.[14] Evidence of increasing social reflexivity and an attendant "softening" to politics stood out in comparison to the 1990s research.

Participants mirrored the authors and audiences of the MEC literature in a number of ways. The vast majority (82 percent) of respondents reported current involvement in MEC enterprises.[15] Ninety-five percent met the definition of "strong Christian," attending church at least once a week. Eighty percent self-identified as either fundamentalist or evangelical.[16] All regions of the United States were represented, with approximately a fifth to a quarter of the group representing the Midwest, Southern Crossroads, South, Pacific, and Middle Atlantic states. The racial makeup of the group met the definition of multiracial provided in the MEC literature (over 20 percent minority group members). Seventy percent of respondents were white, 18 percent were African American, and the remaining 13 percent identified as Asian, Latino, Native American, or mixed race.[17] Consistent with the fact that MGN is a network geared toward pastors and most evangelical pastors are male, 83 percent of respondents were male. The majority (54 percent) were pastors of some sort (not necessarily lead pastors); 25 percent identified as lay leaders (for example, Sunday school teacher); and 17 percent as having some other sort of interest in MEC building (for example, through a funding or umbrella organization). Respondents' experience level in MECs was fairly diverse; approximately one-third (31 percent) had been involved in MEC efforts for three years or less, 18 percent for four to six years, and fully half for six years or more.

A range of MEC types were represented in the survey. In just over half (53 percent) of the group, whites currently occupied the majority in the church. Another quarter of the church builders worked in majority-black MEC congregations. Eleven percent were majority Asian; 9 percent majority Latino; and 11 percent marked either mixed race or "no majority racial group." The lion's share (89 percent) of respondents reported having attended monoracial churches before becoming involved with their current MEC. Consistent with the evangelical meaning-making practice of identifying the hand of God's direction in their personal lives, 55 percent of respondents reported that their primary reason for getting involved in MEC work was that they "felt called by God to get involved (with no prior connection to a multiethnic church)." The remainder cited having either read about MECs or found one through social or neighborhood networks.

MGN survey respondents were passionate in their perception of racism as a social issue that the Christian community needed to address. When asked how important addressing racism and/or racial inequality ought to be as a Christian priority, 93 percent marked important or very important on a Likert scale. A bare majority (51 percent) worried that racism was more pervasive *within* rather than outside the Christian world. (Thirty-four percent marked the latter, and the remainder saw racism as equally pervasive.) And their embrace of the notion of a spiritual mandate to build MECs was clear. Asked, "Do you believe there is a 'theological mandate' in the Bible for Christians to worship in multiethnic communities when possible?," 85 percent affirmed.[18]

Several Likert scale questions probed MEC participants' perspectives on whether and to what degree MEC communities could foster involvement in race-related social change issues within and beyond the church. Following Emerson and Smith's (2000) work, I was also interested in the extent to which respondents favored person-to-person relational approaches to racial change in comparison to more recognizably systemic or structural interventions. The results were surprising. For example, while *all* respondents marked "building an individual relationship with someone from another racial/ethnic group" as an important way to work against racism, nearly as many (90 percent) also cited getting involved "in local issues that especially impact poor and minority communities (example: public education, housing)" as important or very important. Fully half of respondents chose "support political candidates who work for greater racial equality" as important.

Asked to evaluate the appropriateness of a number of different approaches to creating racial change through the MEC, some items being apolitical (for example, volunteering for a charitable group) and others quite political, respondents were similarly warm toward political engagement. For example:

- 92 percent supported working against structures of racial inequality outside the churches;
- 85 percent supported participating as church representatives in public discussions about race-related issues;
- 80 percent supported working against socioeconomic inequality outside the churches; and
- 75 percent supported taking a public position against inequalities in the public education system.

Finally, asked whether, in general, "it is better for churches and denominations to take stands on social and political issues consistent with their theology (for example, challenging poor public housing conditions)" or whether, rather, "taking such stands should always be up to individual Christians," survey respondents were quite strident: 80 percent said churches should "always" or "sometimes" take public stands. Only 12 percent chose the individual-only option.

Whether people see an issue as appropriate or not on a Likert scale is not the same as personally getting involved or supporting one's church in doing so; such survey questions only measure people's warmth toward topics presented in the abstract. Fifty-one respondents answered an open question, "Are there any social issues that you believe are particularly important for Christians to get involved in *as Christians* (as opposed to just ordinary citizens)?" More than half of respondents listed abortion, but also mentioned were human trafficking, food/hunger/poverty, war, the global slave trade, AIDS, health care, and human rights. The MGN survey also probed respondents' views toward two specific policy areas that interviews and fieldwork (as well as *Christianity Today* race discourse) showed as registering to MEC participants as relevant to the work of their churches the more deeply they became invested in multiethnic communities. These were immigration and public education.

If *Christianity Today's* coverage of immigration in the 2000s signaled that evangelicals might be considering race-related issues in more complex ways than in the past, the survey results suggest that MEC participants, even while majority white, are quite amenable to pursuing progressive political approaches to the issue. In fact, when asked to consider the appropriateness of a list of interventions related to immigrants, MGN members looked like a fairly liberal group. Although supporting political policy positions on immigration was less popular than relational interactions (such as welcoming immigrants to church), respondents were fairly supportive of churches taking a public stand on behalf of immigrant-supportive policies. Ninety-three percent saw welcoming immigrants to church, whether legal or not, as appropriate, and, correspondingly, three-quarters saw churches welcoming *only* legal immigrants as *in*appropriate. Eighty-four percent supported assisting undocumented immigrants with processes of becoming legal. When asked about working to address legal obstacles immigrants face in the United States relative to housing, work, and so forth, some respondents (nearly 20 percent) moved toward a neutral position, but 67 percent registered support. The most overtly political item offered, "working to help change immigration policy to make the immigration process less difficult," also garnered a majority (57 percent) of respondents. The conservative approach of "working to curb illegal immigration" attracted the least support (less than 33 percent), and over 10 percent of respondents marked that as inappropriate.[19]

Equality issues in public education generated similar warmth toward political responses, though somewhat more cautiously.[20] MGN members seemed somewhat ambivalent about whether churches ought to promote Christians sending their children to public or private Christian schools. Thirty-one percent thought it appropriate for churches to encourage members to send children to public schools; a similar percentage thought encouraging *Christian* school attendance was inappropriate. Half or more were neutral toward those questions. Large percentages of 80 percent or higher valued church-based programs to support parents and children in the local public school system, such as after-school tutoring. But considerable majorities (over 60 percent) also saw it as appropriate for the church to speak out in public forums about equality in education, to work with other organizations to improve public education policy, and to support proposed laws to improve the public education system. A similar 65 percent considered it inappropriate for churches to stay out of debates about public education policy.

Overall, respondents in the MGN survey did not seem nervous about interpreting the mission of the MEC in social justice terms and were expressly amenable to at least some forms of political engagement *by the church*.[21] Also interesting is that when offered a list of nine social and political issues and asked to gauge each issue's relevance to the MEC church on a Likert scale, traditional marriage and abortion fell lower on measures of enthusiasm than other social issues.[22] The following topics generated the largest percentages of respondents selecting "relevant" or "very relevant" for churches to support: building more racially and ethnically diverse church leadership (98 percent); working against ongoing racial inequalities in society (97 percent); fighting conditions that create poverty (95 percent); and working to prevent homelessness (93 percent). Opposing abortion and supporting traditional marriage as the only legal marriage form were popular but generated a lesser 90 percent and 85 percent, respectively.[23] In other words, structural, systemic socioeconomic issues appeared to register as more immediately relevant to MEC participants than the "moral values" issues that galvanized evangelical Christians in the 1980s and 1990s.

Combined, these results paint a picture of an MEC community that is fairly social justice friendly—and, indeed, perhaps more friendly than aversive even when considering political engagement as an expression of MEC work. Racial reconcilers in the 1990s tended to be bifurcated, in that they either gravitated toward the politically aversive viewpoint, mostly though not exclusively represented by whites, or a pro–social justice/activist perspective largely represented

by people of color. This largely unnamed divergence heightened tensions between the groups in racial change settings. In the absence of effective etiquettes
(norms of speech and silence) for engaging underlying conflict between members, especially political conflict, the customs of evangelicalism for the most part
silenced discussion and limited paths to social reflexivity.

In contrast, MGN members by 2010 did *not* demonstrate an aversion to
considering socioeconomic equality issues. In MEC settings, most participants
seemed to have moved into more vulnerable, and more varied, territory. They
also appeared to be demonstrating greater social reflexivity in considering how
others might interpret issues, seeing problems through "different" members'
perspectives, and asking more questions about how things were done in the
past. Some articulated sensitive perceptions of power structures and politics and
seemed amenable to MEC churches taking more engaged positions. In short,
the MEC community of the 2000s seems to open up a range of perspectives that
disrupts the bifurcation of older race narratives in evangelicalism. This suggests
that where leadership exists in MECs in the direction of political engagement,
many members might be inclined to follow.

Did these patterns repeat on the ground of MEC communities? Also, did local MEC participants have an awareness of the sorts of critiques Emerson and
Smith had made of the evangelical world, and, if so, how did they respond to
those critiques?

Transcending Polarized Narratives

In the interest of building rapport with the MEC participants I met and because
it made for a more natural conversational flow, I waited until about two-thirds
of the way into interviews (which lasted between thirty minutes and two hours)
to raise questions about the potential political implications of MEC work.[24] Participants were first asked about their background, their current churches and/
or MEC ambitions, their views on what MEC-building means, and their critiques of MEC strategy and ideas about the movement's future. They also had
time to reflect on things they had learned about the MEC environment (even if
only through the conferences they attended, if they weren't yet part of an MEC)
and social dynamics they may have observed in their efforts, either within the
MEC context or in the communities surrounding the MEC. The interviews then
moved into questions like the following:

- Are there any structural, social, or policy issues in the larger world that you
  see affecting members of your multiethnic church? (For example, inequali-

ties in public education systems; or immigration policy affecting church members.)

- Would there be any circumstances under which you could imagine your church taking a stand on any of the above issues?
- Does multiethnic church building have any relevance to social justice? How would you define social justice?

Some of the old hesitations and cautions about "losing the gospel" to political engagement were evident in the interviews. But as with the MGN survey results, many MEC participants expressed a striking openness toward engagement on matters of racial-social inequality compared with their predecessors in the racial reconciliation era.

The vast majority of participants who responded to the questions about potential political implications of MEC work fit into one of five categories. These are mapped in figure 5 onto a spectrum from what we might see as least to most politics friendly.[25] Although individuals sometimes made statements consistent with more than one of the positions, interviews were coded based on the overall thrust of the speaker's viewpoint. Most expressed perspectives that placed them in the middle two positions, either ambivalent or nervously interested. To my surprise, the number 3 position, nervously interested, was the one most often articulated. Politics-aversive and activist positions were outliers. However, many MEC participants often began at the left end of the spectrum and moved along it toward the activist end the longer and more deeply invested they became in a successful MEC and the surrounding community.

Politics Aversive

No interviewees expressed perfectly unequivocal aversion toward political responses to race- and ethnicity-related matters on the part of churches or church leaders; most could envision at least some rare circumstance in which it would be appropriate for churches to take a political stand. (An example might be a group being rounded up by the government or prevented from voting, as happened to the Japanese during the Second World War.) However, I met and observed a number of people who expressed consistent enough resistance to political engagement as an outgrowth of multiracial church efforts that they could not fairly be categorized into the next position, ambivalent.[26] MEC participants categorized in Position 1 expressed aversion to politics either because they couldn't identify any relevant connection between politics and MEC building, or because they considered political engagement dangerous for their specific congregation.

Pastor Matt, a white man in his early forties leading a successful MEC in

Figure 5   Political orientations spectrum

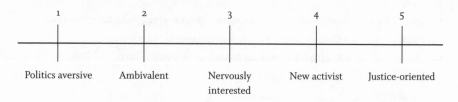

the southwestern suburbs of Illinois, captured the first variety. When presented with the questions about whether the MEC should relate in some way to politics or social justice, Matt seemed to draw a blank and redirect his responses back to the idea that the MEC is a space for ethnic inclusivity. This may have been a matter of background and temperament, but just the topic of politics seemed to make him distinctly uncomfortable. His comments were suggestive of a lack of a developed civic etiquette in his home culture. "You know, my persuasion may be Republican, but I grew up—it wasn't one of those—we don't talk about religion or politics in our house, it's just that we didn't—my folks, we never intermingled our church with politics, per se," he began. At another point in the interview he circled back to the question. "Is what we're doing a political thing?" he reflected. "No, it's not a political thing. I think it's a spiritual thing." At interview's end he insisted that the organizers of the MEC track of the workshop we were attending did not really have politics on the radar. "We've spent lots of hours, hashing and rehashing the movement. And a political component has been little to none," he said.[27] This pastor did not seem able to envision where politics fit in in the MEC vision, although he referenced civil rights leaders as examples of appropriate Christian activism. He tended to categorize these figures and events as relics of the past, and politics as simply irrelevant to the goals of building churches that reflect the diverse body of Christ.[28]

Pastor Sal was a Latino church-planter of a largely first-generation Mexican American church in Tennessee, in the process of becoming increasingly multiracial. He articulated aversion to politics from a different vantage point than Matt. "I told my congregation the other day that there is no hope in the government," he said. "We're not gonna solve [inequality issues, particularly regarding immigration], and I don't see Hillary Clinton or Obama or the next president solve this problem in the next five, six years. So we're not gonna depend on them 'cause they're not gonna solve the problem. But there's one God that can solve this problem. Whether we're here legal or illegal, he's gonna protect us here. We're gonna depend on him and not on the government, not on the United States."

The thrust of Sal's comment echoed other patterns visible in 1990s reconciliation contexts: the concept that religious faith trumps any kind of public authorities, whose motives cannot be trusted, or political processes. However, his viewpoint also reflected feelings of vulnerability on behalf of immigrant communities, and perhaps Latinos' experiences of being betrayed by other governments abroad. These experience-based perspectives arose in other interviews with people of color. Sal's emphasis that Christians trust material circumstances to God rang more of fatalism than of an ideological opposition to political engagement. "Just trust in the Lord," he reported telling his parishioners who may worry about being deported. "Be faithful and be full of the Holy Spirit, and if God wants you here, you'll be here [in America]. If he wants you to go back to your town, he will use you there wherever he will take you."

A steadfast aversion to politics as an extension of the MEC was a minority perspective (only three interviewees fit squarely in the category). Position 1 takes the approach that while inequalities that stem from racism may be societal, the MEC's role is to provide a more holistic environment and sanctuary for its members, not to try to mobilize them.

Ambivalent

Some participants expressed views consistent with ambivalence or confusion rather than outright aversion to political engagement as an outgrowth of MECs. Position 2 folks consistently stumbled around the topic of politics in interviews, or expressed confusion when asked what one thing (for example, social justice) might have to do with the other (their MEC). They did not appear opposed in principle to making connections. Rather, they tended to speak in seemingly contradictory terms, expressing interest in church-based social justice, on the one hand, and rejecting it a breath later.

The Position 2 viewpoint was common among but not unique to white evangelicals. As in the 1990s, however, people of color often raised distinctive concerns regarding political engagement. For instance, two Latino pastors, despite describing social justice as an important mandate for Christian churches to pursue in theory, nevertheless argued that politics was a suspicious arena in which the church had to be very careful engaging. Said Pastor Angél, who was raising up a multiethnic Latino church in Kansas: "I come from a different country [Mexico] and I don't—Mexicans, a lot of Mexican people come to work in construction or whatever . . . but I think our churches should do something and I know it's still hard for our churches. . . . Maybe a little bit [of social justice work] here, a little bit there but, I mean, it's been hard for me to see [the connection]." This pastor's perspective was partly born of direct experience that suggested political engagement is likely to be unsafe for MECs that include undocumented or brand new immigrants.

Another Latino pastor of a rural church relayed a story about going to court to support a parishioner who had been sentenced to two days in jail. "I made the mistake [of speaking up for him] and got him four days because I was trying to defend him. Sometimes when you try to protect people you just make it worse," he surmised. Although this leader could clearly recognize the sorts of political structures and justice issues that impacted his members, he was ambivalent about the tangible risk of the church or him as pastor getting involved.

A Chinese American, Pastor Jon, who led a suburban MEC, expressed the ambivalent position through advocacy of only the mildest forms of political engagement. He explained that his church advocated a five-step approach to community building, the last step being a "call to action." This, he said, might include individual activities, like writing a letter to a congressperson or "standing up against" local injustices like the placement of a toxic industrial plant in a neighborhood. This seems like a fairly politics-friendly position. Yet the pastor was adamant that his church should *avoid* political discussions as a group:

> I think part of the culture that we're developing [in his MEC] is that we want to advocate tolerance and acceptance of all people, and if it means avoiding discussing certain hot buttons then we would do it. And politics is one of those hot buttons. . . .
>
> There are too many irons in the fire. I want to choose my battles very selectively. Politics is not one of those battlegrounds that I want to choose to fight. . . . If there's any of those nerves that I want to hit, it's the issue of racism. So I show movies, like *Mississippi Burning*. I'm choosing not to talk about politics; that could really muddle the focus.

Ambivalence seeps through this combination of statements. Churches must speak out about injustice, but focus on racism, not politics—as if there is no pertinent connection between them, at least from the church's perspective. At the same time, the pastor explicitly encourages an etiquette of *avoidance* of political discussion, and thereby seems to inhibit political reflexivity. He reduces racism to a matter of personal prejudice, yet his model of MEC work encompasses forms of political engagement on behalf of victims of injustice. There is almost a schizophrenic quality to such ambivalent messages, which would seem to cultivate politically ambivalent paralysis. This orientation is reflective of the kind of "customs" inhibitions, wherein speech norms in a given subculture (in this case, the church) discourage sorts of talk that might reveal or generate underlying conflict.

Other quotes from interviews capture how the social justice–aversive narrative, so dominant especially among white evangelicals in the 1990s, still weaves through the ambivalent position on the political orientations spectrum, even as many participants seem to feel a pull *toward* some forms of engagement. Here we see the old bifurcation of pro– and anti–"social justice" orientations:

> [Social justice] is part of, you know, what—at least in terms of practical applications, what the gospel is supposed to do. I think the problem has been, among evangelicals, when you combine social justice with the gospel, that that becomes the gospel. In other words, the whole liberalism, the reason that became—people shied away from those issues because social justice issues ate up the church. (Korean American male pastor, Southern California)

> I do think there's a danger about politics in the multiracial setting because it's so charged, and I just—personally I feel that our politics today have gotten so hostile to each other; both sides. And to bring that to a setting [race] where, you know, there's a history of being hostile and rude to each other. . . . So you've got plenty of things, why bring in politics? (African American male parishioner, Texas)

Position 2 participants on the whole tended to be either unsure about the appropriate connections between the MEC and political engagement, or worried that politicization of the MEC mission as a "social gospel" mission could threaten the interpersonal racial bridging that a multiracial church requires in order to bond. They weren't necessarily averse to political engagement in principle (though they might have come from communities that were), and in many cases they were becoming aware through the direct experiences of their own church members that opportunities existed for the church to engage on issues that might bear on politics. Their comments nevertheless reflected a distinct wavering back and forth regarding whether engagement fit the mission of the MEC.

Nervously Interested

By far, most MEC participants I interviewed expressed a nervously interested orientation, rather than the more explicit aversion or ambivalence we saw among ERC advocates in the 1990s. These interviewees were noticing politics and/or justice-related issues that impacted their members or the surrounding community, and were beginning to see at least some sorts of political engagement as relevant to the multiracial church, even though they still registered considerable ambivalence about themselves or their churches moving toward politics. As in the MGN survey, immigration policy and education surfaced in the interviews as potential arenas in which MECs might get involved. Position 3 church-builders were nevertheless anxious about what political involvement meant for them as pastors or members, and for the movement as a whole. An emergent social reflexivity was also evident, as many interviewees reflected on experiences of groups whose perspectives they had not known much about prior to the MEC context. For the more seasoned MEC participants within this group, such social reflexivity seemed to be expanding to encompass relationships with other groups, even non-Christians.

Pastor Lauren, a white woman leading an MEC outside of Chicago that had become a mecca for new immigrants in the past decade, had, through her congregants, become aware and increasingly critical of the bureaucratic and political obstacles immigrants face when applying for citizenship. Responding to this increased social reflexivity, she wanted to do something, but also worried about making a fragile situation more so. "For me to raise the [political] questions in the church right now . . . it's too much. Because they're all overwhelmed; they're mostly immigrants. We can't ask them to do any more [than they already do]. But it's us becoming aware; how can we help?" As with others in Position 3, Pastor Lauren was anxious that nurturing "unity" across all kinds of difference in an MEC was already difficult enough; to add the risky topic of politics to the plate might just be too much. Nor was she sure she had the relevant skills to guide church members toward political engagement.

Nervously interested folks often worried about what it meant for church members or their congregation as a body to talk openly about, much less "take a stand on," politics—especially on political party platforms or specific candidates. MGN leader Mark DeYmaz, speaking of his own MEC in Little Rock, Arkansas, articulated the common concern prominent among evangelicals in cross-racial settings that just talking about politics would create or amplify tensions in the church. In Position 3 narratives, the white conservative evangelical "social justice critique" commonly surfaced, as it did in DeYmaz's:

> My [MEC building framework] gives proper attention to the reason for doing this *and that is for the gospel, not for social justice, social agenda*, racial reconciliation. All those are wonderful by-products, if we get the mission right, and then reconcile with the churches, all that other stuff's gonna flow from that. . . . I've got strong Republicans, strong Democrats [in my church], so I love them all, in the name of Christ. So I can't just come out and go, hey, we're all for Barack Obama, or we're all for this.
>
> And so then I have to step back and say, what in a positively constructive way, how can we begin to address situations of social justice, that being [for example] education, in a way that is really elevating conversation and not, um, *taking a side*, if you will, and making people think, "here's what we think"? (emphasis added)

Despite these concerns, DeYmaz *had* become involved in a number of quasi-political engagements as extensions of his MEC work. He mentioned having served on a public panel debating the death penalty, as the only representative of a conservative evangelical church. (He was on the panel because he had become increasingly concerned about socioeconomic and political inequalities that made blacks and Latinos overrepresented on death row.) He had sought ways to help undocumented immigrants in his church, and had begun to think more critically about immigration policy than he had in the past. He had become involved in public forums about ongoing inequalities in Little Rock's public education system. He even organized a panel of representatives from different religions to discuss faith and culture as lenses on difference (a truly rare thing for a conservative evangelical to do).

Though many had less experience in MEC work than DeYmaz (and others had more), people in Position 3 tended to recognize issues they could imagine MECs politically engaging around through sympathy with the personal experiences of their church members. The MEC setting clearly seemed to facilitate this basic outgrowth of social contact. As Pastor Lauren put it, "I'm not sure how to [address immigration policy]. But more and more I interact with people who are going through struggles with their visas, and there's a HUGE injustice, not only in our system, but in the way their [countries of origin] handle them, to help them or to hinder them. . . . That's an issue on our table: What's our next step?" Others registered increasing awareness of how health care policy, poverty, and racial profiling impacted members of their MEC church communities.

At Resurrection Bible Church in Colorado, many church members could be described as squarely in or moving toward Position 3. As I elaborate in chapter 8, the better acquainted people became with the challenges the surrounding community faced, and especially to the degree that church members actually lived in diverse neighborhoods, the more the political dimensions of a number of issues began to emerge on people's radar.

New Activist

Interviews and fieldwork suggested that occasionally a person who becomes committed to MEC work can, under the right circumstances, undergo a kind of conversion process in which he or she becomes drawn to faith-based activism despite previous inexperience. This is the position of the new activist, and it was the position of Pastor Cutler at Resurrection and some of his staff.

For the new activist, something shifts with the depth of investment in the MEC community, to the degree that a person begins to actively engage *beyond the church setting* with an issue or issues that enter awareness through some aspect of MEC involvement. The ability to move toward activism may be attributable to personality or temperament; social movement scholarship indicates that certain personality types gravitate toward activism (Block 2006; Carlson 1980). But in the context of church communities that contain significant numbers of at least formerly conservative evangelical Christians, a turn toward political activism is indicative of a paradigm shift. An indicator of this shift for Cutler was the evolution of his comments on the distinctions between "the gospel" and "social justice" over two and a half years.

Before he opened the doors of Resurrection, Cutler's views on the church as a vehicle for the pursuit of political justice issues (or not) were filtered through his upbringing in the very conservative, very white Independent Fundamental Baptist church. In his first interview, he employed the social justice–aversive viewpoint so routine among white evangelicals. Enumerating each element of the church's stated mission, he mentioned "compassionate serving" as relevant to the MEC mission. This would start with listening. "We would say, what are the needs of the community and how can we help? At the same time, we try to avoid the mistake from our perspective of the liberals who just went into social action and lost the gospel."

Less than a year later, Cutler had become deeply involved in outreach and fund-raising efforts for the homeless, local public school reform efforts, immigration reform, and issues related to poverty as it impacted families in the neighborhood. This transformation occurred through the social reflexivity that began to happen as Cutler became invested in the community, both as a church leader who wanted to make an impact and as an individual citizen. Through his children attending the underfunded public elementary school, for example, he was gaining a sense of the massive discrepancies in school resources across the city, such as lack of air-conditioning in poorer schools. "To me, it's an injustice," he commented. "If I have to, I'll go down to [the outdoor mall downtown] and sit in a Plexiglas box for two weeks to prove the point. If that's political, so be it."

Through this newfound familiarity with how structural inequality impacted not only his family but also people he knew in the church, he, like Barbara, found himself reconsidering his old conservative training. "I come from conservative training that says you are supposed to save souls—you know, as opposed to the Rauschenbusch social gospel approach that [conservatives argue] hurt the church. Now I'm saying, you can't separate the gospel from the *work* of Christ. My conservative 'Boomer' friends would be critical; 'its not the job of the church to do this stuff,' they'd say. [I think] there's a time for a sermon, but there's a time to go advocate, to help." When I asked Curt if this meant he was rethinking politics, he affirmed, even as he seemed surprised himself. "Technically, I'm moving into social justice. It's more than social action. And the minute you talk justice you're talking politics. But it's my life!" The pastor found himself directly experiencing things he'd formerly only understood in the abstract. He never expected to lobby on behalf of local school board candidates, but over time this began to make sense as a natural outgrowth of his evolving religious perspective.

Like Cutler, people in the new activist position often move from resistance through ambivalence, to nervously interested, and finally to a place in which their attraction to engagement on issues impacting themselves, members of their churches, or their surrounding communities overcomes their previous hesitance. This process sometimes echoes the conversion narratives so prominent in evangelical culture: a believer (in racial justice) was once in the dark (isolated and afraid of engagement), but comes to be transformed through having her or his heart changed as a result of insights and events that God orchestrates (like meeting people in the neighborhood). Indeed, it is possible that evangelical cultural customs, which emphasize "becoming a new person" through religious epiphanies, render MEC participants more open to shifting their perspectives on politics than they might otherwise be. The new activist doesn't necessarily have a sophisticated understanding of politics, but she or he is ready to get her or his feet wet.

Justice Oriented

People in Position 5, the most politics-friendly position, articulated the perspective that at least a natural and possibly a necessary outcome of a healthy theologically grounded MEC should be some level of church-based political engagement on matters of racial and/or socioeconomic equality. These participants had a more developed framework for conceptualizing the value of political engagement than people in Position 4 and expressed a significant variation on the "biblical mandate" of the MEC. In these respects they broke from—or never bought in to—the customs and etiquettes that characterized both 1990s racial reconciliation settings and other positions on the spectrum identified here.

The belief articulated by justice-oriented interviewees was that MEC building entails a "call" to apply the gospel to social injustice, whether or not local church congregants have such issues on their radar. That call to engagement, they argued, justifies church members—or the church as a body—advocating or challenging political policies, especially local policies, that impact race and class issues and likely affect church members. Three of the advocates for the activist perspective in interviews were African American and consciously drew from the black church tradition of civic engagement. One white pastor (married to an African American woman) and a multiracial contingent he brought with him also saw their mission in this light. These pastors were already involved in forms of political engagement through their MECs. They also expressed interest in creating conversational forums in MEC communities that could facilitate greater social reflexivity.

Pastor Benjamin, who attended Exponential 08, led a church in gentrifying Crown Heights, Brooklyn, New York. The church used to be all African American but now attracted mostly Caribbean Americans, African Americans, "young white people," and Latinos. He came to an MEC workshop series to gather ideas and resources for leading his changing church, while recognizing that as a left-leaning pastor, he was a political minority at this particular conference. "I'm liberal," he noted. "What that means for me is I have a deep concern for the poor and for the oppressed, and for those who have been left on the margins of society. I think the government should have a role in helping people have a strong leg up." He identified a host of social justice issues relevant to the church, including "racism, poverty, environmental issues, peace, housing, education; many things." Such matters, he said, "are at the heart of the gospel; people can't be whole unless they have access to those things, and the gospel speaks very clearly to that."

Churches, the pastor maintained, must find ways to engage in political topics, even if it involves conflict. "We have to have a prophetic voice that's not compromised by the political process, although I think the church needs to be engaged in the political process. We need to be bringing people together to have conversations and to have fights around these issues. The church can be a safe place for conflict and to push people towards power. Because I think it's important for poor and working people to have power. What that means for the churches is that we have to challenge those, nonviolently, who are in the corridors of power." The comments about "having conversations" and even fights and being willing to engage conflict demonstrate the Position 5 support for social reflexivity within Christian communities. From this perspective, church-sponsored conversational space about potentially loaded issues is a path from religious bonding to bridging social difference and even building social capital.

Jeremiah, a white politically invested pastor who led an MEC in a Nebraska city, voiced a similar interest in the church being willing to create safe space for "healthy discussion." "Even though it's going to be very messy, the process of bringing together, let's say Democrats and Republicans, to talk about issues, it can be very healthy if you see all the contributing pieces as being helpful to the ultimate solution, knowing that the solution is what you have to keep in your focus. But if you don't keep that solution in your focus, your process can get [too messy]," he said. Jeremiah acknowledged that white evangelicals probably have a "steep learning curve" as far as being willing to take a social justice stand. To address this, an organization he was leading sought to create forums for helping people move from what I here have been calling resistance, through ambivalence, and toward collective engagement: "Right now I think the evangelical church as a general rule has not been very social justice oriented. And so the first step is, in this network we have in [our city], we start with racial reconciliation. We call it 'A journey from Reconciliation to Justice.' So it's this movement that starts with reconciliation, relationships, but gets to justice."

Pastor Jeremiah was explicitly attuned both to the fear of some pastors that outright politicization will split churches along racial lines, and to the reality that white and black evangelicals draw from different religious racial traditions. He nevertheless advocated political engagements beyond the church. "You talk to black Christians, they want to talk about justice; you talk to white evangelicals, they want to talk about reconciliation. And so when I think about the church that we will be building . . . we will start taking real stands in the area of justice, in the area of change—which is real different from the white evangelical church." Both Pastors Benjamin and Jeremiah saw church-based engagements with political matters as something of a "no-brainer," in that, for them, political realities create social realities. "We definitely wouldn't take a political stand [to support a political party], but we think it's important to talk about politics and race and to take on those issues . . . because it's life!" as Jeremiah put it.

At a regional MEC conference in Lancaster, Pennsylvania, in 2008, a young African American in his early twenties, Pastor D.H., led a workshop that advocated a Position 5 framework in the clearest terms I have heard any MEC participant use. In his talk, "From Behind the Curtains to Beyond the Front Porch," this associate pastor of a small church in Lansdale, Pennsylvania, urged participants to become "unofficial sociologists"—observers of what's happening in their local communities—and "unofficial theologians" who can interpret the relevance of the gospel in light of immediate sociological dynamics in their midst. Then, he urged, MEC churches must engage on the ground. D.H. modeled this process for workshop participants, explicitly drawing from *Divided by Faith* and other academic literature, to offer a structural analysis of social injustice in the United States, and then pairing scholarship with theological grounding.

An MEC culture attuned to structural injustices, he argued, "means careful consideration for both organized and organic parts of our society that harm a segment of the community through their decisions. Regardless of whether it's done consciously, the decisions of the dominant culture can still harm those who are socially, politically, and economically powerless." He used examples of substandard schools in low-income neighborhoods, and communities of color being "terrorized by over-incarceration and police brutality." He then suggested ways churches can "partner to influence justice in communities"—effectively, bridging social capital. For example, a Philadelphia church he works with partnered with other organizations to challenge Temple University's purchase of real estate in poor neighborhoods that effectively drove out low-income people. D.H. suggested that MECs pursue the "felt needs" of the local community, and use those as a bridge (in his words) to minister to other (spiritual) needs.[29]

Because they felt passionate about a social justice mission and drew from a tangible framework to connect theology to that mission, people in Position 5 offered the clearest articulation of the relevance of politics to MEC building. Most MEC participants did not express such clarity. Not only did Position 5 participants explicitly embrace the mantle of pursuing modes of social change that could influence racial inequities grounded in political and institutional structures, they also seemed to have access to traditions, customs, and etiquettes that rendered political engagement more organic and less ideologically threatening than others on the orientations spectrum outlined here. People in the ambivalent, nervously interested, and new activists positions often had to "work through" their indoctrinated resistance to church-based social activities in order to move toward activism.

After *Divided by Faith* diagnosed the sources of racial fracture, in *United by Faith* Curtiss Paul DeYoung, Michael Emerson, and their coauthors promoted the MEC as a space in which evangelicals could build substantively diverse social networks and through that process develop a more realistic grasp of the structural and systemic inequalities that foster real differences between whites and people of color in the United States. *United by Faith* laid out a case for multiethnic congregations as "an answer to the problem of race" in the United States. *United* was a religious treatise and a plea to the evangelical community to deliver on its sociological potential, far more than it was a political manifesto, but in light of *Divided*'s assertions, it entailed implicit hopes for meaningful progress. If Christians of different racial, ethnic, and class backgrounds actually knew each other, DeYoung et al. hoped, if they better understood the circumstances that differentially impacted one another's lives, if they actually sat next to each other in their church pews, they might begin to "get it" about race and injustice, and finally become relevant to closing not just the social but also the socioeconomic divides.

The research assembled here paints a picture of a wave of ERC efforts in the 2000s that looked measurably distinct from the racial reconciliation activities in the 1990s, even as they carried forward some residual relics of that much more politics-phobic era. Rather than clustering along two oppositional poles, with whites invariably in the social justice–aversive position, evangelicals involved in the MEC movement in the first decade of the new century seemed to be fanning out along a spectrum of orientations toward political engagement. Moreover, most MEC members articulated not just an ambivalence toward race-related politics (and political conversation) but rather a nervously *interested* attraction toward "getting involved" in some way, shape, or form, with efforts to ameliorate inequalities that they or members of their church communities faced. Sometimes—though not necessarily or automatically—these shifting orientations seemed to nurture an emerging social reflexivity. Breaking purposefully from well-worn patterns in American evangelicalism, such as HUP-based churches, MEC advocates began to see themselves as pioneers and rebels, at least to some degree, and to bond as kindred outsiders to the old monoracial norms. As they did, they began to ask questions: How were our communities wrong in the past? How could things be different than they are now? How can we preach a biblical mandate for diversity and not consider the obstacles that our members face in their everyday lives? Why shouldn't the church take a stand sometimes? Some MECs, in turn, became forums for increased social reflexivity.

These findings suggest that the American evangelical community, and certainly the community of racial change advocates I have been tracking, has become less bifurcated on the question of political engagements around race issues than it has ever been. It *means something* that the MEC movement works to replace a long-standing model that was complacent (at best) to racial homogeneity with what proponents consider a "biblical mandate" for racial and ethnic diversity in Christian churches. There is space for a shift, and that space is energized. MEC advocates assail HUP-based church models on principle (though that critique is becoming more nuanced as the MEC movement develops). Between this open challenge to the HUP-based church-growth paradigm; the direct, personal experience of participating in MEC communities; and the growing awareness of larger socioeconomic and political factors that impact some of their members by virtue of cross-group contact, MEC participants seem to be broadening their cultural etiquettes and building new mechanisms that foster social reflexivity. An emerging oppositional mentality created by the kindred outsider experience creates new ways of bonding, rearranges social boundaries, and fosters speech norms and conversations that, in many cases, are considerably more open to talk about—and even to action around—politics than we saw in the 1990s.

Within the emerging spectrum of orientations about politics we see in the MEC community, the old bifurcation between activist and politics-aversive orientations toward race remains evident. But two positions on the spectrum, new activist and justice-oriented, provide models of engagement that stand to influence the ambivalent and nervously interested MEC participants who cluster in the middle. These significant developments signal the possibility of a sector of the evangelical community building tools that may in fact help them bridge racial divides in meaningful, and possibly structural, ways.

In the final chapter, I look to the story of one young MEC to consider whether and how this kind of emergent social reflexivity develops, what it changes about evangelical customs and etiquettes, whether it is likely to foster a more politicized MEC movement, and whether this church's experience is representative of a larger phenomenon.

8 On the Ground, In the Moment
Growing a Young Multiethnic Church

———————————————————————————————— +

There were things I thought were Christian that I came to learn were just Anglo.
—Pastor Curt Cutler

Entering a Sunday service at Resurrection Bible Church (RBC), a first-time visitor might wonder if she or he has stumbled into the wrong place—a public meeting about local police activities, perhaps, or a delegation of international tourists. Walking into the worn but well-kempt halls of the public high school Resurrection leases for services, the visitor is greeted by volunteers of all colors and backgrounds around an archipelago of tables arrayed in the makeshift lobby. Each station offers something: pamphlets about the church and its growing hydra of programs and services; headsets for simultaneous translation in Spanish and Swahili; sign-in for children's church; platters of homemade cookies, empanadas, and other refreshments. Amplified live music drifts out of the auditorium where dozens of congregants mingle. More spill into the lobby, conversing in Spanish, English, and African languages. Sunday dress ranges widely, from jeans and T-shirts, to suits and ties, to elegantly decorated African gowns with matching head wraps. It is hard to imagine any space in Denver, Colorado, in which this particular mix of populations would be together on purpose. Many Denverites aren't aware their city is this diverse.

The high school is a fitting choice for this multiethnic church (MEC) as it expands, a symbol of Resurrection's efforts to "establish a presence" in a changing urban neighborhood. Once an institutional jewel of the local African American community, the high school has suffered painful reorganization efforts in recent years after the district declared it "failing" on account of high drop-out rates and low test scores. It serves mostly low-income black and Latino students, despite a surrounding neighborhood that is growing whiter and solidly middle class due to rising real estate values. Like many urban schools, it struggles to regain confidence within a fraught and increasingly class-segregated public school system.[1] Resurrection began leasing the auditorium after outgrowing a smaller church sanctuary.

My first visit to RBC's new location reminds me of how far, in many respects, lead pastor Curt Cutler and his young church have come in a short time. I have watched the church grow from a mishmash of individuals attempting to build an "inner-city church community" to this lively, expressive, and still sometimes awkward crazy quilt of cultures, languages, and music styles. The learning curve is steep, but Resurrection has an undeniably vibrant messiness beyond what its pastor ever envisioned. "If it's a marathon, I'm at mile three," he sighed in one of our last interviews, reflecting on Resurrection's progress and early setbacks. Though we never said it, I'm not sure either of us was convinced, when we first met, that the church would still be standing three years out.

Resurrection started in 2008 with a small group of well-intentioned and, Curt admits in retrospect, "deeply naive" white ex-fundamentalists from the suburbs. Although borderline monoracial at first (having begun with about 90 percent white congregants), today the church clearly meets the definition of a multiethnic congregation. Approximately 25 percent Latino, 10 percent African immigrant (mostly Burundian refugees), 5 percent African Americans and other minorities, and the remaining 60 percent Anglo, the diversity of the church's base is obvious.[2] By mid-2012, Sunday services at Resurrection averaged about 260 people, about half of whom had formally become members. At this writing, there is a core team of five paid pastors (four Anglo, one Latino), and the church is working to replace one of the white pastors with an African American. There are also five paid elders, twenty-five deacons, and sixteen paid staff. While the majority of the staff are also white, some key paid positions are held by people of color, and other kinds of diversity are represented among them: some live below the poverty level; others are or were homeless.[3] The leadership team aims to bring the ethnic makeup of its leadership into alignment with its Sunday morning composition, but that is no easy task, Curt reports.

I met Curt serendipitously in the summer of 2008, when I received a visit at my front door from an enthusiastic member of his church-planting team. (I live two blocks from RBC's current location.) The church was looking for people to join their brand-new congregation, and I happened to be looking for the right local multiethnic congregation to study. Curt's team had canvassed the surrounding neighborhoods with glossy flyers inviting folks to visit this "multi-ethnic, multi-cultural church in the heart of the city."[4] I called Curt, who was then thirty-four years old, to set up an interview, and attended the church's opening service in September 2008.

Though there were other, more established MECs in the area, in Resurrection I saw an opportunity to track an MEC-building attempt in its infancy (since I had already interviewed more established MEC leaders through the Mosaix Global Network). In those early days, Resurrection had no connection to other MECs, and was unaware that a larger movement existed.[5] Whether or not it succeeded, I could observe the church's early development to glean more close-up information about how MEC participants were or weren't thinking about issues of power, political engagement, and social change. What challenges and tensions arose in the process of trying to grow a young MEC? Did the meaning-making practices of this local MEC increase or decrease opportunities for participants to recognize systemic and structural inequalities and regard responses to them as relevant to their overall mission?

From 2008 through 2011, I met or communicated with Curt every few months or more, visited church services and special meetings and events regularly, listened via podcast, and interviewed over a dozen current and former church members, some of them paid and lay leaders, and a few more than once. I used a similar questionnaire as the one I distributed to Mosaix Global Network participants, though the case study interviews tended to be more loosely structured and wide-ranging, allowing the interviewees to direct the conversation into their own areas of interest.

It bears mentioning before introducing my findings that politics and policy tended to be slippery topics for RBC members I interviewed, although for some this seemed to change over time. Many did not *automatically* regard those terms as relevant to what they were doing. Sometimes it was if I were asking what Popsicles had to do with MEC building: Popsicles were handy on a hot day, but what did one thing have to do with the other? Observing Resurrection's early growth, I learned that people attracted to MECs seek many different, and not always mutually compatible, things from the MEC environment, including recognition and representation of their unique cultural background(s), spiritual guidance, personal nurturing, a harmonious experience of community, material and emotional resources, and strong leadership from pastors. Between a nearly infinite list of expectations and the broader cultural customs and etiquettes in evangelicalism, the act of raising topics that bear on politics, even issues that directly impact church members, can be socially complicated if not threatening. It is often hard enough for people to navigate the social and administrative challenges specific to their church. Becoming involved in complex arenas beyond the church, even if only related to the local neighborhood, may feel unworkable. Even so, those complex arenas did register on the radar of this young church, and some members found themselves gravitating undeniably toward active political engagement. Others weren't sure what they thought, but were generous enough to explore their impressions with me. I attempt to relay a range of their perspectives in this chapter.

Warming Trends and Cold Spots

Analysis of the RBC case study material led to four central observations I suspect will reward further investigation in other MEC environments. I offer them as working assessments of political climates (conceived broadly) within MEC culture. Overall, the case study provided more evidence for the warming trends toward political engagement suggested by the Mosaix Global Network survey and interviews, and analysis of *Christianity Today* race discourse. But it also surfaced some intervening factors operative in MECs that merit a textured understanding.

1. *Warming through relationship.* The case study confirmed that relational frameworks do provide paths to social action for some MEC participants by increasing people's interpersonal contact across race and difference and, through those experiences, their awareness of systemic and structural inequalities that impact people they know. However, the likeliness of pursuing political engagement in some form is mediated by the ways in which leadership provides conceptual support for seeing such activity as a natural extension of participants' faith-based perspective. The extent to which MEC church culture is comfortable with and amenable to open "political" discussion and social reflexivity matters. MEC leadership can *cultivate recognition* of the connections between personal and political, familiar and systemic, the church's mission and its relationship to the surrounding world. I apply Stanczak's (2006) term "perceived reciprocal legitimacy" to elaborate this. In the Resurrection case, Pastor Curt himself exemplified this warming to politics, but other members of his leadership team also demonstrated aspects of it.

2. *Competing racial discourses.* The range of positions within the congregation and leadership to the two competing racial discourses within evangelical Protestantism influences the warmth of any given MEC toward political engagement. If members are inclined toward social justice activities, and if they *also* have the ability to articulate that perspective in theologically persuasive terms, political engagement by members or by the church itself may be uncontroversial. If the church includes substantial camps under both racial narratives—which is likely if the congregation contains white evangelicals *and* African Americans and Latinos— the ability to openly engage political topics will depend on the community's facility with navigating open conflict and conversation within the church.

Change in the direction of more activist engagement (or even open discussion of politics-related topics) requires cultivating mechanisms to revise or replace social justice–aversive frameworks, some of which may be unconscious, and helping members conceive of getting involved as a legitimate aspect of their Christian identity.

3. *Subcultures within.* Internal subcultures within an MEC can be countervailing influences on members' inclination and ability to collectively engage with sociopolitical issues. This is not just about race; internal subcultures draw from distinctive religious-cultural experiences, etiquettes and customs that make it harder or easier to navigate tension or open conflict. Discussing political dimensions of social problems requires the ability to at least sit with the tension inherent in encounters with divergent viewpoints. In the Resurrection case, four such groups (some of whose members have overlapping identities therein) were former fundamentalists, new immigrants, African Americans, and Latinos. Former fundamentalists, most of whom were also white, tended to be uncomfortable with and unskilled for navigating open discussion of tension and conflict—yet were overrepresented in church leadership. As a result, some minority members in the church, especially people of color, experienced frustration with the lack of open channels for addressing tension, and some became disillusioned with the church. Such dynamics raise important questions about *internal* power structures and cultures of collective expression in MECs.

4. *Social reflexivity.* The above observations point to a need in MECs for socially reflexive customs and etiquettes for openly addressing tension and conflict if MECs are to flourish, and especially for those wishing to find paths of relevant political engagement through the church. Such mechanisms must align with the meaning-making systems the church embraces—factors like its theology, leadership systems, and authority structures. But conflict-management strategies (perhaps "conflict engagement" is a better term) must also be flexible enough to allow members from divergent backgrounds to take risks, build trust, be vulnerable, say the "wrong" things, abide lack of resolution, expose and heal deep wounds, and ultimately mend relationships. This is difficult, not only because potentially engaging conflict directly exposes church leaders' own personal blind spots and limitations. If those mechanisms are not available for MEC members to address the "ordinary stuff" that arises just as a result of participating in a diverse community, members will also be less likely to engage in high-risk prospects like talking about their views on political power, officeholders, and controversial policy issues that do impact their members. Social reflexivity entails "a collective process of imaging; it requires talking about differences and similarities straightforwardly, in the midst of forging relationships beyond the

group" (Lichterman 2005, 47). Where such imagination is lacking, political engagement is nearly impossible.

Several threads of Resurrection's story illuminate these observations.

"Pulled" to the City

Like many churches, Resurrection draws energy and torque from its magnetic lead pastor. With his warm, commanding presence, focused gaze, and quick energy, Curt Cutler has moved more swiftly and definitively than most of his congregants from a politics-averse position to a new activist orientation on the political orientation spectrum identified in chapter 7. This has undoubtedly influenced his church members' perspectives on the potential connections between MEC work and politics (though he does not impose a political mission on the church). But Curt's galvanization may also reflect the trajectory of a unique individual with a particular personality and evolving vision for manifesting a vibrant MEC. His awakening and struggles along the way illuminate patterns alongside which other church members' perspectives come into relief.

When we first met over coffee to talk about opening his new church, Curt described his decision as a kind of coming full circle. Raised in the Midwest during childhood, his father relocated the family to a Colorado suburb in the wake of near financial collapse. After their parents converted from Catholicism to Christian fundamentalism (more on which below), the children spent their teen years in a religiously conservative but in Curt's words "pretty dysfunctional" home. (The father had addiction problems.) In high school, Curt and some of his brothers became rebellious; he and two others were expelled, though Curt later "rededicated his life to Christ" and attended a conservative Bible college in the upper Midwest.

Perhaps as an instance of his rebellious spirit, Curt "always felt a magnetic pull to the city." Despite having an ambivalent relationship to church as a youth, he was deeply imprinted by Sunday bus trips his father coordinated, in which the family's white, middle-class church would transport low-income African American children from "downtown" (Denver's inner-city area) to their suburban congregation.[6] The transported children, however, were made to attend a different Sunday school than the suburban children. Though he described this "character training" of economically disadvantaged kids as outrageously paternalistic in retrospect, the weekly experience of riding on the buses and getting to know kids of color was nevertheless "transforming" for him.

Curt's early church experiences were imprinted by the strict, isolationist culture of the particularly Spartan brand of American orthodox Christianity that is the Independent Fundamental Baptist (IFB) world. IFB is not a formal denominational entity; rather, it is a nondenominational network of churches, educational institutions, and parachurch organizations united by a theologically orthodox, culturally strict, politically conservative set of values.[7] (IFB churches are a product of the split between the "fundamentalist" and "evangelical" camps of early twentieth-century Protestantism described in chapter 3.) Bob Jones University in Greenville, South Carolina, perhaps the highest-profile IFB institution, was famous in the 1990s for its ban on interracial dating, which was finally lifted in 2000 after national critique and protests from its own student activists, including Barbara from chapter 7.[8] IFB church communities typically demand very conservative dress codes (women wear long skirts and are forbidden from wearing "provocative" outfits), sing traditionalist hymns and ban music with a drum or bass beat, discourage open spiritual expression (such as raising hands in praise), and rear their children in strict, authoritarian households.

During his IFB college years, Curt developed into something of a maverick within fundamental Baptist culture. Based on conversations among his friends, he began creating discussion forums in which participants challenged the cultural sacred cows of IFB doctrine. Young believers, in effect, were questioning the old guard.[9] This later led to the creation of a website that became an influential hub for a new wave of young, "thinking," culturally savvy fundamentalists making use of the Internet as a communication vehicle.[10] Curt gained a measure of fame for his involvement with the site. Although he eventually "jumped stream" from fundamentalist culture before founding Resurrection, a number of Resurrection's early members had essentially followed this charismatic, influential person into his new urban church-planting project.[11]

In his twenties Curt returned to Colorado, where he was hired by his home (IFB) church and eventually ascended to a good position as a youth pastor at the predominantly white congregation. He served there for eleven years, building a strong reputation on his ministries to youth and recovering addicts, and his outreach skills. The church was in an area of town experiencing a rapid influx of Hispanics, and after some discussion the congregation decided to relocate to a more racially homogenous (white) neighborhood rather than change its culture to attract Spanish speakers. Shortly thereafter, frustrated with the Homogeneous Unit Principle "Domino's Pizza for Jesus" model of church growth, Curt decided to follow his instincts to pursue a multicultural church community "downtown."[12] Although he didn't know at the time (2006–8) that a larger MEC network was getting organized across the country, he secured an interim salary to support his investigation; spent a year raising start-up money from larger, mostly white suburban churches; and began familiarizing himself with the church

landscape downtown. Despite trying to recruit some current or former fundamentalists of color he knew to join him, nineteen of his original, informal leadership team of twenty were white men.

Settling In and Waking Up

In its first year, Resurrection pursued a more ambitious agenda than it could
possibly have fulfilled, one sure to make some members nervous. This is partly
attributable to Curt's self-described "project-driven" personality. In addition to
trying to raise up "strong believers" who understood the gospel and kept a commitment to Christ, RBC worked on several simultaneous fronts: attracting new
members from the surrounding neighborhoods; cultivating relationships with
local leaders, especially of color; becoming a presence in the downtown community and online; organizing small groups and classes for Bible study and member support; making meaningful contact with interested visitors from minority
cultures; and finding ways to make the church services resonant for all kinds of
members.

Originally RBC leased out the former sanctuary of an African American Baptist church after the Baptists had upgraded their building. When RBC volunteers
were preparing that space for their first services, they noticed that members of
the homeless, ex-homeless, ex-felon, and substance recovery communities hung
out in the public park next door. They recruited the willing among them to help,
paid them for their services, and ultimately managed to attract a number as regulars. Though RBC leaders had hoped to appeal to African Americans from the
neighborhood, in its first year only a handful had joined. So after about eighteen
months the church shifted its attention to attracting the growing number of Latinos in the area. A few new immigrant families from Africa also joined, and
eventually brought others.

The leadership team discovered early on that to have any chance of attracting an ethnically diverse congregation, they needed, at the very minimum, to
cultivate a cross-culturally resonant music ministry. The Christian contemporary soft-rock style of the church band, while it represented a cultural shift for
the "former Fundies" (for whom any kind of percussion in church music was
foreign), was not going to bring in African Americans and Latinos.[13] It was not
enough for the white band members to expand their musical repertoire; visitors
from nonwhite cultures wanted to see people who looked like them and hear
music that resonated for them if they were to going to become regulars. Curt and
his staff began to explore ways to build a more diverse music ministry. This took
about two years. Today the praise ministry changes every Sunday, from a black

gospel band, to a racially mixed Christian contemporary band that plays some songs or verses of songs everyone knows in Spanish or Swahili, to a Latin ensemble, to some combination of the all of these. Most song lyrics are translated on a large screen.

Many of Resurrection's outreach and diversification objectives required material expansion and financial investment. The church was located in a neighborhood at the intersection of several demographic dynamics. Long-term African American residents lived beside incoming loft-dwellers and home renovators, most of whom were white. Public housing units were dispersed throughout the area, and the hub of homeless outreach organizations downtown was located three blocks from the church. The neighborhood also hosted a retail economic development district bisected by a light rail line. Within a few months of opening, Curt and the church steering committee began looking for concrete ways to minister to the pressing needs of some of the core constituencies within the church and in the surrounding area. These (at least from RBC's viewpoint) included drug rehabilitation, personal counseling, and job skills training for former convicts, people who are homeless, and/or those addicted to drugs; tutoring and after-school activities for youth; a food bank; support services for single parents; a religious education center; and a place for housing summer missions and internships.[14]

In late winter 2009, Resurrection launched a fund-raising campaign to purchase a building in the neighborhood that would become a nonprofit community center (a 501c3) run by the church. Drawing on personal connections across the country, from church members, and from interested outside donors, Curt managed to raise well over $300,000 within a few months—a feat he attributed to God's intervention but which also had a lot to do with his many heartfelt e-mail "asks" from potential supporters. After some renovations on the new building, the church had several programs up and running by the summer, including tutoring and state-supported rehab services.

While crafting fund-raising pitches for the community center, Curt was on a kind of parallel track, becoming intimately involved with the politics of homelessness, school funding, and education reform in Denver within the first few months of opening the church.[15] His arc over time evidences the potentially positive relationship between relationalism and warming toward political engagement, as well as how the competing racial narratives in evangelicalism were often at play in his thinking process.

Having moved his family into the neighborhood shortly before launching Resurrection, Curt and his wife, Amy, a full-time mother who also helped in a number of respects with the church, sent their children to the nearby K-8 public school. Ninety-five percent of the students there were black and Latino and eligible for the free-lunch program (which is to say, poor). The school had been twice closed down by the Denver Public School District for underperformance, and was working under the leadership of a new (white, female) principal to stabilize. Through Curt's personal connection to the school, he quickly learned how besieged the inner-city schools were as a result of underfunding, excessive turnover of teachers and leadership, and periods of abandonment by the school district power brokers.

As he transformed into a public advocate for the school, Curt's orientation toward political engagement shifted fairly dramatically. Not only did he now know other families, teachers, staff, and administrators who cared deeply about the school's success and wanted the best for their children, but he'd also begun to see the impact on urban schools of socioeconomic structures and decision making by political power holders. He found himself feeling increasingly incensed over the extent of inequality in the American public school system, the lack of air-conditioning in some classrooms being just one symptom.

Characteristically goal-oriented, Curt saw the knot of public school politics as a challenge. Nine months after enrolling his children, he teamed up with the principal and a local (also white) businessman who wanted to give back to Denver and had "adopted" the school with a pledge of $250,000. The three plunged their energy into crafting an eleventh-hour application for the school to operate under the category of "innovative school" the following year. The classification would exempt the school from certain teachers' union rules, enable greater flexibility over budget and time-usage, and allow more autonomy, though it met with some initial resistance from some teachers (Meyer 2009). The state ultimately approved the application, after which Curt took a part-time job working for the school, partnering closely with the primary donor and principal to expand resources and increase student performance.[16]

In essence, the pastor went from neophyte in public education reform—or any kind of activism—to paid school advocate in a matter of months. In so doing, he felt some tension between this dawning political awakening and his upbringing in the IFB church and, as relayed in chapter 7, had to rethink the appropriateness of political activism as a Christian. Although he realized he was "technically moving into social justice" by getting involved in school reform, and he said that "the minute you talk justice you're talking politics," he felt personally invested in the issue and suddenly aware of its effects on other people.

Curt was naive in many respects, and tended to jump into issues without full awareness of or consultation with the local activists who had pursued the same issues for years. But as he moved along a fast learning curve from nervously interested in political engagement to at least minimally activist, he did exhibit some expanding social reflexivity, in the form of "reflective talk about [his and] the group's concrete relationships to the wider social world" (Lichterman 2005, 47). One expression of this was an emergent self-awareness about how his own racial privilege might be woven into his new experiences in school reform politics. Was it possible, he wondered, that white privilege potentially gave him more influence and efficacy on the school reform issue than African Americans and Latinos in the neighborhood, who had long worked to attract more equitable resources to their school? "The hard part," he mused a bit anxiously in the wake of the victory with the innovative school application, "is that I'm seeing success that other people worked for decades toward and didn't see. Is that white privilege or is that just timing?" This indicated an awareness of identity and power configurations he had not initially exhibited in Resurrection's heady first days. He had begun to see the differences between earned and unearned power and, perhaps for the first time, recognize the unfairness of racially loaded systems.[17]

Too, Curt noted that he had become increasingly aware of a related dynamic: most whites in his congregation, the majority of whom had come from suburban, monoracial IFB congregations, were still having trouble even *recognizing* white privilege. "When I talk about race with whites in the church, like talking about the need I see to build more diverse ministry leadership, I'd say 25 to 30 percent of them react negatively. They're like, 'Are they qualified? Are there going to be quotas now?' Like race has nothing to do with [our success] as a church!" Such astonishment from a pastor who had only just begun to educate himself on dynamics related to race and privilege reflected a dawning awareness that these church members needed to be more educated about privilege and equality, and that it mattered for the church that they do so. If white RBC members were to responsibly engage in the racially diverse community at all, he was realizing, they *needed* to be aware of how race and class privilege worked and not stuck in their kneejerk reactions.

As the pastor found himself veering from a previous position of avoidance and toward asking how he, his family, and his church should relate to the larger neighborhood, city, and American civic community—arenas of increased reflexivity on his part—a gap became evident between him and some of his congregants. As manifestations of privilege and inequality grew more visible to him, the need to attend to his white-privileged congregants' education became more obvious. He realized many among them lacked skills to identify and address race-related power structures.

Curt's increasing social reflexivity in one topic area seemed to nudge him to others. For instance, as he expanded his network of contacts in the city, he began to come into contact with gay and lesbian organizations interested in some of the same issues. One nationally prominent LGBT rights organization is based in Denver. In 2009, as part of a neighborhood council, Curt was soliciting financing to produce an original play about Dr. Justina Ford, an early twentieth-century African American physician who served low-income downtown residents in an era when few had access to standard health care. Believing (and having preached) that homosexuality is a sin, not a legitimate lifestyle, Curt worried about "moving into dangerous waters" by reaching out to an LGBT organization for financial support. He ultimately overrode his hesitation and approached the foundation on behalf of the neighborhood group, not his church.

Though the partnership did not materialize due to timing, the experience of meeting with the organization led to some reflexivity about how, as a theologically conservative pastor, Curt should engage with members of the LGBT community, people he met in the fields of education, homeless outreach, recovery services—and even a few who had started attending his church. "You know, unlike Baby Boomer evangelicals, I actually *know* gay people," he mused in one of our meetings. He wondered if there was any way to adopt a "welcoming, but not affirming" stance toward gay, bisexual, lesbian, or transgender individuals who showed up at Resurrection, despite the fact that the RBC membership manual explicitly excludes people who practice homosexuality from membership.[18]

Curt was eager to run these thoughts by me, the first open lesbian he felt he knew fairly well, and in the process raised basic, honest questions about the LGBT community. What, he asked, is the estimated percentage of people in the general population who have had homosexual experiences? How many gays and lesbians are "in-your-face" activists? How exactly are lesbians discriminated against? What does homosexuality have to do with gender norms? He wondered if I would be willing to come speak to the congregation about my experience someday. Curt's inquiries might seem elementary, belated, or inadequate to people from secular or liberal perspectives. But his new interest in engaging at least the beginning of a dialogue with members of a community that had previously seemed entirely foreign to him did reflect an emergent social reflexivity that was new to him.[19]

Reciprocal Legitimacy: From Ideal to Lived Experience

As more real-life issues became visible to Curt in his new social location in a mixed-class neighborhood, where only the poorest children attended the neighborhood public schools and many residents were homeless, addicted, involved in gangs, or single-parenting with little support, a new perspective seemed to be taking shape in his awareness: a notion that maybe these inequities require broader-thinking responses, and that these could be consistent with his religious beliefs. "What would Jesus have done?," Curt wondered aloud in our interviews, as if considering Christ's message in socioeconomic context for the first time. If his church is committed to facilitating diversity, harmony, unity, and equality in the body of Christ, shouldn't such commitments lead to action in the face of injustices? Wouldn't actions that create meaningful, long-term change, such as lobbying to increase resource allocation for inner-city public schools, be a more effective expression of Christ's command to take care of the poor and downtrodden than simply pitching in some volunteer hours, as important as that was? Could not only the outreach and service programs Resurrection was initiating through the 501c3 but also some direct activism by Curt or other church members if they felt called be consistent with their church's mandate?

Here Gregory Stanczak's (2006) concept of "perceived reciprocal legitimacy" provides conceptual traction. In the context of American MECs, reciprocal legitimacy is a means through which "religious authority legitimizes the attempts to [racially or ethnically] integrate the community, while successful integration of the community confers legitimacy back upon the religious claims and demands of the church" (857).[20] In other words, MECs typically articulate their racial inclusivity goals through religious tenets that become credible to members, such as the idea of the "biblical mandate" for an MEC (Becker 1998).[21] To the degree that members successfully *experience* integration in their church community, they, in turn, reinforce the authority of the church's religious claims that building multiethnic community is important. So, in a thriving MEC, the lived experience of inclusivity reiterates the religious tenets promoted by the church, and vice versa. Stanczak finds that the church community's public articulation of goals, its organizational structures and resources, and the experiences of its members all contribute to the likelihood of achieving perceived reciprocal legitimacy (Stanczack 2006, 856).

Stanczak does not extend this concept of perceived reciprocal legitimacy to questions of political engagement within the MEC mission. However, I believe it is applicable. Members of an MEC might move from the biblical *ideal* of a diverse "New Testament community" modeled after the first-century church, to the *lived experience* of participating in a multiracial community, to, in turn, feeling friendly toward or even participating in political conversations or activities related to race. As members' reservoirs of personal experience deepen, as they build cross-racial relationships, and as they become committed to and convinced of the MEC mission's theological legitimacy, some, like Curt, experience declining ambivalence toward politics-inclusive approaches to social change. In essence, they come to regard their more politics-friendly perspectives as consistent with their Christianity, in an organic way. Entering into more diverse social networks or learning more about problems impacting their congregants and surrounding community, some begin to see political engagement as not only a reasonable outgrowth of their commitment to the multiethnic community but potentially a necessary one. Therefore, a church's attention to the range of positions on race and justice within the congregation can potentially influence members' orientation(s) toward political engagement by increasing perceived reciprocal legitimacy.

Through the community center and Curt's role in neighborhood school reform initiatives, Resurrection was becoming a presence in the center city community between its first and third years. I met with several more RBC members during this time. I observed both an increase in social reflexivity from the pulpit, and a slow opening (albeit tentative, for most) toward race-related political engagement in and beyond the church. Some were surely influenced by their lead pastor's transformation into a citizen-activist with a much more heterogeneous social network and complex political perspective than he started with. Others who moved toward politics or at least public engagement described experiencing awakenings to the existence of structural and systemic inequalities and unearned privileges they hadn't been aware of before, through the relationships they were building with other members. Some members viewed the church primarily through the lens of whatever specific community they identified with, such as single mothers. Still others, especially the handful of influential members of color, expressed concern that Resurrection might be barreling forward too fast, without sufficiently attending to underlying dynamics *within* the congregation itself.

Nervous Interest in Church and Citizen

An example of warming toward political engagement, through both relationalism and perceived reciprocal legitimacy between the church's core MEC mission and outside engagement, is illustrated in the attendance of three other RBC members at a public event. The "Immigration Reform Prayer Vigil" at the Colorado capitol in early 2010 (about six months after Curt's initial involvement in public school reform) was organized by a collaboration of urban churches in Denver in support of the comprehensive immigration reform legislation nearing debate in the U.S. Congress. Part of a national initiative of the Christian Community Development Association's (CCDA) Evangelical Witness for Immigration Reform, the event coordinators had asked Curt to attend the planning meetings and encourage some of his staff and members to get involved.[22]

When Curt e-mailed me about the event, I was surprised Resurrection was even peripherally involved. The church was still figuring out where it stood—or if it should take stands—on political matters. Meanwhile, some of my most activist students at the local university, liberal Democrats, were supporting the same legislation. But another local white pastor who had been urging evangelicals to speak up in support of the new immigration reform and rights of immigrants, prompted Curt to pitch in.[23] "A lot of [conservative Christians]," the pastor told a local newspaper beforehand, "have relationships with immigrants, but we're lamenting the fact that [evangelical churches] were not participating in the public debate around immigration reform. . . . Our tradition in the last century hasn't done a lot of speaking up about the systemic and institutional issues behind poverty. It's new territory for us."[24] The vigil was an open demonstration of support for, if not a particular law, then at least the *thrust* of new immigration reform legislation.[25] Ultimately, although Curt attended the planning meetings, he was not able to attend the vigil, but he sent a few of his staff with his blessing.

As I arrived at the event, I saw RBC's Osahon (or "Osa" for short) and Nate signing people up to get more involved. A few minutes later, Enrique walked over and joined us. Nate was a white youth minister in his mid-twenties raised in southern Colorado who was doing outreach with neighborhood teens and helping run an after-school Christian group at the aforementioned neighborhood high school.[26] He said he'd come because Curt asked him to. Also, he added, he personally knew young people whose lives were affected by immigration policy, either because they were undocumented or their parents had been or potentially could be picked up by Immigration Customs and Enforcement (ICE) and disappear from their lives.

Osa and Enrique were themselves immigrants. Enrique was a naturalized citizen whose Columbian family had moved to the United States in the 1980s when his father was in graduate school. After Curt asked him to consider coming to Denver to guide small group ministries at Resurrection, Enrique sold everything and left his job at an MEC in upstate New York.[27] Osa was a young, black, Nigerian seminary student whom Enrique had befriended and invited to join Resurrection during its first year. His bright smile frequently greeted Resurrection churchgoers on Sundays. Though both men were highly sensitized to immigration issues and sought to help serve immigrants, neither had been activists for immigration politics, so this modest public gathering for the purpose of learning and praying about political legislation was well outside their comfort zones.

"This is the first thing like this I've basically ever been to," Enrique told me somewhat sheepishly at the rally. "I really don't know anything about politics; I don't know if these kinds of things even make any kind of difference. But, you know, the immigration system is broken, and we have to do something, and I feel like evangelicals are really behind the eight ball on this thing." Here was a note of emerging social reflexivity as the pastor considered how his faith community was interfacing with new immigrants who were, in fact, showing up at the church. Before I left, though, he appended his statement slightly: "This is great. But what turns the tide is personal relationships. Like, there's a single mom in our Wednesday night group [at church]. She's undocumented, raising three kids; a great lady! Her kids are citizens. We're trying to get her to speak to Resurrection members, because when they see people face-to-face, they get it." So while interested in the rally as a tangible statement of collective engagement, Enrique qualified his endorsement of it through the well-worn evangelical theme of relationships at the heart of social change. Good people, good *Christians*, would do the right thing, almost automatically, he implied, if they simply understood the challenges real immigrants experience, by getting to know them. Bad laws would shift, he seemed to assume, as good people demonstrated greater neighborly Christian care. This didn't necessarily require a rally at the capitol.

Such comments could be seen as empty of political content, but this interpretation would miss important underlying dynamics at work. Six months before the vigil, Enrique had remarked in an interview that as a former conservative Republican, he was "still trying to wrap my head around what our [the church's] position should be on [immigration]. Like what if an illegal walks in and wants to be a member? I don't know! So I think we're wrestling with that; I don't really have an answer for that." In general, he had suggested, individual members and families of RBC could support political causes, "rather than Resurrection *as a church*" doing so. After the rally, though, he was hoping to inspire others in his church to support immigration reform. Two years later, in a Facebook posting I saw that Enrique was slated to testify on behalf of in-state tuition rates for undocumented immigrant Coloradans at statehouse legislative hearings. Despite his initial wariness, he had become a public activist within a few short years.

Both Enrique's participation at the vigil and the redoubled commitment it inspired within him to incorporate and accommodate immigrant families in the church—which helped him build the Latino ministry at RBC—were outgrowths of a church environment that, at least through its founding pastor, had become encouraging of racial change activism. Not only was the lead pastor personally demonstrating support and encouragement for some forms of civil and political engagement, but even in Enrique's mind the perceived legitimacy of Resurrection's work in and commitment to the inner city hinged, in part, on the members becoming conversant with the challenges faced by immigrants. A combination of relationalism (get to know the immigrants in your pew), a warming racial justice perspective, and perceived reciprocal legitimacy between the church mission and support for legal and political changes influenced Enrique's evolving viewpoint.

For some, getting "politically" involved meant weighing in on actual policy-making decisions; for others, building relationships and volunteering on an issue area were the more familiar paths. In our earlier interview, Enrique's wife, Caitlin, who is white, described a process of awakening to inequalities and challenges she hadn't previously noticed, but expressed uncertainty about what the proper response of Resurrection as a church should be. She raised a widespread problem in Denver (and which the immigration reform bill in 2009 tried to address), of children of illegal immigrants who'd attended American schools being ineligible to attend state-funded universities. "I think the more time we spend in this city, around people, I become more and more aware of the infrastructure," she said. She elaborated on her view of faith-based social justice engagement:

> I think of [it] more on the grassroots level. I don't think of it as much as going to Washington, going to the capitol or whatever. For example, Focus on the Family has a lobbying arm, but if Resurrection had a lot of families whose kids were at [the local K-8 school], and they had a meeting to lobby the school district, that would be political. And Resurrection families would show up at the meeting and say, "Hey, we're going to weigh in on this." Or, "We think state legislators who help make this policy bill, we want to change these things in the name of equality."

In this statement, Caitlin coded politics as a natural outgrowth of direct experience, which might take the form of citizen-based collective action.

Other RBC members who had moved into the neighborhood spoke about similar ways they thought they could or perhaps should be involved in social or political issues in the area. The church, for instance, had begun an annual winter event called "Night in a Box," in which church members camped overnight in a parking lot downtown to demonstrate solidarity and raise awareness about homelessness (and funding for their work with single parents at the community center). Though the event is geared primarily toward educating the church's own members and supporters to the struggles homeless people face, sleeping outside in the cold is a more activist gesture than the more typical church activity of distributing food or running a shelter. (RBC supported the latter activities as well.) Moreover, through this event church leaders became acquainted with the networks of homeless advocacy and service providers in the city, and more attuned to the socioeconomic conditions contributing to homelessness. Over time, events like this became part of church culture, signaling to members that social activism was acceptable.

Awakening and Whiplash

Sometimes the concern arose that all this "reaching out to the world beyond Resurrection" talk was happening too fast. Enrique, for example, was at one point
involved in helping organize after-school programs to support minority youth
in the neighborhood, and to increase parents' education about the problems
their children faced, while working part-time at the local K-8 school as a security guard. But, he cautioned, he regarded different communities' needs *inside*
the church as at least equally important as these "outreach" goals. He hoped the
church would not lose track of that. The number of Hispanics at RBC was nowhere near the 60 percent of Hispanics living on the northeast side, he noted,
which is why he worked hard to get simultaneous translation technology up and
running. Enrique also feared the church's understanding of race and culture
becoming restricted to the American black and white experiences, and wanted
Resurrection to concentrate more of its outreach efforts on Latino families (an
effort that became the RBC's Hispanic Initiative), and to help the music ministry
become more culturally conversant so it would resonate with Latinos and African Americans. It was exhausting!

As he talked about this, underlying concerns about RBC's cultural environment surfaced, reflecting differences among subcultures within the church. "A
lot of our whites are from the suburbs, and they think [the church is] multiethnic because there are black people," he noted. Too, "a lot of [the whites] are not
from the city so they don't naturally build relationships with their neighbors. We
keep trying to get people to sell everything and move to the city, build relationships here." He feared that many of the white members at RBC were too culturally isolated to understand what other members, much less what people in the
neighborhood, were dealing with.

Another issue Enrique raised was leadership style. While he deeply admired
Curt's enthusiastic visionary approach to growing RBC, he wondered if it sometimes dispersed the church community's energy too widely. "Strengths: [Curt]
is an unbelievable leader, very inspiring, he inspires people to sell everything
and go. He has a lot of vision. That's a huge strength. He's great at giving people
tracks to run on. He's spinning people off to their own ministries. He's great
at unleashing people and telling them to go do it. So that's a strength, but that
could also be a weakness. Because we are spinning a lot of things, and we lose
energy, our energy gets diluted. We need some more balance, which could be a
weakness." Enrique asserted that he and the other three pastors working alongside Curt sometimes needed to rein him in, so as to focus on process.

To foster diversity in the congregation and its programming, as well as "deeper conversations," Enrique hoped the church would pursue the suggestion of hosting open, facilitated conversations about race, through which all members could discuss dynamics unfolding in and beyond the church.[28] Hopefully, this would surface some underlying conflict: "I will know we're in the right place when the whites start complaining, saying we've gone too far. That's when I know we're making progress. We're not anywhere near that yet. We don't want to change the flavor of Resurrection. . . . The preaching is life-changing, Christ-centered; I don't want to change that. But we do need to be more diverse," he said, underscoring that the process through which this might happen mattered, as did leaders taking the initiative.

As RBC members like Enrique and Caitlin were becoming sensitized to the varying needs within the church and in surrounding communities, hoping to develop new mechanisms for engaging reflectively across difference, others were still finding their bearings in the first sociologically diverse settings they had ever been a part of. Especially for those members raised in ultraconservative IFB settings ("former Fundies," as they often called themselves), addressing the tensions that simmered and occasionally boiled over when diverse groups tried to create a shared community could be a fraught experience. In terms of thinking about political responses to inequalities, some members, including Curt himself, reported that inherited ideology was a factor: to consider political engagement as an extension of membership in the MEC community meant overcoming an ingrained aversion to so-called liberal Christianity, which most fundamentalists had been taught diluted the preaching of the gospel and distracted believers' energies. Former Fundies, in other words, tended to have been raised on the social justice–aversive end of evangelicalism's competing racial narratives.

But amplifying that tension was the fact that most former fundamentalists had little experience with openly discussing *any* kind of conflict in church environments, even when politics *wasn't* at issue. That RBC leadership had a limited protocol for addressing it amplified this challenge. One story in particular illustrates how social dynamics specific to a church's makeup can be countervailing influences on members' ability and inclination to approach sociopolitical issues.

Losing Gordon

Terry was a respected RBC elder in his midfifties. Thin, with gray hair and a salt-and-pepper beard, his blue eyes reflected gentleness, humility, and the gravitas of someone who had been to hell and back. Usually dressed in jeans and a plaid shirt, Terry often led the opening prayer or performed the scriptural reading on Sundays, and occasionally preached a sermon. Young people were drawn to his wise counselor style of leadership. His wife, Anita, was a warm woman, generous with hugs, whose shy smile revealed a person only recently comfortable making proclamations on her own behalf. Terry and Anita followed Curt from his former church and, as I was closing this project, were looking to uproot from the suburbs where they'd been for decades in order to move downtown and dedicate more time to the church. Our interview took place during RBC's second year.

When I told them about my interest in emerging orientations toward political engagement in MECs, Terry and Anita mentioned that they'd both been conservative Republicans (their words) most of their adult lives and grown up in communities that were almost entirely white. After decades of marriage and child rearing, Terry and Anita's relationship had been nearly destroyed by a pornography addiction that Terry eventually confessed. Attending recovery ministries together, the couple became deeply involved with "Bible-driven" support groups where they met Curt and another friend I interviewed, Christine, who eventually gravitated with them toward RBC.

Part of these folks' draw to Curt was that, in addition to being a talented minister, he broke "the unwritten code that you have to figure out" in IFB culture. By this they meant the social expectations at fundamentalist churches, where one didn't speak openly about one's personal problems or get involved with others' struggles. Through the recovery ministries he led, "Curt had the courage to open the Pandora's box of the hurting people," said Christine, "where most ministries do not want to do that." Curt didn't measure religious fidelity to social conformity; he was "authentic," they said, and he "didn't put people in boxes." Unlike in suburban churches in which "there was always a [social] crusade," but it was usually a onetime outreach and people weren't interested in building relationships over the long term, Curt's vision for socially engaged Christianity seemed committed and in many ways radical. "I was really up for it," Terry remembered, "because [in recovery] you get all kinds of people with problems. And that's what I liked, when people weren't fine. Where I went to church before, everybody was ok. Nobody had a major problem except maybe not finding a parking spot."

Anita said that originally when she came to RBC, she was just following her husband. "I just didn't think I had the emotional capacity, for one thing, to deal with all these things [urban social problems] that were beyond somebody making a dent in it in an hour or year. It was way out of my comfort zone in every way, and I didn't—I guess I didn't think I could do it, and I didn't think God was big enough to change me to be able to fit in anywhere in [RBC's efforts]." Despite her reservations, Anita and Terry joined Resurrection in the spirit of receptivity. "We were going in [to the church and the city] to learn what was already there," Anita remembered. "We're going in as listeners and learners. I heard things about New Testament church, you know, it's like, nobody's doing this! Well, they did it in the New Testament, you know, can we do it now or not?"

Once the couple got involved in life at RBC, they quickly learned how little they and the rest of the well-meaning suburbanites really knew about the communities in the city or about connecting with people from other backgrounds in substantive ways. They were surprised, for example, to learn how hard it was to attract African Americans from the neighborhood to the church. While a number of individuals and couples had visited Resurrection and offered input on the church's hope of fostering a warm, multicultural community, few had committed to remain for the long term. Sometimes people would show up for a while, but not return.

Terry found this discouraging and hoped that "listening more" could give him insight. He had trouble, though, identifying how or why the culture of RBC (whose leadership structure, music ministry, and small Bible study groups were still majority white) might not be attractive to people of color. Granting his own inexperience, he hoped that in getting to know individuals better he might gain more insight. When I asked why he thought some visitors of color had not stayed, he said:

> I don't think it was anything in particular, it just didn't fit. There's one guy who's an African American that I asked to be able to listen to him. . . . I'm looking for a person who's willing to be able to stick it out and walk me through the process because I'm so deficient in any kind of perspective, because I'm just trapped in my own perspective, in my own skin. And I'm looking, I'm asking him to stick with it in order to teach and just have an atmosphere where he can bring that out. So I think I'm learning to try to listen and try to let them teach.

I asked Terry if what he wanted was a relationship with someone of color who could help him walk through the complexities of cross-racial engagement. "Yeah," he said, "a transitional person. I mean, because without that there's no way I will get there. I just can't get there unless someone makes a bridge for me to cross into that world. So I've been praying for that." From Terry's perspective, he was open to learn, but needed patient instruction.

The African American Terry referred to was Gordon. Twenty-five years old, a tall, handsome, keenly intelligent man married to his college sweetheart, Katie, a white woman, Gordon had grown up just blocks from the site of RBC, when it was a much rougher neighborhood. Abandoned by his father at four years old and raised by a strong single mother, he had initially attended the local public schools, then transferred to a mostly white high school in the suburbs, later earning entry into one of the large state colleges. During RBC's first year, he was earning his master's in theology from the local conservative seminary, from which several RBC leaders had graduated. Accustomed to navigating mostly white institutions, Gordon was searching for a nurturing MEC community in which he and Katie would feel comfortable. "We were looking for a church that was ok with some tension," he later reflected, a church "that wouldn't try to solve everything, but let us live in that, because our whole [marriage] relationship involves tension." Not long after Resurrection officially opened its doors, the couple began attending regularly.

Gordon and Katie were exactly the kind of members RBC was looking to groom for leadership. Indeed, only about six months after their arrival Curt invited Gordon to deliver a Mother's Day sermon, for which the leadership staff offered input during preparation and rehearsal. (That Gordon was a student at the conservative seminary boosted his theological credentials among white RBC leadership.) I attended Gordon's moving tribute to his mother's strength and narration of his own journey to faith and forgiveness as a young man raised in an atmosphere of racial oppression, family violence, and poverty, but also love. Two months after the sermon, we met for our first interview, and periodically followed up over the next two years. During this time, he became frustrated with the church, made his complaints known to the leadership, and, dissatisfied with their approach to MEC building, ultimately left in anger and frustration.

In our first interview, after seven months attending, he said he'd only recently begun to feel at home in the "predominantly white church." Being in a biracial marriage and sharing a "heart for the city," Katie and Gordon didn't feel entirely comfortable in the traditional black churches they visited. They sought a church that was "theologically grounded" and cared not just about a specific cultural tradition but also about "changing the world around them." They had been optimistic about Resurrection's potential for this. Their first Sunday, Enrique had preached about race, and, Gordon remembered, "we were like, 'Wow, this is great!' I've never heard race preached about in a church, and something resonated with that." Plus, he said, "we didn't feel like we got strange looks, strange vibes [as an interracial couple]." Gordon also felt drawn to Curt's preaching and his "deep caring" personality. "I feel like they get it. I feel like Curt gets it. And at my old [monoethnic] church, they didn't get it."

As they got to know Gordon, Curt and the other RBC leaders made it clear that they'd been praying for black leadership at the church and wanted him to think about becoming an elder and perhaps "coming on as a staff member pretty soon." Gordon knew a lot about African American history and theology and hoped to bring that to Resurrection. Moreover, he believed in the MEC as a model for Christian community and felt personally called to the ministry. "It shows the fullness of God, because I don't think God can be represented by any one people, because he's so breathtakingly big," he noted.

When I asked him early on what he thought was most important for MECs to focus on, he, like Enrique, emphasized the value of relational processes over outcomes or content areas. But his emphasis was not just on relationships per se as a reflection of multiethnic engagement or as a mode of spiritual commonality that transcended difference. Rather, he hoped to cultivate communication processes that could help people identify and address the tensions between them that might not change. For starters, this meant "being honest with each other. Me being able to be honest about my fears and what I dislike without being judged, without coming across that I'm being rude or selfish," he said. "Because, culturally, there are going to be some things that come up from ethnic folks when [a church has been] started by an all-white leadership that we're going to bring up that are going to seem very self-centered. Things like the music is hard to listen to—I don't know any of these hymns. I wasn't raised in an African American church, but I know I don't like that. . . . [It's] very white music."

In Gordon's framework, honesty required digging below the surface of comfortable relationships to real points of pain. "I think it was Teddy Roosevelt who said, 'I never trust a man unless he walks with a limp.' And a variation of that: 'You don't really know someone until you've fought with them.' So I think this whole reconciliation thing is very superficial until we've had arguments that hurt and when we come back to the table. And I don't think that's happened yet at Resurrection. We're in the same room, we're saying we're reconciled—but we haven't had those sharp cuts and then come back to the table." Coming to the table in a multiethnic community, Gordon suggested, meant taking both emotional and material risks, being open to vulnerability.

Even so, he felt a bit wary of some things about RBC leadership's approach. For example, he worried about the church's encouragement of young, white suburban Christians to move into urban core neighborhoods and help build the church's mission-driven efforts to reach "underserved" communities. Here he echoed the nervousness Enrique had also expressed about whites' relative cultural isolation. "A lot of folks are moving down to the city—yuppie types moving to the city—and they say they love the city. To me you can't love the city until you've been hurt by the city and you come back to the city.[29] I mean, your love is not deep yet. So to me what needs to happen—it's just going to take time. It's gonna take time. It's gonna take people being robbed, and they come to church on Sunday crying, and they see some healing there." Cultivating honest engagement and meaningful risk also required indigenous leadership, Gordon believed, meaning leadership drawn from within the communities RBC hoped to reach.

"And I don't know how that works with a white male as a pastor, and I'm exploring it with Pastor Curt and other pastors (because there's a lot of white males [at RBC]," he commented, chuckling. "I think it takes indigenous leadership without it being snuffed out by white culture—which I've never seen happen, but I think it could happen here."[30]

About two months after our first interview, however, I received an e-mail from Gordon containing a carefully composed letter directed to the members of RBC's core leadership team. Explaining that he had been in conversation with some of the other African American congregants (which was probably less than a dozen people at the time), Gordon expressed increasing frustration with the philosophy, approach, and internal culture of the church, which he thought I, as a researcher, might want to know about. Consistent with his desire for honesty even at the risk of confrontation, he directed three specific critiques to church leadership, each bearing on what he saw as blacks' growing alienation and even "bitterness" about the direction Resurrection was taking. First, the church's systems (leadership structures, community groups, and ministry) did not, he believed, reflect blacks' "experiences, values or knowledge." Second, there were no clear channels for members of color to express their perspectives; instead, white perspectives were, he thought, given more weight by a white-dominated leadership structure. Third, he argued, RBC practiced a "savior mentality" in relation to the populations it hoped to reach, and exploited minority members' stories for attention and fund-raising.

Gordon's letter expressed dismay that "the leading and most authoritative voices which have formed the theology of our leadership" have been those of white males. He believed that neither certain theologians' perspectives (naming Frederick Douglass and Origen) nor African American "community styles," such as oral traditions of discussion and debate, were welcomed in the small community and Bible study groups RBC encouraged its members to join. He worried that as the church pushed its agenda to get the aforementioned community center (501c3 organization) going, it gave more weight to the feedback of funders and other outsiders on how the center should be used than to the perspectives of local ethnic church members who had grown up in the area. At any rate, he believed the church had not established any meaningful channels for people to offer feedback. "Dialogue is a better medium for many ethnic people to express themselves, yet because our church is filled with empirical leadership, our style of communication is often devalued," he wrote.

He closed his letter by analogizing his experience at RBC to that of a homeless child invited to live with a friendly family, but whose living parameters are set by a system in which the child has no input. "To really be part of the family, the kid would need to have authority in decisions, to be given a key to the front door and have an outlet of expression. Otherwise he is not family, but rather a well-treated, long-term guest. Are the people of color at RBC guests or family?"

Gordon's provocative letter did not, from what I gathered from him and others, go over well. At least one young white pastor, Chris (whom I was not able to interview but who had been the original RBC canvasser who came to my front door), was offended, replying to the rest of the leadership with a strongly worded e-mail ("harsh," according to Gordon), stating that the church needed real commitment and people who would "bleed" for the multiethnic cause. Gordon, he implied, had been too quick to criticize church leadership and philosophy, indicating weak commitment. Gordon responded with his own strong words, stating he'd literally bled for the cause of racial equality his whole life and felt condescended to.

The elders ultimately brokered a mediation and tentative reconciliation between the two men, asking them to apologize for personal attacks and inflammatory remarks. The exchange did not lead, from what I understand, to a formal conversation within the leadership about the issues Gordon had raised, though of course one-on-one conversations did happen. Curt said (and Gordon confirmed) that he tried to keep Gordon engaged in RBC, asking him to stick it out for the time being and bring his skills to a church that might be changing more slowly than he might like. Gordon, however, had lost confidence and stopped coming to the church altogether shortly afterward.

As this conflict was unfolding, Terry, the white elder mentioned previously, had tried to reach out to Gordon, hoping to "cross into that world" of comprehending Gordon's perspective while assuming the structural role he occupied as mentor. When Gordon left, he felt confused and disappointed. Gordon, reflecting on this a year later, said Terry's outreach could not have changed things at the time: "The spirituality and theology that I needed was inseparable from my experience as a black man. Though he was good-hearted, he couldn't offer [meaningful guidance] to me because he himself was clueless about race and culture. That's what eventually stopped our relationship." Terry would likely have agreed that he was "clueless," but his hope had been that in cultivating one-on-one relationships able to endure crisis, he would become more educated as an MEC member, both people would grow, and the church as an whole would benefit.

In many ways Gordon was an outlier at this particular MEC. He was black (the smallest racial minority at the church), was from the neighborhood, had experience with white-dominant institutions, had attended secular schools until studying for his master's degree, and was critical of racialized and gendered dynamics within the church, such as "white" and "masculinist" leadership styles.

He knew more about racial history and dynamics of privilege than many of the RBC leaders, who were entering multiracial arenas for the first time, and some of his social views were quite radical. All these differences from RBC's core members, especially former fundamentalists, made it unsurprising he chose not to invest more time and emotional energy in a church that was at such early stages of growth. He didn't want to have to "educate" the whites around him, he told me, as he had done most of his life. Despite his distinctness, however, Gordon's story is pertinent to RBC's arc, because it represents a significant early challenge that reflected the church leadership's assumptions, its internal processes (or lack thereof), and the hurdles it faced in attracting more people of color, especially African Americans.

After the dust had settled somewhat, I asked Curt for his perspective on what happened. "That was really hard," he said. "He wanted change faster than we could provide at the time." The pastor described the situation as "a bit of a Catch-22," in that if the church pursued the kinds of shifts Gordon wanted to see, especially when Gordon wasn't in any official leadership position yet, it would have alienated other leaders and members by catapulting him into a position of higher influence. But by not being able to change quickly enough, the church lost the opportunity to work with the kind of young, local, potential leader of color that RBC leaders hoped to attract. From Curt's view, losing Gordon was one of the side effects of Resurrection's jagged learning curve.

Broaching Tension

Easily overlooked in this scenario are the influences on the different players' orientations toward conflict of underlying cultural dynamics intertwined with race but not necessarily *direct* products of racial difference. For example, Gordon, who had long learned to navigate white-majority cultures but felt more at home, in some ways, in African American culture, yearned for an MEC community that could engage open dialogue, tension, and even outright conflict in ways that drew on the cultural styles of non-Anglo groups in the church. In this regard, he was open to tension and willing to engage conflict. But instead he found that the "hierarchical, male leadership" structures of the church, which emphasized formal protocol, one-on-one conversations, obedience, and careful "discipling" of emergent leaders by more experienced ones, created no room for such dialogues.

Meanwhile, Terry's experience with conflict drew from at least three subcultures: the culture of recovery, in which individuals are held accountable partly through one-on-one "sponsoring" relationships; the culture of evangelical Christianity, which values faith-based mentoring through metaphors of shepherds (elders and pastors) and flocks and builds leadership structures on those; and fundamentalist cultures, in which open conflict is minimized in favor of ordered mechanisms of control and general silence. White culture could be seen as a fourth influence, though of course white ethnic groups differ in their approach toward conflict. Just at the level of cultural tools, folks like Terry are at the front end of a steep learning curve about culture. To cross the bridge toward understanding Gordon's perspective required resources beyond those Terry could individually access through his existing experience.

In contrast to Curt's resigned disappointment, Gordon's view a year and a half in retrospect had hardened to bitterness, both on the matter of his having been cultivated for leadership and on the question of RBC's trajectory as a church. "I was being groomed for leadership, but by the wrong people," he noted. "I don't see how suburban people from the city can groom indigenous leaders. I had too many white leaders who were trying to 'raise me up' but didn't understand my existence. I realized, why am I trying to be raised up by folks that don't get it? That was the breaking point."[31]

In the wake of the experience, Gordon experienced a deep disillusionment with the possibility of multiethnic Christian community, and had developed a more thoroughgoing critique of white-led MECs:

> After RBC, I couldn't go to church for a year; it took me a year to recover from that experience. [The church] to me reflects what's wrong in America—not just spiritually but socially. It's spiritual colonialism—coming into a certain place, to these "poor, downtrodden" black folk and saying that we [whites] have the answers to these problems, rather than seeing that they have the power to do it themselves. When Curt talks about having a vision for the city from God—to me it sounds like Columbus—it sounds as castrating and dehumanizing as Columbus, coming in in a very patriarchal manner. . . . Change may be happening [at RBC]. I believe it's slower than I was ready for.

In my last interview with him, Gordon's anger was still palpable, reflecting deep concern that the church had become the kind of mission-based "outreach" enterprise that might "contribute more to the problems than it helps." For Gordon, the reciprocal legitimacy of an MEC, if such legitimacy existed, depended on the intentional balance it struck between its mission as a diverse community, its processes of navigating the conflicts that arose from that diversity, and its ability to let members of the communities it sought to reach not only have input but also truly lead. Gordon wanted MECs to model radical visions of Christian social justice, in which participants transformed themselves and the conditions of their existence, rather than outsiders coming in to lead.

The crisis with Gordon was one of many bumps in the road on a winding journey of RBC's first three years, from which I have selected just a few threads. But the conflict and the issues the church has tried to address in the wake of it illustrate how the church navigates the subcultural dynamics within it, how it retains its sense of reciprocal legitimacy, and how political perspectives emerge in their own organic context.

Resurrection had moved into its third year as I closed out my interviews and fieldwork. As Curt and I sat in a coffee shop with my ubiquitous tape recorder between us, he recounted, with much greater humility and self-reflection than when he'd begun, where the church was now. RBC had morphed from a small congregation of well-meaning, upstart white suburbanites fumbling for ways to build a community that valued difference in theory, to a proud, multieithnic assemblage. Slowly, members were learning each other's languages, getting to know friends in social settings, and figuring out ways to address the tensions and conflicts that arose in the process. The church leadership structure had shifted from a lead pastor model, in which most power and decision making flowed through Curt, to a shared leadership structure, in which the five core pastors made all important decisions together and could, if they chose, vote any member, including Curt, out. They were currently "courting" an African American to replace one of the white pastors.

Given what happened with Gordon, what mechanisms, I asked, had the church built in order to address conflicts when they arose?

"Oh, we suck at it," he sighed. "It's the hardest thing." He then relayed a series of anecdotes that, to me, suggested the church had actually made progress. The week prior to our interview, for example, "we had a 'come to Jesus' with the Latinos," who complained that RBC wasn't "Pentecostal enough" in its worship styles, and that the new, shared leadership structure decentered the kind of central patriarch pastor many of them preferred. Rico, the Latino pastor RBC had hired to coteach the Spanish-language services, helped explain to other whites why male leadership was so important in many Hispanic cultures. The five pastors realized they could meet this need through Curt (whom the Latinos liked) performing symbolic headship functions, while structurally retaining their shared power model.

The music ministry had been drastically improved, with Sundays now alternating between black gospel, white Christian rock (with some songs sung in Spanish), a full Latino band, and some combination of the these. "Everyone's uncomfortable some of the time," Curt noted, echoing what has become a central refrain in the MEC movement. "One white woman walked out after the all

African American, loud gospel service last week, saying she had a headache." But that was probably a good sign, he figured. "You know, sometimes I just want to sing songs I know, too," he noted. "But that's part of it."

At any given time there were worries that went along with steps forward. With split, simultaneous single-language sermons on Sundays to accommodate some of the "preservationist" Latinos who wanted services in Spanish, the pastors wondered whether people were really getting to know each other across culture. Were they building real relationships that could be sustained over the long term? They'd also recently screened a film, *Traces of the Trade*, which documented how legacies of American slavery still influenced both white and black Americans. Having learned from past experience that they needed a "culturally competent" person to help navigate the subsequent conversation, they brought in a certified facilitator, an African American woman, to guide the ninety-minute-long conversation afterward. The discussion did generate some "backlash" in the form of Anglos feeling defensive and "mad that we were making them feel guilty for what past generations did," Curt reported, but he was pleased to see that the facilitator was able to convey how blacks in the church received the video, and one of the main white complainers ultimately backed down.

One of the biggest challenges was people being at all different levels of experience with multiethnic engagement. "Some are right at the beginning; step one. Others are way down the road. It's easy to assume you know," Curt reflected. "But you forget what being at step one was like. There were things *I* thought were Christian, that I came to learn were just Anglo." One example he gave was the studious avoidance of tension, which he recognized had been part of his own church upbringing. RBC had begun to think about how to more systematically educate members about issues relevant to the church. To this end, they had added a section on poverty and race to their membership training program, and were hoping to do more cultural competency training in small Bible study groups.

I asked Curt what fears arose for him at this stage, what he worried about. "The nuclear meltdown," he answered. He always felt aware of the risk that underlying tensions could some day explode a community. "I like tension because tension is where you kind of sit there and go, it's time to change. Well, a lot of people don't value tension at all. They value tranquility. So I think sometimes we could have, like, a hurricane. A perfect storm. All of a sudden, boom, and there's a mass exodus. And I think it'd be so deflating to a church that tried so hard and worked so long—and then now you probably have a reputation because people fled and [spoke negatively about it afterward]."

In this context, he had become acutely aware that as a "programmatic style" leader, he was attracted to step-by-step models for working toward specific goals—and this was not always the best approach. He gave the example of an idea he had for getting Anglo and Latino families in the church to "learn to fall in love with each other" through a yearlong commitment to monthly social engagements, dinners in each other's homes and so forth. "But everyone shot me down," he laughed. "You know, [saying] that's such a program, so sterile, and so blah. And I was like, 'Well, I don't understand. We're all big kids, right? If we've got problems and we don't know how to solve them, let's do something.' And they're like, 'Well, it needs to be organic.' But if it's organic," Curt conceded, "you've got to give more power to the subdominant culture," so he had to let go of his idea of how it might work.

Realizing that his own approach was not necessarily culturally neutral or resonant for others in the church, Curt was learning to let go of certain kinds of control. The group ultimately came up with an idea called La Mesa, in which church members met on Sunday afternoons for ten weeks. Participants started in conversations at mixed-language tables, then broke for language classes in Spanish or English (English speakers learned Spanish, and vice versa; speakers of African languages specifically asked for English-language classes). Afterward, they practiced the language skills they'd learned, over mixed-group meals.

Curt reported an "explosion" in people's ability to build new relationships in the church as a result of La Mesa. He calls these "gospel conversations," conversations that come down to the nature of Christianity. When people make sincere efforts to foster Christian relationships across difference, they have to make the kind of personal sacrifices that, he argued, a lot of Americans actually don't like making when it comes to church: "American churches have become so laissez faire, so much about a performance on the weekend, so consumer driven, that this to me is a great way to challenge people, their whole faith. . . . This [multiethnic community] makes us have whole new conversations. Because this involves sacrifices, it involves pain, it involves learning new things—these are all Christian values. And it gives me a real crucible issue to shepherd people through." Committing to MEC community was a true test of faith he felt aware of daily.

Politically, he was continuing to engage. This was no small thing for a white evangelical who in a short time had gone from reciting how "social justice hurt the church" to a someone who saw these kinds of activism as consistent with the risky adventure of building a multiethnic community. He remained involved with education reform through his participation in the reform effort on behalf of his children's school. He had canvassed to help elect a local school board member, and was even considering running for the board himself. He attended a Teach for America conference about education in Washington, D.C., and was thinking about writing about how faith-based groups could address structural inequalities in public education. "The evangelicals I come from wouldn't have gotten that," he noted.

On immigration, he had even lobbied five Republican state senators in an effort to pass legislation that would give undocumented immigrant children in-state tuition rates. (The legislation failed that year.) Though he had never done something like it before, and Rico, the RBC Latino pastor who helped organize the lobbying, had not been able to get another white pastor to come down to the legislature, Curt saw it as a "no-brainer." "What changed my views on immigration?" he reflected. "Just being in contact with immigrants. Watching a third grader cry because her dad is deported. And I talk about 'family values!'" He even wanted to host a forum on race and politics in the church, in which he would bring in people he had met through his own personal experiences. In our last interview, he said he believed RBC members should engage politically, but was reflecting on about how to encourage that "meaningfully, with strength and courage," without Resurrection losing its identity as a church.

Three years of observation generates a mountain of information even in the case of one small church. But a case study can only render a snapshot of one community, at one moment in time, from one observer's invariably incomplete perspective. In a constantly morphing environment like a new church, wherein the formal membership rolls are inconstant, selected interviews, field notes, and visits cannot produce a perfectly comprehensive picture of all the factors at work, or all participants' viewpoints.[32] RBC is dynamic; it will look different in six months, and a year from then. Moreover, as a (white, female, non-Christian) scholar from the state's largest private university, my own social positioning surely informed what church participants chose to share with me. While the results should not be generalized to the diverse array of MECs around the country, this investigation provides an ethnographically textured sketch, and an informed interpretation for readers to consider.

In an MEC, progress is always a matter of perspective. Attracting meaningful diversity and then fostering a livable environment within which members can build substantive community across difference is difficult enough, even before considering broader social or political engagement. As Michael Emerson and the coauthors of *United by Faith* hoped, relational frameworks can and do provide paths to social action for MEC participants—as they certainly have for Curt and others. Even for people inclined toward structure-blind, individualized interpretations of socioeconomic inequalities, as white evangelicals have traditionally been, political orientations can shift when people understand the impact of concrete policies (for example, immigration) on real people they know. But that is surely unlikely if members feel uncomfortable broaching subjects with one another, if friendships feel delicate, or if church leadership suffocates the expression of cross-cultural conflicts.

Even though they themselves were on a learning curve, Pastors Curt, Enrique, and Rico were out ahead of many of RBC's white former fundamentalist members, for whom multiethnic community and the foundational process of building of cross-racial relationships were foreign experiences. Many well-meaning members, like Terry and Anita, required encouragement and resources, both for entering into meaningful cross-cultural relationships and for building the capacity to abide tension, conflict, and uneasiness within the church when they encountered it. But for someone like Gordon, church leaders did not move courageously enough toward the kind of cross-cultural engagement—and attention to power dynamics within the church—in which he could feel welcome. The conflict he catalyzed and his resultant departure illustrate the relevance of internal subcultures on MEC members' inclination and ability to collectively engage with sociopolitical issues inside and beyond the church.

Important questions about power and privilege dynamics within MEC church culture are relevant here. The dominant cultural group, especially if that group enjoys the privilege of whiteness, is often the *least* aware of its own assumptions and practices, and may tend by default to impose its own values on minority groups within the churches without noticing it is doing so (Bush 2004). If there is no mechanism for identifying and addressing these patterns, resentments can simmer, which in turn may lead to upheaval or, alternately, foster avoidance of certain subjects within the congregation that may in the long run be counterproductive. Often carrying extra burdens within these dynamics are members whose identities exist at the intersections of more than one group—for example, people of color experienced in white-dominant settings, mixed-race people, and those who identify as bridge-builders or peacemakers within the church. Such pressures may estrange these members from the church.

Even amid these complex variables, social reflexivity can be nurtured through the creation of customs and etiquettes that resonate with the church's constitution and mission. At RBC, through trial and error, members were learning to run new ideas by each other before implementing them, to create forums to discuss simmering tensions, and to stop to reflect (and talk, and pray) before making decisions. Inherited cultural etiquettes of silence and discomfort around conflict were gradually being exposed and shifted, as an organic result of different cultural groups becoming committed members of the community willing to challenge leadership. Even more critically, the leadership was learning to recognize and decenter "white" styles of leadership and support more representative power structures within the church. Members were learning that conflict in an MEC (which is always also multicultural) is inevitable.

New customs can, in turn, lead to meaningful ways of collectively engaging with broader social and political questions, such as the systemic underpinnings of inequality that affect members and/or the surrounding community. While some members of the church might never become activists, others begin to see political engagement as a natural extension of the Christian principles that drove their interest in the MEC in the first place. RBC did not seem likely to become an activist congregation any time soon, but some of its members and its founding leader had made that transition in a relatively organic way, without seeing it as incongruent with their faith. What matters more than cultural differences or inherited political orientations seems to be what mechanisms a faith-based community is able to build to surface and navigate conflict when necessary, and to channel it productively, rather than shut down against it.

Epilogue

When I began following early racial change efforts among American evangelicals in the 1990s, the movement was not much more than a hatchling. Although a few tireless pioneers had long been broadcasting pleas for transformation, most white evangelicals were tucked too comfortably into their racially homogeneous church cocoons to notice.

Today the influence of two decades of racial change efforts is undeniable. The well-coordinated multiethnic church (MEC) movement led by Mosaix Global Network (MGN) steers toward its ambitious 20/20/20 goal: "of seeing 20% of local churches throughout the United States achieve 20% diversity within their congregations by the year 2020."[1] Guided by a mix of seasoned MEC pastors and interested academics, the movement is enjoying momentum and influence beyond its base.

Whereas people hoping to plant an MEC in the past mostly had to improvise in isolation, today they have access to a bounty of resources and networking opportunities. On MGN's website members can find downloadable presentations, e-books, podcasts, and live teleconferences on emerging trends and best practices. The organization hosts seminars, retreats, and conferences all year long. Aspiring pastors of MECs can be paired with established churches for weekend "Encounter Visits." Experienced practitioners have access to "Leadership Communities" to support one another, brainstorm, and compare strategies, and can access coaching and advanced research in strategizing demographic outreach. The directory of MECs on the MGN website lists hundreds of congregations dedicated to the MEC mission. And for the past several years MGN has been running a special preconference and main conference track on MEC building at Exponential, the annual national church-building conference. The movement is, for all intents and purposes, becoming institutionalized.

Institutionalization is helpful for this kindred outsider community as it confronts a larger body built on demographic insularity and not always eager to change. Mark DeYmaz, the movement's putative spokesman, crisscrosses the country, speaking, training practitioners, and promoting the movement within the broader evangelical community.[2] Through the vehicle of MGN, he practices message discipline like a military commander, emphatically reinforcing the "biblical mandate" behind multiethnic community as a radical Christian imperative (DeYmaz 2007; DeYmaz and Li 2010). Constant messaging reinforces the meaning-making systems that ground the movement, but also enables DeYmaz to challenge leaders of traditional monoethnic churches to consider where they are on a "continuum of learning" about the value of pursuing intentional multiethnicity in the church. He urges conventional churches to take even "baby steps" to make their congregations more welcoming to people with different backgrounds without tokenizing them.[3] In doing so, he asserts a compelling new norm.

While offering practical guidance, DeYmaz does not soft-pitch his critique of mainstream evangelicalism. He publicly accuses the broader evangelical community of "completely lacking credibility" when it comes to race issues, pointing out that 92.5 percent of American churches remain racially segregated. Suffering from institutional racism itself, he asserts, evangelicalism cannot engage in "honest dialogue" across race until it deals with these issues in its own congregations, because dialogue requires trust, and trust is only formed through ongoing, substantive relationship.[4] Christianity "has the answer to the race problem" in the biblical command to "cross ethnic boundaries for the glory of God." But if believers don't use that power to "change the world," they lose it. This direct institutional push is one way of confronting power configurations that have reproduced racial segregation and inequality (even if not always intentionally) within American Christianity.

As I have argued, to reject status quo practices in American evangelicalism and provide a concrete alternative is to challenge a power system and thereby to engage a not insubstantial political stance within the larger body. Considering how long it took white evangelicals to begin addressing their racial past and engaging in meaningful dialogue with their counterparts of color, the contemporary MEC movement instantiates how a growing portion of the evangelical population has measurably shifted beyond fracture and inertia. Vibrant, diverse churches creating meaningful boundary-crossing opportunities dislodge entrenched cultural habits and create new forms of social engagement that change people and communities for the better. Moreover, as we have seen, many participants in evangelical racial change (ERC) efforts show signs of becoming organically engaged in larger political issues the more committed they become to multiethnic communities. I emerge unequivocal that the MEC movement does, in these respects, constitute significant social change. Given the context of rapid demographic change in the United States and the movement's by now well-argued "biblical case," I believe it has a good chance of impacting the main body of evangelicalism in positive ways over time.

Yet perplexities remain, which observers of the movement and those committed to it should keep in view. Like many ambitious social change initiatives around the world, some of the meaning-making systems and practices at the very heart of the ERC phenomenon persistently inhibit its potential reach and relevance. Foremost is this: while the movement's very existence reflects a collective faith in human beings' capacity (albeit with God's help) to change in ways that are "miraculous" from the perspectives of history and human psychology, it persistently avoids perceiving itself as a change agent (or agents, in the case of individual churches) in the shared political world of democratic community. The ERC movement as a whole reads the larger arena of politics (public debates, policy battles, party ideologies, and so on) as "other" in some fundamental way— as dangerous, contaminating, or simply impotent to create meaningful change. This problematic, of faith in the social miraculous combined with ambivalence about its worldly applicability, may be its major crutch.

This dynamic becomes more glaring as increasing numbers of people of color, new immigrants, and low-income, homeless, and other economically struggling people become no longer external to the movement but represented *within* it. The inequities they experience are propelled by systemic and structural forces in American society and, indeed, globally. It is one thing to build relationships and bridges across class, race, or culture through faith-based resources, but another entirely to attend to the material sources of growing material inequality that groups of people, economies, and nations face. Can the racial change movement speak meaningfully to these realities, or will it fall back on reducing sociopolitical phenomena to sinful "attitudes," or un-Christian behavior?

In closing, I want to sharpen this challenge to political engagement by offering one last concrete example, and a possible interpretation of the problematic through political theory.

In March 2012, MGN hosted a teleconference entitled "What Does the Trayvon Martin Case Say About the Church . . . And Why Is the White Evangelical Voice So Silent?" in the aftermath of the Trayvon Martin shooting.[5] Martin, a seventeen-year-old unarmed African American walking through a gated community in Florida, was attacked and ultimately shot dead by George Zimmerman, a neighborhood watch organization volunteer. Zimmerman (who is multiracial

Hispanic) had decided, against orders from police, that Martin was a danger.[6] A controversy arose after police initially released Zimmerman without charge, accepting his story of self-defense at face value. MGN's DeYmaz was joined on the conference call by his church's copastor, Anthony Hendricks, an African American. Several listeners contributed to the conversation with questions and comments.

During the call, DeYmaz and Hendricks agreed that the white evangelical church had been shamefully silent in the national conversation. DeYmaz attributed this to evangelicals' "lack of credibility" on race. Hendricks suggested that even if most white evangelicals are relatively isolated in racially homogeneous congregations, their silence on the injustices still perpetrated on people of color is evocative of the same quiet complicity Martin Luther King Jr. identified in his calling out of white southern churches in his letter from the Birmingham, Alabama, city jail. Such silence, Hendricks argued, perpetuates indignities and mistreatment routinely experienced by people of color at the hands of the criminal justice system. White evangelicals' muteness is a "shame" because the outside culture does not have the answer to overcoming racism, and Christianity does, through the reconciling model of Christ.

Curiously, though, the conversation that promised to "talk about it" did not actually talk about *it*—the actual systems, structures, and overt or implicit policies that reproduce socioeconomic inequities in the United States. Hendricks's mention of insidious institutional practices like a criminal justice system that people of color experience as hostile and whites generally don't was the only moment that the conversation threatened to veer in a political direction. Instead, the discussion stayed in a holding pattern, pivoting around why evangelicals *didn't* talk about race effectively. These MEC leaders repeatedly suggested that the answer is in fostering cross-cultural competence, ideally through building more multiracial congregations. Christians thereby get to know more people different from themselves and build relationships and trust. *Then,* Hendricks suggested, "you ask questions like, 'Can you help me understand how blacks might perceive this situation?'" and continue in dialogue.

This study has taught us enough to recognize that such an approach is resonant of the same faith-based relationalism Emerson and Smith critiqued in *Divided by Faith,* albeit in a more updated form. Sounding much like the racial reconcilers of the 1990s, Hendricks and DeYmaz repeated the mantra that "racism is a spiritual problem" that "can't be legislated or educated," although, they conceded, political efforts can bring some advancement (like lifting Jim Crow laws). "The culture," the pastors repeated, "does not have the answer to racism and prejudice," whereas "Christians do." Another iteration of this was the refrain that for all its attempts at legal and policy remedies, for all its "multiculturalism" (a word evangelicals reject for what they see as its relativism toward different religions and lifestyles), society (or government; the terms seem to be used interchangeably) "still hasn't solved racism or healed our divided culture."

Why remain attached to such refrains? After all, Jim Crow laws, racialized voting restrictions, and educational segregation did not crumble because Christians' hearts suddenly changed. Indeed, it wasn't "Christians" per se who rendered racist laws and institutions constitutionally invalid, though of course the role of African American Christians, first and foremost, and mainline Christian, Jewish, and other religious groups in the civil rights movements is undeniable. Those changes occurred through "the culture," through activists in a secular world—meaning, a community of religious and nonreligious citizens under a common, religiously neutral state—by way of a political system and laws that citizens *demanded* be changed, and worked to change. Whatever white evangelicals' "gospel" commitments were, many, especially conservatives, were behind the curve if not active obstacles to racial progress in the United States.

Whites in today's ERC movement acknowledge this fact. They even acknowledge their historic failures in their presentations about racism in the church. Do they really want to claim that religiously driven "heart change" will somehow magically transform broad-scale racial injustice person by person, without Christians having to take public stances in the world consistent with their stated values, and to do that in the name of protecting the gospel? Can evangelicals possibly remain so stubborn, or is political ambivalence a way to keep certain people among them, like white conservatives unwilling to alter their political ideologies or party alliances, comfortable? At any rate, are they willing to allow that to *appear* to be the case?

Here the twentieth-century political theorist Hannah Arendt provides a perspective worth considering (Arendt 2006). In her essay "What Is Freedom?" she argues that the most important characteristic of human existence, the "supreme gift" unique to human beings—indeed, the faculty of freedom itself—is to create new beginnings in the world. Drawing from Augustine, who articulates the apostle Paul's radical Christian notion of free will, she writes, "Man does not possess freedom so much as he, or better his coming into the world, is equated with the appearance of freedom in the universe; man is free because he is a beginning and was so created after the universe has come into existence. In the birth of each man this initial beginning is reaffirmed. . . . Because he *is* a beginning, man can begin; to be human and to be free are one and the same. God created man in order to introduce into the world the faculty of beginning: freedom" (166).

Arendt argues that we exercise the only meaningful kind of freedom, not by *willing* things to be (in other words, through free will per se), but by *acting* in the world—even if that action is simply a public assertion of faith (2006, 163). Action, for Arendt, takes place in common public space, through open intercourse with others wherein we communicate ideas, defend principles, hear others' views, and make choices—in short, in a politically organized world in which individuals continually assert themselves, through words and deeds. This requires a public political realm. "Without a politically guaranteed public realm, freedom lacks the worldly space to make its appearance" through human action (147).

Arendt looks primarily to Greek and Roman classical antiquity to develop her theory of political action. The Christian tradition interprets free will as an *interior* faculty of human consciousness. This, she argues, is a deeply antipolitical notion of freedom. Alongside other developments in Western philosophy, she notes, the emphasis on interiority informed a flawed modern concept of freedom as individualized retreat, or freedom *from* political life (Arendt 2006, 148, 156). However (in a somewhat surprising move, given that Arendt was Jewish), she finds the most "extraordinary" understanding of the power inherent in human freedom to be articulated precisely by Jesus of Nazareth in the New Testament. Not human free will but faith, or, more accurately, the *product(s) of faith*, produce what the Gospels call "miracles." Miracles, "those performed by men no less than those performed by a divine agent," are "interruptions of some natural series of events, of some automatic process, in whose context they constitute the wholly unexpected" (166). The "power to remove mountains" is produced, as it were, by faith *in action* (166). Likewise in the contemporary political world: it is only through action that human beings disrupt the stagnation that tends to "creep" into human affairs and through which tyranny and other forms of unfreedom enslave humankind (167).[7] To exercise freedom, Arendt affirms, we must continually act in extraordinary and political ways, because "no single event, can ever, once and for all, deliver and save a man, or a nation, or mankind" (167).

Looking back at the religious racial history of the United States, in Arendtian terms we can say that some Christians *acted* on behalf of the vision of racially egalitarian community compelled by their faith. Their adversaries also acted—supporting racist hierarchies through other biblical narratives. Other Christians retreated from the responsibility of deciding to act. Still others employed religion to defend themselves from change. But those early dissidents who fought against the grain for racial justice—those evangelical abolitionists, civil rights activists, and desegregationists within and beyond American churches—created new beginnings in American political life. In acting, over and over, through their faith, they fostered miracles—the end of slavery, voting rights, the slow destruction of racial prejudice.

It is, as it always has been, tempting for evangelical Christians to shy away from engaging in the political world—unless (as in the case of abortion or homosexuality) they can be convinced it's a dire emergency. "Do not be conformed to this world," wrote the apostle Paul, "but be transformed by the renewal of your mind" (Romans 12:2). Evangelicals are constantly being told that "this world in its present state is passing away" (1 Corinthians 7:31). So why "go there," why get one's hands messy in the acrimony of the world, they might wonder. Yet the apostle who wrote these passages is the same Paul who articulated Christ's vision of a spiritually mandated, boundary-crossing Christian body, the central idea that anchors today's MEC movement. If MEC advocates have any core conviction it is that the Christian church on earth is called by God to resemble the diverse unity of humanity in heaven.

Evangelical racial reconciliation efforts in the late twentieth century marked an important beginning. Given the complexities of racial and religious history in the United States and how hard it was to cross those old lines, it may have been appropriate, for a time, to draw a circle around their movement and keep the focus on the essentials: addressing the past, apologizing, working toward relationship building and healing, and figuring out how to relate meaningfully across cultural, ethnic, and racial difference. All those efforts will certainly be ongoing.

But now what? If the larger movement continues to bracket off the pursuit of "heart change" from social change in the world, it muffles important avenues of reflection and handicaps action. Why persist in distancing from "the world's" supposedly misled approach to redressing racial inequities, when the movement's own members are impacted by those inequalities and may see engagement as an imperative? In the case of something like the Trayvon Martin incident, what if MEC advocates, with all their experience navigating multiethnic settings, encouraged their fellow practitioners to begin challenging local police on their interrogation practices, or sponsored public forums in which suburban whites and people of color across town might discuss their respective fears, anxieties, and hopes vis-à-vis racial stereotyping and inequalities in the criminal justice system? Could these not be small beginnings, steps toward politically meaningful action?

MEC leaders report that nurturing multiethnic environments involves invariably offending people's culturally constructed sensibilities. ("One hundred percent of the time you'll be offending someone," says DeYmaz.) When this happens, they urge people to "keep the ring on," to maintain the commitment and not flee during the rough patches. Why not extend this ethic, and the customs and etiquettes that support it, to an open discussion of what sort of racial politics should follow from the commitments to racial change—or at least what kinds of political behavior definitively undermine these goals?

The ERC movement is one of the most interesting faith-based social movements in the contemporary landscape and, in itself, a kind of social miracle. Born from and in many ways still entangled within the United States' interwoven religious and racial history, it is also a product of its own unique cultural contours, customs, evolving practices, and blind spots. Though it demonstrates the potential for bursting into our national conversations about race, class, and other inequalities in a truly public register, the movement as a whole is—complexly— ambivalent. Time will tell if it will redound to matters of engaged, faithful citizenship and justice for all.

Notes

Introduction

1. Surveys vary, but one-quarter of the population is a consistent average count of Americans who identify as evangelical. See Green 2004.

2. Conservative evangelicals, as opposed to left-leaning or "progressive" evangelicals, are defined according to several main characteristics: They place a primary, often literalist emphasis on scripture; believe in a transformative conversion ("born-again") experience; prioritize evangelism; and lean socially conservative on matters related to gender relations, procreation, and the family (Hunter 1987; Wuthnow 1988; Smith 1998). Although the term "evangelical" has been mainly applied to white populations, many African American, Latino, and Asian Protestants share many of these beliefs and practices. See Lewis 2003 and Egan 2005.

3. In these respects, this book advances my ongoing theorization of the intersectionality of race and religion in American political life, discussed further in chapter 1 (Jacobson and Wadsworth 2012; Wadsworth 2008b).

4. On the shift from a moral values to a racial justice strategy by conservative Christian proponents of school vouchers, see Foreman 2007. On evangelicals and immigration, see Jacobson 2011.

5. For an important pioneering work on how Americans avoid politics in everyday life (which I discuss in chapter 7), see Eliasoph 1998; on evangelicals' political avoidance, see Moon 2004.

6. I have written about some of evangelicals' political strategies vis-à-vis gay and lesbian rights battles in Wadsworth 1997, 2008a, 2011.

1. The New Paradigm of Racial Change

1. Though I do not capitalize either term, "white" and "black" in this book denote constellations of ascribed racial identities, whose designation according to color has meaning in the context of U.S. racial stratification systems. I sometimes use "African American" interchangeably with "black."

2. Scholars have defined social movements variously. Goodwin and Jasper (2003) cite "a collective, organized, sustained, and noninstitutional challenge to authorities, powerholders, or cultural beliefs and practices." Meyer (2007, 10) cites "collective and sustained efforts that challenge existing or potential laws, policies, norms, or authorities, *making use of* extrainstitutional as well as institutional political *tactics*." As a constellation of faith-based communities across all major regions of the United States pursuing a shared set of objectives, I consider ERC efforts to comprise a social movement, though it has only recently begun to organize a formal network. Even where it fails to challenge political entities, it does challenge cultural beliefs and practices within evangelicalism. I also sometimes use the term "subculture," by which I refer to the distinctive belief frameworks,

cultural expectations, practices, discourse, and rituals that characterize evangelical multiethnic settings. Many social movements are characterized by distinctive subcultures (McAdam 1999).

3. For a fuller chronology of the movement, see DeYoung et al. 2003, chapter 4.

4. There has also been a racial change movement within mainline Protestant and Catholic churches in the last few decades, but this study focuses primarily on theologically conservative evangelicals. On the mainline movement, see Alumkal 2004; Garces-Foley 2007; and Walsh 2006. As of this writing (2012), Garces-Foley is working on a new, comparative study of ERC efforts among Protestant mainline, evangelical, and Catholic churches.

5. A third wave, which predates and influences both these waves, is the Christian Community Development movement led by John Perkins and others, which has focused on urban development initiatives and is in many respects more politically oriented than RR or MEC efforts. I incorporate some discussion of Perkins's influence on ERC efforts, especially in chapters 4–5, but do not focus in depth on the community development model here. Still a fourth wave could be the reconciliation work led by left-leaning Jim Wallis and his *Sojourners* magazine. This study is limited to ERC efforts by evangelicals who, for the most part, identify as much more theologically conservative than Wallis et al.

6. The movement tends to prefer the term "multiethnic" to "multiracial," because the term "multiethnic" can encompass monoracial churches composed of different ethnic groups (for example, a Latino church with different Central and South American members) as well as multiracial churches. I occasionally use the terms interchangeably.

7. "Strong evangelicals" were those scoring high on markers of church attendance, belief, and theological conservatism.

8. See also the Multiracial Congregations Project, http://www.congregations.info/facts.html. Mark DeYmaz, one of MGN's leaders, suggests that the MEC should be more broadly defined to include diversity of vocational and volunteer leaders, styles of worship, and "cross-cultural transferability of forms and practices of ministry within the congregation." Mark DeYmaz, "By the Numbers?" *Kaleidoscope Newsletter* 1, no. 1 (May 11, 2010), http://www.mosaix.info/resources/newsletter.

9. http://www.mosaix.info/directory.

10. http://www.mosaix.info/.

11. Unless otherwise indicated, I have used pseudonyms to protect the identities of individuals and churches in this study.

12. Weddle examines some of the commonalities and differences in miracle belief across global religious traditions. Always "highly interpreted," social narrative events (meaning that humans communicate about them through stories), miracles generally have the quality of challenging expectations about what is or has been and manifesting some kind of transcendent power, as in that of a god or gods (Weddle 2010). "Across traditions [miracles] are commonly regarded as rare and wondrous signs of a domain of being that utterly surpasses the laws and limits of our world" (3).

13. See, for instance, Diamond 2000. Putnam's latter waves of social capital (2007, 2010) work are exceptions to this dismissive pattern.

14. A few examples of work on the Religious Right that largely omit race include Greenwalt 1988; Wuthnow 1988; Diamond 1989; Himmelstein 1990; Jelen 1991; Snowball 1991; and Soper 1994. Examples of studies of American racial politics that overlook religion have been more the norm than the exception until about 2004. Examples include Gilliam 1975; Perry and Parent 1995; Walton 1994; Goldfield 1997; Persons 2001; Sears 2000; and Carmines and Sniderman 2001.

15. The participation of other racial groups within American evangelicalism, such as Korean Americans, has also been overlooked in much political science scholarship.

16. Such scholars built from sociologist Howard Winant's (2004) influential "white racial projects" schema, which identified five major categories on a spectrum of racial frames circulating in U.S. political culture in the late twentieth century. My elaboration of arguments against the reading of ERC efforts as neoconservative weaves through chapters 3, 4, and 5.

17. Well regarded in the academic community, Emerson and Smith's work was also inclusive of an insider audience—evangelicals interested in understanding more about trends within their communities. Emerson is considered an architect in the MEC movement today (a topic discussed in chapter 7).

18. Emerson and Smith's work inaugurated a new line of research, which I refer to as the DBF, or "Divided," literature. For a review of this literature, see Johnson 2011.

19. Emerson and Smith's conclusions partly built from Smith's earlier (1988) findings that evangelicals (referring mainly to whites) tend as a population to resist tethering theology to long-term social change or political initiatives. American evangelicals, Smith noted, have a transhistorical habit of approaching complex social problems primarily through an individualistic spiritualist framework, due to an awkward contradiction: they are persuaded that a Christian moral framework offers the only truly relevant solution to social problems and the only path to salvation, yet they "simultaneously believe that everyone should be free to live as they see fit, even if that means rejecting Christianity" (97). They thereby often "render themselves . . . largely incapable of seeing how supraindividual social structures, collective processes, and institutional systems profoundly pattern and influence human consciousness, experience, and life chances" (197).

20. This finding is certainly not specific to white evangelicals; other scholars have identified such attitudes as common indicators of white privilege. See Bush 2004; Steyn 2001; and Kimmel and Ferber 2003.

21. My research is not limited to black and white evangelicals; about one-third of my interviewees, and many of the MEC participants I witnessed in ethnographic settings but did not interview, were Latino, Asian, Native American, or mixed-race. However, I, like Emerson and Smith, found that the black-white relationship still dominates evangelical racial discourse in many settings.

22. As discussed in chapter 6, Lichterman argues that civic groups need more than incisive social criticism to become politically engaged.

23. This term is indebted to Lichterman's (2005, 2008) concept of "race bridging" among American religious groups. He defines a bridge as "a *routinized* relationship that a civic group has to individuals or groups that it perceives as outside the group" (Lichterman 2005, 44).

24. For more on my methodological approach, see nancywadsworth.com/AMmethods.

25. Wedeen, in Schatz 2009, also offers an excellent discussion of the sources of resistance in political science to political ethnography.

26. I am relying on a broadly Foucaultian definition of "discourse" here—designating not just conversations and other speech acts, but writing, semiotic texts, and meaning-making practices that stem from disciplinary knowledges (for example, theology, social sciences, medicine, and so forth). Jackson calls this interpretive approach "textual ethnography" (2006, 272).

27. This resonates with what other scholars call identifying "common vocabularies" or "rhetorical commonplaces" in which language shapes meaning in culturally specific and historically demarcated ways. See Soss 2006; Jackson 2006.

28. Looking at Latino faith-based organizations in the United States, political scientist Cath-

erine Wilson introduces the concept of *religious identity politics* to capture "the content and context of religious values, beliefs, and culture that drive social and political action in community life" (2008, 3). Through religious identity politics, Latino faith-based organization leaders navigate competing ways of interpreting the Christian narrative in order to authorize political involvement and engage with the larger social and political order (17).

29. As Wedeen puts it, "The task of an interpretivist is often to analyze the sort of work categories such as 'black' and 'white' or 'Sunni' and 'Shi'a' do, while accounting for how they come to seem natural and taken for granted, when they do" (2009, 81). The interpretive lens also allows recognition that all outsiders' observations are "necessarily mediated by the act of observing" (Allina-Pisano 2009, 55).

2. Evangelical Race Relations in Historical Context

1. The term "evangelical" is somewhat slippery in as broad a historical review as I offer in this chapter. I refer primarily to that branch of revivalist Protestantism that developed through two Great Awakenings in the United States in the eighteenth and nineteenth centuries and ultimately produced two of the largest Protestant denominational groupings, the Methodists and Baptists. Most black Protestants emerge from these two traditions and can be considered evangelicals in terms of expressive style and some doctrinal elements. Pentecostalism, another denomination discussed here, emerges from charismatic evangelical traditions at the end of the nineteenth century. For a good discussion of definitions, see Wheaton College's Institute for the Study of American Evangelicals, http://isae.wheaton.edu/defining-evangelicalism/.

2. Noll demonstrates how the interwoven factors of race and religion drove three of the four key transformations in U.S. political history: the antebellum period, Reconstruction, and the civil rights movement period. While I am informed by his work here, I distinguish my approach from his by placing a steady emphasis on the dynamic of intersectionality versus simple relatedness between religion and race.

3. For a valuable review of the core contributions to this literature, see Strolovich 2007, 22–27; and Hancock 2007. See also Crenshaw 1991; Collins 1991; Razack 1998; and Hancock 2007.

4. The academic field of intersectionality, however, has been underdeveloped in relation to religion. See Jacobson and Wadsworth 2012.

5. American religion also developed in intersection with gender and sexual norms, but for the purposes of this project I focus primarily on race.

6. For more on my conception of the differences between identity and foundational intersectionality and for more engagement with the intersectionality literature, see Wadsworth 2011.

7. My term "religious racial traditions" builds from two main sources: political scientists Desmond King and Rogers Smith's (2005) notion of "racial orders" (long-term and often institutionalized systems of race-based social and political organization); and the historian Paul Harvey's (2005) study of major religious traditions that have defined the race-religion crossover in the American South. For a longer discussion of my divergences from the King-Smith framework and the value of the religious racial traditions concept for understanding American political development, see Wadsworth 2008b.

8. I follow Harvey here by using the lowercase "s" in "southern" when referring generally to Christians living in the American South. I use the capital letter when referring to members of the Southern Baptist Convention. See also Harvey 1997, 130.

9. King and Smith (2005, 76) call this the "white supremacist order." On the other end of their racial orders spectrum is the "transformative egalitarian order."

10. Jews' beliefs and blood, many Christians asserted, rendered them impossible to convert and therefore *permanently* inferior and therefore second-class (see Fredrickson 2002, chapter 1).

11. The "Curse of Ham" drew from a passage in Genesis 9:20–27 to hold that Canaan, one of the sons of Noah, and his descendants were cursed by God as a result of Canaan having seen his father passed out drunk and naked. Many white Americans, particularly in the eighteenth and nineteenth centuries, read the story to justify enslavement and persecution of people of black ancestry, seen to have been "marked" with darker skin.

12. By 1910, a full 40 percent of white churchgoers and 60 percent of black churchgoers belonged to Baptist congregations. The majority of the remainder belonged to other Protestant denominations (Harvey 1997, 3). For a contemporary regional demographic analysis of religious membership, see Silk 2008.

13. See also Eighmy 1987.

14. This is not to imply that Christianity in African American communities did not sometimes serve as an obstacle to black liberation, as some have argued.

15. For more information on the denominational trajectory of Pentecostalism, see http://www.religioustolerance.org/chr_pent.htm.

16. Mainline Protestant denominations define a group of civic- or public-minded communities that came to increasingly identify with progressive causes by the late nineteenth and early twentieth centuries. Most became active supporters of the Federal Council of Churches and later the National Council of Churches and have been seen by evangelical Protestants as too liberal. Much has been written about mainline groups in the civil rights movement, but for starters, see Wuthnow and Evans 2002; Findlay 1997, 255; and Friedland 1998. On Jews, see Webb 2001. On Mennonite struggles with religious racial orders, see Tobin Miller Shearer in Wadsworth and Jacobson 2012.

17. See also Kelsey 1973.

18. On the contemporary use of top-down frameworks to promote racial diversity in mainline congregations, see Antony Alumkal in Wadsworth and Jacobson 2012.

19. Political scientists have often missed this point in their focus on resource mobilization and other theories of collective action in the civil rights movement. Johnny E. Williams (2003) offers a nice discussion of this in his introduction.

20. See also Chappell 2004; Payne 1995; and Morris 1984.

21. Different groups broke off from the original NBC (which became NBC USA, Inc.) at different times. NBC of America, Inc. formed in 1915, the Progressive National Baptist Convention in 1961.

22. It also seems likely that the racially progressive viewpoint in the SBC was represented by higher-status whites. Ammerman (1990) discovered that "the world of moderates was almost exclusively a white collar and professional world, while fundamentalists were distributed broadly across farming, blue collar, white collar, and professional occupations" (129).

23. The fairly large moderate southern Baptist entity the Cooperative Baptist Fellowship (CBF) emerged from this break in the 1990s. Racial justice issues have been central to the CBF as a response to perceived racial attitudes in the SBC. Most of the moderate Baptist churches in the South are now associated with this quasi-denominational entity (Jeffrey Satterwhite, personal correspondence, December 15, 2011).

24. The Graham crusade hired its first black preacher in 1957 (Gilbreath 1998). I discuss Falwell's about-face in chapter 4.

3. Competing Racial Narratives in the Post–Civil Rights Movement Period

1. Martin Luther King's famous "I Have a Dream" speech at the National Mall in 1965 is a classic expression of this challenge. See also Cone 1969, 2007; and Lincoln 1999.

2. Audio of the speech is available online at http://www.youtube.com/watch?v=rkhAwpyYt5A. Journalist Edward Gilbreath, who wrote for *Christianity Today* in the 1990s and later chronicled his experiences in *Reconciliation Blues: A Black Evangelical's Inside View of White Christianity*, notes the signal importance of Skinner's address (Gilbreath 2006).

3. Arminianism contrasted with the formerly dominant Calvinism, which held that only an "elect" body of Christians would be admitted to an afterlife in heaven. This idea was challenged by the more egalitarian denominations that emphasized free will, conversion by choice, and equal access to an afterlife for believers. See Carwardine 1993, 487; and Abzug 1994.

4. Dochuk 2007, 308–9. Indeed, as Himmelstein (2000, 119) notes, a late-1970s Christian Right organization called the Christian Voice focused part of its resources on protesting IRS efforts to challenge the tax-exempt status of Christian schools accused of racial segregation.

5. Dochuk (2007) also tells the interesting story of a transplanted Texan named J. Frank Norris who channeled southern evangelical energies through Baptist churches planted in Detroit and Fort Worth. Norris eventually built a network of political activists mobilized against liberals like Franklin Roosevelt and Harry Truman, "and their legacy of government power concentrated in Washington, D.C." (310).

6. For more on this, see Harding 2000, Introduction note 24. In response to Falwell's segregationism, activists from the Congress of Racial Equality (CORE) performed a kneel-in on his church steps in 1964, much to his surprise.

7. "Ronald Reagan's 1980 appearance at the Religious Roundtable meeting of southern pastors and laypersons in Dallas, in which he endorsed his audience's contributions to the Republican cause and singled out their special role in his political revolution, was in essence confirmation of a relationship that had been nurtured in California for years," Dochuk writes (2007, 316).

8. Denominational divisions in evangelical organizations will be discussed further in the next chapter.

9. For more on Wagner's biography, see http://www.globalharvest.org/peter.htm.

10. This is McGavran's phrase from his book *Understanding Church Growth* (1970, 198); Wagner quotes it in *Our Kind of People* (32).

11. Interestingly, McGavran and Wagner were sensitive to the idea, also discussed by anthropologists, that in some cultures Western individualism was an inappropriate framework for delivering a new meaning system like Christianity. Conversion to a faith would be better approached through cultural frames that emphasized the collective—leading to en masse rather than one-on-one conversions. This is a curiously culturally "sensitive" missionary model that nevertheless promotes Christianity in what can be critiqued as a colonialist mode.

12. This relief is articulated in the back cover blurb of *Our Kind of People*, which read: "Wagner attacks the Christian guilt complex arising from the civil rights movement and puts it to rest with a skillful mixture of scriptural precedent and human psychology. In doing so, Wagner transforms the statement that '11 a.m. on Sunday is the most segregated hour in America' from a millstone around Christian necks into a dynamic tool for assuring church growth" (DeYoung et al. 2003, 124).

13. "My own inclination is to follow the wording of the Lausanne Covenant, which says that 'in the church's mission of sacrificial service evangelism is primary'" (Wagner 1979, 17). Wagner is also the architect of "harvest theology," which he describes as "the presentation of the gospel which results in the actual decision of nonbelievers to follow Jesus Christ as Savior and Lord" (Wagner, Arn, and Towns 1986, 291).

14. Wagner cites the Lilly Endowment–funded study by a group called the Hartford Consortium, which produced a report in 1979 called *Understanding Church Growth and Decline 1950–1978.* Wagner participated in the consortium.

15. Indeed, in *Our Kind of People* he argues that whereas the United Methodist Church is losing members due to a failed attempt at creating more racially "integrated" churches, the Southern Baptist Convention is multiplying as it pursues an HUP-based church-planting approach, starting new churches geared toward, for example, Korean and Haitian communities. Wagner asserts that the SBC has been falsely "stereotyped" as racist (thereby evading acknowledgment of its longer history) (1979, 11–12).

16. In June 2011, Mosaix Global Network, the national network of the evangelical multiethnic church movement, self-published its first e-book entitled *Should Pastors Accept or Reject the Homogeneous Unit Principle?* by movement leader Mark DeYmaz. According to the Mosaix newsletter, the e-book "challenges long-held, erroneous, assumptions concerning the Homogeneous Unit Principle. Far from bashing it, however, the book shows how the principle more accurately and biblically applies to church planting, growth and development today" (Kaleidoscope, *Mosaix Global Network Newsletter* 3, no. 8 [December 21, 2011], author's e-mail archives). Most contemporary multiethnic churches, while critical of past use of the HUP, acknowledge some merit in offering single-ethnicity or monolingual services in MECs as one way of valuing the church's diversity and gradually integrating members, especially new immigrants.

17. Jane Lampman, "Targeting Cities with 'Spiritual Mapping,' Prayer," *Christian Science Monitor,* September 23, 1999. See also http://www.apologeticsindex.org/797-c-peter-wagner.

18. Another example: in 1972, Billy Graham and Bill Bright prominently featured African American evangelical pastor E. V. Hill at their "Explo" convention of evangelicals, where Richard Nixon addressed the crowd. Hill remains a favorite partner of white evangelical conservatives.

4. Religious Race Bridging as a Third Way

1. Again, this is not to imply that *all* blacks were social justice oriented and all whites resistant to justice framings; that is not the case. But among evangelicals, the general race-divided trend holds true.

2. This exemplifies a well-documented tendency of whites as a dominant racial group to remain oblivious to their own racial identity and privilege. See Steyn 2001; Bush 2004; Roediger 1991; and Olson 2004.

3. This lens is similar to what Pachirat describes as "the importance of problematizing everyday, and therefore more normalized and naturalized, instances of power relations" (2009, 147).

4. As I elaborate in chapter 6, my use of this term is a variation on Lichterman's term "race bridging." Lichterman (2005, 2008) explores similar efforts in evangelical and mainline Protestant settings.

5. The influence of etiquettes and customs is discussed in chapter 6. Religious race-bridging models will differ according to the specific meaning-making practices of different religious groups. For more on this in the context of U.S. history, see Prentiss 2003.

6. In this respect, evangelical religious race-bridging attempts have differed from mainline Protestant approaches to race, which have drawn more explicitly on secular and academic frameworks (for example, multiculturalism, diversity, and social justice literatures). See Alumkal 2012.

7. As of February 2012, CT claimed to reach 634,000 people through the magazine and millions more online and through newsletters. See http://www.ctiadvertising.com/print/christianity-today/.

8. Phone conversation with Edward Gilbreath, May 10, 2010. Gilbreath, a former writer for CT, noted that after the magazine had been perceived to stray from its traditional readers in the 1990s, its editorial board made a concerted effort to return to catering to the "core audience of the white, male, fifty-one-year-old leader."

9. For more on my coding approach, see nancywadsworth.com/AMmethods. In the 1980s, most "current events" stories fell under the first three categories, so I coded them there, whereas in the 1990s more free-standing, race-related news pieces appeared, which were coded in a stand-alone category.

10. Examples include Locklear 1980; Carney 1981; and Frame 1983.

11. Such slippages are not exclusively the case; in 1981 two Latino-related news reports do offer perspectives from Latino church leaders, and in 1985 a greater sensitivity to the need for cross-cultural understanding seems to surface, as indicated by Frizen 1985.

12. A noteworthy example of this cross-current was a profile of Tom Nees, a white pastor working in inner-city Washington, D.C., who attested to seeing more "authentic Christianity" in urban black culture than in the self-serving white church that "ignore[s] the needs of the poor" (Thompson 1984). Such critiques resurfaced in subsequent decades.

13. For example, the 1985 piece "The Rationalization of Racism" critiqued the faulty theology justifying South African apartheid and only peripherally mentioned ongoing theological racism in the United States.

14. Others have used the term "thin pluralism" in other theoretical contexts. See Dzur 1998, 378.

15. http://www.ccda.org/about.

16. Two early features on Latinos indicative of this change were Neff 1990 and Tapia 1991.

17. Though I was unable to pursue this line of investigation, it would be fascinating to conduct a social networks analysis of the behind-the-scenes relationships that may have existed between CT editors, authors, and the public figures and ERC movement leaders they profiled.

18. For the full text, see http://www.the-nbea.org/articles-documents.html.

19. Although the framing is black/white, the feature's introduction discusses complexities related to Latino and Asian populations as well.

20. In another part of the article, even Billy Graham weighs in on the moral and spiritual "sin" of racism among evangelicals (Graham 1993, 27).

21. The speaker is Chip Murray of Los Angeles.

22. See also "A Bus Ride Beyond the Comfort Zone" (Anonymous 1993a, 22).

23. Books from the racial reconciliation flood include Grant 1995; George 1995; Collun 1996; Matsouka 1995; Loury 1995; Mabry 1995; Palau 1996; and DeYoung 1995.

24. There had been an earlier SBC resolution against racism in 1989 that did not mention slavery. For text of the 1995 resolution, see http://www.sbc.net/resolutions/amResolution.asp?ID=899.

25. Later in 1995, CT produced a long profile of black SBC churches (Maxwell 1994).

26. For the list of promises, see http://www.promisekeepers.org/about/7promises.

27. While the organization still exists as this book goes to press, and continues to host na-

tional conferences, it is much smaller than it was at its peak around 1997. See http://www.promise
keepers.org/.

28. Statistics from Diamond 2000, 224–25.

29. Diamond 2000, 226 and note 19. Diamond argues that PK leveraged race to forward its conservative (patriarchal) gender agenda. While there is some truth to this, scholars have overlooked the passion and commitment expressed by many PK members and leaders to the racial reconciliation promise. Indeed, given that many PK members came from communities that took the gendered framework for granted, the faith-based race work may have felt much more innovative and transformative.

30. CC lost its tax-exempt status in 1999 due to partisan canvassing. After leaving, Reed presided over Century Strategies, a Georgia-based consulting firm. A losing lieutenant governor run in 2006 marked his first move from consultant to candidate. Century Strategies biography of Ralph Reed, www.centstrat.com.

31. "Ironically, the curse of Ham has now fallen on us; evangelical whites are *the new marginalized community*, those most likely to be reviled for our political activism, in part because of the religious bigotry of our foes, but also *because of the sins of our forefathers*" (Reed 1996a, 236, emphasis added).

32. For example, in 1997 Reed directed the CC to spend $100,000 broadcasting pro–school choice radio spots on minority stations and distributing literature in churches of color. He also advocated religious conservatives working more actively within the Democratic Party to connect with minority voters (Reed 1996a, 245).

33. http://neopolitique.org/Np2000/Pages/Interviews/Articles/reedinter.html.

34. Reed was notorious in his tenure at the CC for using war analogies in his rhetoric—a habit he discusses in *Active Faith* and later repudiated.

35. Although at least one article appeared on affirmative action, in the 1990s *CT* rendered the subject in such broad strokes as to dissolve the policy implications. When it *was* covered, the discussion narrowed to the question of bridging gaps by finding common ground: On the one hand, the magazine asked, how could white-dominant evangelical organizations institute effective voluntary policies that would expand access and participation of minority groups "while avoiding the hazards of government mandates" (Zipperer 1994, 44)? On the other hand, the magazine noted, some Christians of color were also suspicious of government-sponsored remedies.

36. The article quoted Rodolpho Carrasco, director of public relations for the Hispanic Association of Bilingual and Bicultural Ministries (HABBM): "The people who passed 187 were white evangelicals, [whereas] Latinos are basically conservative, but they are liberal on some basic social issues that the Democrats pick up on."

37. The Christian Right had a broader strategy of reading welfare reform through its "profamily" policy, as discussed by Williams 2010.

38. See also Sherman 1996, 35–36; and Wilson 1996, 25.

39. Alumkal (2004) helpfully identifies how the evangelical racial reconciliation phenomenon may reflect a "rearticulation" of a white neoconservative racial project through evangelicalism (and vice versa). Through racial reconciliation, he argues, white evangelicals can assuage the anxieties of a white identity crisis in the post–civil rights movement period while retaining power by resisting meaningful redress, through politics, of racial and class inequities (204–5). While there is truth to this, as subject chapters of this book illustrate, Alumkal is too dismissive of the power and transformational potential of even these individually and spiritually oriented racial change efforts.

5. Epiphanal Spaces of Evangelical Culture

1. All individual and organizational names have been changed in these stories.

2. As a parachurch organization, PK reflected many of the same meaning systems and practices one finds in evangelical churches. Because the PK movement attempts to involve Christian men across the United States, the organization tends to speak of the Christian community in terms of a broad spectrum of denominations, worship styles, and individual communities with different, sometimes competing interests and issues. Most of the PK representatives I spoke with were in a position to interface with diverse communities—portions of ethnic, urban, local, and regional communities across the country. Thus, their discussions about community tended to revolve around the complicated interaction *between* diverse communities in the interest of growing a vital movement within an even larger, overarching Christian community.

3. The flipside of the prominence of biblical authority is an epistemological orientation that is often selectively skeptical if not hostile toward secular sources of authority such as academia. See Noll 1994, 274.

4. Miller's (1997, 201) study of new paradigm Christians revealed a slightly higher percentage of people (65 percent) who believed the Bible to be the inspired Word of God, granted that "some verses are to be taken symbolically rather than literally," but 32 percent of the group still believed the Bible to be totally inerrant. Eighty-five percent of new paradigm Christians were found to read the Bible two to three times a week or more. For current numbers, see the American Religious Landscape study at www.pewforum.org.

5. As Miller (1997, 130) writes, "new paradigm Christians do not see the Bible as a legalistic 'rule book' so much as an instrument through which the Holy Spirit speaks to them. . . . When they read the Bible, they claim, the Holy Spirit speaks to them regarding things they should change in their behavior, people they should nurture and care for, and new directions they should take in their career or service to God."

6. This is also called the "Great Commission," a term to which many evangelicals I met routinely referred.

7. As a person in the room who happened to be employed at the time in an organization that served sexual assault survivors, I felt critical of the role Bob assumed after Vanda shared her rape experience. I worried that the spontaneous ritual essentially coerced her into forgiveness of her perpetrators. Vanda, however, described the experience as transformative, which to me was indicative of our cultural differences.

8. The reference is to Colossians 3:11.

9. Ephesians 2:11–18; Acts 10:28–36.

10. African American pastor.

11. African American reconciler.

12. A minority of my interviewees referred, at least obliquely, to a different line of theoretical reasoning about sin to account for separation among different groups of people. What I call the "Tower of Babel" account asserts that God created the initial separation between races to thwart the arrogance of human enterprise (the attempt to be like, or too close to, God), by causing human beings to speak different languages. Later, through Christ's sacrifice, God created the mechanism by which different ethnic groups could recombine, *as Christians united* to the glory of their god. The Tower of Babel account never stood on its own in individual narratives; it was always presented alongside the standard explanation of human separation resulting from sinful separation from God.

13. For more on this, see Wadsworth 2000.

14. This perspective bears relevance to the old debate discussed in chapter 3 between fundamentalist pre- and postmillennialists regarding whether Christians will be raptured prior to or after a thousand-year reign by Christ. I did not pursue the details of this with the 1990s reconcilers. People who believe Christians will be raptured after Christ's return have a more vested interest in pursuing a Christian-dominated society on earth. From what I know and heard, I assume that most believe they will be raptured before Christ's return, though I cannot confirm that.

15. Latino reconciler.

16. Asian American reconciler.

17. White reconciler.

18. These practices are discussed at greater length in Wadsworth 2000.

19. This quote is from James 2:9. Other biblical verses used here are Galatians 2:6: "But from those who seemed to be something—whatever they were, it makes no difference to me; God shows personal favoritism to no man—for those who seemed to be something added nothing to me," and 1 Timothy 5:21: "I charge you before God and the Lord Jesus Christ and the elect angels that you observe these things without prejudice, doing nothing with partiality."

20. As one Latino reconciler put it, "To me, reconciliation is restoring a trust that was broken. And in every racial tension in this country there's been a violation of trust."

6. Troubled Waters under the Bridge

1. Emerson explained to *Christianity Today* editors in preparation for an October 4, 2000, review of *Divided* that he had approached the project expecting to write a book about all of the positive efforts evangelicals were making in the 1990s, inspired by the wave of racial reconciliation activities happening that decade. But in researching the book, he moved his white family into a majority black neighborhood in Minneapolis and, between that and the survey results, realized "that these followers of Christ were speaking different languages, perceiving different worlds, and living separate lives" (Neff 2000, 117).

2. "The first new step evangelicals might consider is engaging in more serious reflection on race-relations issues, in dialogue with educated others," rather than jumping into their characteristic backlash-oriented activism (Emerson and Smith 2000, 171).

3. Stricker (2001) observed that conceiving of racial change as something that happens through personal relationships tends to serve white evangelicals disproportionately, at least when a white-dominant framework like "race-blindness" is employed. For example, in Promise Keepers men's movement settings, whites assumed their Christian love helped them "not see" or "see beyond" race, and that this was a positive thing. Their counterparts of color often sought more direct acknowledgments of, and even confrontations around, difference. Partly influenced by different cultural etiquettes, they wanted avenues for grappling with differences and finding real areas of commonality. When harmonious relationships are an overarching goal (emphasis here on not just "relationships" but also "harmonious"), whites can avoid interrogating their own racial privilege as well as the unfair results of unequal structures and institutions.

4. See Lichterman 2005, Appendix II, for a discussion of the literature and methods that ground his study of customs at work in group interaction.

5. These patterns still apply to many relationship-based religious race-bridging settings today.

6. It is worth mentioning the kinds of things *not* generally discussed within evangelical spiritual etiquette, such as whether God really exists, whether Christ was literally the son of God, what other religions' tenets are, and so forth. This suggests an unspoken taboo against questioning basic

theological claims. Some suggest that the "Emerging Church" is challenging this taboo (Carson 2005).

7. Bartowski and Ellison encapsulate some of the literature on the phenomenon of authority hierarchies helping modulate or tamp down what otherwise might manifest as conflict: "The widespread preoccupation with establishing and defending the legitimacy of biblical authority is one facet of a broader conservative Protestant worldview that Kenneth Wald and his colleagues (1989) have termed 'authority-mindedness.' Many commentators maintain that the general concerns of authority and obedience permeate virtually every aspect of conservative Protestant life. . . . Crucially, they indicate that two types of hierarchical relationships in contemporary conservative Protestant thought and practice—(1) between God and creation, and (2) between pastor and congregants—establish a paradigm for social relationships that is generalized to other spheres, especially the family" (1995, 23).

8. Social reflexivity, according to Lichterman, also entails "a collective process of imagining; it requires talking about differences and similarities straightforwardly, in the midst of forging relationships beyond the group" (2005, 47).

9. Lichterman concludes, "The church groups' customs bid the volunteers to establish interpersonal relationships from scratch; doing otherwise threatened not just their beliefs but their own constitution as groups. Mutual friendliness proved to be an undependable bridge for relationships across social gaps that volunteers recognized dimly but could not discuss" (2005, 169).

10. I also saw differences in the two periods under observation. In the 1990s, reconcilers consistently identified relationship as the missing element leading to the failure of other historical initiatives to permanently correct the social problem of race. In the 2000s, such statements became more qualified, as we will see, but continued.

11. This would be consistent with Winant's (1997) "white racial projects" framework.

12. In the 2000s, partly as a result of the theological frames for multiethnic church building outlined in *United by Faith* and other guides, the language about "kingdoms" changes, and ERC advocates frame race bridging as a necessary means of creating "God's kingdom" on earth. I discuss this shift in chapter 8.

13. In the 1990s, I saw a deep lack of awareness among evangelical reconcilers of other reconciliation movements in the world—for example, between indigenous groups and governments; in South Africa; across ethnic hostilities; and so forth.

14. They offered, for example, a "parable" likening white evangelicals' narrow understanding of the effects of long-term structural inequalities on racial minorities to asking an overweight person to lose weight while surrounded by nothing but junk food and television, and with no access to exercise equipment. His or her competitor, meanwhile, has access to healthy food, free gym use, and a personal trainer. (White evangelicals are like the winning dieter who blames the disadvantaged "failure" for not showing enough personal initiative) (Emerson and Smith 2000, 111–15).

15. Only 38 percent of white evangelicals, Emerson and Smith found, support "integrating residential neighborhoods" as the best way to reduce racism. Ninety percent support "getting to know a person of another race" as the best choice, and 83 percent "working against discrimination in jobs" (2000, 122).

16. See comments by Packer and Lyons (Ellis and Lyon 2000, 42).

17. "We're not here to become stakeholders in the American Dream," commented Edward Ellis. "We're here to be transformational presences. And those two things are not one and the same" (Ellis and Lyon 2000, 44).

18. Willow Creek's John Ortberg, for instance, commented: "[At Willow Creek] the only way you can move people is developmentally—one step at a time. So we encourage people to take the next step, and then provide them with opportunities to serve—from weekend plunges to long-term missions, commitments" (Ellis and Lyon 2000, 47).

19. Each individual article was nonetheless coded under only one category, for the sake of a clear total.

20. DeYoung et al. use the term "multiracial" congregation in *United by Faith* to denote not just communities that include members of different races but also congregations from one racial community that include different nationalities or ethnicities (for example, Latinos or Asians). They do, though, encourage congregations that attempt to bridge racial as well as ethnic divides.

21. Richard Land, president of the Ethics and Religious Liberty in 2004: "In 1970 we were almost totally a white denomination by choice. As of 2000, 20 percent of Southern Baptists were ethnic" (Green 2004). Rick Warren: "I found those 2,000 verses on the poor. How did I miss that? I went to Bible college, two seminaries, and I got a doctorate. How did I miss God's compassion for the poor? I was not seeing all the purposes of God" (Morgan 2005, 3).

22. Articles on cross-racial political alliances could also have been coded under "policy," thereby expanding that category by almost 50 percent, but a primary focus on alliance building suggests political strategy, potentially around numerous policy issues. It therefore merited a stand-alone category.

23. The main policy-related topic covered in *CT* in this period (that is, not directly race-focused) was "family values," with a fixation on same-sex marriage, particularly during George W. Bush's second election in 2004.

24. Other articles related to policy included health care and needs of the urban poor, but given that participants typically employed "social justice" language to emphasize grassroots social change methods in such contexts, these were usually coded under social justice.

25. The article notes, "three quarters of the Latinos surveyed said they want their churches or religious organizations to aid undocumented immigrants even when it would be illegal" (9).

26. A representative sample includes Neff 2000; Morgan 2005; Tennant 2006; Rutledge 2008; Galli 2009; and Moring 2009.

7. Politics, Culture, and the Multiethnic Church

1. DeYoung et al. primarily use the term "multiracial," but others, such as Mark DeYmaz (mentioned below), use "multiethnic" to include boundary-crossing churches that may contain mostly members of one racial group. Asian and Latino multiethnic groups would be an example. Most MECs are also multiracial. I prefer the more encompassing "multiethnic."

2. Interview length averaged about thirty-five minutes, though some lasted over an hour. Either live or after the event, I listened to thirteen speakers or workshop leaders, five of whom I interviewed. Further details provided upon request.

3. Participants represented six U.S. regions, ten states, twelve cities, seventeen men, four women, and four racial groups. MEC networking forums are geared toward pastors and lay leaders; all but five respondents were leaders in their local churches or the MEC movement (a few were interested parishioners who did not identify as leaders). As pastoral and ministry staff tends to be male in conservative evangelical settings, I had fewer chances to interview women.

4. To protect people's identities, I have used pseudonyms for all churches and participants interviewed, except for Mark DeYmaz, pastor of Mosaic Church in Little Rock, Arkansas, and

cofounder and directional leader of Mosaix Global Network. The sociologist George Yancey (University of North Texas) is the other cofounder of Mosaix. Both Yancey and DeYmaz are public, published leaders of the MEC movement.

5. For more on the study of micropolitics in political science, see Kubic 2009 and Pachirat 2009.

6. DeYoung et al. (2003, 130–32) challenge the HUP in explicit terms. See also Yancey 2003, 30–38.

7. Personal recording of lecture at Exponential church-planting conference, Orlando, Florida, April 22, 2008. While DeYmaz has stridently critiqued the application of the HUP to American church building, since about 2011 he has also gone to some pains to defend McGavran's original *intentions* as nonracist—for example, at http://markdeymaz.com/2011/08/should-pastors-accept-or-reject-the-hup.html. An e-book he published in late 2011, *Should Pastors Accept or Reject the Homogeneous Unit Principle?*, differentiates appropriate versus inappropriate uses of McGavran's model (http://www.mosaix.info/resources/hup).

8. Cutler described his MEC project as inherently challenging the HUP growth model wherein "you cater to a market. We've given people what they wanted, we've attracted that crowd and it worked, the marketing worked. . . . But if we created a church in where people walk in and see people together who normally would never associate with one another in society, that to me would demonstrate part of the gospel. To me it was either that or Trenton. Either that or Africa. I wanted to give my life to something that counts and I thought, *this would be the riskiest, most dangerous, highest possibility of failure thing that I could do, something like this.*" Interview by author, June 27, 2008.

9. For a helpful discussion of the social costs, particularly to racial minorities, of engaging in volunteer efforts in diverse churches, see Christerson and Emerson 2003, 163–81.

10. The gist of kingdom theology in the context of the multiethnic church is the idea that Christians are called by God (as evidenced in Christ's earthly ministry) to create a Christian community on earth that looks much like God's heavenly kingdom—which means overcoming all external divisions. See Padilla 2010; DeYmaz 2007, 206; DeYmaz and Li 2010; and Woo 2009.

11. The first third of DeYmaz's influential manual *Building a Healthy Multi-Ethnic Church* (2007) delineates in scripture-laced passages the biblical call of multiethnic witness and worship as a lighthouse to the world. "In order to build a healthy multi-ethnic church, planters [of new churches] and reformers [of monocultural churches] alike must be rooted in an understanding of God's word and his revealed will for the local church. We must find our inspiration in none other than Christ himself, *who calls us to be one so that the world would know God's love and believe* (John 17:23)" (xxviii, emphasis added).

12. Critical to the MEC hermeneutic is the rejection of ethnic assimilation (to the standards of the majority group in the church) as a measure of oneness. A staple of the MEC literature is the embrace of different cultures' uniqueness as a reflection of God's love of diversity, and necessary to the whole of the Christian "body" (church). Movement architects take pains, however, to insist that the embrace of cultural difference does not equate to promoting "pluralist" and "relativist" values frameworks that proponents read as non-Christian (see DeYoung et al. 2003, 128, 139).

13. In his consultation with churches working toward multiethnicity, Mark DeYmaz emphasizes this message, often tapping into the language of "spiritual warfare." "It is a hard time to be a Christian," he told a small group of leaders at Resurrection. "Because you're working in Satan's territory and Satan is a great divider" (field notes and personal recording, July 11, 2010). Such statements link MEC membership with resistance to satanic influence in the world.

14. Survey questions and results available at www.nancywadsworth.com/2010MECsurvey.

15. Of the remaining 18 percent, most stated they either had been involved in MECs in the past or were simply interested in becoming involved.

16. Most of the remainder (24 percent) identified as mainline Protestant.

17. Respondents were allowed to choose more than one racial category if they identified as mixed race; therefore the total percentage is over 100.

18. Nine percent answered "No"; 10 percent "Don't Know."

19. Curiously on this question, almost 50 percent of respondents selected the "neutral" option, perhaps suggesting discomfort but not outright opposition with a restrictionist approach toward immigration.

20. This issue was chosen in the survey because equity in public education surfaced as one of the main concerns of MEC members I interviewed through Mosaix and through the Colorado case study.

21. At least one outlier critiqued the notion of political engagement in the context of the MEC. In a comments option at the survey's end, she or he wrote: "The survey design reflects a very deficient understanding of the biblical mandate, therefore concepts are imposed upon the diverse church that threaten to make much of the survey results invalid. Put another way, the political model works at cross purposes with the biblical model." I also received dozens of comments that the survey was well crafted and tapped into important questions in the MEC. Despite some critiques, the survey results demonstrated high enthusiasm about at least some forms of basic political engagement as an outgrowth of the MEC.

22. Survey data suggested that MGN members were distinctly ambivalent about how to engage matters related to homosexuality in MEC churches. Some worried about equating sexual difference with racial and ethnic difference. Others wanted to cast a welcoming tone to gays and lesbians without "endorsing their lifestyle." Few were enthusiastic about working politically to protect traditional marriage, even though they endorsed it. Such results merit further analysis.

23. A separate question asked, "Do you think issues of sexual orientation are relevant to the overall mission of the church? (For example, God's views on homosexuality, and/or the church's position on treatment of homosexuals)." Respondents were given the option to elaborate their answers. Sixty percent said "Yes," 18 percent "No," and 17 percent "Not Sure." In comments, many argued that homosexuality shouldn't be singled out over other sins, including divorce, poverty, abortion, and racism, and that churches shouldn't treat homosexuals in a "condemning manner." Though space prevents an elaboration of this, an interesting question emerged in these comments about whether sexual orientation should be rightly compared to race or ethnicity.

24. Full MEC questionnaire at www.nancywadsworth.com/AMAppendices.

25. Here I am just counting those formally interviewed, although speakers and workshop leaders I did not interview could also fit into these categories.

26. The fact that pastors, who for the most part received a fair amount of education, were overrepresented in my interviews may account for the paucity of interviewees in this position.

27. In fact, however, some of the organizers I interviewed did articulate more extensive thoughts about politics than Pastor Matt.

28. For example, he had trouble seeing King's methods of political engagement as relevant to the MEC movement. "I mean, my understanding was that he was speaking equality for the black person. He was a leader in that. . . . And so absolutely, there will obviously be political implications [of MEC efforts], but I think the majority of leaders are gonna focus on Christ's call for us to be one."

29. Personal recording of conference talk, Second Annual Mosaix Northeast Multi-Ethnic Ministry Conference, Lancaster Bible College, Lancaster, Pennsylvania, November 15, 2008.

8. On the Ground, In the Moment

1. Denver is a "choice" city, meaning that children may attend any public school in the district and are not restricted to neighborhood schools funded by the local property taxes. In practice, this "choice" privileges families with greater resources to support their children traveling long distances to school, and essentially ghettoizes the poorest neighborhoods.

2. Numbers reported in interview with Cutler by author, March 22, 2011.

3. Phone interview with Cutler by author, October 25, 2011.

4. RBC "Dear Neighbor" flyer, author's archives, n.d.

5. After I told Curt about the existence of Mosaix Global Network, the clearinghouse for communication, training, and resource sharing among MECs, he did connect with the movement. Resurrection has since become an active member in MGN.

6. Interview by author, July 15, 2008.

7. For a self-description of the group's identity and history, see Abrams 2007 and http://bible-truth.org/BaptistHistory.html. Interestingly, the group rejects belonging in the umbrella category of Protestant (see subhead in link above).

8. In 1983, Bob Jones University lost a Supreme Court case (*Bob Jones University v. United States*, 461 U.S. 574) in which the school defended its racially segregationist policies as "sincerely held religious beliefs." The school's tax exemption was revoked by the IRS based on the court's decision.

9. For example, Curt developed a survey of IFB members in which he asked about beliefs, behaviors, and even sexual habits—revealing that many of those in IFB were not respecting strict IFB-endorsed practices. His results showed, among other things, that at least as many people raised in IFB culture had homosexual experiences as people in the larger culture did.

10. I omit naming the site to avoid identifying details. The site remains a popular open forum for discussion and critique by, for, and of people in IFB culture, and some who have left it. It is not without its critics, who claim that the forum inadequately challenges IFB institutions. The limits of this chapter prevent me from discussing those viewpoints, but a full study of these conversations within and beyond IFB culture would be very useful.

11. The material on Curt's development as an IFB challenger from interview by author, July 10, 2009.

12. "I went to Willow Creek, I went to Saddleback and those places. Cause I was curious, when are people going to reach their communities? [The drive to build a multiethnic church] just came down to the fact that it shouldn't be the homogenous church principle at work. Really the gospel's supposed to go to all peoples, all nations, giving out the message. So I drove down here and I saw a place where the gospel could be on its greatest display." Interview by author, July 15, 2008.

13. Resurrection did sponsor a "visiting" music service or two from First Central Baptist Church at the beginning. Indeed, as strains of black gospel music wafted up from the larger Baptist church sanctuary from which RBC rented its space, I often wondered why Resurrection hadn't taken more advantage of the musical resources right next door. However, for other reasons the relationship between the two churches was no more than polite; each church mostly left the other alone and kept to itself.

14. Newsletter, April 1, 2009.

15. Space limits prevent me from writing about RBC's evolving relationship to the issue of homelessness in Denver.

16. Denver Public Schools Communications Office, http://communications.dpsk12.org /announcements/cole-arts-and-science-academy-receives-innovation-approval.

17. When Curt learned in our first interview that I teach courses on race and other topics related to power and privilege, he asked me for a list of resources, including resources on the topic of white privilege. A quick study, Curt had read a number of these sources by our next meeting a few months later. This indicates that his social reflexivity regarding white privilege may have been informed by my influence as an outsider/expert. However, his initiative is a relevant factor in the process; another pastor may not have solicited and followed up on suggestions.

18. Personally, I doubted that incomplete membership could constitute "welcoming." However, I remained in conversation with Curt on the issue of homosexuality, and have also accepted Mark DeYmaz's invitation to engage in a similar one-on-one dialogue about the topic of homosexuality and Christianity. This is huge, complex subject, one that I hope to develop in another project entirely.

19. Interestingly, the next sermon Curt delivered at RBC (June 28, 2009) after our first conversation about LGBT rights was on the topic of wives obeying their husbands. Listening to the podcast of it, I was surprised to find that Curt had done more homework on the history and demands of the U.S. feminist movements (some of which I had relayed to him in a previous interview) than I had expected. Even as he remained a staunch gender traditionalist in some areas (like male headship of the family and church), his social reflexivity seemed to be expanding.

20. Stanczak followed a very diverse MEC in Los Angeles.

21. As we have learned, in conservative evangelical churches where scriptural grounding is prioritized, a common assertion is that Jesus's teachings in the New Testament amount to a command to foster diversity among Christians as a model to the world. "Proof texting" is another name for this act of finding biblical quotes to support a position. See Becker 1998, 458, quoting Ammerman.

22. As readers may recall, the CCDA was started by John Perkins, whose participation in evangelical racial reconciliation was discussed in chapter 4. See http://www.ccda.org/history.

23. Melanie Asmar, "For Christ's Sake: Local Evangelicals Plan Civic Center Park Rally for Immigration Reform," *Westword*, January 22, 2010. Curt and Enrique also independently mentioned being inspired by a professor at the local conservative seminary who they believed would be "changing the conversation" among evangelicals about immigration ("Immigration Reform Vigil Set for Tuesday," January 25, 2010, http://www.denverpost.com/news/ci_14265399.)

24. Asmar 2010. See also http://coloradoimmigrant.org/article.php?id=594.

25. "The group stated the rally would 'raise awareness of the broken immigration system in the United States, to act on the biblical mandate of compassion and justice toward immigrants, and to lament that the evangelical tradition has been late to join other Christian traditions and faiths in advocating for more just immigration laws'" (Asmar 2010).

26. Nate helped run a weekly Bible study club at the high school, through Young Life, a Christian organization. He also worked through Volunteers for America to help build "advisory groups" to help support students materially through graduation (interview by author, July 7, 2009). Nate later left RBC, though I am not clear as to why.

27. Before joining the ministry, Enrique had been a well-paid engineer. He also raised the much of the funding to support the family through the one-to-two-year start-up period at RBC. At the

time of our interview, he had just gotten part-time work in security at the local middle school. Interview with Enrique and his wife, Caitlin, by author, August 4, 2009.

28. Curt asked me to help facilitate one or more of the conversations. I suggested other, more experienced facilitators, though I did offer to present a standard lecture I give on white privilege. RBC never followed up on the request, though I think not from disinterest.

29. Here he related stories that he and members of his family had been racially profiled by Denver police.

30. Gordon was the only RBC member I interviewed who did not take the church's male leadership structure for granted and raised a gender critique of the church. He thought that the church minimized women's leadership and suffered from a "patriarchal" orientation that was invariably influenced by the broader history of racial imperialism in modern Christian history. This, among other things, put him considerably to the left of most other RBC members.

31. Phone interview by author, October 8, 2011.

32. It would be fruitful, for example, to use a schema like the political orientations spectrum described in chapter 7 to plot where *every* member of the church fit in their perspective on the legitimacy of political engagement as an outgrowth of church work. For the time being, I can only rely on data for selected members.

Epilogue

1. http://www.mosaix.info/About/history.

2. http://www.mosaix.info/Services/speaking.

3. DeYmaz has an e-book on the topic of the HUP principle, but a concise statement of his views can be found in the MGN Teleconference, "Best Practices: Accept or Reject the Homogeneous Unit Principle," http://www.mosaix.info/_literature_131747/HUP.

4. Teleconference, "Frontline with Mark DeYmaz and Anthony Hendricks: What Does the Trayvon Martin Case Say About the Church?" March 29, 2012, http://www.mosaix.info/_literature_129404/Trayvon_Martin_Case.

5. http://www.mosaix.info/_literature_129404/Trayvon_Martin_Case.

6. Zimmerman later commented on Fox News that he believed the shooting was part of "God's plan," but this comment was made after the MGN conference call. http://www.latimes.com/news/la-naw-zimmerman-interview-20120718,0,4171414.story.

7. "What usually remains intact in the epochs of petrification and foreordained doom is the faculty of freedom itself, the sheer capacity to begin, which animates and inspires all human activities and is the hidden source of production of all great and beautiful things" (Arendt 2006, 167).

Bibliography

Abrams III, Cooper B. 2007. "A Brief Survey of Independent Fundamental Baptist Churches." http://bible-truth.org/BaptistHistory.html.

Abzug, Robert H. 1994. *Cosmos Crumbling: American Reform and the Religious Imagination*. New York: Oxford University Press.

Alford, Deanne. 2007. "Nightmare of Nightmares: Virginia Tech's Korean Christians Wrestle with the Aftermath of a Massacre." *Christianity Today* 51(6): 52.

Allina-Pisano, Lisa. 2009. "How to Tell an Axe Murderer: An Essay on Ethnography, Truth, and Lies." In *Political Ethnography: What Immersion Contributes to the Study of Power*, edited by Edward Schatz, 53–76. Chicago: University of Chicago Press.

Alumkal, Antony. 2004. "American Evangelicalism in the Post–Civil Rights Era: A Racial Formation Theory." *Sociology of Religion* 65(3): 195–213.

Ammerman, Nancy Tatom. 1990. *Baptist Battles: Social Change and Religious Conflict in the Southern Baptist Convention*. New Brunswick, N.J.: Rutgers University Press.

Anderson, David, and Bridgeway Community Church (Columbia, Md.). 2004. *Multicultural Ministry: Finding Your Church's Unique Rhythm*. Grand Rapids, Mich.: Zondervan.

Anonymous. 1980. "Buffalo Churches Rally in Response to Race Murders." 1980. *Christianity Today* 21(20).

———. 1981. "Inter-Varsity Generates Soul to Reach the Heart of the City." *Christianity Today* 25(3): 72.

———. 1982. "Hispanics: The Harvest Field at Home." *Christianity Today* 26(18): 68.

———. 1989. "The Christian Legacy of Martin Luther King." *Christianity Today* 33(9): 33.

———. 1990. "NAE, NBEA Groups Join to Condemn Racism." *Christianity Today* 34(4): 35.

———. 1993a. "A Bus Ride Beyond the Comfort Zone." *Christianity Today* 37(11): 22.

———. 1993b. "How Should Evangelicals Respond to Border Problems?" *Christianity Today* 37(15).

———. 1996a. "Christians Protest Welfare Cutbacks." *Christianity Today* 40(2): 106.

———. 1996b. "States, Nonprofits Shoulder Welfare-Reform Burden." *Christianity Today* 40(2): 100–101.

———. 2000. "A CT Special Section: Divided by Faith?" *Christianity Today* 44(11): 34–65.

———. 2006. "Blessed Are the Courageous." *Christianity Today*.

———. 2007. "I Was a Stranger (A CT Poll)." *Christianity Today* 51(9).

———. 2009. "The Soul of the Border Crisis." *Christianity Today* 53(6): 18.

ARDA. 2000. *Association of Religion Data Archives Report 2000*. Association of Religion Data Archives. University Park, Pa. http://www.thearda.com.

Arendt, Hanna. 2006. *Between Past and Future*. New York: Penguin Classics.

Asmar, Melanie. 2010. "For Christ's Sake: Local Evangelicals Plan Civic Center Park Rally for Immigration Reform." *Westword*, January 22.

Balmer, Randal Herbert. 1989. *Mine Eyes Have Seen the Glory: A Journey into the Evangelical Subculture in America.* New York: Oxford University Press.

Barkun, Michael. 1994. *Religion and the Racist Right: The Origins of the Christian Identity Movement.* Chapel Hill: University of North Carolina Press.

Bartkowski, John P., and Christopher G. Ellison. 1995. "Divergent Models of Childrearing in Popular Manuals: Conservative Protestants vs. the Mainstream Experts." *Sociology of Religion* 56(1): 21–34.

Bartkowski, John P., and Helen A. Regis. 2003. *Charitable Choices: Religion, Race, and Poverty in the Post Welfare Era.* New York: New York University Press.

Becker, Penny Edgell. 1998. "Making Inclusive Communities: Congregations and the Problem of Race." *Social Problems* 45(4): 451–72.

Beers, V. Gilbert. 1983. "If Not Abortion, What Then? Why Prolife Rhetoric Is Not Enough." *Christianity Today* 27(9).

Bercovitch, Sacvan. 1978. *The American Jeremiad.* Madison: University of Wisconsin Press.

Bjork, Don. 1985. "Foreign Missions: Next Door and Down the Street." *Christianity Today* 29(10): 17.

Black, A. E., D. L. Koopman, and D. K. Ryden. 2004. *Of Little Faith: The Politics of George W. Bush's Faith-Based Initiatives.* Washington, D.C.: Georgetown University Press.

Blank, R. M. 1997. "Policy Watch: The 1996 Welfare Reform." *Journal of Economic Perspectives* 11(1): 169–77.

Block, Jack, and Jeanne H. Block. 2006. "Nursery School Personality and Political Orientation Two Decades Later." *Journal of Research in Personality* 40(5): 734–49.

Blunt, Sheryl. 2003. "Saving Black Babies." *Christianity Today* 47(2): 21.

Boles, John B., ed. 1988. *Masters & Slaves in the House of the Lord: Race and Religion in the American South, 1740–1870.* Lexington: University Press of Kentucky.

Bonilla-Silva, Eduardo. 2010. *Racism without Racists: Color-Blind Racism and the Persistence of Racial Inequality in the United States.* Lanham, Md.: Rowman & Littlefield.

Bush, Melanie E. L. 2004. *Breaking the Code of Good Intentions: Everyday Forms of Whiteness.* Lanham, Md.: Rowman & Littlefield.

Buursma, Bruce. 1985. "Concerns of the Evangelist: Interview with Billy Graham." *Christianity Today* 29(6): 22.

Cadwalader, Sandra L., and Vine Deloria. 1984. *The Aggressions of Civilization: Federal Indian Policy since the 1880s.* Philadelphia: Temple University Press.

Campbell, D. E., and J. Q. Monson. 2008. "The Religion Card: Gay Marriage and the 2004 Presidential Election." *Public Opinion Quarterly* 72(3): 399–419.

Carlson, James M., and Mark S. Hyde. 1980. "Personality and Political Recruitment: Actualization or Compensation?" *Journal of Psychology* 106(1): 117–20.

Carnes, Tony. 2003. "'The Peoples Are Here': Record Immigration Pushes American Christians Out of Their Comfort Zones." *Christianity Today* 47(2): 76.

Carney, Clandion W. 1981. "Black Americans: Still Looking for the Promised Land." *Christianity Today* 25(7): 32.

Carrasco, Rodolpho. 1996. "Pivotal Minority Movements Strive for Racial Unity." *Christianity Today* 40(1): 70.

——. 2001. "Catching Up with Hispanics." *Christianity Today* 45(14): 66.

Carson, D. A. 2005. *Becoming Conversant with the Emerging Church: Understanding a Movement and Its Implications.* Grand Rapids, Mich.: Zondervan.

Carwardine, Richard. 1993. *Evangelicals and Politics in Antebellum America*. New Haven, Conn.: Yale University Press.

Chappell, David. 2004. *A Stone of Hope: Prophetic Religion and the Death of Jim Crow*. Raleigh: University of North Carolina Press.

Chaves, M., M. E. Konieczny, K. Beyerlien, and E. Barman. 1999. "The National Congregations Study: Background, Methods, and Selected Results." *Journal for the Scientific Study of Religion* 38(4): 458–76.

Christerson, Brad, and Michael O. Emerson. 2003. "The Costs of Diversity in Religious Organizations: An In-Depth Case Study." *Sociology of Religion* 64(2): 163–81.

Christerson, Brad, Korie L. Edwards, and Michael O. Emerson. 2005. *Against All Odds: The Struggle for Racial Integration in Religious Organizations*. New York: New York University Press.

Collun, Danny D. 1996. *Black and White Together: The Search for Common Ground*. Maryknoll, N.Y.: Orbis Books.

Colson, Charles W. 1985. "Standing Tough Against All Odds." *Christianity Today* 29(12): 26.

Cone, James. 1969. *Black Theology and Black Power*. New York: Seabury Press.

———. 2007. "Liberation and the Christian Ethic (God of the Oppressed)." In *On Violence: A Reader*, edited by Bruce B. Lawrence and Aisha Karim, 351–62. Durham, N.C.: Duke University Press.

Crenshaw, Kimberle W. 1988. "Race, Reform, and Retrenchment: Transformation and Legitimation in Antidiscrimination Law." *Harvard Law Review* 101(7): 1331–87.

Crosby, Cindy. 2003. "Healing Salve." *Christianity Today* 47(11): 82.

Dailey, Jane. 2004. "Sex, Segregation, and the Sacred after Brown." *Journal of American History* 91(1): 119–44.

Daly, John Patrick. 2004. *When Slavery Was Called Freedom: Evangelicals, Proslavery, and the Causes of the Civil War*. Lexington: University Press of Kentucky.

DeYmaz, Mark. 2007. *Building a Healthy Multi-Ethnic Church: Mandates, Commitments, and Practices of a Diverse Congregation*. San Francisco: John Wiley & Sons.

DeYmaz, Mark, and Harry Li. 2010. *Ethnic Blends: Mixing Diversity into Your Local Church*. Grand Rapids, Mich.: Zondervan.

DeYoung, Curtiss P. 1995. *Coming Together: The Bible's Message in an Age of Diversity*. Valley Forge, Pa.: Judson Press.

DeYoung, Curtiss P., Michael O. Emerson, George Yancey, and Karen Chai Kim. 2003. *United by Faith: Multiracial Congregations as a Response to the Racial Divide*. New York: Oxford University Press.

———. 2005. "All Churches Should Be Multiracial." *Christianity Today* 49(4): 32.

Diamond, Sara. 1989. *Spiritual Warfare: The Politics of the Christian Right*. Boston: South End Press.

———. 1995. *Roads to Dominion: Right-Wing Movements and Political Power in the United States*. New York: Guilford Press.

———. 2000. *Not By Politics Alone: The Enduring Influence of the Christian Right*. New York: Guilford.

Dochuk, Darren. 2007. "Evangelicalism Becomes Southern, Politics Becomes Evangelical: From FDR to Ronald Reagan." In *Religion and American Politics: From the Colonial Period to the Present*, 2nd ed., edited by Mark A. Noll and Luke E. Harlow, 297–325. New York: Oxford University Press.

DuBois, W. E. B. 1903. *The Souls of Black Folk*. New York: New American Library.

Dzur, Albert W. 1998. "Value Pluralism versus Political Liberalism?" *Social Theory* 24(3): 375–92.

Eckholm, Eric. 2012. "Southern Baptists Approve Steps Aimed at Diversity." *New York Times*, June 15.

Edsall, Thomas Byrne, and Mary D. Edsall. 1992. *Chain Reaction: The Impact of Race, Rights, and Taxes on American Politics*. New York: Norton.

Edwards, James. 2006. "Seeking Biblical Principles to Inform Immigration Policy." *Christianity Today*.

Egan, P. J. 2005. *The Politics of Same-Sex Marriage*. Cambridge: Cambridge University Press.

Eighmy, J. L. 1987. *Churches in Cultural Captivity: A History of Social Attitudes of Southern Baptists*. Knoxville: University of Tennessee Press.

Eliasoph, Nina. 1998. *Avoiding Politics: How Americans Produce Apathy in Everyday Life*. New York: Cambridge University Press.

Ellis, Edward, and Charles Lyon. 2000. "We Can Overcome." *Christianity Today* 44(11): 40–49.

Emerson, Michael O. 2001. "Costs and Benefits of Multiracial Congregations." In *Changing Terrain of Race and Ethnicity Conference*. Chicago: University of Illinois.

Emerson, Michael O., and K. C. Kim. 2003. "Multiracial Congregations: An Analysis of Their Development and a Typology." *Journal for the Scientific Study of Religion* 42(2): 217–27.

Emerson, Michael O., and Christian Smith. 2000. *Divided by Faith: Evangelical Religion and the Problem of Race in America*. New York: Oxford University Press.

Emerson, Michael O., and Rodney M. Woo. 2006. *People of the Dream: Multiracial Congregations in the United States*. Princeton, N.J.: Princeton University Press.

Findlay, James F. 1997. *Church People in the Struggle: The National Council of Churches and the Black Freedom Movement, 1950–1970*. New York: Oxford University Press.

Finke, Roger, and Rodney Stark. 1993. *The Churching of America, 1776–1990: Winners and Losers in Our Religious Economy*. New Brunswick, N.J.: Rutgers University Press.

Foner, Eric, and Schomburg Center for Research in Black Culture. 1993. *Freedom's Lawmakers: A Directory of Black Officeholders during Reconstruction*. New York: Oxford University Press.

Formicola, Jo Renee, Mary C. Segers, and Paul J. Weber. 2003. *Faith-Based Initiatives and the Bush Administration: The Good, the Bad, and the Ugly*. Lanham, Md.: Rowman & Littlefield.

Foster, C. R., and T. Brelsford. 1996. *We Are the Church Together: Cultural Diversity in Congregational Life*. Valley Forge, Pa.: Trinity Press International.

Frame, Randy. 1983. "Why Black Brethren Embrace Politics." *Christianity Today* 27(9): 34–37.

———. 1986. "The Cost of Being Black." *Christianity Today* 30(13).

———. 1988. "Race and the Church: A Progress Report." *Christianity Today* 32(4): 16.

———. 1989. "For Black Evangelicals, a Silver Anniversary." *Christianity Today* 32(8): 43.

———. 1997. "Welfare Reform: God in a Box?" *Christianity Today* 41(4): 46.

Fredrickson, George M. 2002. *Racism: A Short History*. Princeton, N.J.: Princeton University Press.

Friedland, Michael B. 1998. *Lift Up Your Voice Like a Trumpet: White Clergy and the Civil Rights and Antiwar Movements, 1954–1973*. Chapel Hill: University of North Carolina Press.

Frizen, Edwin. 1985. "Cross-Cultural Vision and Challenge." *Christianity Today* 29(10): 20.

Fukuyama, Francis. 2007. *America at the Crossroads: Democracy, Power, and the Neoconservative Legacy*. New Haven, Conn.: Yale University Press.

Gabelein, Frank. 1981. "Booker T. Washington: Freeing the Spirit for Service." *Christianity Today* 25(17): 2.

Gallay, Alan. 1988. "Planters and Slaves in the Great Awakening." In *Masters & Slaves in the House of the Lord: Race and Religion in the American South 1740–1870*, edited by John B. Boles, 19–36. Lexington: University Press of Kentucky.

Galli, Mark. 2006. "Blessed Is the Law—Up to a Point." *Christianity Today.*

———. 2009. "Making the Local Church a Hero." *Christianity Today* 53(3): 32.

Garces-Foley, Kathleen. 2007. "New Opportunities and New Values: The Emergence of the Multicultural Church." *Annals of the American Academy of Political and Social Science* 612(1): 209–24.

Garcia Bedolla, Lisa. 2007. "Intersections of Inequality: Understanding Marginalization and Privilege in the Post–Civil Rights Era." *Politics & Gender* 3(2): 232–48.

Gilbreath, Edward. 1996. "A Prophet Out of Harlem." *Christianity Today* 40(10): 37.

———. 1998. "The Jackie Robinson of Evangelicalism." *Christianity Today* 42(2).

———. 2004. "One Lord, One Faith, Many Ethnicities." *Christianity Today* 48(1): 52.

———. 2006. *Reconciliation Blues: A Black Evangelical's Inside View of White Christianity.* Downers Grove, Ill.: InterVarsity Press.

———. 2007. "Racism vs. Gracism." *Crosswalk.com.* http://www.crosswalk.com/11622744/.

Gilbreath, Edward, and Mark Galli. 2005. "CT Roundtable: Harder Than Anyone Can Imagine." *Christianity Today* 49(4): 36–43.

Gillespie, E., B. Schellhas, N. Gingrich, and D. Armey. 1994. *Contract with America: The Bold Plan by Newt Gingrich, Dick Armey and the House Republicans to Change the Nation.* New York: Random House.

Gilliam, Reginald Earl. 1975. *Black Political Development: An Advocacy Analysis.* New York: Dunellen.

Glaude, Eddie S., Jr. 2000. *Exodus!: Religion, Race, and Nation in Early Nineteenth-Century Black America.* Chicago: University of Chicago Press.

Goffman, Erving. 1979. "Footing." *Semiotica* 25:1–29.

Goldenberg, David M. 2005. *The Curse of Ham: Race and Slavery in Early Judaism, Christianity, and Islam.* Princeton, N.J.: Princeton University Press.

Goldfield, Michael. 1997. *The Color of Politics: Race and the Mainsprings of American Politics.* New York: New Press.

Grady, J. Lee. 1994. "Pentecostals Renounce Racism." *Christianity Today* 38(14): 58.

Graham, Billy. "Racisim and the Evangelical Church." *Christianity Today* 37(11): 27.

Grant, George, and D. J. Kennedy. 1995. *The Changing of the Guard: The Vital Role Christians Must Play in America's Unfolding Political and Cultural Drama.* Nashville, Tenn.: Broadman & Holdman.

Green, Amy. 2004. "Southern Baptist Surprise!" *Christianity Today* 48(9): 54–56.

Greenwalt, Kent. 1988. *Religious Convictions and Political Choice.* New York: Oxford University Press.

Haider-Markel, D. P., and M. R. Joslyn. 2005. "Attributions and the Regulation of Marriage: Considering the Parallels between Race and Homosexuality." *PS: Political Science and Politics* 38(2): 233–39.

Hancock, A. M. 2004. *The Politics of Disgust: The Public Identity of the Welfare Queen.* New York: New York University Press.

Harding, Susan. 1991. "Representing Fundamentalism: The Problem of the Repugnant Cultural Other." *Social Research* 58(2): 373–93.

———. 2000. *The Book of Jerry Falwell.* Princeton, N.J.: Princeton University Press.

Harlow, Luke E. 1990. "Slavery, Race, and Political Ideology in the White Christian South before and after the Civil War." In *Religion and American Politics: From the Colonial Era to the 1980s*, edited by Mark A. Noll, 203–24. New York: Oxford University Press.

Harvey, Paul. 1997. *Redeeming the South: Religious Cultures and Racial Identities among Southern Baptists, 1865–1925*. Chapel Hill: University of North Carolina Press.

———. 2005. *Freedom's Coming: Religious Culture and the Shaping of the South from the Civil War through the Civil Rights Era*. Chapel Hill: University of North Carolina Press.

Heagney, Meredith. 2009. "Southern Baptists Seek More Diversity." *Columbus Dispatch*, July 9.

High, Brandon. 2009. "The Recent Historiography of American Neoconservatism." *Historical Journal* 52(2): 475–91.

Himmelstein, Jerome L. 1990. *To the Right: The Transformation of American Conservatism*. Berkeley: University of California Press.

Horsman, Reginald. 1981. *Race and Manifest Destiny: The Origins of American Racial Anglo-Saxonism*. Cambridge, Mass.: Harvard University Press.

Howard-Pitney, David. 2005. *The African American Jeremiad: Appeals for Justice in America*. Rev. and expanded ed. Philadelphia: Temple University Press.

Howe, D. W. 1991. "The Evangelical Movement and Political Culture in the North during the Second Party System." *Journal of American History* 77(4): 1216–39.

Hughes, Paul. 2008. "Continental Divide." *Christianity Today* 52(2): 14–15.

Hunter, James Davison. 1987. *Evangelicalism: The Coming Generation*. Chicago: University of Chicago Press.

Inouye, Stanley K. 1989. "The Mirror of God." *Christianity Today* 33(4): 25–43.

Jackson, Patrick Thaddeus. 2006. "Making Sense of Making Sense: Configurational Analysis and the Double Hermeneutic." In *Interpretation and Method: Empirical Research Methods and the Interpretive Turn*, edited by Peregrine Schwartz-Shea and Dvora Yanow, 264–80. Armonk, N.Y.: M. E. Sharpe.

Jacobson, Matthew Frye. 1998. *Whiteness of a Different Color: European Immigrants and the Alchemy of Race*. Cambridge, Mass.: Harvard University Press.

Jacobson, Robin Dale. 2011. *The New Nativism: Proposition 187 and the Debate over Immigration*. Minneapolis: University of Minnesota Press.

———. 2012. "The Stranger Among Us: The Christian Right and Immigration." In *Faith and Race in American Political Life*, edited by Robin Dale Jacobson and Nancy Wadsworth, 170–86. Charlottesville: University of Virginia Press.

Jacobson, Robin Dale, and Nancy Wadsworth 2012. "Intersecting Race and Religion." In *Faith and Race in American Political Life*, edited by Robin Dale Jacobson and Nancy Wadsworth, 1–29. Charlottesville: University of Virginia Press.

James, Larry M. 1988. "Biracial Fellowship in Antebellum Churches." In *Masters & Slaves in the House of the Lord: Race and Religion in the American South 1740–1870*, edited by John B. Boles. Louisville: University Press of Kentucky.

Jelen, Ted G. 1991. *The Political Mobilization of Religious Beliefs*. New York: Praeger.

Johnson, Dean J. 2011. "Critiquing the Soul of White Supremacy and the Spiritualities of Whiteness: Narrative and Everyday Praxis." Ph.D. diss., Iliff School of Theology.

Jordan, Winthrop D. 1974. *The White Man's Burden: Historical Origins of Racism in the United States*. New York: Oxford University Press.

Kantzer, Kenneth S. 1985. "Varsity Racism?" *Christianity Today* 29(16).

———. 1989. "Listening to America's Ethnic Churches." *Christianity Today* 33(4): 25–43.

Katz, Michael B. 1996. *In the Shadow of the Poorhouse: A Social History of Welfare in America*. New York: Basic Books.

———. 2001. *The Price of Citizenship: Redefining the American Welfare State*. New York: Metropolitan Books.

Kauffman, Richard A. 1997. "Leaders Pursue Unity in Fighting Poverty." *Christianity Today* 41(7): 60–61.

Kellner, Mark A. 1994. "Divided Pentecostal Groups to Pursue Unity." *Christianity Today* 38(5): 50.

———. 1996. "Conservatives Debate Church's Role." *Christianity Today* 40(2): 101.

Kelsey, George D. 1973. *Social Ethics among Southern Baptists, 1917–1969*. Metuchen, N.J.: Scarecrow Press.

Kennedy, John. 1996. "Racial Reconciliation Steps Proceed Slowly for NRB." *Christianity Today* 40(3).

King, Desmond S., and Rogers M. Smith. 2005. "Racial Orders in American Political Development." *American Political Science Review* 99(1): 75–92.

King, Martin Luther, Jr. 1986a. "An Experiment in Love." In *A Testament of Hope: The Essential Writings and Speeches of Martin Luther King, Jr.*, edited by James M. Washington, 16. San Francisco: Harper and Row.

———. 1986b. "Letter from Birmingham City Jail." In *A Testament of Hope: The Essential Writings of Martin Luther King, Jr.*, edited by James M. Washington, 289. San Francisco: Harper and Row.

Kristol, Irving. 1995. *Neoconservatism: The Autobiography of an Idea*. New York: Free Press.

———. 2003. "The Neoconservative Persuasion." *Weekly Standard* 8(47): 23–25.

Kubic, Jan. 2009. "Ethnography of Politics: Foundations, Applications, Prospects." In *Political Ethnography*, edited by Edward Schatz, 25–52. Chicago: University of Chicago Press.

Larsen, Larissa, Sharon L. Harlan, Bob Bolin, Edward J. Hackett, Diane Hope, Andrew Kirby, Amy Nelson, Tom R. Rex, and Shaphard Wolf. 2004. "Bonding and Bridging: Understanding the Relationship between Social Capital and Civic Action." *Journal of Planning Education and Research* 24:64–77.

Lee, Helen. 1995. "Racial Reconciliation Tops NAE Agenda." *Christianity Today* 39(4): 97.

Lemelle, Anthony, and Juan Battle. 2004. "Black Masculinity Matters in Attitudes toward Homosexuality." *Public Opinion Quarterly* 47(1): 39–50.

León, Luis. 2005. "César Chávez and Mexican American Civil Religion." In *Latino Religion and Civic Activism in the United States*, edited by Gastón Espinosa, Vergilio Elisondo, and Jesse Miranda, 53–64. New York: Oxford University Press.

Lewis, Gregory B. 2003. Black-White Differences in Attitudes toward Homosexuality and Gay Rights. *Public Opinion Quarterly* 67(1): 59–78.

Lewis, Gregory B., and C. W. Gossett. 2008. "Changing Public Opinion on Same-Sex Marriage: The Case of California." *Politics & Policy* 36(1): 4–30.

Lichterman, Paul. 2005. *Eusive Togetherness: Church Groups Trying to Bridge America's Divisions*. Princeton, N.J.: Princeton University Press.

Lichterman, Paul, Prudence Carter, and Michele Lamont. 2008. "Race-Bridging for Christ? Conservative Christians and Black-White Relations in Community Life." Presented at "The Conservative Christian Movement and American Democracy" conference, April 27–29, 2007. New York: Russell Sage Foundation.

Liebman, Robert C., Robert Wuthnow, and James L. Guth. 1983. *The New Christian Right: Mobilization and Legitimation*. Hawthorne, N.Y.: Aldine.

Lincoln, C. Eric. 1999. *Race, Religion, and the Continuing American Dilemma*. Rev. ed. New York: Hill and Wang.

Lindner, Eileen W. 2001. "The Fevered Frenzy Over Faith-Based Initiatives." *Yearbook of American and Canadian Churches* 14.

Locklear, Jimmy. 1980. "Theology-Culture Rift Surfaces among Evangelical Blacks." *Christianity Today* 24(10): 44.

Loury, Glenn C. 1995. *One by One from the Inside Out: Essays and Reviews on Race and Responsibility in America.* New York: Free Press.

———. 2002. *The Anatomy of Racial Inequality.* Cambridge, Mass.: Harvard University Press.

Lugo, Luis, Sandra Stencel, John Green, Timoth S. Shah, Brian J. Grim, Gregory Smith, Roberty Ruby, et al. 2006. "Spirit and Power: A 10-Country Survey of Pentecostals." Washington, D.C.: Pew Forum on Religion and Public Life.

Luker, Ralph. 1991. *The Social Gospel in Black and White: American Racial Reform, 1885–1912.* Chapel Hill: University of North Carolina Press.

Mabry, Marcus. 1995. *White Bucks and Black-Eyed Peas: Coming of Age Black in White America.* New York: Scribner.

Macdonald, G. Jeffrey. 2006. "On Immigration Issue, Big Evangelical Groups Conspicuously Mum." *Christianity Today.*

MacHarg, Kenneth D. 2000. "Immigration: Separation Anxiety?" *Christianity Today* 44(5): 26.

MacRobert, Ian. 1988. *The Black Roots and White Racism of Early Pentecostalism in the USA.* New York: St. Martin's Press.

Manis, Andrew Michael. 1987. *Southern Civil Religions in Conflict: Black and White Baptists and Civil Rights, 1947–1957.* Athens: University of Georgia Press.

Maracle, John E. 1989. "The Lost Nation." *Christianity Today* 33(4): 25–43.

Marino, Gordon. 1998. "Me? Apologize for Slavery?" *Christianity Today* 42(11).

Marsden, George M. 1980. *Fundamentalism and American Culture: The Shaping of Twentieth Century Evangelicalism, 1870–1925.* New York: Oxford University Press.

———. 1991. *Understanding Fundamentalism and Evangelicalism.* Grand Rapids, Mich.: W. B. Eerdmans.

Mathews, Donald. 2004. "Lynching Is Part of the Religion of Our People: Faith in the Christina South." In *Religion in the American South*, edited by Beth Barton Schweiger and Donald Mathews, 153–94. Chapel Hill: University of North Carolina Press.

Matsouka, Fumitaka. 1995. *Out of Silence: Emerging Themes in Asian American Churches.* Cleveland: Pilgrim Press.

Maust, John. 1980. "The Exploding Hispanic Minority: A Field in Our Back Yard." *Christianity Today* 24(14): 12.

Maxwell, Joe. 1995. "Black Southern Baptists." *Christianity Today* 39(6): 26.

———. 1998. "Obituary: Racial Reconciler Spencer Perkins." *Christianity Today* 42(3).

McAdam, Doug. 1999. *Political Process and the Development of Black Insurgency, 1930–1970.* Chicago: University of Chicago Press.

McCartney, Bill, and David Halbroo. 1997. *Sold Out: Becoming Man Enough to Make a Difference.* Waco, Tex.: Word Publishing.

McDonald, Robin. 1992. "Stretch Your Racial Comfort Zone." *Christianity Today* 36(7): 14.

McGavran, Donald. 1955. *The Bridges of God: A Study in the Strategy of Missions.* New York: Friendship Press.

———. 1970. *Understanding Church Growth.* Grand Rapids, Mich.: W. B. Eerdmans.

McGill, Denise. 2007. "The Town That Loves Refugees." *Christianity Today* 51(2).

Meyer, Jeremy P. 2009. "Cole Steps toward Innovation." *Denver Post,* April 4.

Miller, Donald E. 1997. *Reinventing American Protestantism: Christianity in the New Millennium.* Berkeley: University of California Press.

Mitchell, Jerry. 1998. "The Preacher and the Klansman." *Jackson Clarion-Ledger.*

Moll, Rob. 2005. "The New Monasticism." *Christianity Today.*

Moon, Dawne. 2004. *God, Sex, and Politics: Homosexuality and Everyday Theologies.* Chicago: University of Chicago Press.

Morgan, Timothy C. 1995. "Racist No More? Black Leaders Ask." *Christianity Today* 39(9): 53.

———. 1996. "Youth Are Key in Moving Past 'Feel Good' Reconciliation." *Christianity Today* 40(13).

———. 2005. "Purpose Driven in Rwanda." *Christianity Today* 10(10).

Moring, Mark. 2009. "Songs of Justice, Missions of Mercy." *Christianity Today* 53(11): 30–33.

Morone, James A. 2003. *Hellfire Nation: The Politics of Sin in American History.* New Haven, Conn.: Yale University Press.

Morris, Aldon D. 1984. *The Origins of the Civil Rights Movement: Black Communities Organizing for Change.* New York: Free Press.

Myra, Harold. 1994. "Love in Black and White." *Christianity Today* 38(3).

———. 1995. "Racial Reconciliation Begins with You." *Christianity Today* 39(3): 18–19.

National Black Evangelical Association and National Association of Evangelicals. 1990. *Statement on Prejudice and Racism.* www.the-nbea.org/uploads/1/0/2/2/10227782/racismbill.pdf.

Neff, David. 1990. "God's Latino Revolution." *Christianity Today* 34(8).

———. 2000. "Different Worlds." *Christianity Today* 44(11): 117–19.

Nelson, Douglas J. 1981. "For Such a Time as This: The Story of Bishop William J. Seymour and the Azusa Street Revival." Ph.D. diss., University of Birmingham.

Newman, Mark. 2001. *Getting Right with God: Southern Baptists and Desegregation, 1945–1995.* Tuscaloosa: University of Alabama Press.

Newton, Judith Lowder. 2005. *From Panthers to Promise Keepers: Rethinking the Men's Movement.* Lantham, Md.: Rowman & Littlefield.

Noll, Mark A. 1990. *Religion and American Politics: From the Colonial Period to the 1980s.* New York: Oxford University Press.

———. 1994. *The Scandal of the Evangelical Mind.* Grand Rapids, Mich.: W. B. Eerdmans.

———. 2008. *God and Race in American Politics: A Short History.* Princeton, N.J.: Princeton University Press.

Norton, Will, Jr. 1982a. "George Wallace: Ten Years Later." *Christianity Today* 26(7): 52–53.

———. 1982b. "An Interview with John Perkins, The Prophet." *Christianity Today* 26(1): 20–23.

Oliver, Melvin L., and Thomas M. Shapiro. 2006. *Black Wealth, White Wealth: A New Perspective on Racial Inequality.* New York: Routledge.

Olsen, Ted. 2004. "Fred Caldwell: Paying the Price for Unity." *Christianity Today* 48(8).

Olson, Joel. 2007. "The Freshness of Fanaticism: The Abolitionist Defense of Zealotry." *Perspectives on Politics* 5(4): 685–701.

Ortiz, Manuel. 1996. *One New People: Models for Developing a Multiethnic Church.* Downers Grove, Ill.: InterVarsity Press.

Pachirat, Timothy. 2009. "The Political in Political Ethnography: Dispatches from the Kill Floor."

In *Political Ethnography: What Immersion Contributes to the Study of Power*, edited by Edward Schatz, 143–61. Chicago: University of Chicago Press.

Padilla, C. René. 2010. *Mission between the Times: Essays on the Kingdom.* 2nd rev. ed. Menlo Park, Calif.: Langham Monographs.

Palau, Luis, and Mike Umlandt. 1996. *The Only Hope for America: The Transforming Power of the Gospel of Jesus Christ.* Wheaton, Ill.: Crossway Books.

Pang, Wing N. 1989. "Out of Chinatown and Back Again." *Christianity Today* 33(4): 25–43.

Payne, Charles. 1995. *I've Got the Light of Freedom: The Organizing Tradition and the Mississippi Freedom Struggle.* Berkeley: University of California Press.

Pearce, Roy Harvey. 1967. *Savagism and Civilization: A Study of the Indian and the American Mind.* Baltimore: Johns Hopkins University Press.

Perkins, John. 1995. *Restoring At-Risk Communities: Doing It Together and Doing It Right.* Wheaton, Ill.: Baker Book House.

Perkins, John, and Thomas A. Tarrants III. 1994. *He's My Brother: Former Racial Foes Offer Strategy for Reconciliation.* Orlando, Fla.: Baker Press.

Perkins, Spencer. 1989. "The Prolife Credibility Gap." *Christianity Today* 33(7): 21.

———. "Integration versus Reconciliation." *Christianity Today* 37(11): 22.

Perry, Huey, and Wayne Parent. 1995. *Blacks and the American Political System.* Gainesville: University Press of Florida.

Persons, Georgia Anne, ed. 2001. *The Politics of the Black "Nation": A Twenty-Five Year Retrospective. National Political Science Review* 8. New Brunswick, N.J.: Transaction.

Prentiss, Craig. 2003. "'Loathsome unto Thy People': The Latter-Day Saints and Racial Categorization." In *Religion and the Creation of Race and Ethnicity*, edited by Craig Prentiss, 124–39. New York: New York University Press.

Pulliam, Sarah. 2007. "Solution Stalemate." *Christianity Today* 51(6): 20–21.

Putnam, Robert D. 2000. *Bowling Alone: The Collapse and Revival of American Community.* New York: Simon & Schuster.

———. 2007. "E Pluribus Unum: Diversity and Community in the Twenty-First Century: The 2006 Johan Skytte Prize Lecture." *Scandinavian Political Studies* 30(2): 137–74.

Putnam, Robert D., Louis M. Feldstein, and Don Cohen. 2003. *Better Together: Restoring the American Community.* New York: Simon & Schuster.

Razack, Sherene H. 1998. *Looking White People in the Eye: Gender, Race, and Culture in Courtrooms and Classrooms.* Toronto: University of Toronto Press.

Reed, Ralph. 1996a. *Active Faith: How Christians are Changing the Soul of American Politics.* New York: Free Press.

———. 1996b. *After the Revolution: How the Christian Coalition Is Impacting America.* Dallas: Word Publishing.

Roediger, David R. 1991. *The Wages of Whiteness: Race and the Making of the American Working Class.* New York: Verso.

Roose, Kevin. 2009. *The Unlikely Disciple: A Sinner's Semester at America's Holiest University.* New York: Grand Central.

Rosen, Robert N. 2000. *The Jewish Confederates.* Columbia: University of South Carolina Press.

Rutledge, Fleming. 2008. "When God Disturbs the Peace." *Christianity Today* 52(6): 30–33.

Sack, Kevin. 1996. "A Penitent Christian Coalition Offers Aid to Burned Churches." *New York Times*, June 19.

Salzman, Jack, and Cornel West. 1997. *Struggles in the Promised Land: Toward a History of Black-Jewish Relations in the United States*. New York: Oxford University Press.

Schatz, Edward, ed. 2009. *Political Ethnography: What Immersion Contributes to the Study of Power*. Chicago: University of Chicago Press.

Scheller, Christine A. 2006. "A Delicate Hospitality." *Christianity Today* 50(3): 48–51.

Schirch, Lisa. 2005. *Ritual and Symbol in Peacebuilding*. Bloomfield, Conn.: Kumerian Press.

Segers, M. 2003. "President Bush's Faith-Based Initiative." In *Faith-Based Initiatives and the Bush Administration: The Good, the Bad, and the Ugly*, 1–24. Lanham, Md.: Rowman & Littlefield.

Sellers, Jeff. 2003. "Hispanic Churches Primed to be More Socially Active." *Christianity Today*.

Sharp, Douglas. 2004. "7 Habits of Racially Mixed Churches." *Christianity Today* 48(8): 60.

Sherman, Amy. 1996. "STEP-Ing Out on Faith—and Off Welfare." *Christianity Today* 40(7): 35–36.

———. 1997. "A Call for Church Welfare Reform (Part 2)." *Christianity Today* 41(11): 46–51.

Sherrod, Sherry, and Herbert C. DuPree. 1993. "The Explosive Growth of the African American Pentecostal Church." In *1993 Yearbook of American and Canadian Churches* 7. New York: National Council of Churches.

Silk, Mark, and Andrew Walsh. 2008. *One Nation, Divisible: How Regional Religious Differences Shape American Politics*. Lanham, Md.: Rowman & Littlefield.

Skillen, James W. 1985. "In Search of Something That Works." *Christianity Today* 29(9): 26.

Skinner, Tom. 1968. *Black and Free*. Grand Rapids, Mich.: Zondervan.

———. 1970a. "The U.S. Racial Crisis and World Evangelism." https://urbana.org/past-urbanas /urbana-70/us-racial-crisis-and-world-evangelism-1970.

———. 1970b. *How Black Is the Gospel?* Philadelphia: J. B. Lippincott.

———. 1970c. *Words of Revolution*. Grand Rapids, Mich.: Zondervan.

———. 1974. *If Christ Is the Answer, What Are the Questions?* Grand Rapids, Mich.: Zondervan.

Smidt, Corwin, ed. 2003. *Religion as Social Capital: Producing the Common Good*. Waco, Tex.: Baylor University Press.

Smith, Christian. 1998. *American Evangelicalism: Embattled and Thriving*. Chicago: University of Chicago Press.

Smith, J. A., Jr. 1989. "The Invisible Church." *Christianity Today* 33(4): 25–43.

Smith, Timothy L. 2004. *Revivalism and Social Reform: American Protestantism on the Eve of the Civil War*. Eugene, Ore.: Wipf & Stock.

Sniderman, Paul M., and Edward G. Carmines. 1997. *Reaching Beyond Race*. Cambridge, Mass.: Harvard University Press.

Snowball, David. 1991. *Continuity and Change in the Rhetoric of the Moral Majority*. New York: Praeger.

Soper, J. Christopher. 1994. *Evangelical Christianity in the United States and Great Britain: Religious Beliefs, Political Choices*. New York: New York University Press.

Soss, Joe. 2006. "Talking Our Way to Meaningful Explanations: A Practice-Centered View of Interviewing for Interpretive Research." In *Interpretation and Method: Empirical Research Methods and the Interpretive Turn*, edited by Peregrine Schwartz-Shea and Dvora Yanow, 127–49. Armonk, N.Y.: M. E. Sharpe.

Spickard, Paul R. 1986. "Why I Believe in Affirmative Action." *Christianity Today* 30(14): 12.

Spring, Beth. 1984. "A Christian School Files Suit to Prove It's Not Racist." *Christianity Today* 28(6): 80–81.

Stafford, Tim. 1995. "Here Comes the World." *Christianity Today* 39(6): 18–26.

——. 2006. "The Call of Samuel." *Christianity Today* 50(9).

Stanczak, Gregory C. 2006. "Stragetic Ethnicity: The Construction of Multi-racial/Multi-ethnic Religious Community." *Racial and Ethnic Studies* 29(5): 856–81.

Stanton, Glenn T. 1994. "Will the Promise Keepers Keep Their Promise?" *Christianity Today.*

Steyn, Melissa E. 2001. *Whiteness Just Isn't What It Used to Be: White Identity in a Changing South Africa.* Albany: State University of New York Press.

Stricker, Mary. 2001. "A New Racial Ideology for the New Christian Right?: The Meaning(s) of Racial Reconciliation within the Promise Keepers Movement." Ph.D. diss., Temple University.

Stumme, W. C. 1995. "The Inclusive Congregation: A Response to 'The Inclusive Church' by Peter Rudowski." *Trinity Seminary Review* 17:13–18.

Swidler, Ann. 1986. "Culture in Action: Symbols and Strategies." *American Sociological Review* 51:273–86.

Synan, Vinson. 1971. *The Holiness-Pentecostal Movement in the United States.* Grand Rapids, Mich.: W. B. Eerdmans.

Tapia, Andrés. 1986. "Political Refugees or Illegal Immigrants." *Christianity Today* 30(2): 68.

——. 1991. "¡Viva Los Evangélicos!" *Christianity Today* 35(12).

——. 1993. "The Myth of Racial Progress." *Christianity Today* 37(11): 16–25.

Tennant, Agnieszka. 2006a. "Social Justice Surprise." *Christianity Today* 50(7): 44–45.

——. 2006b. "What's Next? International Justice." *Christianity Today* 50(10): 72.

Thompson, Barbara. 1984. "In the Ghetto: Where Authentic Christianity Lives." *Christianity Today* 28(3): 29–31.

Thumma, Scott, and David Travis. 2007. *Beyond Megachurch Myths.* San Francisco: Jossey-Bass.

Tinker, George E. 1993. *Missionary Conquest: The Gospel and Native American Cultural Genocide.* Minneapolis: Fortress Press.

——. 2004. *Spirit and Resistance: Political Theology and American Indian Liberation.* Minneapolis: Fortress Press.

Trammel, Madison. 2007. "No Sick Child Left Behind." *Christianity Today* 51(5): 21.

Wadsworth, Nancy D. 2000. "'God's Timing': Conservative Evangelicals and the New Racial Reconciliation Discourse." Ph.D. diss., New School for Social Research.

——. 2008a. "Race-ing Faith and Fate: The Jeremiad in Multiracial 'Traditional Marriage' Alliances." *Race/Ethnicity: Multidisciplinary Global Contexts* 1(2): 313–41.

——. 2008b. "Reconciling Fractures: The Intersection of Race and Religion in United States Political Development." In *Race and American Political Development,* edited by Julie Novkov, Joseph Lowndes, and Dorian T. Warren, 312–36. New York: Routledge.

——. 2010. "Bridging Racial Change: Political Orientations in the United States Evangelical Multiracial Church Movement." *Politics and Religion* 3(3): 439–68.

——. 2011. "Intersectionality in California's Same-Sex Battles: A Complex Proposition." *Political Research Quarterly* 64(1): 200–216.

——. Forthcoming. "Of Milestones and Millstones: Intersections of Race and Religion in the 2012 Election." In *Religion and American Cultures Encyclopedia,* edited by Gary Laderman and Luis Leon. Santa Barbara, Calif.: ABC-CLIO Press.

Wagner, C. Peter. 1979. *Our Kind of People: The Ethical Dimensions of Church Growth.* Atlanta: John Knox Press.

——. 1996. "A Season of Reconciliation." *Charisma* 61:3.

Wagner, C. Peter, Win Arn, and Elmer Towns, eds. 1986. *Church Growth: The State of the Art.* Wheaton, Ill.: Tyndale House.

Wald, Kenneth D. 1994. "The Religious Dimension of American Anti-Communism." *Journal of Church and State* 36(3): 483–506.

Walker, Ken. 2007. "Trusted Guides." *Christianity Today* 51(9): 17.

———. 2009. "Counting Controversy." *Christianity Today* 53(9): 17.

Walsh, Katherine Cramer. 2006. "Elusive Togetherness: Church Groups Trying to Bridge America's Divisions." *Political Science Quarterly* 121:171–72.

Walton, Hanes. 1997. *African American Power and Politics: The Political Context Variable.* New York: Columbia University Press.

Washington, Raleigh, Glen Kehrein, and Claude V. King. 1997. *Break Down the Walls: Experiencing Biblical Reconciliation and Unity in the Body of Christ.* Chicago: Moody Press.

Watson, Justin. 1999. *The Christian Coalition: Dreams of Restoration, Demands for Recognition.* New York: St. Martin's Press.

Webb, Clive. 2001. *Fight against Fear: Southern Jews and Black Civil Rights.* Athens: University of Georgia Press.

Weddle, David. 2010. *Wonder and Meaning in World Religions.* New York: New York University Press.

Wedeen, Lisa. 1999. *Ambiguities of Domination; Politics, Rhetoric, and Symbols in Contemporary Syria.* Chicago: University of Chicago Press.

———. 2002. "Conceptualizing Culture: Possibilities for Political Science." *American Political Science Review* 96(4): 713–28.

———. 2008. *Peripheral Visions: Publics, Power, and Performance in Yemen.* Chicago: University of Chicago Press.

West, Cornel, and Eddie S. Glaude Jr. 2003. *African American Religious Thought: An Anthology.* Louisville, Ky.: Westminster John Knox Press.

Wilcox, Clyde. 1992. *God's Warriors: The Christian Right in Twentieth-Century America.* Baltimore: Johns Hopkins University Press.

Williams, Jean. 2011. "Battling a 'Sex-Saturated Society': The Abstinence Movement and the Politics of Sex Education." *Sexualities* 14(4): 416–43.

Wilson, Catherine. 2008. *The Politics of Latino Faith: Religion, Identity, and Urban Community.* New York: New York University Press.

Wilson, Everett L. 1996. "Saving the Safety Net." *Christianity Today* 40(8): 25.

Winant, Howard. 1990. "Postmodern Racial Politics in the United States: Difference and Inequality." *Socialist Review* (January): 121–46.

———. 1997. "Behind Blue Eyes: Whiteness and Contemporary U.S. Politics." In *Off White: Readings on Race, Power, and Society,* edited by Michelle Fine, 40–55. New York: Routledge.

———. 2004. *The New Politics of Race: Globalism, Difference, Justice.* Minneapolis: University of Minnesota Press.

Wise, Tim. 2010. *Colorblind: The Rise of Post-Racial Politics and the Retreat from Racial Equity.* San Francisco: City Lights.

Woo, Rodney. 2009. "The Color of Church: A Biblical and Practical Paradigm for Multiracial Churches." Nashville, Tenn.: B&H Academic.

Woodberry, Robert D., and Christian S. Smith. 1998. "Fundamentalism et al.: Conservative Protestants in America." *Annual Review of Sociology* 24(1): 25–56.

Wuthnow, Robert. 1988. *The Restructuring of American Religion: Society and Faith since World War II.* Princeton, N.J.: Princeton University Press.

Wuthnow, Robert, and John H. Evans. 2002. *The Quiet Hand of God: Faith-Based Activism and the Public Role of Mainline Protestantism.* Berkeley: University of California Press.

Wyatt-Brown, Bertram. 1971. "Prelude to Abolitionism: Sabbatarian Politics and the Rise of the Second Party System." *Journal of American History* 58(2): 316–41.

Yancey, George. 1999. "An Examination of the Effects of Residential and Church Integration on Racial Attitudes of Whites." *Sociological Perspectives* 42(2): 279–304.

———. 2003. *One Body, One Spirit: Principles of Successful Multiracial Churches.* Downers Grove, Ill: InterVarsity Press.

Yancey, Philip. 1990. "Confessions of a Racist." *Christianity Today* 34(1): 23–26.

Yanow, Dvora, and Peregrine Schwartz-Shea. 2006. *Interpretation and Method: Empirical Research Methods and the Interpretive Turn.* Armonk, N.Y.: M. E. Sharpe.

Youngren, J. Alen. 1981. "Can Christian Colleges Mix with Minorities?" *Christianity Today* 25(19): 44–48.

Zipperer, John. 1995. "Immigration Debate Divides Christians." *Christianity Today* 39(2): 42–43.

Zoba, Wendy Murray. 1996. "Separate and Equal." *Christianity Today* 40(2): 14–24.

Zuckerman, D. M. 2000. "Welfare Reform in America: A Clash of Politics and Research." *Journal of Social Issues* 56(4): 587–600.

Zylstra, Sarah Eekhoff. 2009. "Black Flight." *Christianity Today* 53(1): 13.

Index